BizTalk Server 2000

Developer's Guide for .NET

Robert Shimonski

Chris Farmer

Henk-Evert Sonder

Milton Todd Technical Reviewer and Contributor

KEY	SERIAL NUMBER
001	P9KM6TF3Q3
002	VF67YHAM88
003	4RF6TFBH8A
004	ZTN75RSAH3
005	U5SNEM5W32
006	DJ4T6PLE4X
007	8VT3DF9PA2
008	G5S4M8KAUQ
009	RF67HN9A4M
010	JN7KM45EDQ

PUBLISHED BY
Syngress Publishing, Inc.
800 Hingham Street
Rockland, MA 02370

BizTalk Server 2000 Developer's Guide: for .NET

Technical Reviewer: Milton Todd
Acquisitions Editor: Catherine B. Nolan
Developmental Editor: Jonathon Babcock
Freelance Editorial Manager: Maribeth Corona-Evans

Cover Designer: Michael Kavish
Page Layout and Art by: Shannon Tozier
Copy Editor: Beth Roberts
Indexer: Rich Carlson

Distributed by Publishers Group West in the United States and Jaguar Book Group in Canada.

Acknowledgments

We would like to acknowledge the following people for their kindness and support in making this book possible.

Richard Kristof and Duncan Anderson of Global Knowledge, for their generous access to the IT industry's best courses, instructors, and training facilities.

Ralph Troupe, Rhonda St. John, and the team at Callisma for their invaluable insight into the challenges of designing, deploying and supporting world-class enterprise networks.

Karen Cross, Lance Tilford, Meaghan Cunningham, Kim Wylie, Harry Kirchner, Kevin Votel, Kent Anderson, and Frida Yara of Publishers Group West for sharing their incredible marketing experience and expertise.

Jacquie Shanahan and AnnHelen Lindeholm of Elsevier Science for making certain that our vision remains worldwide in scope.

Annabel Dent of Harcourt Australia for all her help.

David Buckland, Wendi Wong, Marie Chieng, Lucy Chong, Leslie Lim, Audrey Gan, and Joseph Chan of Transquest Publishers for the enthusiasm with which they receive our books.

Kwon Sung June at Acorn Publishing for his support.

Ethan Atkin at Cranbury International for his help in expanding the Syngress program.

Jackie Gross, Gayle Voycey, Alexia Penny, Anik Robitaille, Craig Siddall, Darlene Morrow, Iolanda Miller, Jane Mackay, and Marie Skelly at Jackie Gross & Associates for all their help and enthusiasm representing our product in Canada.

Lois Fraser, Connie McMenemy, Shannon Russell and the rest of the great folks at Jaguar Book Group for their help with distribution of Syngress books in Canada.

Contributors

Scott Roberts (MCSE+I 4.0, MCSE 2000, MSF, MCDBA, MCT, MCP + Site Building) was one of the first 1600 MCPs in the world. He has a long history with Microsoft products and technology and is currently employed as a Senior Consultant within the Microsoft Consulting Services, Platform Consulting Organization. This group develops and deploys solutions for Enterprise customers focused on the .NET Server platform. Prior to joining Microsoft, Scott was the President/CEO of Enterprise Technology Group Inc., a Windows 2000 and e-commerce development, consulting, and training company. He has also been a featured conference speaker on messaging and e-commerce topics throughout the country.

Chris Farmer (Ph.D., MCSD) is a consultant at SciTegic in San Diego, CA where he specializes in integration of scientific applications for pharmaceutical and biotech companies using SOAP and other XML-based technologies. Chris's recent background includes design and development of .NET-based Web applications and extensive e-commerce database development and integration with legacy systems using XML with IT-Age Corporation in Atlanta, GA. Chris holds a bachelor's degree from the University of Virginia and a Ph.D. from the University of Georgia. Chris currently lives in sunny San Diego, CA with his wife, Michelle.

Robert J. Shimonski (CCDP, CCNP, NNCSS, MCSE, MCP+I, Master CNE, CIP, CIBS, CWP, CIW, GSEC, GCIH, Server+, Network+, Inet+, A+) is a Lead Network and Security Engineer for Thomson Industries Inc. Thomson Industries is the leading manufacturer and provider of linear motion products and engineering. Robert's specialties include: network infrastructure design with the Cisco and Nortel product line; network security design and management with CiscoSecure and PIX Firewalls; network management and troubleshooting with CiscoWorks and Sniffer-based technologies; systems engineering and administration with Microsoft NT/2000/XP, UNIX, Linux, Apple, and Novell Netware technologies, and developing a host of Web-based solutions for companies securing their market on the Web. He has also contributed to hundreds of articles, study guides, and certification preparation software for Web sites and organizations worldwide, including Brainbuzz.com and SANS.Org. Robert's background includes positions as a Network Architect at Avis and Cendant Information Technology. Robert holds a bachelor's degree from SUNY, NY and is a part-time Licensed Technical Instructor for Computer Career Center in Garden City, NY teaching Windows-based and networking technologies. Robert has previously contributed to the Syngress Publishing title, *Configuring and Troubleshooting Windows XP Professional* (ISBN: 1-928994-80-6), and is the Technical Editor of the forthcoming *Sniffer Network Optimization and Troubleshooting Guide* (ISBN: 1-931836-57-4).

Henk-Evert Sonder (CCNA) has over 15 years of experience as an Information and Communication Technologies (ICT) professional, building and maintaining ICT infrastructures. In recent years, he has specialized in integrating ICT infrastructures with secure business applications. Henk's company, IT Selective, works with small businesses to help them develop high-quality, low cost solutions. Henk has contributed to several Syngress Publishing titles, including the *E-Mail Virus Protection Handbook* (ISBN: 1-928994-23-7), *Designing SQL Server 2000 Databases for .NET Enterprise Servers* (ISBN: 1-928994-19-9), *VB.NET Developer's Guide* (ISBN: 1-928994-48-2), and *Configuring and Troubleshooting Windows XP Professional* (ISBN: 1-928994-80-6). Henk lives in Hingham, MA with his wife Jude and daughter Lily.

Technical Reviewer and Contributor

Milton Todd is a software engineer at InterKnowlogy, LLC in Carlsbad, CA. InterKnowlogy is a consulting firm and Microsoft partner providing custom software and infrastructure solutions for secure and effective use over the Internet. Milton has focused the last year on developing BizTalk solutions, primarily to the insurance industry. Previously, he developed front- and back-end applications in the e-commerce and manufacturing industries, depending heavily on Microsoft technologies.

Milton holds a bachelor's of science in Mechanical Engineering and spent several years in the design and construction field, experience that has provided a firm grounding in practical problem solving and the design process. When possible, he continues to teach mathematics. Milton currently resides in Diamond Bar, CA with his wife, Lida.

Contents

Answers to Your BizTalk Questions

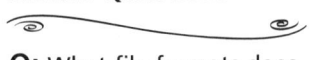

Q: What file formats does BizTalk Server support?

A: XML, flat files (delimited and positional), and EDI (ANSI X12 and EDIFACT) documents. In addition, it has an open binding architecture that allows for additional third-party add-ons to increase this support using the supplied SDK that ships as part of the Enterprise Edition.

Complete Coverage of BizTalk Server 2000

BizTalk Server 2000 includes the following tools:

- BizTalk Orchestration Designer
- BizTalk Document Tracking
- BizTalk Editor
- BizTalk Mapper
- BizTalk Messaging Manager
- BizTalk Server Administration

Implementing BizTalk Server

⊶━━━━━━━━━━━⊷

- Use the methods of the Interface object to exchange a business document between an application and BizTalk Server 2000 directly.

- You can use the BizTalk Server Administration tool to create receive functions.

- The Submit method is used to submit documents in an asynchronous fashion without waiting for a receipt document.

NOTE

When configuring an ordinary channel that processes a document requesting a receipt, you must provide details of the receipt channel that will handle the receipt. Therefore, you must configure the receipt channel and its associated messaging ports prior to configuring the ordinary channel that uses it.

The Functoid Palette

BizTalk Document Tracking

- Document tracking data is stored in the SQL Server 2000 InterchangeDTA database.

- Document definitions and channel configurations provide the means for selecting individual document fields to persist to the database.

- The BizTalk Server Administrator allows you to configure the server to log all interchanges and document content to the tracking database.

Assessing Employees' Roles

Perform the following steps to assess the roles of employees who will be working with the BizTalk application:

1. Make an overview of all the roles and put them in groups, based on the type of use they will make of the application. Try to minimize the number of groups—the more groups, the more administration involved, and the greater the chance of error.

2. Determine for each group which parts of the BizTalk solution they will need to use, and what type, or level, of access this will require. Be very strict about this. If users only need read-only access, that should be all they get.

3. Add only the usernames of the employees you have identified as needing access to the BizTalk solution to the groups. Review these group members at least twice a year, since employees have a tendency to change jobs.

4. Never give access rights at user level, as this only complicates the system administration tasks.

Developing & Deploying...

Binding Order

You might want to check your binding orders if running multiple protocols. Try to make TCP/IP (or the protocols most used) the first protocol to be looked at first when bound to the NIC cards by placing it at the top of the binding order in you network and dial-up connections settings. This can be found in the **Advanced** menu under **Advanced Settings....**

Chapter 10 Troubleshooting   461

**Defining Schedule
Status Displayed in
XLANG Monitor**

Icon	State
Green dot	Running XLANG schedule
Blue lines	A suspended/ paused schedule
Blue snowflake	A dehydrated schedule
Red dot	Complete schedule— with errors
Black dot	Complete schedule— successful

Foreword

BizTalk Server 2000 is Microsoft's much-needed solution the issue of interoperability. BizTalk Server 2000 provides a tool for closing the gap on how dissimilar services, specifications, and products communicate over the World Wide Web. The Internet (as well as other communication media) allows users and companies to get from point A to B, but if Company A speaks Japanese and Company B speaks English, they will have a problem communicating. So what's the answer? Does Company A spend time learning English in order to do business with Company B? If Company B goes to visit Company A is it assumed that Company B will be able to speak the language of Company A? Absolutely not—this is where BizTalk Server 2000 comes into play. BizTalk is the middleman for the future of data exchange, a translator for the cyber cities of business data. With the ultimate power of translation, demand for this product will increase exponentially in the coming years. Companies will see more and more B2B connections and extranets emerging faster than IT departments can keep up with implementing them. So now what? You connect, but can you really do business together? If the companies are similar and trust each other to implement similar systems…Stop! You know as well as I do that the IT world simply does not work this way. The solution is to deploy BizTalk Server 2000.

With BizTalk Server 2000 users and companies are now able to integrate Purchase Orders from home grown systems, SAP ERP packages, Peoplesoft software applications, and other various product lines, or even various specifications such as X12 or EDIFACT without serious communication problems. Users have the power to connect these dissimilar systems with a tool that acts as the middleman to your B2B implementation. The push in the past five years was for businesses to implement thousands of different systems, and for homegrown software applications to interact together. Additionally, all of these objectives must be achieved within strict budget constraints. BizTalk Server 2000 eliminates that previous need of implementing various systems, and streamlines data exchange, resulting in significant savings.

How does *BizTalk Server 2000 Developer's Guide for .NET* improve your skills, and how will it impact your deployment of BizTalk? Well, this book is designed to bring you into BizTalk Technology full blast. It is not a beginner's guide, as we have tried to inundate this book with "Heads-up," "Watch out for…," and "You may really have a problem with…" types of answers to your .NET questions on BizTalk Server 2000. It is by no means a definitive guide; it would be a Herculean a task to attempt to encompass all of the nuances of this powerful product. This is where we point you to additional complementary resources online to answer more of your questions. We also provide a means to answer your ongoing questions and provide regular technology updates via the Syngress Publishing Web site devoted to the title *BizTalk Server 2000 Developer's Guide for .NET*. Simply browse to www.syngress.com/solutions to activate your membership. Much of this book was written before, during, *and* after live implementations on test and production networks with BizTalk heavily involved. We hope our countless hours of testing and research will greatly improve your understanding of this product, and save you some time down the road.

This book is for a very wide group of people. The earlier chapters provide cornerstone information on Microsoft's .NET initiative with a particular emphasis on the role of BizTalk Server 2000 within the initiative, while the later chapters provide advanced information for developers and engineers. Although there may be quite a few books out on the market about BizTalk, honestly, none of them are enough—all the documentation in the world would not be enough. BizTalk Servers connect systems that are too big, too all encompassing, and too massive to ever foresee all the problems that you may encounter. Think about it…the trick five years ago was to integrate NT 4 servers into your pre-existing Novell Netware 4.11 environments. At the time, that seemed like an *enormous* task. However, looking back that task seems trivial compared to having to integrate a SAP /R3 ERP system with another company's ERP system over the Internet, through a set of DMZ's and firewalls with XML and XSLT code.

BizTalk Server 2000 Developer's Guide for .NET is a collaborative work that will provide readers with access to some of the brightest minds in the BizTalk community. This is a book written by a group, for a group, and we look forward to your feedback as a group. We hope you enjoy this book as much as we enjoyed writing it for you. It was truly gratifying to work with developers, and systems and network engineers to bring you a book that we believe is both unique and a valuable resource. The authors that wrote this book are just as diverse and driven as the systems they implement—Enjoy!

—*Robert J. Shimonski*
CCDP, CCNP, NNCSS, MCSE, MCP+I, Master CNE, CIP, CIBS, CWP, CIW, GSEC, GCIH, Server+, Network+, i-Net+, A+

Chapter 1

The Role of BizTalk in the .NET Server Family

Solutions in this chapter:

- Overview of Microsoft BizTalk Server 2000
- Why Use BizTalk?
- BizTalk 2000 Application Model
- BizTalk 2000 Administration Model
- Implementation of Open Standards
- ☑ Summary
- ☑ Solutions Fast Track
- ☑ Frequently Asked Questions

Introduction

BizTalk Server 2000 is Microsoft's next initiative for supporting e-commerce and Enterprise Application Integration (EAI) solutions. Built on open industry standards, BizTalk 2000 provides the capabilities to build intercompany workflow solutions and/or control the flow of information required to complete a business task while enforcing business rules.

This chapter introduces BizTalk's role in the new .NET initiative from Microsoft and provides an understanding of the concepts upon which BizTalk is designed. BizTalk Messaging and BizTalk Collaboration services provide the foundation to which we can provide solutions with the marketplace. We also talk about how BizTalk provides the capabilities to talk with other non-Microsoft systems, and we delve into the framework that specification 2.0 provides.

Overview of Microsoft BizTalk Server 2000

Application integration has been around for a very long time. For years, businesses have been developing systems to communicate electronically instead of relying on humans for direct interaction. The problem that we have always faced is that different groups within a company use applications that natively cannot communicate with each other, let alone communicate with companies outside of the organization. The problem just gets worse when we start looking at connecting these businesses to automate business processes with trading partners. Differences in software, hardware, and network protocols produced difficult barriers to overcome in the past. There were solutions that attempted to solve these problems, but most were very expensive to implement, very time consuming, and did not react well to any change in the structure of the information.

BizTalk Server 2000 addresses these concerns by acting as the universal translator between the disparate systems that have evolved within an organization and between organizations. It is based on open industry standards and specifications to allow communication for application-to-application interactions. We will use BizTalk Server 2000 to create, integrate, manage, and automate business processes for the exchange of business documents. BizTalk Server 2000 is part of the .NET family of Enterprise Servers designed to work together to provide e-business solutions. The .NET Enterprise Servers are based on open Web standards such as XML to allow an organization to integrate and orchestrate their applications and service needs into a single comprehensive solution.

The .NET Enterprise Servers

Microsoft's .NET strategy is comprised of five basic parts: the User Experience, Clients, Services, Tools, and the Enterprise Servers. These Enterprise Servers will be the underlying platform that will provide the foundation for all of the other parts of the .NET strategy. For example, on the Services front we have the Microsoft XML Web Services, codenamed "Hailstorm," which will rely on the presence of these .NET Enterprise Servers. The .NET enterprise servers will work together to meet the needs of business-to-consumer online transaction systems and business-to-business electronic fulfillment systems. Table 1.1 lists the different server titles and their descriptions.

Table 1.1 The .NET Enterprise Servers

Server Title	Description
Microsoft Application Center 2000	A deployment and management tool that enables Web applications that are built on Microsoft Windows 2000 to achieve a high availability through software scaling for mission-critical availability.
Microsoft Commerce Server 2000	A comprehensive system for building scalable, personalized, business-to-consumer (B2C) and business-to-business (B2B) e-business solutions on Windows 2000, as well as tools for analyzing site activity.
Microsoft SQL Server 2000 (SQL)	For Web-enabled database applications, Microsoft SQL Server 2000 provides data storage and analysis, indexing and searching, and security and auditing for enabling scalable Web applications.
Microsoft Internet Security and Acceleration Server 2000 (ISA)	Provides secure Internet connectivity, fast Web access through delivery of Web content through a Web cache, and unified firewall management.
Microsoft Exchange Server 2000	Offers solutions for e-mail delivery as well as real-time collaboration. In e-business scenarios it provides automation of transaction acknowledgments.

Continued

Table 1.1 Continued

Server Title	Description
Microsoft Host Integration Server 2000 (HIS)	Much of the data and business processes of today's large corporations are still handled by legacy systems. HIS provides access and integration opportunity with systems and your e-business applications, protecting and leveraging your existing investments.
Microsoft Mobile Information 2001 Server	A reliable and scalable platform for wireless solutions that bring together wireless users and corporate data.
Microsoft BizTalk Server 2000	A comprehensive solution that allows both business analysts and developers to work side by side to automate business processes and leverage each of the other .NET servers.

An Example of .NET Server Integration

Let's walk through an example to illustrate how BizTalk Server 2000 fits into the .NET enterprise family. This is just one example; BizTalk Server 2000 can work in a mixed environment just as easily as in a complete .NET solution.

We will start with a customer purchasing an item through our company's Web site. Our Internet connection is protected via ISA Server 2000, allowing access to just a protected segment of our network (called a DMZ). Our company can use Application Center 2000 to manage the cluster (Web farm) of servers that make up our Web site, and we can use features like Windows load balancing to distribute the load across all the servers in the cluster.

The Web site will communicate through a second ISA Server firewall to our private segment. The customer can query product information from our Web site, with the query being handled by Commerce Server 2000, which passes it on to SQL Server 2000 to retrieve the product list from the database. Commerce Server 2000 processes the product list for presentation to the customer. Once the order is placed on the Web site, it is handled by Commerce Server 2000, updating the SQL database as well as handing the order over to BizTalk Server 2000 for processing.

BizTalk Server 2000 will transform the document into a form understood by our legacy host system, which is still handling all order fulfillment and processing. It will communicate through Host Integration Server 2000 for the delivery of the document into the host system. The host system could send an acknowledgment that it has received the order back to BizTalk Server 2000, which could then trigger an e-mail notification to be generated via Exchange Server 2000. If we did not have the item in stock, the host system could generate, through BizTalk Server 2000, a purchase order for a business partner. BizTalk Server 2000 would handle the conversion of this request from our document format into a document format that could be understood by the business partner.

This request could be delivered into an existing system for handling or to another BizTalk Server 2000 running at the partner location. The order processing system at the trading partner could then generate an order confirmation response that our BizTalk Server then receives, transforms, and submits to our order processing system. BizTalk Server would also then update the status information by submitting documents to Commerce Server 2000, or sending additional e-mails through Exchange Server 2000.

Features of BizTalk Server 2000

BizTalk Server 2000 has a powerful set of tools and services that allow you to rapidly build and deploy integrated business processes within your organization and with your trading partners. This suite of tools and services is designed to make it faster and more efficient to develop these EAI systems. Communication can be established in a secure and reliable fashion and quickly implemented independently of operating system, programming models, or languages.

BizTalk Server allows organizations to document and then automate their business processes using dynamic GUI tools. The BizTalk Orchestration Designer allows business analysts to work side by side with developers to create these BizTalk-based solutions in a common design environment. BizTalk Server is based on creating and using XML-based documents, so that integrating with business partners is made much more simple. The XML document exchanges are in W3C standard XML along with support for the emerging specifications.

The BizTalk Framework 2.0 gives us a standard, reliable way of building messages that can be shared with business partners. The BizTalk Framework 2.0 specification is compliant with the SOAP 1.1 and provides for exactly one delivery of documents. BizTalk Server has very flexible document delivery capability with its support of HTTP, SMTP, WebDAV, and network file-sharing mechanisms. In addition to the full support of Internet protocols for transmission, BizTalk Server 2000 has full support for public key infrastructures, digital signatures, MIME, and S/MIME, plus third-party plug-in security modules. Microsoft and SAP have even worked together to provide an SAP R/3 application integration component.

The features of BizTalk Server can be broken down into some general categories. At this point, we are not going to delve into the specific tools or options, but we will discuss the high-level features that BizTalk Server provides.

Administration

There are many functions that administrators will have to configure. The following is a list of the general duties that can be required in the day-to-day operations as a BizTalk Server 2000 administrator:

- The creation and management of servers and server groups.

- Administrators may want to consider the creation of multiple receive functions. The ongoing administration of these receive functions will be very important.

- Configuration of the properties that will apply to all the servers within a group (global properties). Items such as the location of the Shared Queue database and Tracking database are easy to administer.

- Configure the setting of the individual servers within each server group.

- As documents are submitted into the server and sent back out, the queues that are holding these documents will have to be monitored and maintained.

- In addition to server administration, there will be the duties of programmatically accessing and administrating the XLANG Scheduler System Manager, group managers, XLANG schedule instances, and XLANG ports.

Document Tracking

In every business transaction there is a strong need to determine the exact status of the transaction at any time. Customers may call in and ask about the status of an order, or the sales department may want to ensure that an item has been shipped to a customer. It is vital that at any point in the process we can get an exact status of the transaction. BizTalk Server 2000's primary tool that can assist us with this monitoring is the BizTalk Server Document tracking tool. We can search for, display, view, and save complete copies of any interchange or document processed by BizTalk Server 2000. We can create queries to find out specific pieces of information to determine the exact status of a transaction. The basic idea of BizTalk Server 2000 is that from the time the documents are submitted to the time of completion, we are able to know exactly what is going on.

Orchestration

Orchestration is Microsoft's term for documenting the business process and then linking to the actual implementation of the process. For the first time, business analysts can use the same interface to describe the business processes that the developers use to programmatically automate those processes. The orchestration services are deigned to manage business processes that could take weeks or months to complete. It literally defines how the data will move between each step within the business process. The user interface for orchestration is presented as a VBA application within Visio 2000 SR-1A; hence, the need for Visio. BizTalk Server 2000 Orchestration Services are implemented by the BizTalk Messaging Services, COM components, Message Queuing Services, and Windows Script components.

Messaging

BizTalk Server 2000 provides a set of messaging services that you can use to automate business processes and the exchange of data. These services are the key for BizTalk Server 2000 to send and receive documents, parse documents, retrieve routing and processing information, and then finally track and deliver documents. The Message Services also include data mapping services, the ability to generate receipts, and manage data integrity and security services.

Development Tools

In the next section, we are going to look at each of these functions and see how they are provided for or managed by a unique set of tools. These tools will be your main interface to the development and administrative functions of your BizTalk-based solutions.

BizTalk Editor

BizTalk Editor will be used to construct your document's required *format, specification, and schema.* These terms are used interchangeably within the BizTalk Server 2000 environment. BizTalk Server 2000 is able to transform a document from one specification to another, but we must first start with valid documents.

BizTalk Editor will be used to construct the documents that we will use to perform validity testing on our documents. BizTalk Editor can handle the following text formats: XML, positional flat files, delimited flat files, mixed positional/delimited flat files, and EDI (X12 and EDIFACT).

BizTalk Editor ships with many sample business documents that you can use as a baseline for your work. Figure 1.1 illustrates what a sample purchase order specification will look like in BizTalk Editor.

Figure 1.1 Sample Purchase Order Specification

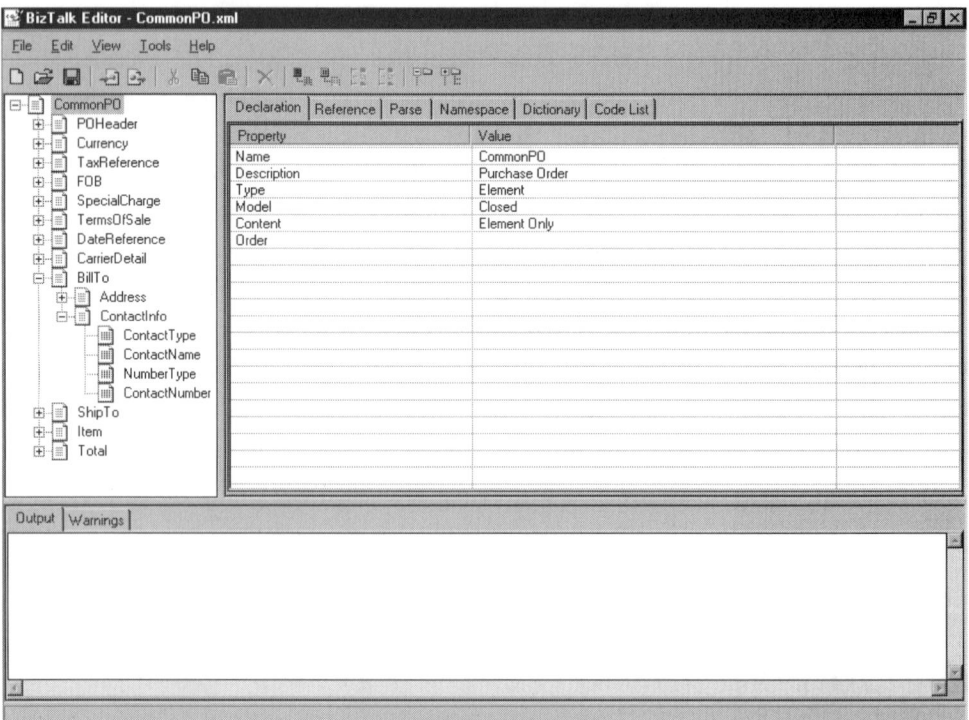

Rather than using the XML schema terms of <ElementType> and <AttributeType> within the interface, Microsoft has chosen to make BizTalk Editor more accessible to people who may not be that knowledgeable about XML schemas. They have instead decided on the database metaphors of *records* and *fields* to describe the specification that you are building.

The files that you save using BizTalk Editor will be XML-DR-based, or XDR schema documents. We will use these schema documents to verify that we are working with valid files and to feed the BizTalk Mapper to construct our transformations. Note, however, that the specifications created using BizTalk

Editor do include some BizTalk Server-specific tags. They are not yet 100–percent interchangeable with XML-DR schemas that you would create with third-party tools. This is due to limitation in the XML-DR schema itself in that when working with non-XML specifications, it cannot capture information about delimiters or positions within flat files.

If you wish to save to the BizTalk Framework schema repository at BizTalk.org, you will need to export your specification to an XML-DR schema because this is the only schema that the repository supports. Furthermore, BizTalk Editor supports importing XML-DR schemas. Once the W3C moves the XML-DR specification into final form, Microsoft has committed to updating BizTalk Server to fully support the released specification.

BizTalk Mapper

Using BizTalk Mapper you can graphically represent the relationship between the records and fields of the source and destination specifications. BizTalk Mapper will create an XLST file that other services will use to apply a transformation to the source document, based on what you defined in your map, into a destination document that conforms to the destination specification. This is the key to the document translation services of BizTalk Server 2000. It allows you to transform a document from any defined source specification such as XML, X12, or EDI-FACT into any type of destination specification.

This allows organizations to share documents with one another without having to worry about converting the data into a format that the destination can receive ahead of time. Each organization can continue to work with their documents in the format with which they are most comfortable, and then BizTalk Server 2000 will convert the data into the desired format for exchange.

Figure 1.2 shows a Purchase Request specification loaded on the left. The right side of the screen is the Purchase Order that represents the desired transformation output format. Notice the lines connecting the fields on the left to the appropriate fields on the right. As part of this transformation process, we can manipulate the data. Notice that the values of the LastName and FirstName fields from the source are combined to create the Contact Name field value. You can manually supply the script code to do this, or use one of the supplied *functiods*. A functiod is an object supplied by BizTalk Mapper to represent many of the most common math, string, and other functions that you might wish to use to transform the data. You can even create your own functiods to represent common manipulations that you need to perform.

Figure 1.2 BizTalk Mapper

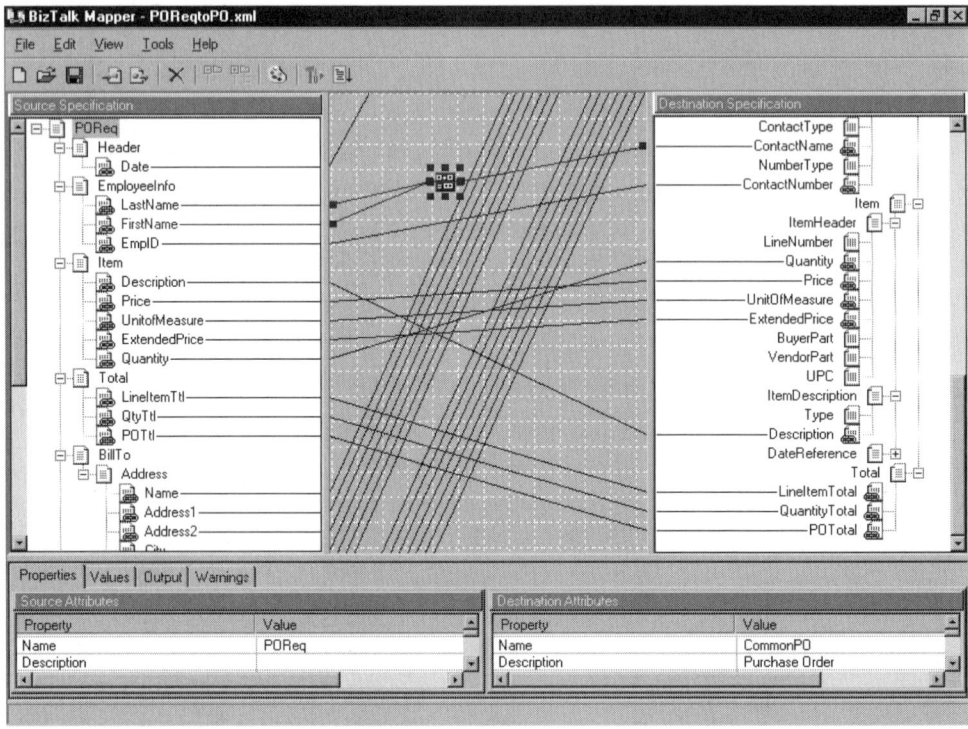

When the developer is finished, he or she will compile the map. This results in an XML transformation (XSLT) stylesheet. This stylesheet is then called upon at the appropriate time by the runtime services to produce the transformation of the document.

BizTalk Orchestration Designer

BizTalk Orchestration Designer is a GUI VBA application that is run from within Vision SR-1A (Figure 1.3). The business analyst will model the business process on the left side so that the developer can then go down the right side, linking each step in the business process to an appropriate implementation of this process. The tool is programmed with all the knowledge required to build an XLANG schedule, which is the XML-based language Microsoft developed to describe this business process and its implementation. Upon saving this business process document, the XLANG schedule is compiled into an XLANG executable. This executable is then handed over to the XLANG Scheduler to be called upon when needed.

Figure 1.3 BizTalk Orchestration Designer

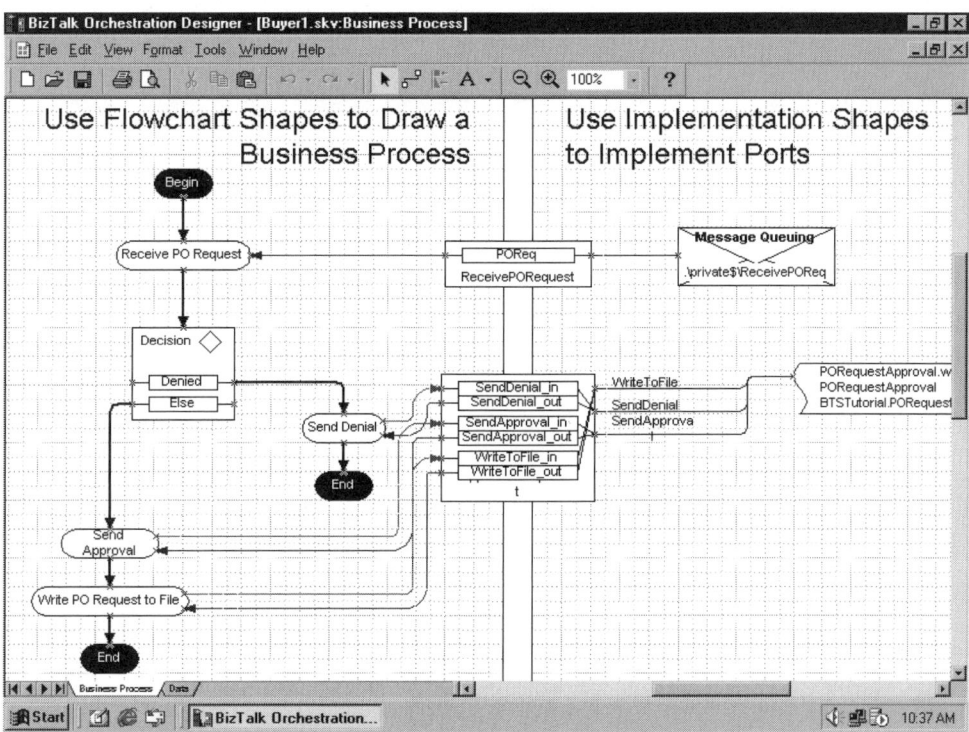

BizTalk Server Administration

The BizTalk Server Administration Microsoft Management Console (MMC), shown in Figure 1.4, provides a visual representation of the tools and services that the system administrator snap-in will manage. This will be the primary tool that you will use to manage your servers and server groups, configure all global server properties, create and modify receive functions, and monitor document queues.

Figure 1.4 shows the four queues that are used to manage the documents while they are being routed and processed though the various states. This MMC is where you will go to configure the document Receive functions and server-related properties. You will also notice a link for the Event Viewer. This is the same Event Viewer MMC snap-in that is found under Administrative tools, but a shortcut is provided for you here as well.

Figure 1.4 BizTalk Server Administration Microsoft Management Console Snap-In

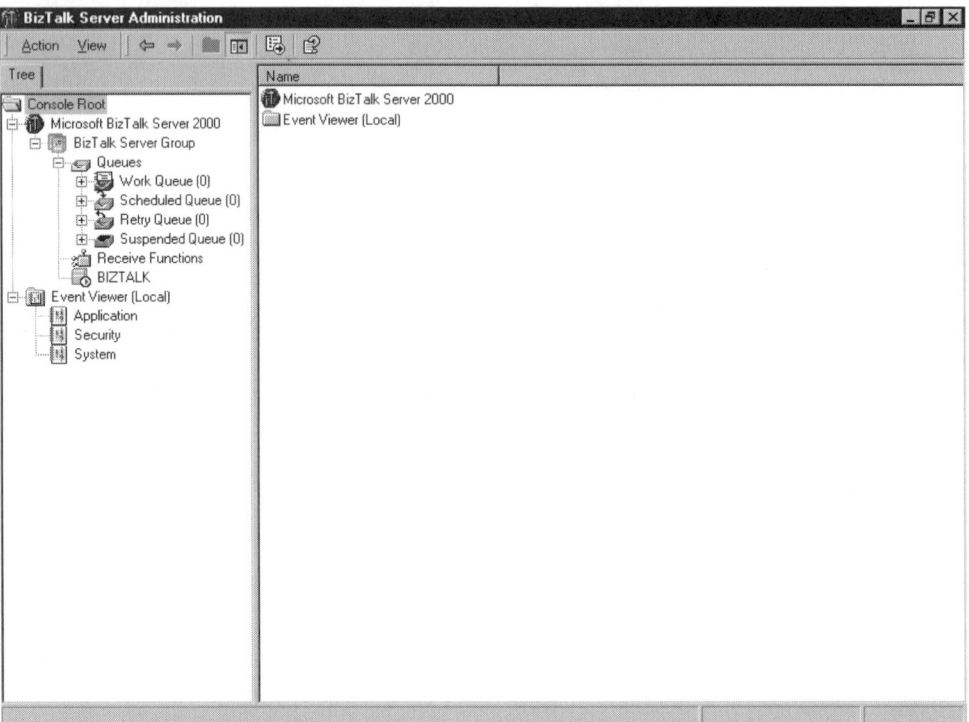

Why Use BizTalk?

Information access is the key for business survival in the Information Age. In order to conduct business-to-business trading over the Internet, there is the need to easily share information. Businesses face numerous challenges when it comes to sharing information. Data exists in a variety of formats and there is no universal standard for sharing this data with others. Many businesses have even deployed applications within their company that cannot easily share data with each other.

There have been technologies and efforts in the past to try to solve this problem. The most well known of course is EDI (Electronic Data Interchange). EDI is a set of specifications for ordering, billing, and paying for parts and services over private value-added networks (VANs) linking dissimilar computer systems.

EDI is used by organizations for many of the same reasons that we are using to build the case for BizTalk Server 2000. The main problem with EDI, however, is that it has always been very expensive to implement, and relatively complex, so it really has been limited to just the largest organizations and their partners. EDI is also based on 1980s technology.

You might ask, isn't this what XML was supposed to fix? Isn't XML the universal language of business now? Well, yes and no. XML does provide a way to truly exchange meaningful data between business partners. The problem is that it provides no guidance on the structure of these messages. For example, one business partner might like to have a FirstName field separate from the LastName field on a purchase order, but the other business partner prefers just to have a FullName field. XML can describe in great detail the documents that each of these partners has created, but we have a fundamental problem of inconsistent document structures.

This is where BizTalk comes in. BizTalk is not just a product, but also a set of initiatives for facilitating application integration within and across organizations. BizTalk uses XML to provide a way to describe the schemas for XML messages and the technology to help you route these XML messages and process them as the messages are transmitted from business to business. The BizTalk initiative comprises:

- **BizTalk Framework 2.0** A set of guidelines put forth from a broad group of businesses on how to define messages to enable e-commerce building on top of existing standards such as XML and the Simple Object Access Protocol (SOAP). The BizTalk Framework 2.0 provides the basis for interoperable reliable messaging in BizTalk Server 2000.

- **BizTalk.org** A Web site where people can learn more about the initiative and, more importantly, a public schema library where people can post their schemas for the business documents they are working with, such as invoices and purchase orders. For example, if you want to send a purchase order electronically what is the preferred schema that they use for their purchase orders?

- **BizTalk products** These products provide support for BizTalk Framework 2.0. BizTalk Server 2000 is Microsoft's implementation of a server product for the Windows 2000 platform that provides for this support. However, the framework is written such that an application can be constructed on any platform using any programming language to support the capability to send, process, and receive BizTalk messages.

This initiative hopes to solve the problems of the past, using new technologies and specifications to truly enable application integration for the masses.

Open Binding Architecture

There have been many attempts in the past at distributed computing. OLE, CORBA, and even Java RMI have all attempted to deliver the promise of scaleable and flexible architectures for distributed computing. All of these systems still resulted in tightly coupled implementations that did not react well to even simple changes in the business process, and none of them by themselves are widely enough deployed to be a standard for B2B e-commerce over the Internet.

This difficulty in allowing cross-platform, Internet-based application communication lead IBM, Microsoft, and several other companies to develop the SOAP specification that has now been submitted to the W3C (www.w3.org/TR/SOAP/). This specification, which the BizTalk Framework 2.0 Specification incorporates, allows for an open binding architecture. Developers or independent software vendors are therefore able to build adapters that allow their products to be accessed from within BizTalk Server. This open mechanism helps connect business processes with any application or component running on any platform over any protocol to enable an "any-to-any" integration.

Language Support

Microsoft provides programmatic support by allowing the creation of Application Integration Components (AICs). These are COM objects developed using any language that supports the COM interface, including Visual Basic, C#, C++, Java, or even Windows script components (formerly called scriptlets). Microsoft even provides support for the pipeline-component model available in Microsoft Site Server Commerce Edition 3.0. The bottom line is that Microsoft has attempted to make it very easy to integrate BizTalk Server into your environment using a programming language with which you are already familiar.

Management Capabilities

We have spent a great deal of time talking about administration and configuration tools. They are all used to create specifications and set configuration options. Now we need to tie everything together and actually start processing messages. There are many items still to configure. We must define all the properties of our organization and business partners, the protocols that we are going to use to transport our documents, and the locations where we are going to receive these documents.

Tools

The remaining tools that provide the ongoing management are the BizTalk Messaging Manager and the BizTalk Document Tracker. Combined, these tools provide the capability to manage the document and message flow of our BizTalk business process. The BizTalk Messaging Manager is used to create and manage channels, messaging ports, document definitions, envelopes, organizations, and distribution lists of objects using a graphical interface. You can also programmatically create and manage these objects as discussed in the next section.

Object Model

Microsoft BizTalk Server 2000 provides support for programmatically integrating your existing applications by using the BizTalk Messaging Configuration object model, or by extending and customizing the functionality of the server to suit your business and information-exchange needs. Although you can use a variety of languages, Microsoft supplies an interface reference that provides all the necessary information for Visual Basic and Visual C++ programmers. Table 1.2 lists the Messaging Configuration object model reference.

Table 1.2 Messaging Configuration Object Model Reference

COM Objects/Interfaces	Description
IBizTalkBase	In C++, the IBizTalkBase interface defines common methods and properties that are inherited by the following objects. In Microsoft Visual Basic, the IBizTalkBase class defines common methods and properties that are implemented by the following objects: BizTalkChannel, BizTalkDocument, BizTalkEnvelope, BizTalkOrganization, BizTalkPort, BizTalkPortGroup.
IBizTalkChannel	Use the methods and properties of the BizTalkChannel object to configure a channel for processing documents.
IBizTalkConfig	Use the BizTalkConfig object to create channels, document specifications, envelopes, organizations, ports, and port groups.

Continued

Table 1.2 Continued

COM Objects/Interfaces	Description
IBizTalkDocument	Use the BizTalkDocument object to identify and describe the document specification of a document.
IBizTalkEndPoint	Use the BizTalkEndPoint object to configure source information for a BizTalkChannel object and destination information for a BizTalkPort object.
IBizTalkEnvelope	Use the BizTalkEnvelope object to configure the envelope format used with documents processed by BizTalk Server. An envelope is the header information for an interchange.
IBizTalkOrganization	Use the BizTalkOrganization object to configure organizations, its organization identifiers (aliases), and the applications within the organization that send and/or receive documents. The application indicates the ultimate source or destination of the document.
IBizTalkPort	The BizTalkPort object configures a one-way transfer of a document between organizations and applications. It identifies the source organization and/or application, the destination organization and/or application, the primary transport type, and, if selected, the associated envelope for transmission.

There are additional object models to do things such as submit documents programmatically and check the status of documents in the message flow using the IInterchange interface (Table 1.3).

Table 1.3 IInterchange Interface (C++) / Interchange Object (Visual Basic) Method Samples

Method	Description
Submit	Submits an interchange to BizTalk Server 2000 for asynchronous processing. This method accepts only a string variable as the document or interchange.

Continued

Table 1.3 Continued

Method	Description
SubmitSync	Submits an interchange to BizTalk Server 2000 for synchronous transmission. This method returns a response if one is provided. This method accepts only a string variable as the document or interchange.
CheckSuspendedQueue	Checks the Suspended queue and returns a list of handles to documents or interchanges in the queue that match the request criteria.

BizTalk 2000 Application Model

When developing a BizTalk *application*, you will find that it is going to be a little different from developing an application in VB or C++. In those environments, you take your source code, compile it into an executable, and you are done. A BizTalk application will be a collection of business process flows, specifications, maps, and defined submit and receive locations that enable our application to function. These systems can be broken down into two basic groupings: BizTalk Messaging Service and BizTalk Orchestration Services. We will break these down in the next section.

BizTalk Messaging Services

BizTalk Messaging Services enable BizTalk Server 2000 to send and receive documents, parse documents, extract routing and processing information, and track and deliver documents. BizTalk Messaging Services also include data mapping, receipt generation and correlation, and data integrity and security services. BizTalk Messaging Services include the following services:

- **Receive functions** These services are designed to communicate with applications that cannot speak directly to BizTalk Server via the COM interface. There are two support types of receive functions: file and message queues.

- **Transport services** Transport services are used to send documents. These services allow for communication regardless of the application's COM support. Transport services include support for HTTP, HTTPS, SMTP, file, message queuing, AICs, and a loopback interface.

- **Data parsers and serializers** The capability of understanding the documents that have been submitted falls to the data parsers. BizTalk includes parsers for many industry standards, such as XML, X12, and EDIFACT. The document validation is handled by the serializers for each document instance that is processed.

- **Reliable document delivery** BizTalk Server has capabilities to send documents at specific times, a configurable number of retries, and a centralized queue so that if one BizTalk Server within a group fails, the others can continue to submit the document.

- **Security** As mentioned previously, BizTalk Server 2000 implements full encryption and digital signature support, public-key encryption support for documents transversing public networks and decryption, and verification mechanisms for received documents.

BizTalk Orchestration Services

BizTalk Orchestration Services allow for a visual link between the business process and the implementation of that process. It supports loosely coupled, long-running transactions that may take months to complete. We discussed the BizTalk Orchestration Designer in the previous section "Features of BizTalk Server 2000," but that was only the surface of what is really going on. Microsoft has developed an entire language called XLANG (based on XML) to document a business process and its link to the implementation of that process. They have shielded the users from this by presenting it within a Visio interface, but the technology is really quite impressive. As mentioned previously, the drawings that you develop in the BizTalk Orchestration Designer are then compiled into an executable form. This executable is called an XLANG Schedule and is run by a service called the XLANG Scheduler Engine. Technologies that are used to implement the business process are the BizTalk Messaging Services, COM components, message queuing, and Windows script components.

BizTalk 2000 Administration Model

Earlier we defined the general areas of administration. Now we want to focus on the most important aspects of the administration model. We start by looking at the different queues that are available and detail the purpose of each. We then introduce the concepts relating to XLANG Schedule management and move on to a discussion of the benefits and administration tasks involved with setting up multiple server and server groups.

BizTalk Queue Management

Since the BizTalk Server is constantly going to be receiving and submitting documents, it is important to have a place to put those documents while we are waiting to process them. Figure 1.5 takes another look at the Administration tool. Now we are going to focus on the queues that you will have to work with as a BizTalk Server administrator.

Figure 1.5 BizTalk Server Administration Microsoft Management Console Snap-In

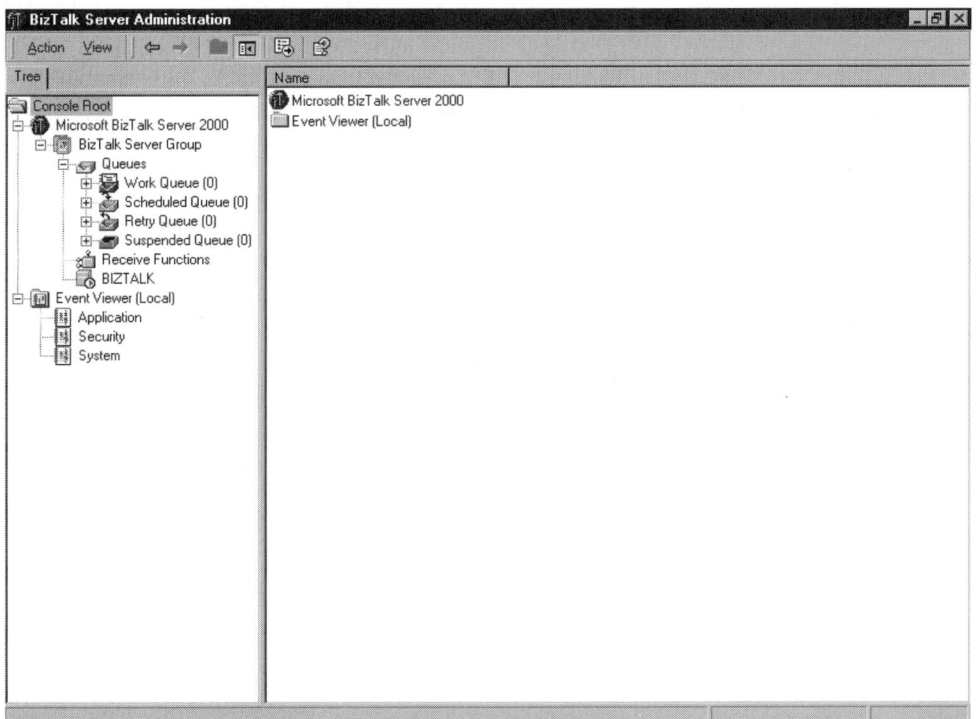

The four queues are defined as follows:

- **Work** The Work queue holds the documents that have been submitted via the IInterchange interface. Documents that are placed in this queue should be processed immediately. It should be rather rare for you to find any documents in this queue. Only when your server or server group has received more documents than can be processed will you find any documents in this queue. If you do find them in this queue, it should be a cause for concern. Ramifications, and if necessary, remedies should be investigated, including additional processing power.

- **Schedule** After documents are picked up from the Work queue, they are placed in the Schedule queue for delivery. Documents that are visible in this queue are ones that cannot be sent to their destination at this exact time, but are scheduled for delivery at another time. They may be waiting for a particular time (such as off-peak hours) for delivery.

- **Retry** If for some reason there is a problem with the message itself (e.g., it is either incomplete or improperly formatted), it will be moved to the Suspended queue. However, if the system is having trouble completing the actual delivery, the document will stay in the Retry queue while attempts to resend the document are made. You can configure how many times the system will attempt a retry on a document, as well as the interval between retries. This setting is under Retry options on the Advanced Configuration page within the Channel Wizard.

- **Suspended** There are a variety of reasons why a document may end up in the Suspended queue. If a document has continued to fail to be transmitted and has arrived at the maximum number of attempts threshold, it will be placed in the Suspended queue. If a document is not properly formatted, it will be placed in the Suspended queue. The list goes on. Normally, we will end up deleting the documents within this queue, but before doing so we can get some interesting troubleshooting information from the documents themselves. We can look at the error information returned from the Messaging Services as well as additional document information depending on the state of the document.

NOTE

For troubleshooting queue problems, consult Microsoft.com online BizTalk Server documentation and look for "Suspended Queue States." Microsoft provides a detailed table which lists common states, error messages, and explanations/suggestions.

XLANG Schedule and Instance Management

An XLANG schedule is executed when you develop an application that instructs the XLANG Schedule Engine to create an instance of an XLANG schedule. This application can be an ASP page, command-line Visual Basic Script application, or a full-blown application written in VB or C++. You can also create an instance of the XLANG schedule by using a message port that has been configured to send a business document to an XLANG schedule. An example of this might be the submittal of a document to a file or message queue.

WARNING

We highly recommend that you create a service account to manage COM+ applications that host XLANG schedules. Otherwise, they will log on using the "Interactive user" account and will stop processing if the interactive user logs off the server.

Remember, XLANG schedules may represent transactions that may take months to complete, and there might be multiple instances of the same XLANG schedule running in memory at one time. It would be impractical to attempt to track the status of these transactions in memory. The Orchestration Persistence database is used to record the current state of every XLANG schedule instance. When an XLANG schedule is currently not needed, it is moved out of memory and its current state is recorded in the database along with all the instance-specific persistence data needed to recreate it at a later time. This process is called *dehydration*, which frees up active memory and returns it to the system. This will occur any time the XLANG schedule is waiting for a message and no other activity is occurring within the XLANG schedule. Only a small portion of the XLANG schedule will stay in memory, waiting for the next event to occur. When this happens—for example, when a message arrives at a port—the XLANG Scheduler Engine will retrieve this instance information and recreate the rest of the object in memory. This is called *rehydration*. This process allows BizTalk Server 2000 to support business processes that can occur over the course of months and persist through server failure, while still providing the required services.

Server and Group Management

Using the BizTalk Server 2000 Administration tool shown earlier, you will con-figure the properties of the individual servers and the global settings that apply to groups of servers. First, we need to discuss the setting for the Messaging Management database. Right-clicking the **Microsoft BizTalk Server 2000** node and choosing **Properties** will produce the screen shown in Figure 1.6. You can also choose **Action** and then **Properties** from the toolbar menu once you have the correct node highlighted. This screen sets the master configuration of your BizTalk installation. This object is placed in the hierarchy above the server groups. If you are creating a custom console, you might have to provide this information. It will read the Messaging Management database for the list of groups and server properties, but you have to tell it where to start. This data will be saved as part of the local machine's registry.

Figure 1.6 Microsoft BizTalk Server 2000 Properties

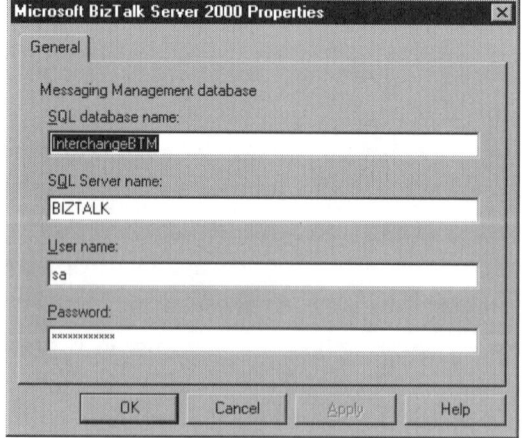

From there, you can look at the properties of the server groups by right-clicking and selecting **Properties**. Four tabs are available for group configuration (Figure 1.7). Remember, these settings will apply to all the servers in that partic-ular group.

- **General** Properties handling SMTP and general Internet protocol settings.
- **Connection** Server and database names for the Tracking and Shared Queue databases, along with login information.

- **Tracking** Settings related to the audit level requested for the group.
- **Parsers** The list of installed parsers and the order in which they are attempted.

Figure 1.7 BizTalk Server Group Properties

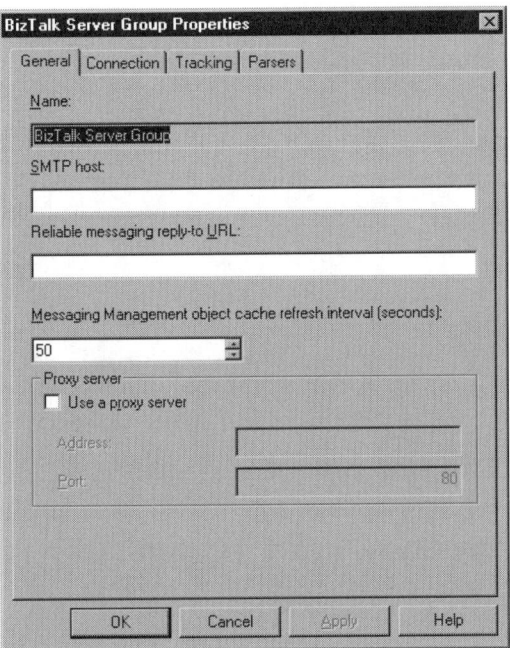

Below the Server Group level in the hierarchy are the individual server settings. Simply right-click and select **Properties** on the server in question (Figure 1.8). This is where you can tweak the properties for an individual server. If you have a server with ample processing power and a large number of documents to process, you can increase the number of worker threads per processor or reduce the latency in the BizTalk Server Scheduler. In the main window, you can also view the status of the server, which will show its active state.

Additional Options

As shown previously, all the servers within a Server group will share the Shared Queue and Tracking databases. If you need to separate the workload into different groups, simply right-click on the **Microsoft BizTalk Server 2000** node and select **New | Group**.

Figure 1.8 Properties of an Individual Server

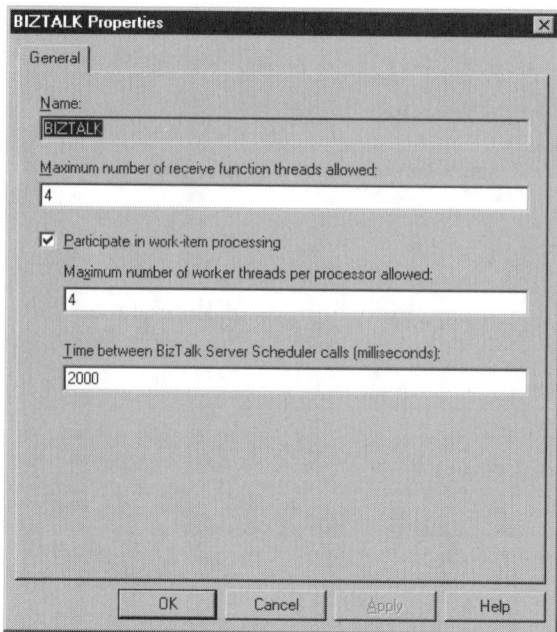

Implementation of Open Standards

One of the core BizTalk Server 2000 features is its capability to transform documents from one format to another. In doing so, Microsoft had to embrace the standards that were available. Microsoft has long been known for creating their own standards and going their own way. However, in the case of BizTalk Server 2000, they really have tried to use the available standards when possible, and to work with broad industry groups to create specifications when there was nothing available.

In this section, we are going to look at Microsoft's use of these broad industry groups and available standards in the BizTalk Framework 2.0, SOAP specification. We also want to spend a little time looking at the other e-business specifications and how they relate to BizTalk Server 2000.

BizTalk 2.0 Framework

As discussed previously, just supporting XML is not enough for large-scale, cross-platform application interoperability. BizTalk Framework is a set of guidelines put forth from a broad group of businesses on how to define documents and messages to enable e-commerce, building on top of existing standards such as HTTP,

MIME, XML, and SOAP. BizTalk Framework 2.0 provides the basis for interoperable reliable messaging in BizTalk Server 2000. The idea behind the framework is that it allows vendors on any operating system or platform to create a server that can understand BizTalk documents and BizTalk messages. This initiative can be as open and interoperable as the vendors choose to make it.

SOAP

When we start to discuss application integration, one topic that always comes up is the desired capability to access the method of objects. Over the years, a myriad of protocols enabled this capability, but all of them faced cross-platform communication barriers. For example, take Microsoft's RPC mechanism, where you have to have a number of ports open on a firewall to allow for communication between two systems using RPCs. Furthermore, forget about trying to invoke a method to a component via DCOM that is running on a Linux server.

This is where the Simple Object Access Protocol (SOAP) comes in. Put simply, SOAP allows you to invoke a method from a remote component and retrieve the result in a cross-platform manner. When first drafted, SOAP was based on XML and HTTP as the transport protocol, but in version 1.1 (which is still in draft form at the W3C), it enables communication over a flexible number of transports, including SMTP. Microsoft recently has been doing demonstrations of this technology, using a layer of applications built upon SOAP dubbed "Web Services" to describe its behavior, codenamed Hailstorm. The benefits of this system are tremendous. It gives us the capability to treat an entire Web site as an object with methods to address. Let's say, for example, that you want to create your own personal investment tracking Web site. With SOAP, you could construct a page that at runtime invokes a query price method and takes a stock symbol as input to a Web site like Microsoft Investor that could then return the current stock prices that you could integrate into your content.

Since SOAP primarily uses HTTP at this point, a SOAP document (which all BizTalk documents are) could pass easily through any firewall for application integration.

Other Frameworks

Since Microsoft is not the only vendor that is making a push into this area, it is important to look at the other frameworks for application integration and business-to-business e-commerce. The two that are the furthest along are RosettaNet and ebXML, which are discussed in the following sections.

RosettaNet

RosettaNet is a consortium of over 400 companies in the technology, electronic components, and semiconductor manufacturing verticals that have developed a series of business-to-business e-commerce specifications. RosettaNet is a self-funded, nonprofit group focused on creating, promoting, and implanting open e-business standards. These standards include the RosettaNet Business Dictionary, RosettaNet Technical Dictionary, RosettaNet Implementation Framework (RNIF), and RosettaNet Partner Interface Processes™(PIPs™). For more information, go to www.rosettanet.org.

Microsoft was one of the founding members of RosettaNet and on April 18, 2001, they announced the development of the Microsoft BizTalk Server Accelerator for RosettaNet. This product provides a series of tools and technical resources that expand BizTalk Server 2000 to significantly reduce the amount of time and resources required to build, deploy, and manage RosettaNet-based solutions.

ebXML

Probably the most direct competition to the Microsoft BizTalk Framework is the ebXML series of specifications. Officially established by the OASIS group and the United Nations (UN/CEFACT) in 1999, with support of companies such as Sun Microsystems and their related partners, they were tasked with facilitating international trade and developing technical solutions for e-commerce. On May 14, 2001, they announced, via a press release, the official approval of the current ebXML specifications by their task force. Their specifications attempt to address many of the same areas of concern in business-to-business e-commerce as the BizTalk Framework 2.0. However, since they have been somewhat late in releasing their solution, Microsoft has a distinct head start. In the long run, only time will tell who will have the greatest success, but we predict that before long you will see an enterprising third-party develop an ebXML to BizTalk component that offers complete integration between these two systems. You can get more information on ebXML from www.ebXML.org. For more information about the ebXML sponsors, go to www.uncefact.org and www.oasis-open.org.

Summary

In this chapter, we introduced BizTalk Server 2000 as Microsoft's next initiative for integrating e-commerce partners and Enterprise Application Integration (EAI) solutions. BizTalk Server differs from legacy solutions such as EDI in that it allows for very loosely coupled, long-running transactions that are easily able to respond to changes in the business process. BizTalk Server 2000 is part of the .NET Enterprise Server family, Microsoft's next-generation platform that will control how users, client applications, tools, and servers will interact in a networked/Internet-based universe.

BizTalk Server 2000 allows organizations to document and then automate their business processes using a set of dynamic, graphical tools. Business analysts are able to work side by side with developers using the BizTalk Orchestration Designer. This tool allows for a Visio-based environment with which an analyst can diagram the business flow, which allows the developer to then connect the implementations within the diagram. We also introduced BizTalk Server 2000 tools such as the BizTalk Editor and BizTalk Mapper, which allow you to create the specifications to describe your documents and the desired transformations that you wish to perform. The graphical BizTalk Administrator, Document Tracking, and Message Manager applications provide us easy access to all the required configuration and troubleshooting facilities the product has to offer.

BizTalk is based on open standards such as XML, SOAP 1.1, and the BizTalk Framework 2.0. It is designed to allow for an open binding architecture that enables BizTalk Server to easily be integrated into a mixed environment. This open binding architecture allows development to take place using a variety of programming languages, including Visual Basic, C++, or even Java. The BizTalk Server product is backed by the BizTalk.org Web site, which allows the capability to trade BizTalk schemas publicly to further facilitate the development of business-to-business e-commerce applications. Its support for XML, X12, EDIFACT, SAP R/3, flat files, and positional files allows it to work with both legacy and modern systems.

Solutions Fast Track

Overview of Microsoft BizTalk Server 2000

☑ BizTalk Server 2000 acts as the universal translator between the disparate systems that have evolved within an organization and between organizations. It is based on open industry standards and specifications to allow communication for application-to-application interactions.

☑ BizTalk is part of the .NET family of Enterprise Server for building and managing your complete IT infrastructure.

Why Use BizTalk?

☑ BizTalk uses XML to provide a way to describe the schemas for XML messages and the technology to help you route these XML messages and process them as the messages are transmitted from business to business.

☑ The BizTalk initiative comprises: BizTalk Framework 2.0, BizTalk.org, and BizTalk products. This initiative hopes to solve the problems of the past, using new technologies and specifications to truly enable application integration for the masses.

BizTalk 2000 Application Model

☑ BizTalk applications are a collection of components working together to automate your business process.

☑ BizTalk Messing Services are the key to receiving, transporting, parsing, and delivering documents.

☑ BizTalk Orchestration Services are the key to developing the business process flow, rules, and logic behind the transformations.

BizTalk 2000 Administration Model

☑ The Graphics BizTalk Server Administration tool makes it easy to configure group and server properties.

☑ Administrators must maintain a watchful eye on the Work, Schedule, Retry, and Suspended queues to ensure proper flow.

☑ The process of dehydration and rehydration of XLANG schedules conserves resources while allowing for very long-running transactions.

Implementation of Open Standards

☑ Microsoft BizTalk Server 2000 is based on the open XML protocol, backed by the BizTalk Framework 2.0 for cross-platform integration.

☑ BizTalk Servers can be developed on any platform.

☑ A BizTalk document is a SOAP 1.1-compliant message for easy integration.

Frequently Asked Questions

The following Frequently Asked Questions, answered by the authors of this book, are designed to both measure your understanding of the concepts presented in this chapter and to assist you with real-life implementation of these concepts. To have your questions about this chapter answered by the author, browse to **www.syngress.com/solutions** and click on the **"Ask the Author"** form.

Q: Is BizTalk another proprietary Microsoft product? Do you have to be in a complete Microsoft environment to derive any benefit from it?

A: No. While there are parts (such as XLANG) that Microsoft had to develop due to lack of existing standards in some cases, none of those parts are exposed to the outside world. BizTalk Server's external interfaces are all based on open interoperable standards.

Q: What file formats does BizTalk Server support?

A: XML, flat files (delimited and positional), and EDI (ANSI X12 and EDI-FACT) documents. In addition, it has an open binding architecture that allows for additional third-party add-ons to increase this support using the supplied SDK that ships as part of the Enterprise Edition.

Q: What platforms does BizTalk Server 2000 really support?

A: While it does claim to support all versions of Windows 2000, including Datacenter Server, Advanced Server, Server, and Professional, you should really consider using Windows 2000 Professional machines in a development or testing environment, and not as production servers.

Q: What database products does BizTalk Server 2000 support?

A: While it does require SQL 7.0 with Service Pack 2 or SQL 2000 for its internal storage, you could use COM components as part of your business process that use data from any ODBC or OLE-DB data source.

Q: What XML specifications does BizTalk Server 2000 support?

A: BizTalk Server 2000 ships with the Microsoft XML Parser version 3.0. This provides support for standard XML documents and SAX2, DOM2, XSLT, and XPATH.

Chapter 2

Planning an Installation of BizTalk 2000

Solutions in this chapter:

- **Identifying System Requirements**

- **Designing and Planning Your Installation**

- **Installing and Configuring SQL Server**

- **Installing and Configuring Visio SR1**

- **Installing and Configuring BizTalk Server**

☑ **Summary**

☑ **Solutions Fast Track**

☑ **Frequently Asked Questions**

Introduction

The first step to a successful BizTalk implementation is the design and documentation of the environment in which your solution will run. Even the smallest implementation should begin with an initial analysis of your current infrastructure. Questions such as, "How will I use BizTalk to help me?" or "How many servers will I need to install BizTalk?" addressed in advance of implementation will help to maintain the administrators' sanity. Frameworks and methodologies such as Microsoft's Solutions Framework or Rational's Unified Process help guide us to provide professional and successful projects.

BizTalk 2000 provides tools for management of both the Messaging and Orchestration services. BizTalk Document Tracking, BizTalk Server Administration, and BizTalk Messaging Manager are the tools provided to assist in the management of the many facets of BTS. BizTalk also provides a rich object model that allows programmatic administration of routine and/or special tasks.

The following sections walk you through your installation of BizTalk Server 2000. We outline the hardware and software requirements for the various BizTalk releases. By the end of this chapter, you will have the knowledge and capability to successfully install BizTalk for both large and small organizations. You will also understand how the various administrative tools are used to manage and maintain your BizTalk installation.

Identifying System Requirements

To successfully install BizTalk Server 2000, you must first identify all the hardware and software requirements and, of course, implement them. Only after you have the proper configuration can you then proceed with the installation. Do not try to take shortcuts. BizTalk Server 2000 is somewhat unlike other products that you might have installed in the past. It is not simply pop in the disc and click-click your way through the installation. Proper time *must* be given to laying a solid foundation for BizTalk. Without that, you are doomed from the start, because BizTalk Server is a very resource-intensive product that can easily overwhelm smaller systems. It is also very configuration intensive with what appear to be minor configuration steps that are easily overlooked and can prevent a successful configuration of the product.

Hardware

We begin by looking at the minimum hardware requirements. As we all know, these minimum requirements are just that, the minimum that you can use. In a true production scenario, the actual hardware requirements will depend on a multitude of factors all relating to what you are actually trying to do with the product.

The significant minimum hardware requirements for a basic installation of Microsoft BizTalk Server 2000 include:

- An Intel Pentium 300 processor
- 128MB of RAM
- A 6GB hard disk

We discuss running BizTalk server in a large-scale environment later in this chapter. For now, we will assume that you are starting with a test or development environment.

Software

The following section outlines the software that must be installed to run Microsoft BizTalk Server 2000. The software that is required will depend on which installation method you choose: Complete, Custom, or Tools. All three installation methods require the following base software or options:

- Microsoft Windows 2000 (Professional, Server, Advanced Server, or DataCenter Server)
- Windows 2000 Service Pack 1
- Internet Explorer 5.0 or later
- Vision 2000 SR1A (required to use BizTalk Orchestration Designer)

The Complete and Custom installation methods require:

- SQL Server 7.0 with Service Pack 2 (SP2) or SQL Server 2000. This could be on the same server or on a different server.

Windows 2000

There are several operating system requirements that you should verify before you begin your installation of BizTalk Server 2000. The following are the required operating system components or options that BizTalk Server 2000 is dependent on:

- **Service Account** You must have an account available that is a member of the local Administration group to use as a service account. If you do not create a service account, BizTalk Server 2000 will configure itself to use the Local system user account. Further, several components will be configured using the **interactive user** account. If the user logs off, the BizTalk Server 2000 services will fail. During installation, this account will be given the **logon locally and act as part of the operating system** user rights. If you forget to specify this account during the installation, you can always come back and do so, but then you will have to manually assign these user rights. Please note that even if you do select a service account during the installation, you will still have to come back and reconfigure some components away from the interactive user account.

- **NT File System (NTFS)** Due to the sensitive nature and importance of the documents involved we need to make sure that we can place tight security on the files and folders within the file system. NTFS allows us to do that.

- **Internet Information Server (IIS)** BizTalk Messaging Manager will not run unless the World Wide Web Publishing Service (provided by IIS) is running.

- **Microsoft Message Queue (MMQ)** BizTalk Server takes advantage of the builtin MMQ service as one of the primary methods to store and route documents. This is a required service for BizTalk Server to do it's job.

- **Service Pack 1** You must install Service Pack 1 before launching the BizTalk Server 2000 installation. SP2 is recommended.

- **Hotfixes** At the time of writing, there are two suggested post Service Pack 1 hotfixes—Q275872 and Q279130 are suggested. Please see Microsoft's TechNet site for more information. These are incorporated into SP2.

- **Internet Explorer** IE should be configured to allow the local server name as part of the Trusted Zone setting and clear the **require server authentication** setting.

There are, of course, also several versions of Windows 2000 that you could be running. These are listed in Table 2.1, along with the benefits associated with each.

Table 2.1 Choosing the Correct Version of Windows 2000 Operating System

Product	Benefits
Windows 2000 Professional	The Windows 2000 Professional operating system is designed for business desktop users. This can be used as a development workstation with BizTalk Server 2000. Although the product allows you to install the full version on Windows 2000 Professional, it is most common to install just the development tools that you would use to create solutions with BizTalk Server 2000 running Windows 2000 Server or higher.
Windows 2000 Server	This will be the typical operating system with which BizTalk Server 2000 is deployed. It provides the best platform for file and print, Web server, and group mail, as well as Biz Talk Server 2000. Scales from 1 to 4 processors and up to 4GB for RAM.
Windows 2000 Advanced Server	If you have enhanced performance and scalability requirements, this would be the appropriate selection, as Windows 2000 Advanced Server scales from 1 to 8 processors and up to 8GB of RAM. Enhanced reliability and availability— provides two-node clustering; 32-node network load balancing.
Windows 2000 DataCenter Server	Best platform for large-scale line-of-business and enterprise .com backend usage. Supports server consolidation and enhanced scalability. Scales from 1 to 32 processors and up to 64GB of RAM. Maximum reliability and availability— provides four-node clustering; 32-node network load balancing.

NOTE

Windows 2000 Service Pack 2 has shipped. It includes the aforementioned hotfixes and this author has installed and configured BizTalk Server 2000 using SP2 with no problems. Furthermore, post SP2, a serious buffer overflow security flaw has been found within the Internet Printing Protocol implementation. This flaw allows for complete root access over HTTP to any server with IIS 5.0 installed. This and several additional related security flaws have been corrected by several post-SP2 hotfixes. It is recommended to install at a minimum SP2 and hotfixes; Q282784 and Q293826. Please see www.microsoft.com/security for the download links and more details for these fixes.

IIS

Internet Information Services (IIS) has a setting that you should configure before installing BizTalk Server 2000. To avoid problems accessing and saving specifications to the BizTalk Server 2000 repository, you must turn off the Enable authoring options within IIS. The following steps guide you in the configuration of this option:

1. On the **Start** menu, point to **Settings**, click **Control Panel**, double-click **Administrative Tools**, and then double-click **Internet Services Manager**.

2. Click the **expand indicator** (+) for the local IIS server.

3. Right-click **Default Web Site**, and click **Properties**.

4. The Default Web Site Properties dialog box appears. Click the **Server Extensions** tab and clear the **Enable authoring** check box (Figure 2.1).

WARNING

Do not install Visio 2002. Although BizTalk Server 2000 SP1 has shipped, it *does not* provide for compatibility with Visio 2002. This will be addressed in a later service release.

Figure 2.1 The Server Extensions Tab of the Default Web Site Properties Window

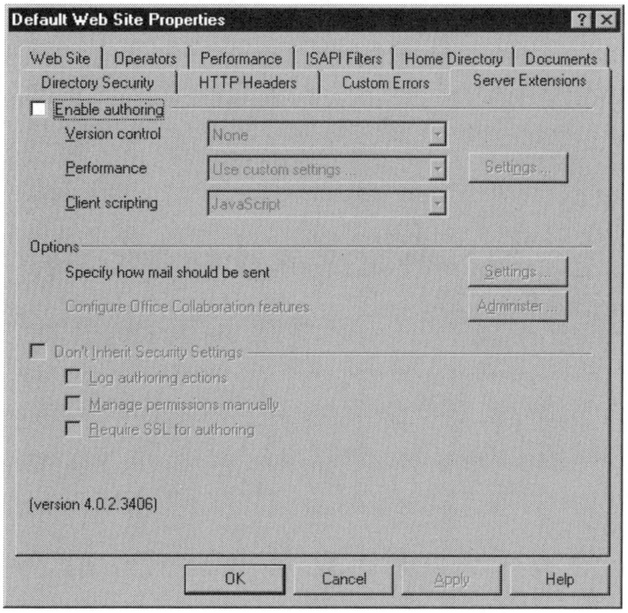

Message Queuing

After the installation of the operating system, you must add the Microsoft Message Queuing (MMQ) component. It is not installed by default. This is required for BizTalk Server 2000 to process messages. Message Queuing servers store messages locally and can send and receive messages even when they are not connected to a network.

To add the Message Queuing, simply go to the **Add/Remove Programs** icon in **Control Panel | Windows Components**, scroll down, and select **Message Queuing Services** (Figure 2.2).

Figure 2.2 Selecting the Message Queuing Services in Windows Components

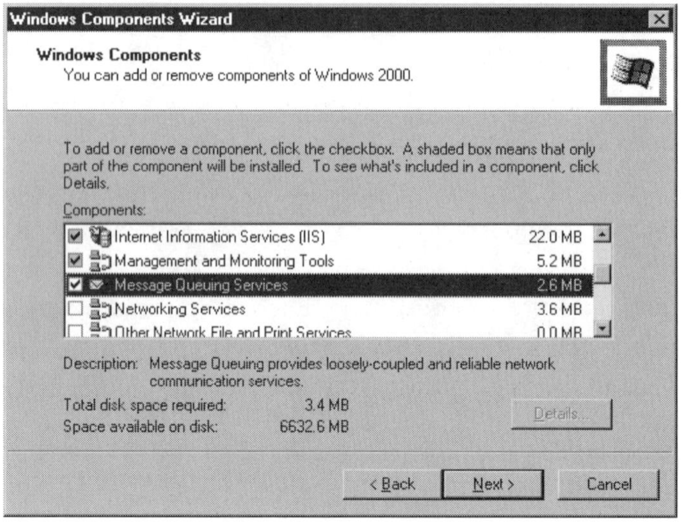

A Summary of Optimal Performance Suggestions Recommended for a Large Organization

There are some special recommendations that you should review if you are going to be configuring BizTalk Server 2000 in a large organization (LORG). This will provide for the greatest level of scalability possible with the BizTalk Server product.

- Microsoft recommends that you build a three-server configuration. In this configuration, one server would run BizTalk Server 2000, you would install SQL Server on the second server for purposes of managing the Tracking database, and then install the BizTalk Messaging Management and Shared Queue databases on a third server.

- It is possible to configure one or more BizTalk servers to be dedicated to processing functions, and one or more dedicated to receiving the inbound document requests. Separate the workload across multiple servers with each server handling one of these duties.

- As with any large-scale solution, you have to look at the underlying hardware. One area of concern is the disk subsystem. The Microsoft recommended configurations include four SCSI II or higher hard disks. You should dedicate one drive to the Windows page file, the second to document tracking and storage, one to the tracking log file, and the final drive to the Distributed Transaction Coordinator (DTC) log. Do no just assume, however, that a RAID 5 array is a faster or better solution. You have to look carefully at the data involved. A RAID 5 array involves calculating extra parity information for each byte of data written. You have to decide if that extra overhead is worth it in each situation.

- It is possible to create multiple instances of receive functions to monitor multiple receive locations for documents that are to be processed. To balance the load of documents across several computers, locate the receive functions on separate computers. Each monitoring location must be unique and must have a separate receive function. You can combine this with features such as Windows load balancing, DNS round robin, or load-balancing products such as Cisco Local Director to evenly distribute the load across multiple servers.

- For more information on these topics, please refer to the BizTalk online documentation, as it has a great deal of useful information to assist you in the planning process for LORG implementations.

Scaling the BizTalk Server Vertically and Horizontally for Large Organizations

BizTalk Server 2000 is capable of scaling to even higher loads by vertical and horizontal design methods. *Vertical* scaling generally means that we will simply increase the capabilities of the same physical number of servers. *Horizontal* scaling means that we will increase the number of physical servers in our design. By increasing the number of processors and amount of memory, you can vertically scale BizTalk Server 2000. The benefits of vertical scaling are that it requires fewer servers and makes server administration less complex. However, it is generally a more expensing solution, as servers that include multiple processors and large memory support are much more expensive. By scaling an architecture horizontally, you are increasing administration complexity, but will be able to increase scalability using lower-cost servers. Moreover, once capacity on existing hardware is maximized, you must begin to scale the system horizontally. A proper approach is to use both scaling methods, balancing the benefits and costs of each.

Vertical Scaling Tips

To experience the highest level of performance with BizTalk Server, we recommend the following:

- A multiprocessor PIII Xeon MHz processor system capable of being upgraded to eight CPUs. You need to make sure you select the correct version of Windows 2000 in order to scale to this level. Windows 2000 Server scales to 4 processors, Windows 2000 Advanced Server scales to 8 processors, and Windows 2000 Datacenter Server can scale to as many as 32 processors.

- A 1 to 2MB L2 processor cache (increases parsing performance).

- 512 MB of RAM per server (more if your organization will be processing multiple-megabyte documents).

- Multiple 100 Mbps (megabits per second), or greater, network cards connected to 100MB switch ports to increase network I/O throughput.

- Consider writing DTC log operations to a central remote server or storage area network (SAN) to offload file I/O contention on the local BizTalk server.

- Use dual honed network interface cards (NICs) in the BizTalk servers to separate HTTP processes from the Shared Queue and BizTalk Messaging Management databases dedicated SQL Server processes.

This is assuming that you are running BizTalk on a dedicated server. If you are sharing this server with additional .NET applications, additional hardware is required.

NOTE

Keep in mind that if you are running Windows 2000 Server on a single CPU, adding three additional CPUs improves performance, but does not increase the processing speed of one CPU by a multiple of four. Moreover, beyond eight processors there is a scale of diminishing returns as you add additional processors, due to additional overhead and context switching. You might want to consider horizontal scaling at that point.

Horizontal Scaling Tips

Scaling horizontally provides many benefits:

- **Performance** Performance is able to exceed what could be cost-effectively accomplished on a single server.

- **Server fault tolerance** By adding several servers into the system that perform overlapping duties, it is then possible to provide for the failure of one of these servers. Should disaster occur, the traffic could be switched over to the remaining server.

- **Separation and custom optimization methods** By placing pieces of the system on different physical servers, you are able to tweak the settings on each server to best suit each component. If everything is installed on the same system, sometimes a setting you want to make to improve one component will negatively affect another component. By having them physically separate, you do not have to make a middle-of-the-road decision.

To achieve the highest performance, it is recommended that you place key components of BizTalk Server 2000 on different physical servers. The key components of BizTalk Server 2000 can be broken down into the following categories:

- **BizTalk services** These services include BizTalk Messaging services and BizTalk Orchestration services.

- **Databases** These databases include the BizTalk Messaging Management, Tracking, Shared Queue, and Orchestration Persistence databases.

- **Transport services** The transport services include HTTP, File, SMTP, and Message Queuing. Each component has unique scaling requirements.

Designing and Planning Your Installation

Like any new product that is deployed, the BizTalk Server 2000 installation process should be thoroughly planned out. We must have a detailed plan of action. Since BizTalk Server 2000 is an Enterprise Application Integration (EAI) server, you must start with an understanding of the existing applications with which

BizTalk Server 2000 will be communicating, and the environment in which it will be running. Next you will need to determine which version of BizTalk Server 2000 is appropriate for your environment.

Documenting Your Environment

Every deployment at this level should be aligned with an organization's enterprise architecture. The Microsoft Enterprise Architecture is a system that describes the four key perspectives within an organization and how they relate to one another to provide information technology-based solutions. It is key to understand the large picture before trying to deploy BizTalk Server 2000. Microsoft defines the four key perspectives within an Enterprise Architecture as:

- The **business** perspective that identifies the goals and objectives of the organization.

- The **application** perspective that represents the collection of applications that support the business processes.

- The **information** perspective that documents what the enterprise needs to know to run its operation, as well as the interactions between the applications and information.

- The **technology** perspective that represents the components and technologies needed to build and run the organization's system;, it also links the technology to the applications and information architectures.

Specifically within the technology perspective, you should document the following:

- Network topologies and backbone infrastructure (routers, switches, etc.)

- Application development environment (do you have a test lab?)

- Security polices and structures such as firewalls

- Other network services such as DNS, WINS, DHCP, Windows load balancing, and IIS

- Database management systems

Each of these items will affect the nature and manner in which you deploy BizTalk Server. One additional item you must document is the anticipated volume of documents that BizTalk Server 2000 will be processing, and from this decide on the scaling choices up front.

If you would like more information about Microsoft suggestions on the contents of an enterprise architecture, we suggest learning about Microsoft's Solutions Framework (MSF), which is part of their Enterprise Services Framework. Please view www.microsoft.com/enterpriseservices for general information. For a specific example of what should go into an enterprise architecture, read the EA whitepaper at microsoft.com/trainingandservices/content/downloads/EnterpriseArchitectureEssentials.doc.

Which Version of BizTalk 2000?

Microsoft has put together several different editions of BizTalk Server 2000. Each edition is targeted to a specific audience and priced accordingly.

Enterprise

The Enterprise edition is targeted at large organizations, business-to-business or business-to-consumer trading exchanges, or any type of digital marketplace. It has unlimited support for application integration and unlimited numbers of trading partners. From a hardware point of view, Enterprise edition is targeted to large servers, as it supports an unlimited number of processors, scale-out clustering, and failover clustering capabilities. It is designed to handle the largest transaction volumes.

Standard

The Standard edition is targeted at small and medium-sized organizations. It has a hard-coded limit of integrating with just five internal applications and business partners such as exchanges or digital marketplaces. The other limiting factor is that BizTalk Server 2000 Standard edition does not have support for multiple processors or clustering environments.

Developer

The Developer edition is designed to give a developer all the tools and technologies that he or she needs to develop a BizTalk solution. It allows BizTalk Server 2000-based solutions to be developed and tested for later deployment into a production BizTalk Server 2000 environment. It ships with the same software as the Enterprise Edition, but is limited from a licensing standpoint to a single developer use. Note that the licensing supports only a *one-time* transfer from a user to another user. In an effort to reduce software piracy, Microsoft is limiting your ability to resell the product once purchased, and it bans indirect transfers (e.g., flea markets, etc.).

Licensing

The licensing system for BizTalk Server 2000 is based on a per–CPU pricing model. Purchasing client seats or Internet connector licenses is not required for BizTalk Server 2000. The Developer edition retails for $499 (unlimited CPUs), Standard edition $4,999 (one CPU), and the Enterprise edition at $24,999 (one CPU). All prices are in U.S. dollars and are the estimated retail.

NOTE

If you have a series of Web servers as the front end for you applications, you should use message queues to submit documents to the BizTalk servers. This is due to the fact that if you install the BizTalk Server COM Object, IInterchange, which allows for submitting documents to BizTalk Server programmatically, on your Web server, you will have to purchase a BizTalk Server 2000 license for each CPU of your BizTalk server *and* for each CPU on your Web server.

Installing and Configuring SQL Server

BizTalk Server 2000 supports both SQL 7.0 with Service Pack 2 and SQL 2000. When you install BizTalk Server 2000, the installation procedure is going to create four databases (the BizTalk Messaging Management database, the Shared Queue database, the Tracking database, and the Orchestration Persistence database) within SQL Server. It is vital that you have a correct SQL Server configuration, as it is the heart of the BizTalk Server 2000 product.

Setup

The SQL Server 7.0 or 2000 installation itself is straightforward if you are installing a fresh copy to support BizTalk Server 2000. The major setting change if you are installing SQL 2000 is that you must configure your SQL Server to support Mixed Mode authentication rather than the default of Windows Only. Figure 2.3 shows the selection during the installation.

If you have already installed the server, you can change this configuration at any time. Figure 2.4 shows where in SQL Enterprise Manager you would go if you wanted to change this after the installation. This is not a problem if you are installing SQL Server 7.0, because Mixed Mode is the default selection. You simply need to verify that this has not been changed from the default setting since the SQL server software was installed.

Figure 2.3 Authentication Mode Selection for a Fresh Installation of SQL Server

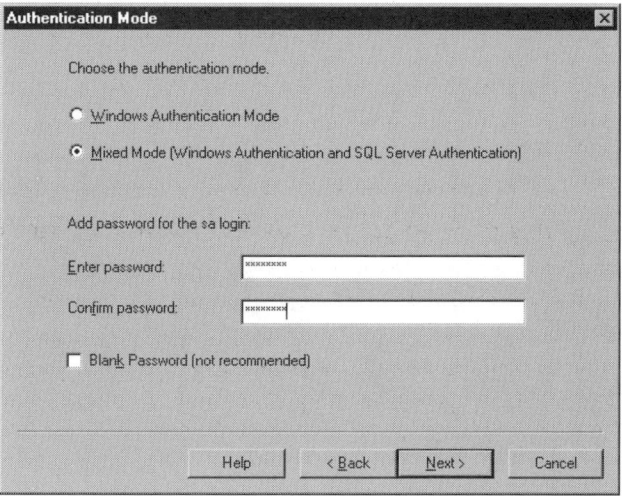

Figure 2.4 Authentication Selection for Existing Servers

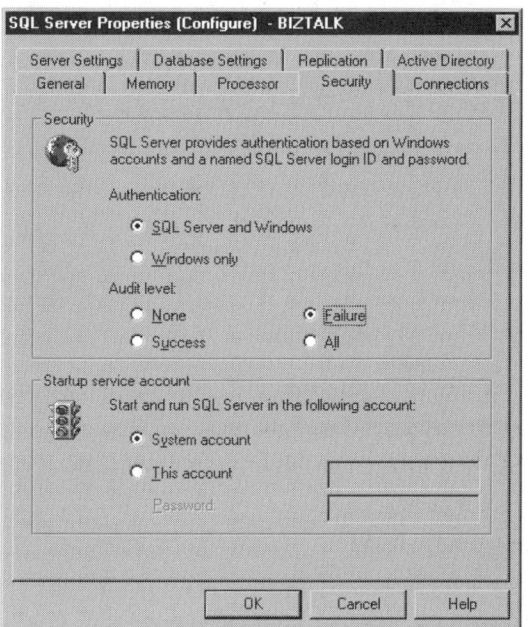

If you are installing SQL Server in an environment where it will be running beside other SQL servers, it is recommended that you select the same Sort Order, Character Set, and Unicode Collation that are in use on your other SQL servers, as this will make moving databases to other servers down the road much easier. See Figure 2.5. Please note that Figure 2.5 is a SQL Server 2000 screen shot.

Figure 2.5 Collation Settings

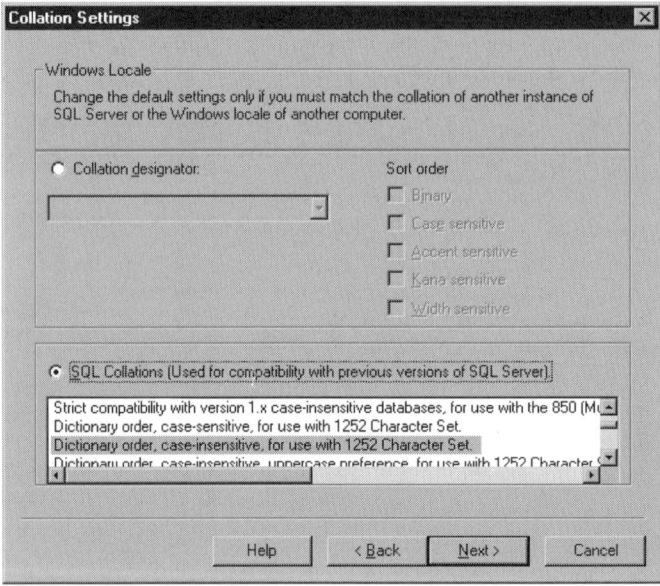

You must be logged in to your server with Administration permissions, and it is preferred that you configure a SQL Service Account as well. In any situation where there is the possibility that the server software will have to communicate on the network, creating a service account will be a required setting versus using the Local system account option. The Local system account does not have network privileges.

Cluster Server Scenarios

BizTalk Server Services are not supported to be used with the Windows 2000 Advanced Server Clustering Services. You can, however, install SQL Server in a clustered environment. If you do so, you will need to install the SQL Client Tools on the BizTalk Server 2000 server in order to be able to communicate to SQL Server properly. To install the SQL Client Tools, simply insert the SQL Server CD-ROM into the BizTalk server and begin the SQL Server setup. However, rather than choosing the **typical** or **custom** setup options, make sure to select

Install Client Tools. This will provide the required connectivity to the clustered SQL server. You need to make sure that you have configured the network library to TCP/IP on both the SQL server and during the installation of the SQL Client Tools. Please refer to the BizTalk documentation on changing the default network library on your SQL servers.

Testing

After you have installed SQL Server, it is vital that you test the installation. First, verify that the SQL Service is starting using the **SQL Service Manager** tool or **Enterprise Manager**. Next, make sure that you have the server in Mixed Mode authentication. You can do this by launching **Query Analyzer**, and in the **Connect using** dialog box, click **SQL Authentication** and then log in using the SA account to verify connectivity to the server.

We can run some basic queries to verify that the installation was successful in creating all the default system objects. Verify that the **master database** is selected, and type **SELECT ★ FROM INFORMATION_SCHEMA.SCHEMATA**. You should see a list of the installed databases: master, tempdb, model, msdb, pubs, and northwind.

It is also vital that you make sure you are using at least Service Pack 2 for SQL Server 7.0. Use **SELECT @@VERSION** to verify that you have upgraded to SQL Server Service Pack 2, and Windows 2000 Service Pack 1. The following is the output you should receive:

```
- - - - - - - - - - - - - - - - - - - - - - - - - - - - -
Microsoft SQL Server  7.00 - 7.00.842 (Intel X86)
     Mar  2 2000 06:49:37
     Copyright (c) 1988-1998 Microsoft Corporation
     Standard Edition on Windows NT 5.0 (Build 2195: Service Pack 1)
```

This will help you verify that you have at least build 842 of SQL 7.0, which is the SP2 build number, and at least build 2195: Service Pack 1 with Windows 2000 applied. If these numbers do not match, go back and make sure you installed the correct service packs.

Installing on Microsoft Windows 2000 Professional

Although you can install BizTalk Server 2000 on Windows 2000 Professional, SQL 7.0 and SQL 2000 do not support Windows 2000 Professional. You will be required to install SQL Server on a computer other than your BizTalk server.

MSSQL 2000

The key thing to remember when installing BizTalk Server 2000 on Microsoft SQL Server 2000 is to select **Mixed Mode** authentication from the default of **Windows Only**. This is sometimes referred to as "SQL and Windows" authentication.

Installing and Configuring Visio SR-1A

As part of the prerequisites for the BizTalk Server installation, you will need to install and configure Visio SR-1A or later. The BizTalk Orchestration Designer is based on the existence of a Visio installation. The manuals lead you to believe that you can technically install this later, but we like having everything installed and tested first, and then install BizTalk Server 2000. If we were to do it in the other order and for some reason the BizTalk Orchestration Designer has problems, we would not really know if it was Visio's fault or BizTalk's fault, and would end up having to remove both to find out. By installing and testing Visio first, any problems that are found would be directly related to the BizTalk Server installation.

Setup

The installation of Visio, while quite long, is rather straightforward. Most likely, before the system starts the actual installation of Visio, it will update a few system objects and require a reboot before you continue the installation. You want to be sure to allow it to reboot, because not doing so can cause this and later installations to fail. In addition, make sure to restart the installation after the reboot. After my reboot, I took some time and started working on a few other things. I then came back to try to finish the Visio installation, and it seemed to have forgotten that it had already initialized the installation and did it again! So, however many times it takes, eventually you should get to the screen shown in Figure 2.6. This shows that Visio has completed the preinstallation initialization and that the system is ready to begin the Visio installation. From there, the installation is very simple: simply choose which templates your want to have as part of your Visio installation and it will proceed. It really does not matter which templates you select; none are specifically required for your BizTalk Server installation.

Testing

After the installation, make sure that one selection in particular is enabled: **Enable automation events** (Figure 2.7). The **Enable automation events** selection should be enabled by default. However, if Visio was previously installed it is possible that someone might have changed this and it needs to be on for BizTalk Server 2000 to successfully install.

Figure 2.6 The Completion of Preinstallation Initialization Screen

Figure 2.7 Checking to See If Enable Automation Events Is Enabled

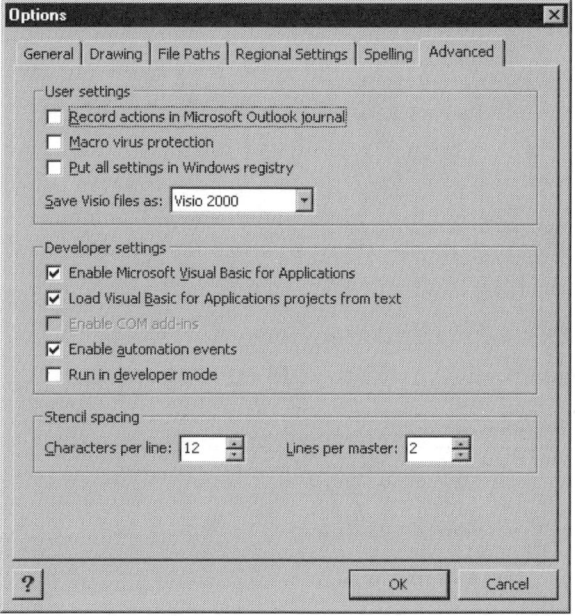

Visio 10/2002

There are some known issues with Visio 2002. It is not supposed to be included with BizTalk Server 2000 at this time. Microsoft is addressing this in an upcoming service release, but for now, stay away from it on any system on which you want to use the BizTalk Orchestration Designer. The BizTalk Orchestration Designer is based on Visio 2000 and will not work properly with Visio 2002.

Installing and Configuring BizTalk Server

In this section, we are going to walk through a complete BizTalk Server 2000 installation. This section explains the differences between the installation methods and the options that you will find during each step of the installation. Please note that the installation is based on a Microsoft Windows Installer Package. This allows for easy removal and repair of failed installations. Microsoft has also provided a setup.exe, which when double-clicked launches the .msi package installation file.

Complete/Custom Installation

The Complete/Custom installation will include all the BizTalk Server 2000 services, tools, and samples. The only difference with the custom installation is that you have the opportunity to override the default choices to select only a subset of features. Before you launch the installation, make sure you are logged on as a member of the local Administrators group on the server in which you are installing BizTalk Server 2000. This installation option requires 52MB of disk space, not including the space required for the databases.

BizTalk Server 2000 Complete/Custom installation includes the following services:

- **BizTalk Messaging Services** Includes a parse, serializer, correlator, and runtime binaries.
- **BizTalk Orchestration Services** Allow you to integrate business processes by providing an executable business-process file called an XLANG schedule.

BizTalk Server 2000 includes the following tools:

- BizTalk Orchestration Designer
- BizTalk Document Tracking
- BizTalk Editor

- BizTalk Mapper
- BizTalk Messaging Manager
- BizTalk Server Administration

The Installation wizard will create four SQL Server databases, and you will have to decide on their location. This location needs to be active during the installation, as it will not complete without being able to set up these databases.

The installation will begin with a basic splash screen. You will not get very far past this if you do not have the perquisite software installed. Figure 2.8 shows that this screen also provides a link to the readme.htm page. You might want to take a few minutes and read this for any additional information that might apply to your particular situation.

Figure 2.8 BizTalk Server 2000 Setup Wizard

The next set of screens relates to licensing. You will be presented with a screen documenting the licensing restrictions. Make sure to read this; it will verify which version of BizTalk Server 2000 you are installing. It would be a disaster to go through a complete installation thinking that you are installing the Enterprise edition, only to find that you installed the Developer edition. This initial license screen is about the only place you can see a difference between the versions. After the licensing agreement screen, the next screen will prompt you for your username, organization, and product key (Figure 2.9). You *must* have a valid license key. Some Microsoft products allow you to supply a generic number, just to get past the screen, but not BizTalk Server 2000. You must have a valid

BizTalk Server 2000 key to move forward. In addition, you have the option of limiting the access to BizTalk Server 2000 to just the person who is doing the installation; however, in most cases you should select **Anyone who uses this computer**.

Figure 2.9 Registration and Licensing Information for Microsoft BizTalk Server

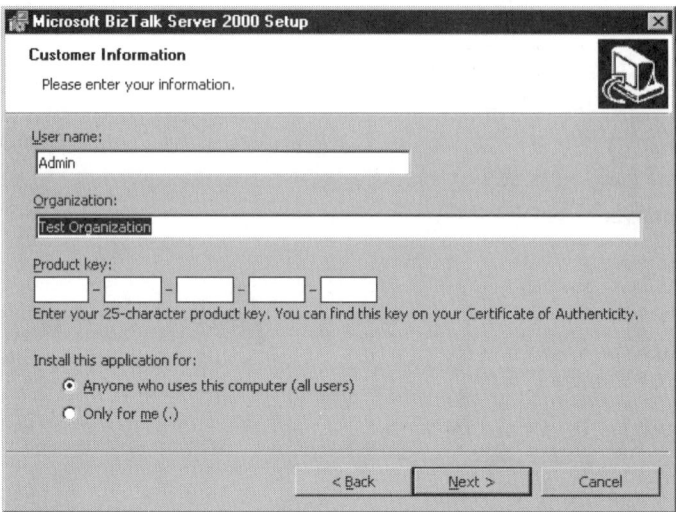

In the Destination Folder screen (Figure 2.10), you have the option of choosing the directory where BizTalk Server 2000 is installed. We recommend leaving it on the default path for development servers, as many of the online tutorial paths will be incorrect and a little more difficult, although certainly still usable. This is a single setting for all of the components, but on the following screen, you can choose a different location for some of the components. Also, note that it is verifying that the location is on an NTFS partition.

After you select the location, you will then be prompted for which type of installation you wish to perform. Note in Figure 2.11 that it also shows the amount of disk space that will be required for each installation, not including databases. For the Complete installation option, 52MB is required. See the next section for a discussion of the Tools installation choice. We will select **Custom installation** to continue our walkthrough.

The Custom option is identical to the Complete option, with the added capability of deselecting components and choosing a different location for some components. In Figure 2.12 you can see the four main choices during the Custom installation, Documentation, Services, Tools, and the SDK and Samples.

Each of the components can be installed in a different location; however, we recommend leaving the default options.

Figure 2.10 Installation Directory Selection

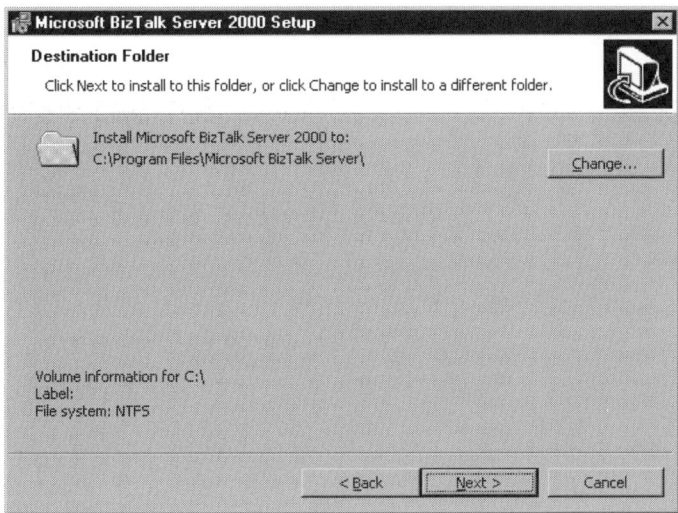

Figure 2.11 Installation Selection for Complete, Tools, or Custom Install Methods

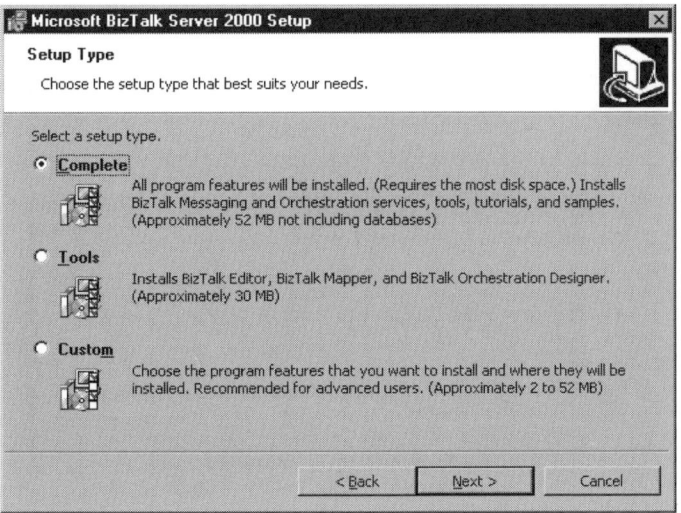

Figure 2.12 The Custom Installation Component Selection

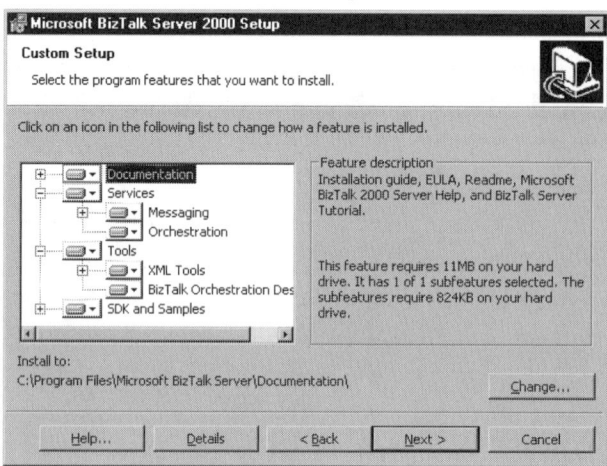

After selecting the Installation method, you will be prompted for the name of the Administration group that BizTalk Server 2000 will create (Figure 2.13). The members of this group will have full administrative control of the BizTalk server, so you should carefully choose the membership. Feel free to rename this group at this point, but unless you have a compelling reason, we suggest leaving the default. If you want to rename the group later, you will have to also edit the Windows Registry under HKEY_LOCAL_MACHINE\SOFTWARE\Microsoft\BizTalk Server\1.0\NTGroups. BizTalk Server 2000 uses this Registry key to point to the group.

Figure 2.13 Configuration of BizTalk Server Administrative Privileges

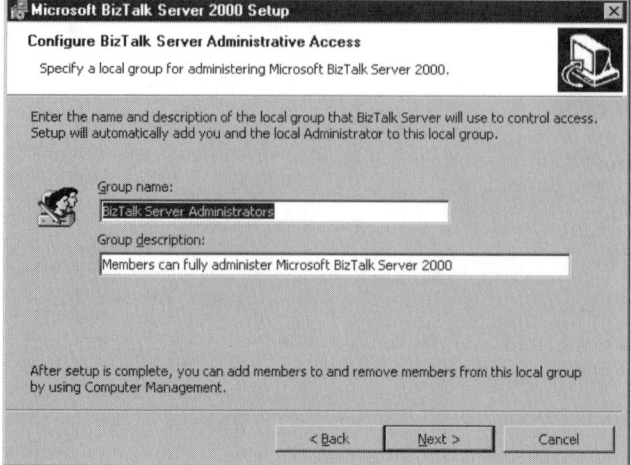

The next screen will be one of the most important selections that you make during your installation. This is one of those famous nonchoices from Microsoft, meaning that you appear to have a choice here, but in a production environment, it's not really a choice. If you truly want to be able to use this installation in a multiserver production environment, you must create and select a service account at this point during the installation. Otherwise, your service will be limited to communicating to itself due to the lack of network credentials. This account should be a member of the local Administrators group and have the "log on locally" and "act as part of the operating system" user rights. BizTalk Server 2000 will automatically grant this user account the "logon as a service" and "act as part of the operating system" user rights if the account does not already have those user rights (Figure 2.14).

Figure 2.14 System Account User Selection

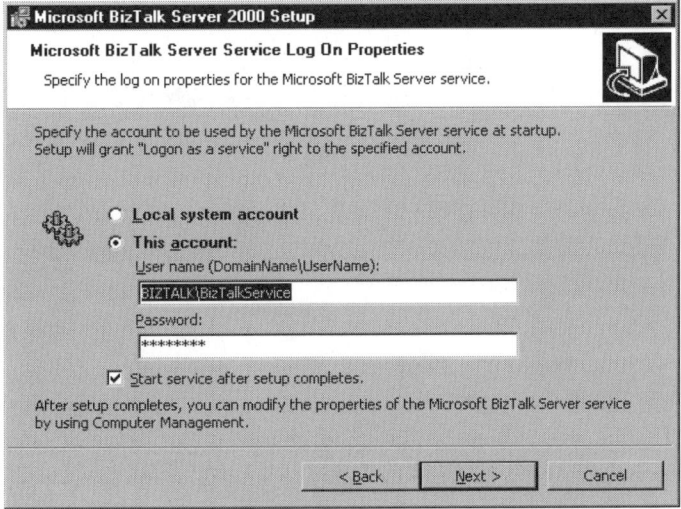

The next screen (Figure 2.15) is your last chance to change any options before the system starts the installation. One thing that will show up is a warning about not having Visio 2000 SR-1A installed. Even if you have it installed correctly, it will still give you this message. The first time I saw this screen I thought it had some sort of problem finding Visio, so I reinstalled Visio just to be safe, relaunched the BizTalk Server installation, and found the same message! Later I learned that it is simply a warning and is not really checking anything at that point.

You will then see the install progress bar (Figure 2.16). At about 80 percent, it will launch the Database Creation wizard. One note of interest is that if you abort out of the installation at any point, it actually will start sliding the progress bar *backward* as it is undoing the installation steps that were completed!

Figure 2.15 Verification of Installation Selections

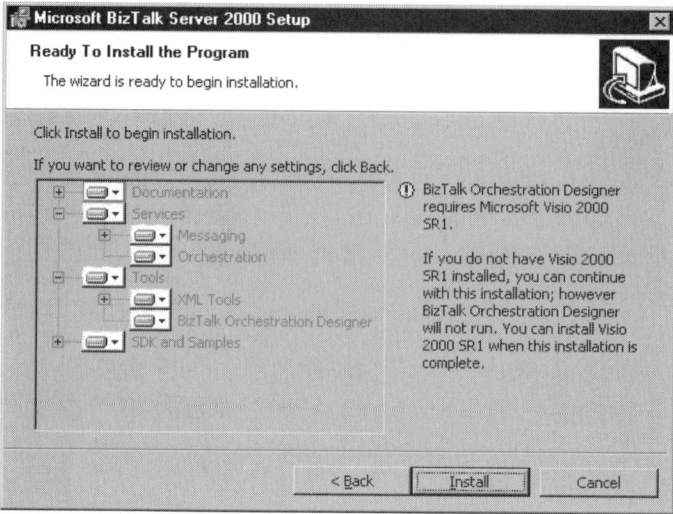

Figure 2.16 Installation Process Screen

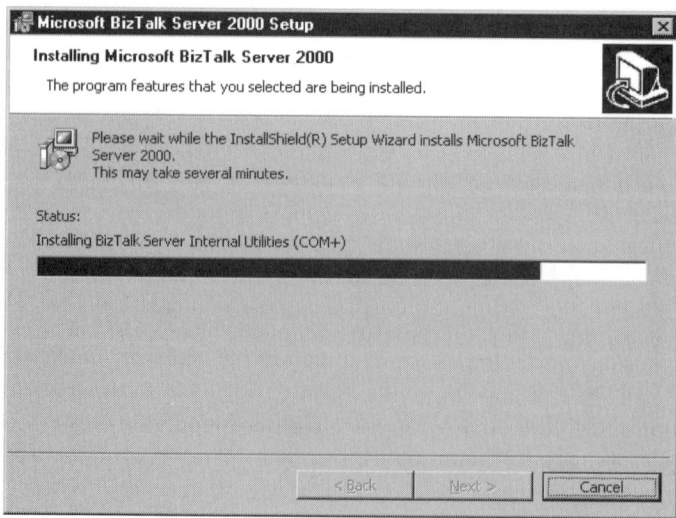

At this point in the installation, you will see the Database Setup wizard, which will walk you through the process of creating or connecting to the four databases that comprise the BizTalk Server 2000 environment. Table 2.2 lists the required databases and an overview of their functionality.

Table 2.2 BizTalk Server Databases and Their Functionality

Database Name	Number Required	Description
BizTalk Message Management	One per organization	This database stores the information that is related to all of the server configurations. This includes group and server settings, receive functions, and all of the messaging configuration information for the objects that are created by using the BizTalk Messaging Manager, or by accessing the BizTalk Messaging Configuration object model.
Tracking	One per server group	The Tracking database enables the tracking of documents that are processed by the server. This database is also used to track the XLANG schedule status.
Shared Queue	One per server group	This database stores all the documents—via a series of four queues—that are processed by BizTalk Server 2000, and the status of each.
Orchestration Persistence	One per server group	When an XLANG schedule is dehydrated, it is stored in the Orchestration Persistence database along with the current status.

After the splash screen (Figure 2.17), you will be prompted for the location of the databases and the necessary information to attach to the SQL server. If you do not want to use the SA (System Admin) account, you will need to use an account with SA access due to the requirement of the wizard to create a login ID. After the installation, you can go back and give BizTalk Server a lower-level account to use. In addition, remember that if you are installing the database on a remote SQL server, such as in the case of installing BizTalk Server on a Windows

2000 Professional machine, you will have to supply the name of the remote server where you installed SQL Server, rather than the local server name.

Figure 2.17 Messaging Database Setup Wizard

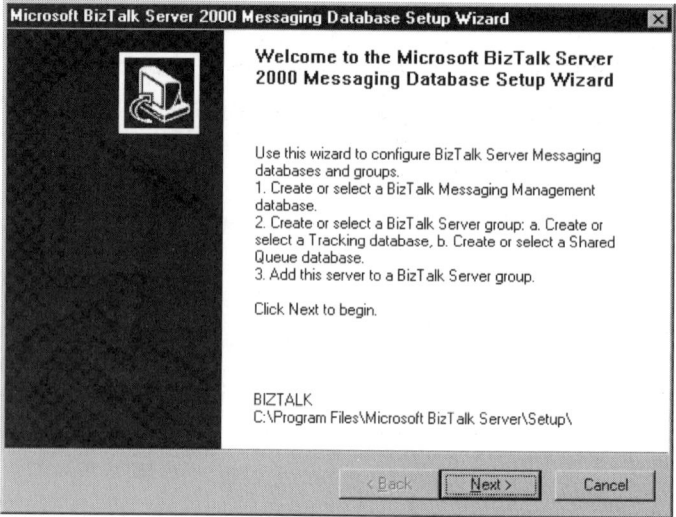

NOTE

If you tell BizTalk Server 2000 to use an existing database, it is recommended that you first delete all contents from the database. This is because the wizard will only check for the existence of a single stored procedure as its determination if the existing database is intact. If it finds this single stored procedure, it will not touch the database and nothing else will be configured. We personally find it to be easier to simply delete the existing databases (if we don't care about the existing data) and let it re-create the databases.

Figure 2.18 is the first of the four database wizard screens that you will see. After supplying the required information for the BizTalk Messaging Management database and clicking **Next**, you will see some screens pop up where it is executing the SQL scripts to create and configure the database. If there are any SQL connectivity problems, you will find out right here! You will generally have one database of this type per organization, so it is placed before you are prompted to select your server group.

Figure 2.18 Configuration of the Messaging Database

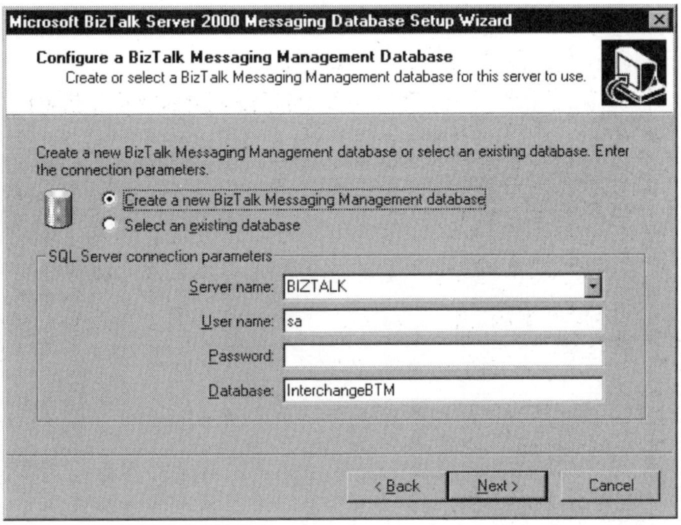

It is important to note that all the SQL databases created by this wizard have the **Automatically Grow Database** option selected. This option ensures that the database will never run out of space , until you fill your hard drive! You will need to monitor the sizes of these databases on an ongoing basis or risk filling your disk. Some of these databases include utilities to help reduce their sizes. You can choose to deselect this option, but you risk having serious problems should the databases fill up until you manually increase their sizes.

The next screen (Figure 2.19) addresses which BizTalk Server group you wish to join. If this is an installation of an additional BizTalk server, you will want to make sure to select the existing BizTalk Server group, unless you specifically wish to create a separate Server group. Earlier we discussed that servers should be in the same server group if you want them to share a common Tracking, Queue, and Orchestration Persistence database. This would be an appropriate choice if you needed to scale the workload beyond a single server, or if you wanted to create some fault tolerance within your design. If one server within a server group fails, the other servers have access to the same databases and are able to pick up where the first one left off. If this functionality is not desired, simply create a new server group. If you are sharing this SQL server with another Server group, you will need to provide a unique name for each instance of these databases. The suggestion is to supply the name of the Server group as part of the name of each of the databases.

Figure 2.19 BizTalk Server Group Membership Selection

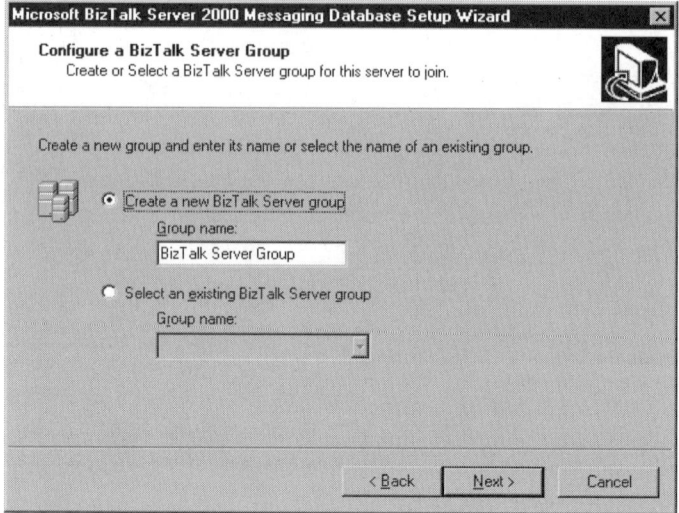

NOTE

BizTalk Server 2000 Service Pack 1 includes a recommendation for the archiving of this database, as well as a SQL script for purging the records in this database. Please review the Service Pack 1 readme.htm for complete instructions on the configuration of such a system and implementation of the SQL scripts.

If you decide to create a new Server group you will be prompted for the location of the document Tracking database (Figure 2.20). You can use the same SQL server for all the databases, or several different SQL servers for scalability. This database will grow quite quickly, as information about every interchange is recorded in this database. The SQL Script DTA_SampleJobs.sql, which is located in the \Program files\Microsoft BizTalk Server\SDK\Messaging Samples\ SQLServerAgentsJobs folder, is provided to help reduce the size of this database by removing records from the dta_debug_doc table if the number of records in the table is greater than 25,000. However, *do not* manually change any of this code or modify the database directly in any way that is not supported. Doing so might cause unexpected behavior, and might corrupt the database or result in the loss of data.

Figure 2.20 Configuration of the Tracking Database

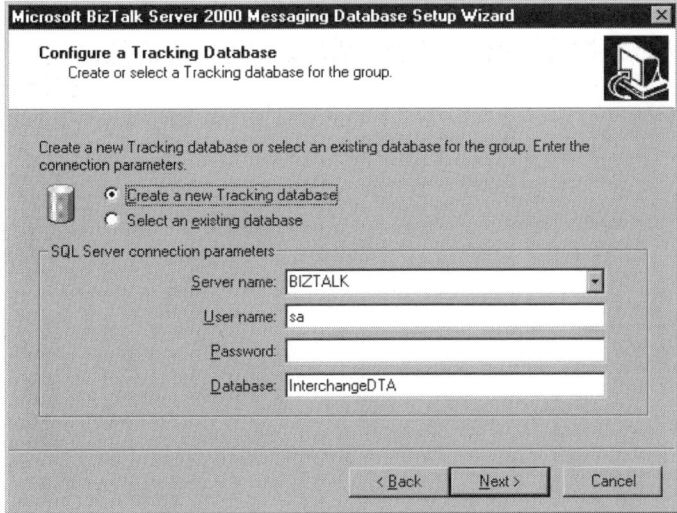

The next selection allows you to configure the Shared Queue database (Figure 2.21). This database maintains the four queues: Work, Scheduled, Retry, and Suspended. It does not have the same type of rapid growth issue as the Tracking database, and does not have any supplied database maintenance tools.

Figure 2.21 Configuration of the Shared Queue Database

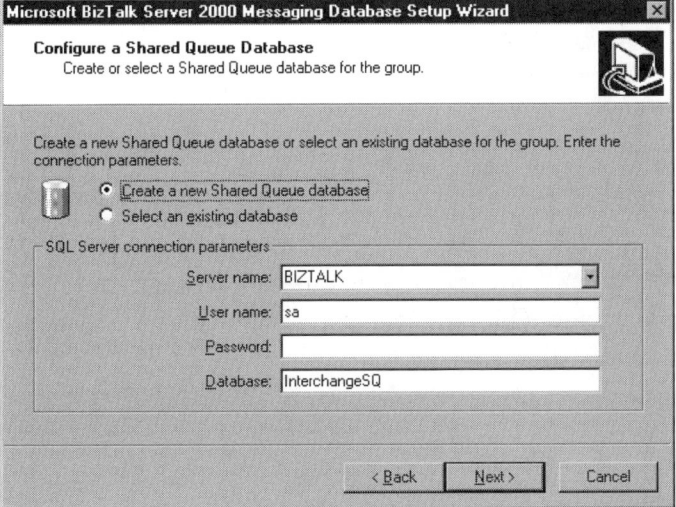

After you configure the first three database options, you will get a summary screen asking you to confirm all the selections. This is your chance to go back and change anything you missed (Figure 2.22).

Figure 2.22 Verify that the Information Is Correct

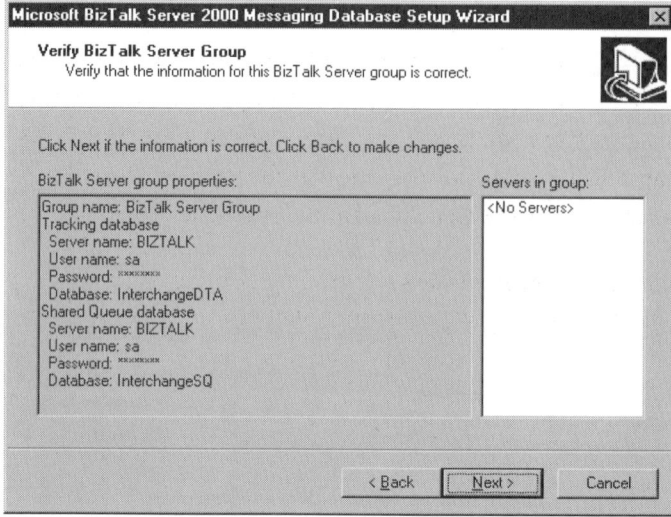

Clicking **Next** will complete the Messaging Database Setup wizard (Figure 2.23).

Figure 2.23 Completion of the Message Database Setup and Configuration

The wizard will then return briefly to the main BizTalk Server 2000 installation script and launch the final Database Setup wizard. This will be for the Orchestration Persistence database where the XLANG schedules are hydrated and dehydrated while we are waiting on the long-running transactions to complete (Figure 2.24). Once you complete these details, you are just about done! This database will grow quite quickly because even the completed schedules will still have audit data in the database. Procedures will have to be created to move this data into a database warehouse and off the production server. Microsoft recommends reviewing their Web site at www.microsoft.com/biztalk for additional whitepapers that discuss maintaining the Orchestration Persistence database and sample scripts that can be created and made available.

Figure 2.24 Configuration of the Orchestration Persistence Database

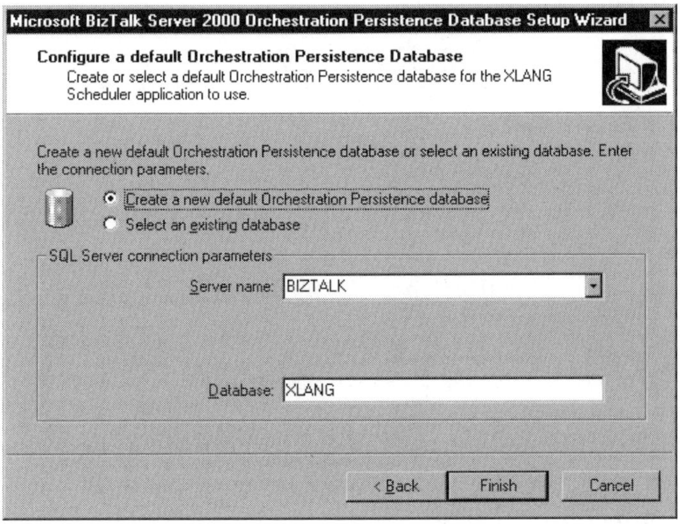

NOTE

BizTalk Server 2000 Service Pack 1 provides a SQL script for the maintenance of the Orchestration Persistence database. Please review the readme.htm that ships with the service pack for complete instructions on how to implement this SQL script.

If you set up everything correctly and made all the appropriate choices during the installation, this is the screen you should get (Figure 2.25).

Figure 2.25 BizTalk Server 2000 Setup Completion

Performance-Enhancing Registry Changes

To increase the performance of the BizTalk Orchestration Services, Microsoft recommends changing the default threading model from **Apartment Threaded** to **Both**. This allows for multiple threads per process, which can dramatically increase the number of threads BizTalk Server can create to handle the required workload. Microsoft has supplied a Registry file to assist with this process. Using **Windows Explorer**, browse to **Program Files | Common Files | System | ado**, and then double-click **adofre15.reg**. A confirmation dialog box will appear; click **Yes**, and then click **OK**. For a more detailed discussion of threading models, please review this TechNet Article: www.microsoft.com/NTServer/appservice/techdetails/prodarch/DCOM/5_ConcurrencyMgmt.asp.

The Internet Explorer Security Setting

After the installation is complete, when you attempt to use the Document Tracker Web application you will receive a security warning dialog box. To prevent this display in the future, follow these steps to add this server to the list of trusted sites:

1. Launch **Internet Explorer**.

2. On the **Tools** menu, click **Internet Options**.

3. After the Internet Options appear, On the **Security tab**, click **Trusted Sites** and click **Sites**.

4. The Trusted Sites dialog box appears. In the **Add this Web site to the zone** box, type the location of the BizTalk Document Tracking server.

5. To find the location of the BizTalk Document Tracking server, on the **Start** menu, point to **Programs | Microsoft BizTalk Server 2000**, and then click **BizTalk Document Tracking**. The location of the BizTalk Document Tracking server appears in the Address list.

6. Clear the **Require server verification (https:)** for all sites in this zone check box.

7. Click **Add**, and click **OK** twice to close the dialog boxes.

Review the Supplied Tutorials

One post-installation step we like to perform is to run through one of the supplied tutorials to make sure the system is functioning as expected. View the online documentation for more information about these tutorials. Figure 2.26 shows one of the completed tutorials screens in the Orchestration Designer.

Figure 2.26 Example of a Business Process Flow within the Orchestration Designer

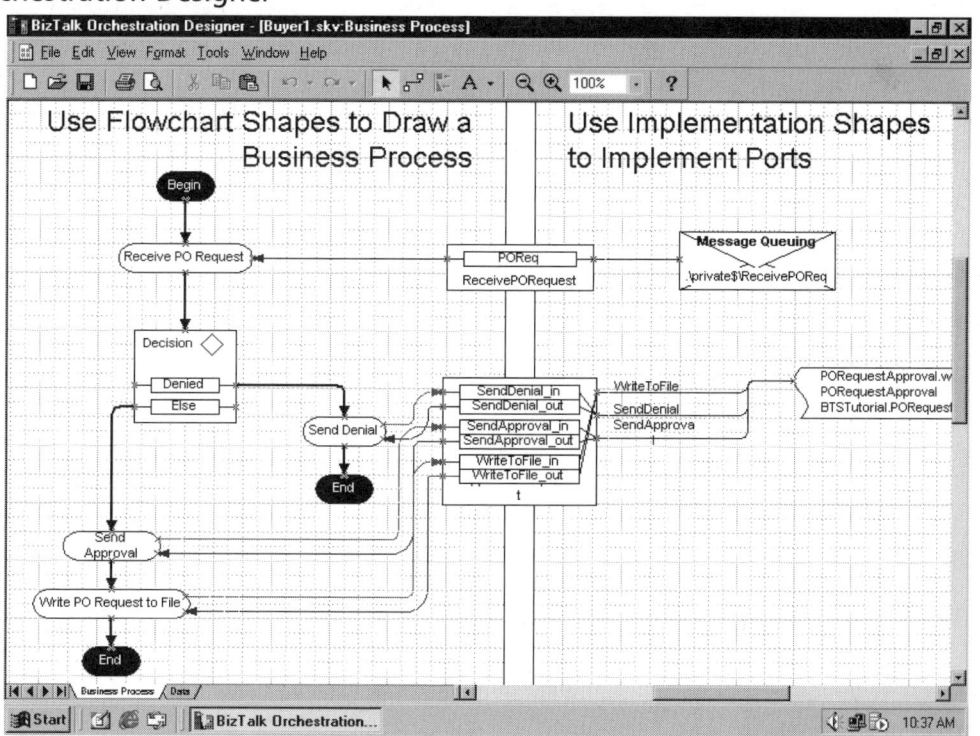

Tools Installation

You can choose to select the Tools installation method if you are in the role of a business process analyst or developer, and the BizTalk server will be located on another server. You will need all the same base software with the exception of SQL Server as outlined earlier.

The Tools installation allows you to install only the BizTalk Orchestration Designer, BizTalk Document Tracking, BizTalk Editor, BizTalk Mapper, and the BizTalk Server 2000 Help components. This installation method will require 2 to 52MB of disk space. This option might be appropriate for a developer or and administrator to use on his or her desktop to remotely support, manage, and develop for BizTalk Server 2000. This does not install any of the server components on the local machine. After the Tools install, you should be able to bring up the default BizTalk Orchestration Designer (Figure 2.27) to verify your installation.

Figure 2.27 Example of a Fresh Business Process Document within the Orchestration Designer

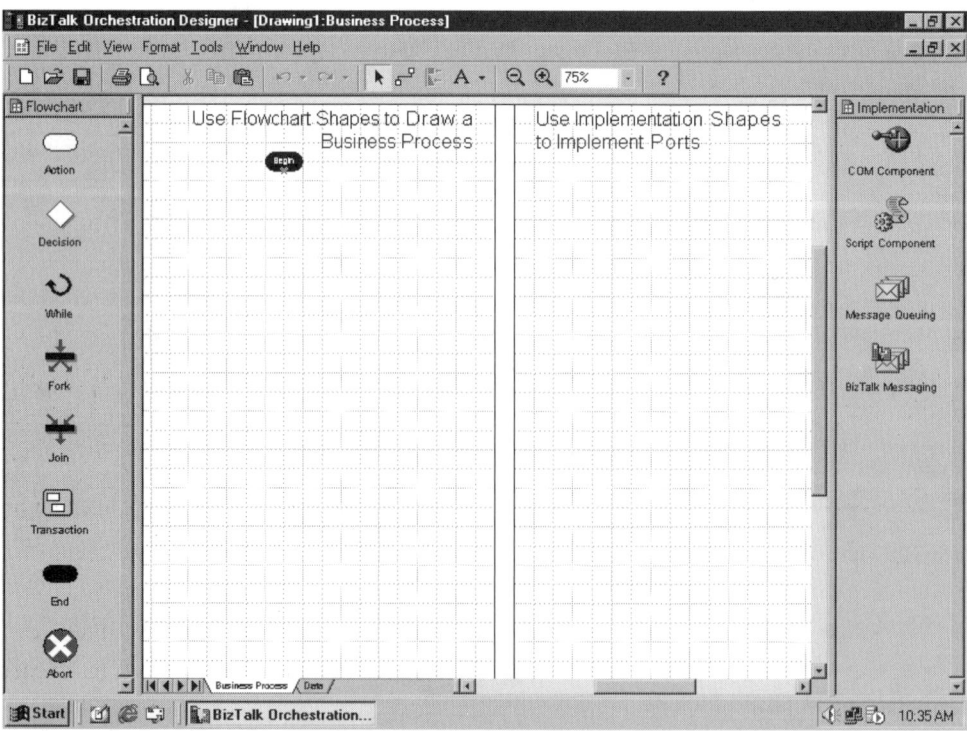

Unattended Options

For situations in which you will be configuring several BizTalk servers either in the same or different server groups, you probably will want to avoid manually performing the installation on each server. Instead, use the silent installation features to help ensure that the servers have identical settings. For example, let's say that we have three servers that are going to be part of the same Server group and share SQL that is installed on a fourth server, such as BIZTALK, BIZTALK2, BIZTALK3, and SQLServer1. For this example, we'll pretend that we have copied the entire CD up to a network share called **BTFILES** on a server called **IMAGESERVER**. We have also created an INI file called **SQLSettings.ini** to contain our SQL Server configuration, and all these servers are a member of a domain called **BTDOMAIN**.

Here is an example command line that will provide for a completely silent installation (this is one line, let it wrap; we broke it down to make it easier to read):

```
msiexec /I "\\IMAGESERVER\BTFILES\Microsoft BizTalk Server.msi"
/qb /Lv*"C:\Temp\install.log"
INSTALLLEVEL=200
BTS_USERNAME="BTDOMAIN\BizTalkService"
BTS_PASSWORD="password"
ALLUSERS=1
PIDKEY="your 25-character product key (without dashes)"
DSNCONFIG="\\IMAGESERVER\BTFILES\SQLSettings.ini"
```

The preceding command line is documented here:

- **ALLUSERS=1** controls the setting that allows the Registry changes made during the installation to be seen by all users. It is required.

- **BTS_USERNAME=** is the domain name and username of the service account you want to configure BizTalk Server to use. Without this, it defaults to the Local system account and is not recommended. You can also use a Local account; in that case, you could supply **.\BizTalkService** to avoid having to change the file for each server you want to use this file with. However, you would still have to create this user account before the installation.

- **BTS_PASSWORD=** is the password for the user specified on the BTS_USERNAME parameter

- **/I** is the command line to install the product rather than uninstall.

- **/qb** is the command line to present a basic user interface (progress bar only).

- **/Lv★** produces a log file based on the location and filename that you specify.

- **INSTALLLEVEL=200** installs the server. If you do not specify the INSTALLLEVEL, the value defaults to 100, which is the Tools installation of BizTalk Server 2000.

- **PIDKEY="your 25-character product key (without dashes)"** is the product key. For example, PIDKEY= AB6CDEFGH7IJK8LMN45LLTT34.

- **DSNCONFIG="\\IMAGESERVER\BTFILES\SQLSettings.ini"** provides DSN installation information to the Setup wizard.

Table 2.3 lists some other possible command-line options, their default values, and their descriptions.

Table 2.3 Other Command-Line Options

Parameter	Default Value	Description
USERNAME	Logged on User Name	The username information from the initial manual installation screen.
COMPANYNAME	Logged on Company	The organization information from the initial manual installation screen.
INSTALLDIR	"\Program Files\ Microsoft BizTalk Server"	The installation root directory.
BTS_GROUP_NAME	"BTSAdmin"	The name of the Windows NT group that the installation will create.
BTS_GROUP_DESCRIPTION	"Member can fully administer Microsoft BizTalk Server"	The description for the Windows NT group.
BTS_SERVER	"localhost"	The name of the BizTalk server.

Continued

Table 2.3 Continued

Parameter	Default Value	Description
BTS_SDK_SERVER	"localhost"	The name of the server for DCOM access (IInterchange).
BTSSETUPDB.INI	""	Instead of DSNCONFIG, this .ini can be broken down into two files. This file path supplies the location of the .ini file containing the information for the Messaging Service Database Configuration Wizard, BTSsetupDB.exe.
XLANGSETUPDB.INI	""	Supplies the file path to the .ini containing the information for the XLANG Database wizard, XLANGsetupDB.exe.

DSN Configuration File

This simple text file contains information about your SQL server, database names, and server group information. There are five basic sections within this text file, which are shown next. If the BizTalk Server group already exists, the rest of the settings are ignored. If the databases already exist, they will be left alone. This makes this script able to be used on the first and subsequent installations. If any of these values are not supplied, it uses a default value in each case. Server defaults to **localhost** and the other defaults have not been changed from the example file shown here:

```
SQLSettings.ini
;----------------------------------------------------------------
; SQL Server connection parameters for BizTalk Messaging Management
  database
; Required section used by BTSsetupDB.exe        .
; Specify new or existing database.
;
[InterchangeBTM]
```

```
Server=SQLSERVER1

Username=sa

Password=

Database=InterchangeBTM


;------------------------------------------------------------------

; Name for BizTalk Server Group

; Required section used by BTSsetupDB.exe        .

; Specify new or existing server group.

;

[Group]

GroupName=BizTalkGroup


;------------------------------------------------------------------

; SQL Server connection parameters for BizTalk Tracking database

; Required section used by BTSsetupDB.exe        .

; Optional if existing server group specified.

;

[InterchangeDTA]

Server=SQLSERVER1

Username=sa

Password=

Database=InterchangeDTA


;------------------------------------------------------------------


;

[InterchangeSQ]

Server=SQLSERVER1

Username=sa

Password=

Database=InterchangeSQ


;------------------------------------------------------------------

; SQL Server connection parameters for Orchestration database
```

```
; Required section used by XLANGsetupDB.exe      .
; Specify new or existing Orchestration database.
;
[Orchestration]
Server=SQLSERVER1
Database=XLANG
```

Uninstallation Instructions

To uninstall BizTalk Server 2000, simply click **Remove** within **Control Panel | Add/Remove Programs**. This uninstallation does not require input and removes almost everything that it installed. However, it will leave some remnants. For example, the installation uses the XML parser version 3.0; after the uninstall, this parser remains. In addition to OS upgrades that are within the system directory, it also leaves some files in its installation directory and miscellaneous Registry keys. These "leftovers" are documented here for your convenience. After doing several installations and uninstallations while using the Sysdiff tool to trace down what is left over, we have found that literally thousands of lines in the Registry remained, all referring to the components that are added to the system root or \program files\common files directories. If you want to attempt to remove BizTalk Server 2000 from a system, leave most of those lines alone; only a small number of items specific to BizTalk Server will need to be manually cleaned off.

These are the items you need to remove manually:

1. Delete the Directory: C:\Program Files\Microsoft BizTalk Server. Here are the leftover files in this hierarchy:

   - BTF1 Envelope.xml

   - CanonicalReceipt.xml

   - CommonAdvancedShipNotice.xml

   - CommonInventoryAdvice.xml

   - CommonInvoice.xml

   - CommonPartnerProfile.xml

   - CommonPO.xml

   - CommonPOAcknowledgement.xml

- CommonPriceCatalog.xml

- CommonShippingAdvice.xml

- CommonShippingOrder.xml

- Simple SOAP Envelope.xml

- CanonicalReceiptTo4010-997.xml

- CanonicalReceiptToD98B-CONTRL.xml

2. Drop all the BizTalk Server SQL databases and delete the associated database files: **C:\Program Files\Microsoft SQL Server\MSSQL\Data**.

- InterchangeBTM.mdf

- InterchangeBTM_log.LDF

- InterchangeDTA.mdf

- InterchangeDTA_log.LDF

- InterchangeSQ.mdf

- InterchangeSQ_log.LDF

- XLANG.mdf

- XLANG_log.LDF

3. Delete the BizTalk-specific Registry keys:

- HKLM\SOFTWARE\Classes\Applications\BzAppDes.exe

- HKLM\SOFTWARE\Classes\Applications\XLANGMon.exe

- HKLM\SOFTWARE\Microsoft\BizTalk Server

- HKLM\SOFTWARE\Microsoft\SystemCertificates\BizTalk

- HKLM\SOFTWARE\SAP

NOTE

Make sure you reboot the system after performing the uninstallation, as any components that are in use will not be removed until the next reboot. Proceeding with a new installation without restarting could corrupt your new install the next time you reboot.

Required XLANG Schedules Post-Installation Configuration

The XLANG Scheduler application, any new COM+ applications that you create, and the BizTalk Server Interchange application default to an **interactive user** account. If these components are left configured with the interactive user, they will shut down if the local user logs off the server. After installation, you must reconfigure these components to use a service account.

You will have to launch the **Component Services Administration** tool, expand down through the **My Computer** and **COM+ Applications** to view the list of packages. Then, right-click on the **XLANG Scheduler components**, select the **Advanced** tab, deselect **disable changes**, and then click **OK**. At that point, you can then go back into the properties of the XLANG Scheduler application component and any other COM+ applications that will host XLANG schedules, click the **Identity** tab, and then choose the **service account** you want. In most cases, this can be set to the same service account that you selected during the installation. See Figure 2.28 for a picture of what this should look like.

Figure 2.28 Configuration of the XLANG Scheduler Using the Component Services Administration Console

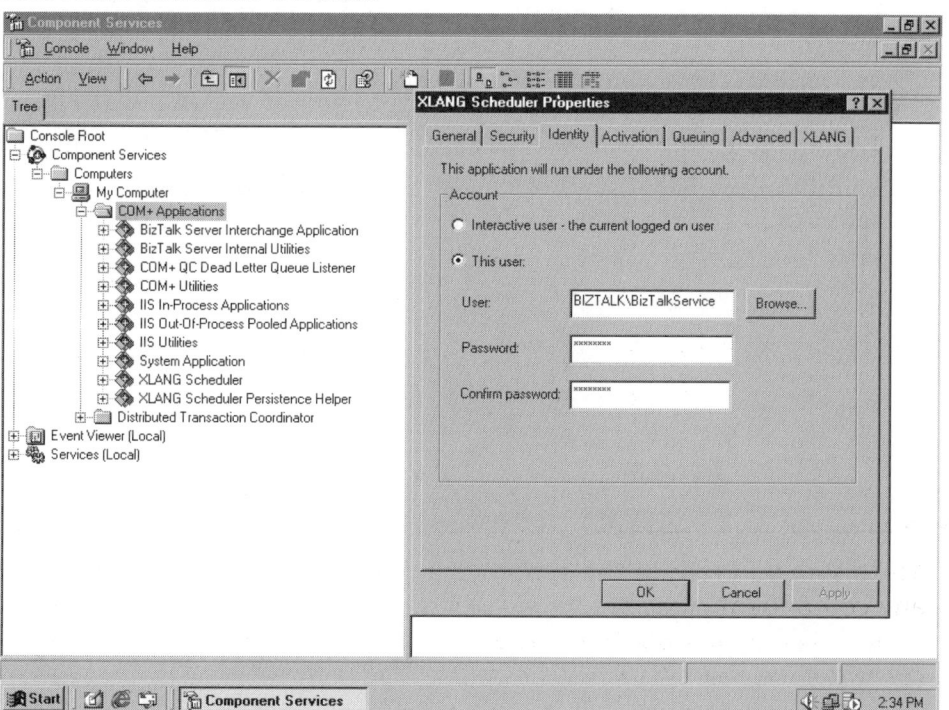

Advanced XLANG Schedule Configuration

If you need to manually configure the link between the XLANG Scheduler application because something happened to your default file DSN, or if you create another COM+ application to host XLANG schedules, you will have to provide the DSN information necessary to allow the XLANG application to know where to hydrate its schedules. You might also need to create multiple XLANG Schedule persistence databases to separate records for different vendors or business partners. Follow the path outlined previously and as shown in Figure 2.28, this time select the **XLANG** tab. On this tab you will have the options to **Create DSN**, **Configure DSN**, and **Initialize Tables**. If you created a new database within SQL Server to use as a persistence database, follow these steps to complete the configuration:

1. Select the **XLANG** tab for the component that will host the XLANG schedules that will be hydrated to the new database you created.

2. Click **Create DSN**. This will launch the ODBC DSN wizard. DSN files are limited in that they do not support connection pooling, but they are easier to share in a networked environment. Typically, System DSN provides all the options you need. Walk through the remainder of the wizard screens selecting your database; in most cases, you can use the defaults.

3. After you finish creating your DSN, you are not yet done—the database is still empty. We must click **Create Tables** on the **XLANG** tab to prepare the data structures that will hold our hydrated schedules. Do not select this option for an existing database, because it will destroy all the current data.

Summary

In this chapter, we introduced the installation process and basic configuration process. We began by making a thorough analysis of your needs to make sure that you selected the hardware and deployment options that will support the level of scalability required.

We discussed the system requirements to install and configure BizTalk Server 2000, the minimum hardware and software requirements, key installation options, and preferred configuration choices. The base installation requires that Windows 2000 with Service Pack 1, SQL Server 7.0 with Service Pack 2, and Visio SR1 are installed before launching the BizTalk Server installation.

We also introduced several key configuration steps. Before starting your BizTalk Server 2000 installation, make sure that the underlying services and configurations are present within Windows. Make sure the Microsoft Message Queue engine is installed. Within IIS, it is recommended that you disable authoring access. BizTalk requires several hotfixes in order to function properly; the easiest way to apply those is to apply Windows 2000 Service Pack 2, and for maximum security, make sure you apply all the post Service Pack 2 hot fixes as well. It is also helpful to create a BizTalk Service account, and select that account when you perform your installation to make management easier later.

Within your SQL Server configuration, it is important that you select **Mixed Mode** authentication. For maximum performance, don't forget to install the ADOfre15.reg file. The final key configuration setting is to verify that you changed the identity of the XLANG scheduler from the system account to the service account after your installation.

By following these basic guidelines, you should have a successful installation of BizTalk Server 2000. You also want to make sure that you review the Microsoft BizTalk (www.microsoft.com/biztalk) and the Microsoft Security (www.microsoft.com/security) Web sites prior to installation to verify if there are any new guidelines or hotfixes that should be included in your installation routine.

Solutions Fast Track

Identifying System Requirements

☑ The significant minimum hardware requirements for a basic installation of Microsoft BizTalk Server 2000 include:

- An Intel® Pentium 300 processor.

- 128 megabytes (MB) of RAM.

- A 6-gigabyte (GB) hard disk.

☑ All three installation methods (Complete, Custom, or Tools) require the following base software or options:

- Microsoft Windows 2000 (Professional, Server, Advanced Server, or DataCenter Server)

- Windows 2000 Service Pack 1

- Internet Explorer 5.0 or later

- Vision 2000 SR1A (required to use BizTalk Orchestration Designer)

Designing and Planning Your Installation

☑ In order to successfully design and plan your installation you must create a detailed analysis of current applications and a detailed analysis of current network infrastructure in addition to carefully planning your scalability requirements.

Installing and Configuring SQL Server

☑ Verify that Service Pack 2 is installed if you are using SQL 7.0, Use SELECT @@VERSION.

☑ Verify that the SQL server is set to Mixed Mode authentication.

☑ To dramatically increase the performance of BizTalk Orchestration Services, in Windows Explorer, browse to **Program Files | Common Files | System | ado**, and then double-click **adofre15.reg**.

Installing and Configuring Visio SR1

☑ Make sure you reboot after the installation upgrades some base OS files.

☑ Verify that **enable automation events** is enabled.

☑ Although the system says that you can install Visio after the fact, do it ahead of time.

Installing and Configuring BizTalk

- ☑ Make sure to choose the edition that meets your current and future needs.

- ☑ Select a service account during the installation rather than 'Local system account.

- ☑ If the SQL databases exist due to a failed or corrupt installation, delete them before a reinstallation.

- ☑ To uninstall BizTalk, launch the uninstallation from within **Control Panel | Add/Remove Programs**, manually clean up the leftover files as listed in the Uninstallation section, and make sure to reboot after the uninstallation before reinstalling the product.

Frequently Asked Questions

The following Frequently Asked Questions, answered by the authors of this book, are designed to both measure your understanding of the concepts presented in this chapter and to assist you with real-life implementation of these concepts. To have your questions about this chapter answered by the author, browse to **www.syngress.com/solutions** and click on the **"Ask the Author"** form.

Q: I uninstalled and then reinstalled BizTalk Server 2000. Everything worked fine until I rebooted. Services would not start and many error messages appeared in Event Viewer.

A: If you uninstall BizTalk Server, the uninstallation does not really finish until the next reboot. Therefore, when you rebooted, it finished the uninstallation from the first install, removing key files upon reboot. The only choice is to uninstall again and reboot, starting over.

Q: What is the command line used to start and stop BizTalk Server?

A: Use **net start btssvc** at a command prompt to start BizTalk Server Service, and **net stop btssvc** to stop it.

Q: What is the best way to reinstall BizTalk Server 2000 Evaluation edition if it becomes necessary?

A: Completely remove or uninstall the product before reinstalling it. In addition, it is easiest if you delete all the InterchangeXX databases that BizTalk Setup created.

Q: What operating systems can run BizTalk Server 2000?

A: BizTalk Server 2000 and client utilities work on any Windows 2000 system. It is not supported on Microsoft Windows NT.

Q: Can BizTalk Server be installed to run on a computer running Windows 2000 Terminal Server?

A: BizTalk Server can be installed and run on a Windows 2000 Terminal Server–based computer. However, there are some limits to how well BizTalk Server works on a Terminal Server computer. Don't Install via Terminal Services, and use Remote Admin mode, not App Server mode.

Chapter 3

Testing the Installation

Solutions in this chapter:

- **The BizTalk 2000 Tutorial**
- **Setup and Configuration**
- **Implementation**
- **BizTalk Server Final Prep and Tests**

- ☑ **Summary**
- ☑ **Solutions Fast Track**
- ☑ **Frequently Asked Questions**

Introduction

BizTalk Server 2000 is installed, you applied necessary service packs and hotfixes, looked it over, and kicked the tires, if you will. Our next challenge is how to stick our heads under the hood and see if the engine is actually running. In other words, was our installation a success? If so, how can we prove it? In this chapter, we look at the downloading and installation of the BizTalk Server 2000 Tutorial, which will provide you with additional insight into the product. We then review "after installation configurations" and introduce many things that will be explored in detail in later chapters. Finally, we look at the last-minute details and preparatory work to make sure the server is ready to go!

The BizTalk Server 2000 Tutorial

BizTalk Server 2000 comes with a complete tutorial that will help guide you through understanding and working with BizTalk Server. If you are already working with the product, this tutorial can still be beneficial, as it can aid in either refreshing certain "forgotten" skills, or possibly expose you to things you might not have known. In any case, you will find it beneficial to follow the next section on installing, configuring, and using this supplemental tutorial.

You will find the BizTalk tutorial on the BizTalk Server CD-ROM, or you can download it from the Internet. You can find this tutorial in multiple places on the Microsoft Web site (either on MSDN or in the Downloads sections of the site), or you can use the links we provide within this section.

The tutorial, referred to as Learning BizTalk Server, is one continuing lesson broken into seven different documents. However, before we discuss what's actually in the tutorial and how helpful it can be, let's install it on your machine.

Briefly, the tutorial is based on a fictional company, "Northwind Traders," a computer hardware retailer ordering computer parts from Contoso, Ltd. The underlying functions are an existing purchasing application at Northwind Traders that generates a purchase requisition and outputs this file to the hard drive in Extensible Markup Language (XML) format. BizTalk Server 2000 will pick up this file and then submit it to the Northwind Traders' order approval process. In this simplified example, the requisition will be approved if it does not exceed $1,000; otherwise, it will be declined. If it is declined, we would normally modify the document indicating the reason, and output the file to the local hard disk. In the starting configuration, the tutorial displays a dialog box to the interactive user indicating that it has been declined. If successful, this sample application then creates an output XML-based purchase order document that is sent (using the HyperText Transfer Protocol commonly referred to as HTTP) to Contoso, Ltd. Once Contoso, Ltd. receives the purchase order document; it passes it to Contoso's business process, which generates an invoice to be delivered to Northwind Traders via HTTP. Finally, Northwind Traders receives the invoice and writes it to the local hard drive. In this tutorial, we will be using one BizTalk server to simulate both trading partners. If you want to modify the sample to use two BizTalk servers, it is relatively straightforward to do so.

This tutorial is well written and helpful. However, should you experience trouble with it, do not despair. As this tutorial is the first contact with BizTalk for many users, it is an extremely popular topic in the newsgroups. As a result, trouble you experience might very well be exactly what many others have experienced, and checking the newsgroup postings could make short work of the solution. This tutorial is designed to help you learn BizTalk Server 2000 and some of its functionality, while testing the components within to make sure they are functioning properly.

Setup and Configuration

This section covers the basics of verifying your setup and doing basic configuration using specific tools, including the tutorial. On April 27, 2001, Microsoft released a new version of a tutorial that is found within the BizTalk Server Online Documentation. This new tutorial should be downloaded and installed, as it is the easiest way to test your BizTalk Server 2000 configuration. You can find the tutorial in several different locations, including:

- **Version 1.5 of the tutorial** www.microsoft.com/downloads/ release.asp?ReleaseID=29392.

- **Main Download page** www.microsoft.com/biztalk/ downloads/default.asp.

The tutorial download consists of the lesson guide, code, and script examples compressed into a single ZIP file. Once you have downloaded the file, we can begin to install it. To take full advantage of the tutorial, we recommend that you have an installed version of BizTalk Server, SQL Server, and Visio 2000 ready to go. Since we covered installs already, it is assumed that this is the case. However, what might not be obvious is the additional software required to open the ZIP file, and Microsoft Word to read the lessons documents. These applications might not be software that you normally would install on your production server, so you might want to run the tutorial on a test machine only.

Installation Instructions

Begin by downloading the file (LearnBizTalk.zip) to your local machine, or finding it on the BizTalk Server 2000 CD-ROM. Once it is where you can access it, follow these steps:

1. Unzip LearnBizTalk.zip to the root of your C:\ drive (or the drive letter you have assigned as the root). This process will create a new folder called C:\LearnBizTalk on your hard disk. This is where the tutorial is expanded and where all of the lesson documents, scripts, XML files, and samples will be located.

NOTE

It is recommended in the readme.txt file that you create the new directory new folder called C:\LearnBizTalk on your hard disk. The benefit of a new directory is that file access might depend on the fact that it is located on the root drive. In any case, it is a tutorial, so if it fails, it should not be too distressing.

2. Once LearnBizTalk.zip is unzipped to the C:\ drive, navigate to the C:\LearnBizTalk\Scripts directory and double-click **Setup.vbs**. The installation script should provide a dialog box once complete.

3. Open Windows Explorer and browse to the installed tutorial.

4. Go to My Computer and open it. Navigate to your C:\ drive (or where you installed BizTalk Server), and go to **Program Files | Microsoft BizTalk Server | Tutorial | Setup**. Within this folder, you will find a Visual Basic Script called Install_PotoInvoice.vbs. The Install_PotoInvoice.vbs script is the script you need to run to install the tutorial pieces with which to test.

5. Open the Messaging configuration script folder and run the Visual Basic Script ConfigureBuyer.vbs.

6. Now, exit the Setup dialog box.

One of the first things to view after running the scripts is the receive function that is created for your viewing and testing. This will help to see that your installation of the system does in fact work and allows you to perform further tests as will be highlighted in the next few sections. To view the receive function, we need to open the BizTalk Server Administration console. This can found by navigating to **Start | Programs | Microsoft BizTalk Server 2000 | BizTalk Server Administration**. The dialog box as shown in Figure 3.1 appears.

Figure 3.1 Viewing the Receive Function in the BizTalk Server Administration Console

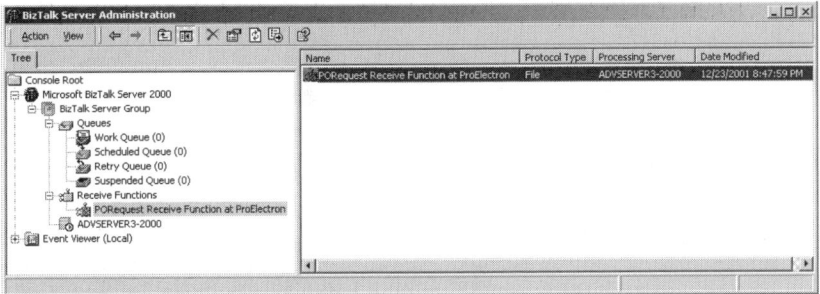

It is important to note that when setting up the tutorial, the script created the PORequest receive function, but rendered it "disabled" by default. You need to first enable it so you can use it.

1. In Figure 3.1, you can see the Receive Functions group within the BizTalk Server Administration tool, and by selecting it, you can view it in the right-hand pane.

2. Right-click this **receive function** and select **Properties**.

3. A dialog box will open as shown in Figure 3.2. This is where you will see the option to disable the receive function.

4. By unselecting the **Disable receive function** check box, it will become enabled. By doing this and closing the dialog box by selecting **OK**, the receive function lose its red "X" and returns to the standard gray icon, indicating that it is now enabled.

Figure 3.2 Changing Receive Function Properties to "Enabled"

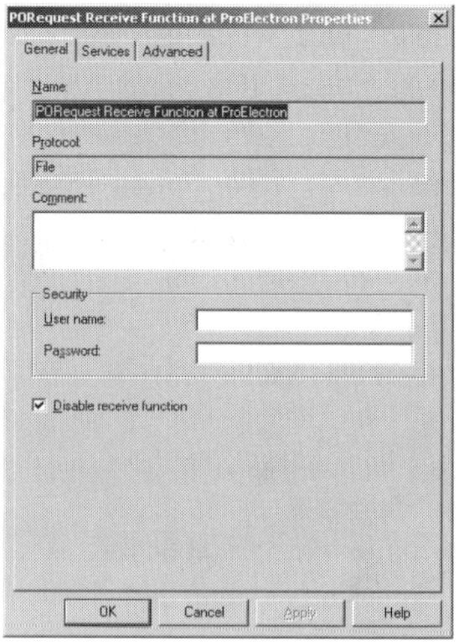

NOTE

A receive function is used to receive documents from a receive location and have them submitted to BizTalk Server 2000. We discuss receive functions more fully later in this chapter.

Testing the Basic Configuration

Now that you understand the basic theory behind this tutorial, and have done the initial preparation, let's see it in action. This section will walk you through testing the basic configuration of the tutorial.

Generating a Purchase Request Rejection

1. Open **C:\LearnBizTalk\Documents\ReqtoDecline.xml**. Review the values of the reqStatus, totalPrice, and reqNumber fields, noting that reqStatus contains a value of "New" and the totalPrice is greater than $1,000.

2. Copy this document into the C:\LearnBizTalk\Pickup directory. Make sure not to move the document, as it will be automatically deleted from this directory.

3. Since the amount is over $1,000, you should see a dialog box stating that this document is being rejected.

Generating a Purchase Request Acceptance

1. Open **C:\LearnBizTalk\Documents\ReqtoApprove.xml**. Review the values of the reqStatus, totalPrice, and reqNumber fields, noting that reqStatus contains a value of "New" and the totalPrice is less than $1,000.

2. Copy this document into the C:\LearnBizTalk\Pickup directory. Make sure not to move the document, as it will be deleted from this directory.

3. Since the amount is under $1,000, you should see a dialog box indicating that the system has approved the purchase request and will be submitting it to Contoso Ltd.'s system.

4. From there, Contoso Ltd.'s system should generate an invoice. This invoice is then sent back to Northwind Trader's system, which writes to the local disk. You will find this invoice in the C:\LearnBizTalk\Output directory.

5. Open this document to see the successful generation of an invoice.

Success! You have just tested your first business-to-business process flow. Continue this tutorial and actually build this setup step by step by reviewing the tutorial documentation located in the C:\LearnBizTalk\Lessons directory.

You can view the actual document movement by using the BizTalk Server Document Tracking tool. To start the Tracking tool, select **Start | Programs | Microsoft BizTalk Server 2000 | BizTalk Document Tracking**. (For detailed information on the use of BizTalk Document Tracking, refer to Chapter 6, "Tracking and Receipts.")

Implementation

A significant purpose to using BizTalk Server is the processing of documents. Whether they are purchase orders, invoices, XML, Electronic Data Interchange (EDI), flat files, or other business-type documents, BizTalk Server's capability to consume, convert, and transport these documents demonstrates its power. When we can get our BizTalk Server installation to perform this task, we are well on our way to a production-worthy application.

Submitting Documents to BizTalk Server

As we begin to use this application, obviously a significant milestone in getting BizTalk Server to work on our system is the successful submission of one of our documents to BizTalk Server. To that end, we will briefly explore two general ways in which we can submit a document to BizTalk Server. One way to submit a document to the BizTalk Server is via the programmatic COM Interchange object, and the other method of submitting documents is via the receive function. We will first explore the receive function.

Receive Functions

The receive function is what administrators create to get the ball rolling and start allowing applications to submit documents from applications that do not speak COM. You will use the BizTalk Server Administration tool to create receive functions.

A question that we need to answer before creating our receive functions is, what type of documents will we be receiving? BizTalk Server has two basic categories, self-routing and non-self-routing documents.

- A self-routing document is one in which the document will contain information about where it should be sent.

- The non-self-routing document, as the name implies, is missing this information, so we will have to provide that routing information as part of our receive function definition.

Another question we have to answer is where will BizTalk Server deliver the documents after receiving them? In order to deliver a document to a destination, we have to define that location by using the BizTalk Messaging Services. These predefined locations are referred to as messaging ports. You can configure a messaging port to deliver a document using any of the supported protocols, which include HTTP(S), Simple Mail Transport Protocol (SMTP), Message Queuing, and custom Application Integration Components (AICs). Channels generally directly precede messaging ports. Channels are where one document can be mapped to another, and are typically the targets of receive functions using non-self-routing documents. Using the BizTalk Messaging Services, we define the properties of specific channels:

- The source organization and application that sent us the document.

- The decryption or digital signature verification, if required, on the inbound document.

- The inbound and outbound document specifications that you create using the BizTalk Editor tool.

- Any mapping you create using the BizTalk Mapper tool that aligns the fields within the inbound document specification to the outbound document specification.

Once we have a channel defined, we can proceed with creating a receive function. BizTalk Server supports two types of receive functions: File receive functions and Message Queuing receive functions. When you define the receive function, you will point it to either a source directory on the local hard disk or to a message queue. This directory is referred to as a polling location, since BizTalk Server will constantly be looking within this location for new documents. It is also possible to have a receive function use a custom component as a preprocessor, but that is outside the scope of this chapter.

Here is an example procedure to create a file receive function to test your installation of BizTalk Server 2000. This assumes that a channel has been defined, along with the required messaging ports, document specifications, and mappings. If you are unfamiliar with these concepts, they are covered more fully in Chapter 4 "Understanding BizTalk Messaging Services," and Chapter 5, "Specifications and Mapping."

1. Launch the **BizTalk Server Administration tool**.

2. On the left side, click the (**+**) to expand the server group to make the receive functions visible.

3. Right-click **Receive Functions**, navigate to **New**, and then click **File Receive Function** as seen in Figure 3.3.

4. You will open a new dialog box as seen in Figure 3.4 that will allow you to create a new Receive Function. Supply the name of the receive function; for example, Sample File Receive.

5. Configure the polling location for the documents; for example, C:\inbound.

6. Supply the file extension to poll for; for example, *.xml.

7. Click **Advanced**.

Figure 3.3 Creating a New File Receive Function in the BizTalk Server Administration Console

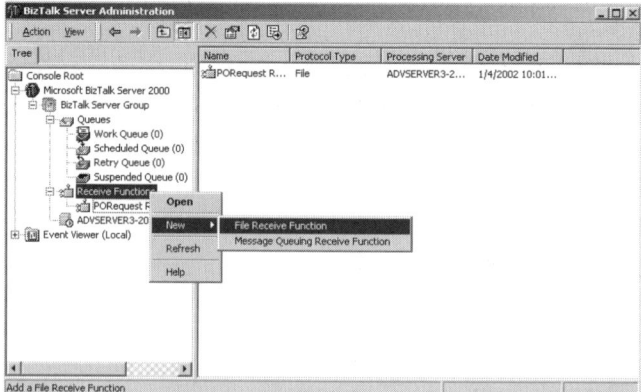

8. The Advanced Receive Function Options window appears. Configure the options as needed, such as whether the document is self-routing, and the channel to use, and then click **OK**.

9. Last, Enter a **Username** and **Password**. In Figure 3.4 the Administrator account was used.

Figure 3.4 Adding a File Receive Function Dialog Box

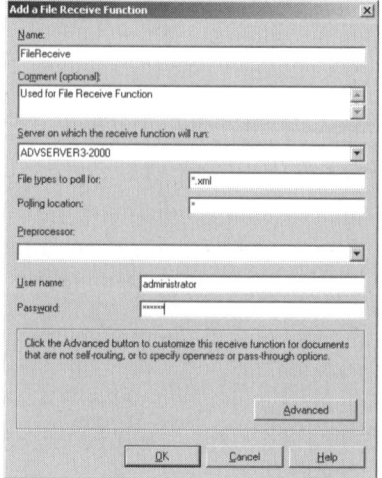

> **NOTE**
>
> If you need to set some properties for dealing with non-self-routing docu-
> ments, you will need to use the Advanced button to manually define the
> source organizations, destination organization, document format, and
> additional properties about the documents with which you are dealing.

Using the Interface Object

We can use the methods of the Interface object to exchange a business document
between an application and BizTalk Server 2000 directly. The Interchange object
is supported by the IInterchange interface. There are two methods of the
Interface object, Submit and SubmitSync. Both of these methods accept a string
buffer or a file path as the business document or interchange. Dynamically calling
Submit or SubmitSync at runtime can give us much more control over the submission process. Rather than having to hard code the channel properties as part
of the definition of the receive function, or make sure that the document itself
contains the required information, we can supply the data we want during runtime as the parameters we send to the methods.

Submit Method

The Submit method is used to submit documents in an asynchronous fashion
without waiting for a receipt document. BizTalk Server places this document in a
message queue until a server is available to process it. An asynchronous submission can also be delivered to multiple destinations.

   If you would like to receive a document via HTTP, you could create an .ASP
page that receives the data posted to the Web site, and then submits that to
BizTalk Server using the Submit method.

   This following code example uses the ADO type library to create a Stream
object. This Stream object then opens the data posted to the ASP page. The data is
then converted from binary format into text format. This data is then submitted
using the Submit method of the Interchange object. To see all the available
options, please refer to Table 3.1.

```
<% Dim objInterface
Dim SubmittedDocumentResult
Dim streamADO
```

```
Set streamADO=CreateObject("ADODB.Stream")

streamADO.Open

streamADO.Type = = adTypeBinary

streamADO.Write Request BinaryRead(Request.TotalBytes)

streamADO.Position=0

streamADO.Type=adTypeText

Set objInterface=Server.CreateObject ("BizTalk.Interchange")

SubmittedDocumentResult=objInterface.Submit (1,streamADO.ReadText, , ,
    "Source Org", ,"Destination Org")

Set objInterface=Nothing %>
```

Table 3.1 Parameters of the Submit and SubmitSync Methods

Parameters	Description
IOpenness	This will be a number that indicates the openness property of the source organization or application, and the openness property of the destination organization or application. 1 = Not Open, 2 = Source is Open, 4 = Destination is Open.
Document	This string contains the submitted document instance. It accepts only a string buffer as the document. This is an optional parameter; however, either the Document or the FilePath parameter must be set—do not set both.
DocName	This string contains the name of the submitted document. Optional parameter.
SourceQualifier	A string that is used to identify the type of SourceID that is being supplied—a name, DUNS number, and so forth. Optional parameter.
SourceID	A string that contains the value of the qualifier of the source organization. For example, if the SourceQualifier is DUNS number, then this is the actual DUNS number of the source. Optional parameter.
DestQualifier	A string that is used to identify the type of DestID that is being supplied—a name, DUNS number, and so forth. Optional parameter.
DestID	A string that contains the value of the qualifier of the destination organization. For example, if the DestQualifier is DUNS number, then this is the actual DUNS number of the source. Optional parameter.

Continued

Table 3.1 Continued

Parameters	Description
ChannelName	The string that identifies the BizTalkChannel object that is executed for this document. This is optional unless the PassThrough parameter is to TRUE.
FilePath	The string that identifies the fully qualified path that contains the document to be submitted. This is instead of directly supplying the document as a string. You can provide URLs, UNCs, and local drive letter paths.
EnvelopeName	This string identifies the name of the envelope. When submitting a flat file, you must create an envelope for this flat file and specify the name of the envelope. Optional parameter.
PassThrough	This is a long data type value that indicates how the server processes the document. If this parameter is set to TRUE, no decryption, decoding, or signature verification is performed, and you must define the parameters as discussed in the following note. If set to FALSE, decryption, decoding, and signature verification are performed.
SubmissionHandle	SubmitSync only. This is a variant data type value that contains a unique identifier for the submitted document. You could use this to query the status of the submitted document.
ResponseDocument	SubmitSync only. This is a variant data type value that contains an optional response document.

NOTE

If the PassThrough property is set to TRUE, the IOpenness property must have a value of 1, and the channel name must be specified. Additionally, you cannot set a value for the DocName, SourceQualifier, SourceID, DestQualifier, DestID, and FilePath parameters.

SubmitSync Method

This method is used to submit documents to BizTalk Server synchronously. Documents submitted using this method are able to receive a receipt document;

in other words, the method returns a document and submits one. Make sure that you submit just one document at a time, and that you have an exact match on the channel name; otherwise, BizTalk Server will return an error.

BizTalk Server Final Prep and Tests

In the previous section, we delved into the BizTalk Server 2000 tutorial, and provided you with an understanding of what is to come in the remainder of the book. More importantly, however, it helped to test your initial installation of the product. In this section, we will look at a few things that you should do to wrap up the final stages of testing your installation and ensure that you are ready to begin developing BizTalk applications in a production environment. That preparatory work includes inspecting the Event Viewer logs and a few trips to Microsoft's Web site.

Inspect the Event Viewer

As an administrator of any platform, you should be checking the Event Viewer regardless of what you install or run. This utility can provide you with a great deal of insight about possible problems, and problems that might be waiting to occur. We are going to visit this utility to see what might have happened during the installation and any possible problems that occurred.

To use the Event Viewer, open the BizTalk Server Administration utility. The Event Viewer is "snapped in" by default. To open the Administration tool, go to **Start | Programs | Microsoft BizTalk Server 2000 | BizTalk Server Administration**. When the MMC opens, you will see the Event Viewer at the bottom of the console as shown in Figure 3.5.

Figure 3.5 The Event Viewer within the BizTalk Server Administration Utility

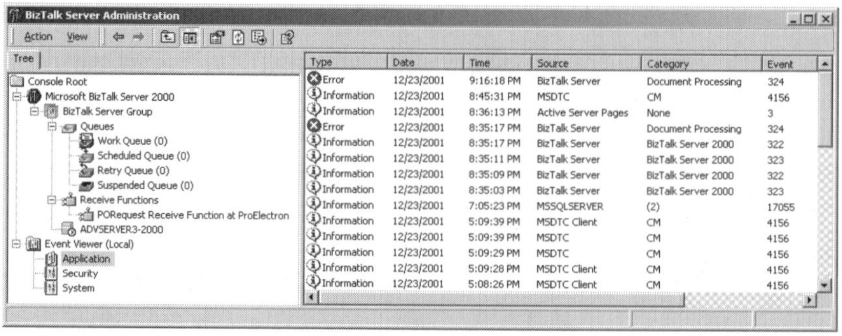

As we look at the console in Figure 3.5, we see that there are errors and informational events associated with BizTalk Server 2000. We should be concerned about all messages that appear, but should pay special attention to the ones identified as errors. (The information events for BizTalk are letting us know that the BizTalk Server 2000 service has started.) Sometimes, these errors will point to a service not running, or an application that suffered a critical error. Regardless of what it might be, by using the reported events, you will be addressing the specific source of your problem, rather than chasing irrelevant hunches and potentially creating more problems. Let's look at the BizTalk Server error a little closer (Figure 3.6).

Figure 3.6 A BizTalk Server 2000 Critical Error Message within the Event Viewer

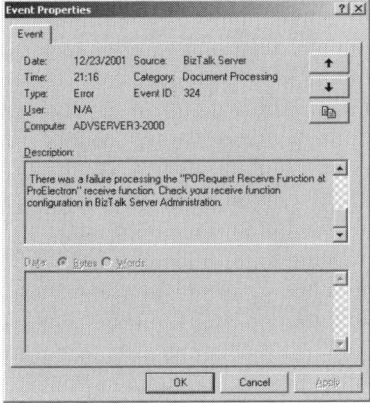

Upon further investigation by selecting the actual error in the Event Viewer, you can see that the receive function experienced problems. This is not a happy occasion, but it is certainly nice to know from the log what the problem might be. The log tells us that BizTalk Server could not process the receive function listed, and thus disabled it. Having been reenabled, it seems to be functioning properly after two days of stress testing. A good practice is to keep monitoring both the Event Log and the receive function in case it happens again. Since the log has not reported any more errors, we could say that it is safe to finish the preparatory and testing phase.

Check the Microsoft Knowledge Base

The Microsoft Knowledge Base should be any technician's best friend. TechNet and MSDN are of course wrapped into this section but they are used more for how to's, and information gathering. The Knowledge Base is more geared toward fixing critical errors.

- **Knowledge Base** http://support.microsoft.com/
- **Downloads section** www.microsoft.com/downloads/search.asp?

This is where you want to go to run a check on BizTalk Server 2000, and every week (seven days on the query pane), run a check on what's new. Definitely run a check on installation issues to make sure you have all the critical hotfixes and service packs you need to continue with deploying your server. The best way to run this query is to run a check on anytime and search for install as seen in Figure 3.7. You will find about two dozen articles about things you might want to check. Finally, you might want to check the Microsoft Downloads page to make sure that all hotfixes and service packs are downloaded and applied to finish the preparation and test of your server.

Figure 3.7 The Microsoft Knowledge Base BizTalk Server Search Query

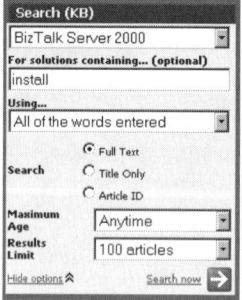

Summary

In the previous chapter, we installed BizTalk Server 2000 onto our hardware. In this chapter, we focused on testing the installation, learning the basics of the accompanying tutorial, and used it to further test our installation. Getting the tutorial in place first was key. We have choices, and we looked at the choices available and where to get them. We also covered the preliminary work of getting the installation of this tutorial in place. After installing the tutorial, we discussed the basics of what it covered and how it is laid out.

Next, we looked at actually maneuvering through this tutorial, which served two purposes. The first was of course to make sure that the installation was in fact tested. By installing the tutorial and running through the exercises, you were testing the components of the system and making sure that they would perform reliably under production circumstances. The second purpose was to get you thinking about how to use BizTalk Server, and introduce you to some of the tools that we will expand on in later chapters. Since this is not a "beginners" guide to BizTalk Server, we needed to bring you up to speed quickly on the basics if you weren't familiar with them:

- Submitting documents to the BizTalk Server
- Receive functions
- Using the Interface object
- The Submit method

Last, we covered the final preparation and test work to make sure that all final checks were in place to start the next chapters with a clean and functioning installation of BizTalk Server 2000. Make sure you always check your logs; it is critical to in order for your systems to run properly. You want to be proactive in solving problems before they escalate to a critical state. We looked at possible post-installation errors or errors involved directly with the running of the tutorial. We also reviewed where you can find Hot Fixes and more information on problems relating to your BizTalk Server 2000 system.

You are now better prepared for the detailed learning, configuring, developing, and mastering of BizTalk Server 2000 presented in the following chapters.

Solutions Fast Track

BizTalk Tutorial

- ☑ The BizTalk Tutorial is a helpful aid that will serve two purposes:
  - Help test your installation
  - Help to demonstrate some of the inner workings of BizTalk Server 2000
- ☑ The tutorial can be found online at Microsoft's Web site in the Download section (www.microsoft.com/biztalk/downloads/default.asp), or on the Installation CD-ROM for BizTalk Server 2000.

Setup and Configuration

- ☑ To set up the tutorial, you will need to first run the script **Install_PotoInvoice.vbs**.
- ☑ Once installed, you will walk through the rest of the documented tutorial installation. Open the **BizTalk Server Administration** console to see that the VBScript installed the necessary components.
- ☑ After the installation and configuration of the tutorial, make sure you read the seven lesson documents that accompany the tutorial. This will aid you in testing the installation of BizTalk Server 2000.

Implementation

- ☑ Use the methods of the Interface object to exchange a business document between an application and BizTalk Server 2000 directly.
- ☑ You can use the BizTalk Server Administration tool to create receive functions. This is covered in the tutorial, and this introduction to it will greatly help in later chapters.
- ☑ The Submit method is used to submit documents in an asynchronous fashion without waiting for a receipt document.

BizTalk Server Final Preparation and Tests

- ☑ Check the Event Viewer logs after installation and consistently thereafter to make sure everything installed properly, that services are running correctly, and to proactively monitor any new issues that might arise.

- ☑ After installation, continue to check the Microsoft Knowledge Base (http://support.microsoft.com) for new issues and problems with BizTalk Server 2000.

- ☑ Visit the Downloads section of Microsoft's Web site to get any hotfixes or needed service packs after installation (www.microsoft.com/downloads/search.asp?).

Frequently Asked Questions

The following Frequently Asked Questions, answered by the authors of this book, are designed to both measure your understanding of the concepts presented in this chapter and to assist you with real-life implementation of these concepts. To have your questions about this chapter answered by the author, browse to **www.syngress.com/solutions** and click on the **"Ask the Author"** form.

Q: I installed BizTalk Server 2000 and tested the installation. Upon applying Service Pack 1 (SP1), nothing seems to work. How do I fix this problem?

A: If you configured the BizTalk Server Messaging service to start under a different user or start manually instead of automatically, these configurations are lost when you install BizTalk Server 2000 SP1. This can cause problems when the configured account credentials are needed to access secure file shares, queues, and so on.

Q: I am having difficulty trying to get the tutorial to work properly. The only thing that was altered was the use of non-ASCII characters. Is this a problem?

A: Using non-ASCII data in the BizTalk Server 2000 Tutorial creates a problem—the BizTalk Server 2000 Tutorial does not work with non-ASCII data. The solution is to change the code for the scripting component (**PORequestApproval.wsc**) to use the XML DOM to write data.

Chapter 4

Understanding BizTalk Messaging Services

Solutions in this chapter:

- **BizTalk Messaging Services**
- **Document Definitions**
- **Specifications**
- **Organizations**
- **Channels**
- **Ports**
- **Distribution Lists**
- **Messaging Services Object Model**

☑ **Summary**

☑ **Solutions Fast Track**

☑ **Frequently Asked Questions**

99

Introduction

If you have ever been part of a project in which your product was responsible for trading information between multiple systems, in multiple locations, between multiple recipients, you will appreciate the robust and feature-rich capabilities found within BizTalk Server. The Messaging Services of BizTalk Server provide administrators and developers alike the ability to configure and manage document exchange between different operating systems, different types of networks, and even different languages. How, you might ask? Microsoft has made a strong effort with their latest .NET servers and framework to support open architecture and to adhere to industry standards. BizTalk Server is no exception to this rule, and provides support for the latest XML-based technologies and operating on industry-aware and publicly available standards such SOAP and the BizTalk 2.0 Specification.

This chapter talks about the various components that constitute the Messaging Services of BizTalk Server 2000. We will discuss items such as specifications and build upon the knowledge of channels, ports, etc. introduced in Chapter 3, "Testing the Installation" Upon completion of this chapter, you will have a solid foundation of the main components of BizTalk Server, and have a better understanding of the new concepts that BizTalk Server 2000 brings to the .NET server family.

BizTalk Messaging Services

The BizTalk Server framework is fundamentally based on messages. In any business process that is automated by BizTalk Server, messages must be received from their source, processed, possibly transformed into another format, and then sent to their destination. While BizTalk Orchestration services are responsible for much of the processing of the messages that arrive, BizTalk Messaging Services manage both the process of moving messages from their source to their destination *and* the process of converting documents between different message formats appropriate for each transaction.

BizTalk Messaging consists of several key objects that must be both understood and properly configured in order to correctly route messages. The main objects are document definitions, document specifications, organizations, channels, messaging ports, and distribution lists. Each of these objects depends on one or more other types of object, so it's important to understand their purpose. A brief description of these objects is given here, and more detail is provided for each later in the chapter:

- **Document definitions** provide information on the type of document used by a channel.

- **Document specifications** describe the exact structure and layout of the document.

- **Organizations** represent trading partners involved in exchange of business documents.

- **Channels** are used to receive source documents from other organizations or other internal applications, and act as "gateways" into your BizTalk Server.

- **Messaging ports** are used to route documents from a channel to another organization or application.

- **Distribution lists** combine messaging ports into a single entity, allowing one message to be distributed to multiple ports.

Even from these short descriptions, you can see that these different objects rely heavily on one another, since BizTalk Messaging cannot perform its job without interactions between these different types of objects. While it might seem initially cumbersome to have so many different entities act in combination to provide these messaging services, it is this decoupling that truly gives BizTalk Server Messaging Services its flexibility and power. Business processes are rarely etched in stone and change frequently. This loosely coupled messaging services architecture allows you to build up your messaging system from smaller parts to accomplish your business needs. When some aspect of your business process changes, you can react by simply updating only those objects that require it (modifying a port to send an invoice to a different URL, for example), rather than redesigning your entire message transport process. The details of the interactions between the different types of messaging objects will become clearer in the sections to follow.

The BizTalk Messaging objects can all be created from the BizTalk Messaging Manager interface, which can be launched from the Start menu via your BizTalk installation. The interface is rather basic and mainly serves as a launching pad for various wizards and property pages from which you can configure your messaging objects. The Messaging Manager interface is shown in Figure 4.1.

Figure 4.1 The Messaging Manager Interface

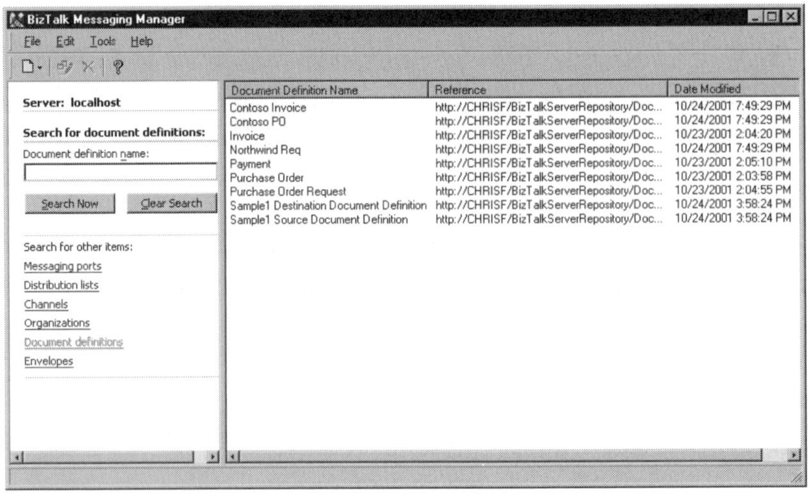

Document Definitions

A document definition describes a specific type of document that's involved in a business process and any tracking or selection criteria that go along with it. It could describe a class of XML document that is received by your BizTalk Server from a business partner, or it could describe a flat-file text document that represents the output of an old legacy system in your enterprise. Document definitions reinforce the flexibility of BizTalk to understand vastly different types of documents. In order to examine how a document definition is created and what kinds of information it contains, let's create one.

1. Choose **File | New document definition** from the Messaging Manager interface.

2. Name the new definition **Invoice**, make sure **document specification** is checked, and specify **CommonInvoice.xml** from the Microsoft subfolder in the WebDAV repository on your BizTalk Server machine.

3. The new document definition property sheet is shown in Figure 4.2.

4. Click **OK** to save this document definition.

The most important items when creating a document definition are the definition name and the document specification. The name allows different messaging channels to reference this document definition. You should choose a name that is descriptive for this type of document. The document specification provides the structure of the XML document referenced by this document definition. The difference between a document definition and its document specification is initially confusing. However, it is important to remember that a document specification provides XML structure and content information in the form of an XDR schema, and the document definition acts as a pointer to that specification. The separation of these two concepts allows multiple document definitions to reference a single document specification, reducing redundancy in your system.

Figure 4.2 Creating a New Document Definition

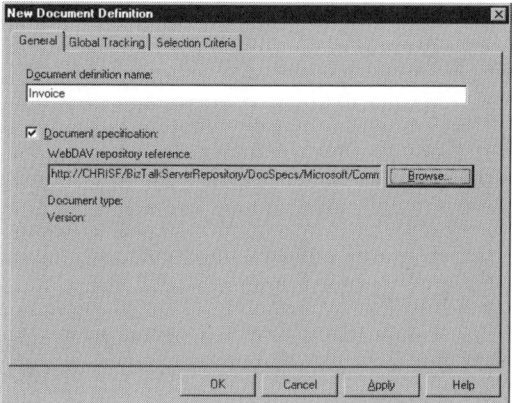

Although it is not strictly required that you select a document specification for a document definition, there are few good reasons not to do so. When you select a document specification, you get the following benefits that you would not otherwise have:

- Validation of the XML document against a schema to reduce errors.

- The ability to use the Messaging Services mapping functionality to transform one document type into another.

- The ability to specify tracking information and selection criteria for the XML document.

Without the document specification, the document definition becomes little more than a named placeholder.

Considerations for Tracking and Querying Document-Specific Data

In addition to the schema validation benefits obtained by using a document specification within your document definition, you gain the ability to track specific
fields in your documents to the BizTalk tracking database in SQL Server. As a
messaging channel receives a document, it looks to a document definition to
describe the format of the document. The document definition describes the
location of key document *fields*, or the important data structures contained by
your document. The fields you select here are known as *global tracking fields*,
because these fields are tracked for all documents imported by all channels that
reference this document definition. This feature is useful in cases where your
business needs require you to have easy access to fields.

In order to better see how to accomplish this and what benefits it yields, we
will now create a new document definition. This document definition will represent an invoice document that we plan to receive from a trading partner. Because
the company management requires access to important information about the
invoices that pass through our system, we will need to track certain pieces of
information for each invoice document that arrives. This document definition
will be named **Tracking Invoice** and reference the same
"CommonInvoice.xml" document specification from before. Field tracking
options are available in the Global Tracking tab of this property sheet, as seen in
Figure 4.3.

Figure 4.3 Selecting Global Tracking Fields

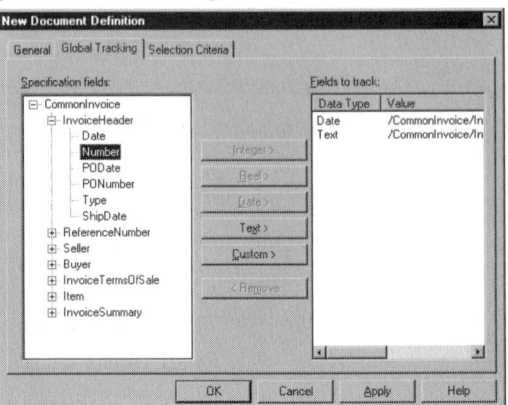

On the Global Tracking tab, the tree view on the left is populated with schema information from the document specification referenced on the General tab. To select a particular field for tracking, perform the following steps:

1. Click the **field** you want to track in the tree view on the left (note that it must be a leaf node).

2. Click the **button** corresponding to the desired data type. (Note that you are not specifically required to use strict data typing, but if you plan to use this information in business calculations later, it is wise to do so.)

The chosen fields appear on the right, denoted by their data type and an XPath expression specifying where to find the field in the source document. In this example, we have specified two fields from the document to track: the "Date" and "Number" fields from the "InvoiceHeader" record. After this document definition is saved and subsequently referenced from one or more channels, any documents that reference this document definition will have these fields logged in the SQL Server tracking database.

NOTE

> Channel configuration gives you the option of tracking documents at the field level. These settings override any settings specified in your referenced document definition and are used *in place* of the fields in your document definition.

Field Level

Global tracking fields specified in the document definition are saved to the SQL Server "InterchangeDTA" database in the "dta_outdoc_details" table. This database can be queried directly by your applications in order to retrieve summaries or information about specific document transactions. Note that the database schema for this table restricts you to tracking only two fields for each of the real, integer, date, and string data types. You can, however, track additional fields using the "custom" data type, which stores your additional fields (name, XPath, and value) in an XML structure in the same database record in "dta_outdoc_details." Since retrieving those values from the XML structure is more computationally intensive than reading single values from a database, you should take care to use your strongly typed values for the fields that are most frequently accessed by your applications, leaving the "custom" structure for the less common information. If you do choose to use the custom structures for commonly accessed information, you will be responsible for parsing the custom XML structure information from the database to retrieve your values of interest and then inserting it into your downstream business logic. It is far easier for both the developer and the processor to use a single, strongly typed field from the database.

In addition to directly accessing the SQL Server database, you can view query-tracking data via the BizTalk Document Tracking Web interface. Unlike the several other Windows-based applications included in the BizTalk Server product, the Document Tracking application is accessed via a Web browser, as seen in Figure 4.4. Internet Explorer 4 or later is required to access the Web-based tracking application, since ActiveX controls are used to provide much of the functionality. This is unfortunate, since by doing things this way, Microsoft has achieved the worst of both worlds. First, due to the nature of HTML-based inter-faces, Web applications are inherently feature-limited compared to their desktop counterparts. Second, by including ActiveX controls in the application, they have restricted access to users of Internet Explorer on the Windows platform. If Microsoft had gone fully either way—either a truly portable Web-based application or a full-featured Windows-based desktop client—their rationale would have been easier to understand.

Figure 4.4 The BizTalk Document Tracking Application

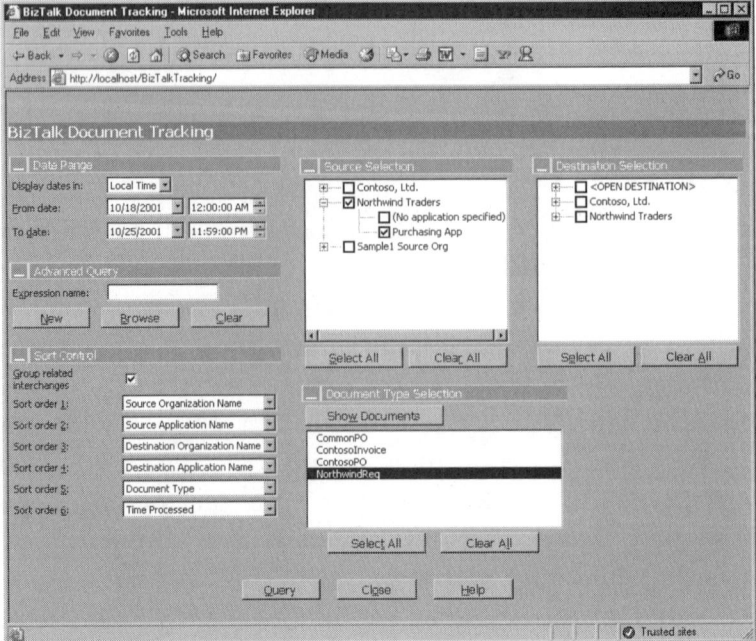

This document tracking page can be used to form virtual queries against the tracking database by selecting the date range of the interchange, source and/or destination organizations, and document specifications for those transactions of interest. The results can be viewed on another screen by clicking **Query**. The Query Results screen is shown in Figure 4.5.

Figure 4.5 Document Tracking Query Results

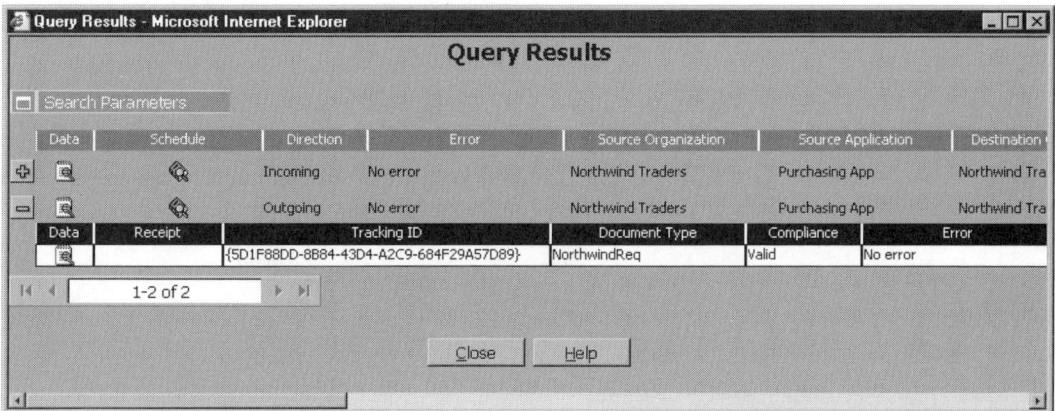

Individual interchanges are the main row entries, while individual documents are shown by expanding the **+** icon on the left of the interchange rows. The data detail contains information about the document itself, including all tracked field data.

Document Level

Tracking can also be enabled at the document level, in place of or in addition to tracking at the field level. Tracking at the document level is enabled from the BizTalk Server Administration application. Right-click on the **BizTalk Server Group**, and choose **Properties**. The Tracking tab allows you to control the logging at the document level, as shown in Figure 4.6.

Specifications

Document specifications describe the internal structure of your document instances. In the previous section, we learned that document definitions reference document specifications in order to provide document validation and mapping capabilities to BizTalk Messaging Services. When a channel initially receives a document, its document definition is queried for (among other things) its document specification. The document specification exists as an extended XDR file, and this file is used to validate the document instance arriving at the channel. XDR stands for "XML Data-Reduced" and is a method for describing the schema (or layout) of an XML document. Use the BizTalk Editor to create new specifications and edit existing document specifications. The editor makes it easy to graphically build and visualize complicated document specifications for various instance document formats, including XML, EDIFACT, X.12, and custom positional or delimited text file formats, although there are some tricks to generating specifications based on flat-file formats.

Figure 4.6 Specifying Document-Level Tracking Options for the Server

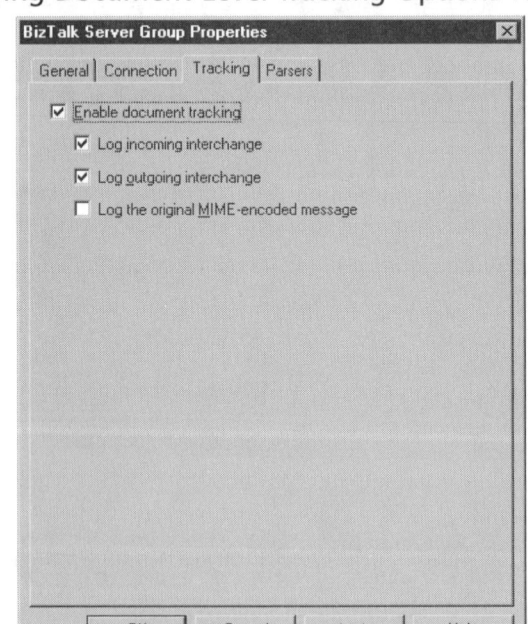

Here are a sample flat-file format representing a simple purchase order, and some tips to using the editor to model this format:

```
Joe  Smith    123 Main Street    Somewhere, CA    92121    123-456-7890
20    56789    Apple Pie                  9.99
5     23232    Box of plastic forks    2.50
```

In the preceding code, the individual lines are delimited by carriage returns, while the fields within each line are tab-delimited. The steps to take to model this file in the BizTalk Editor are as follows:

1. Create an XML tree in your specification to look like Figure 4.7.

Figure 4.7 Modeling a Flat-File Format in the BizTalk Editor

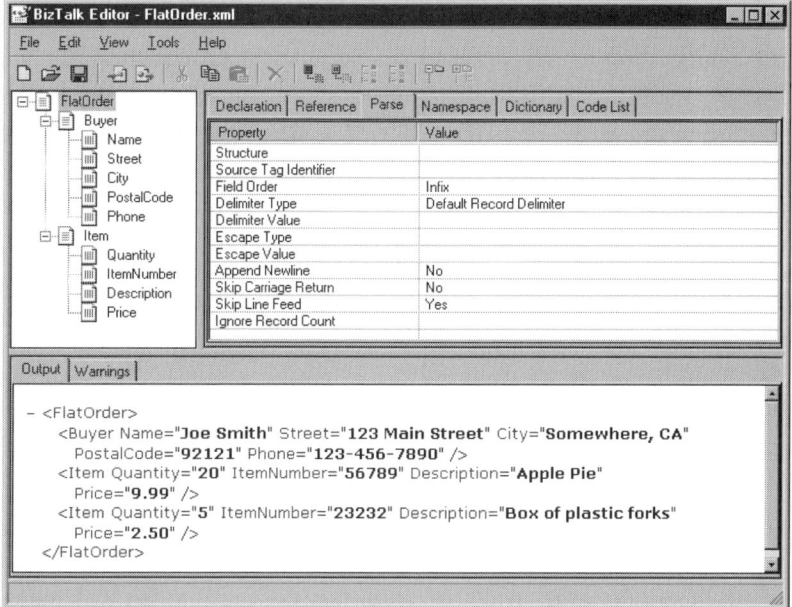

2. Select the **FlatOrder (root) node** in the tree view on the left and the **Reference** tab on the right, then change the **Standard** property to **CUSTOM**. Changing this property is required to parse and validate any non-XML documents.

3. Change the **Default Record Delimiter** value to **CR (0xd)**.

4. Change the **Default Field Delimiter** value to **TAB (0x9)**.

5. Next, select the **Parse** tab on the right pane, and change the **Field Order** property to **Infix**. This tells the validator to look for the delimiters between different records or fields, but not before the first field or after the last field.

6. Change the **Skip Carriage Return** property's value to **No**.

7. Duplicate these property settings for the Buyer node and the Item node to explicitly set the validation properties for these nodes.

8. Finally, select the **Item** node and its **Reference** tab. Change the **Maximum Occurrences** value from **1** to *****. This is necessary to allow multiple items to be ordered in one instance of a document.

The document specification is now complete, and an instance document can be validated from the **Tools | Validate instance** menu option. Selecting the simple order flat file (Figure 4.7), we see the internal XML representation of the file resulting from BizTalk reading this document instance and parsing and validating it against our newly created document specification.

There is a substantial benefit to separating the document definition from its document specification. The document specification provides abstract information about the types and structures of document instances, while the document definition provides specific information about the document instance. One of the benefits lies in the ability to have multiple document definitions that reference the same document specification. This might be necessary if you sometimes need to enable global tracking fields, but not always. For example, the specification contains metadata information about the document standard (i.e., XML, EDIFACT, etc.), document type, and version, in addition to the document schema information inherent in an XDR schema. Furthermore, a simple built-in versioning mechanism is provided here, since the document specification is imported into the internal configuration database whenever you create a document definition. For example, you reference a version of a specification in a document definition and use that definition to execute your business rules. Several weeks later, you update the specification to accommodate a slightly different schema based on requirements from a new business partner, and then you create another document definition to reference the revised specification. Even when the underlying original specification file changes, your original document definition remains valid. This allows you to accommodate different versions of a document specification, each of them actively participating in your business practices at any given time.

NOTE

Sometimes the term "BizTalk Independent Document Specification" is used in information describing BizTalk. This term is more accurately the "BizTalk Framework," since it describes the internal, SOAP-based formatting of BizTalk documents in transit. "Document specifications," as we're discussing, are concerned with the body of the internal SOAP message, which represents our original business document.

Industry Awareness

Industry awareness and acceptance is growing constantly for XML-based transfer of business documents and for the BizTalk initiative in particular. At the time of this writing, over 500 unique schemas and specifications have been deposited in public registries such as those at www.biztalk.org and www.xml.org. These documents have been published publicly to encourage adoption of standards for data exchange within particular industries, and to facilitate communication between disparate organizations within those industries. For example, various specifications exist for human resources, transportation, and banking, and are freely available for organizations within that industry to use to enable communication between them.

One of the greatest benefits of the BizTalk initiative is that the framework itself makes no demands on the types of information that can be transferred with it. Those choices are left to those best able to determine what's best for a particular industry or organization: the industry leaders themselves. The BizTalk Framework only specifies the packaging of the business message, requiring nothing in particular from the message itself.

Source and Destination

Another powerful feature of BizTalk Server 2000 is the ability to convert one document specification into another. This functionality is provided by the BizTalk Mapper, accessible from the BizTalk Server group in the Programs folder in the Start menu. The BizTalk Mapper allows you to create a *mapping* between a source and destination document specification, thus enabling BizTalk Server to translate one format to another as required by your business. This mapping functionality is implemented internally as an XSLT style sheet, an XML-based way to facilitate transformations between different documents. Simple one-to-one transformations can be done with simple drag-and-drop operations. More complex operations (e.g., totaling the prices for all items in an invoice and applying the result to a single field in the destination format) can be modeled by using what are known as *functoids* by the BizTalk Mapper tool. A functoid encapsulates some bit of logic to aid in the transformation of your document formats. Functoids are represented in the resulting XSLT as VBScript functions. BizTalk Mapper ships with 65 different functoids, divided between several tabs on the Functoid palette, ranging in function from string manipulations to math functions to extracting information from a database. For any function that's off the beaten path and is not covered by the other included functoids, there exists a *scripting* functoid that enables you to write your own custom function to perform your transformation logic. Figure 4.8 demonstrates a map of the simple order form that was used earlier to the "PaymentSpec.xml" specification that's included with BizTalk Server.

Figure 4.8 Using the BizTalk Mapper to Map One Document Specification to Another

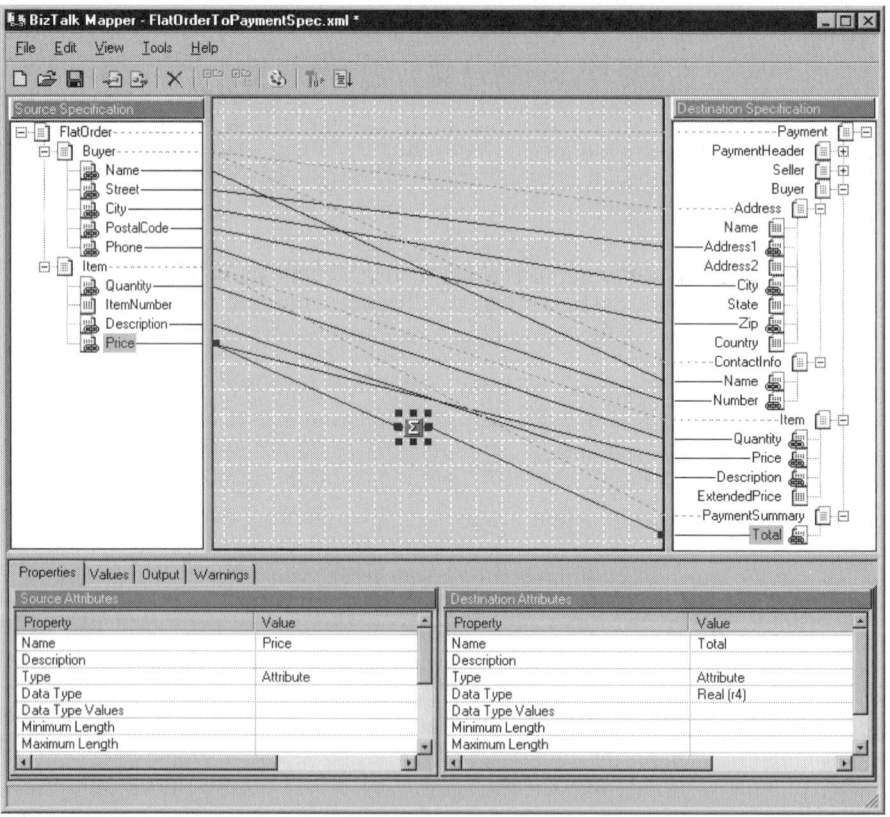

Each mapped field is a simple one-to-one mapping, except for the highlighted functoid mapping. The functoid shown is the "cumulative sum" functoid, and in this case, it sums the prices for each of the items in the source document and applies that value to the Total field in the destination specification.

The functionality of document mapping and its use within BizTalk Messaging is discussed in greater detail later in this chapter, specifically in the discussion on Channels.

Developing & Deploying...

BizTalk Mapper Pitfalls

To open a source and destination specification from within the BizTalk Mapper, go to **File | New**. You will then be prompted to select a source specification and a destination specification. If you first attempt to use **File | Open** to open a source and destination specification, you will be prompted with an unintuitive error message similar to the one in Figure 4.9, even though the file is a valid document specification.

Figure 4.9 BizTalk Mapper Warning

The **File | Open** option is used for opening an existing Mapper output file, which internally contains the source specification, the destination specification, and the XSLT to transform between the two.

Organizations

The reception and routing of BizTalk messages uses organizations as source and destination endpoints. Organizations in BizTalk are high-level identifiers for the trading partners that are the source and the destination of business documents. There are two fundamental types of organizations in BizTalk Server: the home (or default) organization, and trading partner organizations. There can be only one home organization (representing your internal business). In contrast, there can be any number of trading partner organizations.

Organization Types

The home organization is a special organization. There can be only one home organization, and it cannot be deleted. The home organization represents your internal business, and it acts as a parent for any number of "applications." A trading partner organization can represent any of the organizations with which you exchange documents, and can act as a source or destination for your documents. A home organization cannot act directly as a document source or destination; rather, the document source and destination documents must be directed at a specific application within your organization. Similarly, a trading partner organization cannot be associated with any specific applications (since you probably do not have knowledge of the specific applications that handle the incoming documents at your business partner, anyway).

Communication between Multiple Organizations

The BizTalk Framework is centered on communication between multiple organizations. With BizTalk Server 2000, you can control the routing and processing of business documents between your home organization and your trading partner organizations. There are several paths that a document can take when routed through your BizTalk Server, depending on your individual business practices:

- **Remote organization source to home organization application destination** A trading partner sends a document into your BizTalk Server that is intended to be received by an internal application.

- **Home organization application source to remote organization** An internal application sends a document into your BizTalk Server that is then routed to your trading partner.

- **Home organization application to another home organization application** An internal application creates a document that is imported into BizTalk Server, processed, and the output document is routed to another internal application. This is useful, for example, when your business has multiple applications that participate in a business process but whose input and output formats are not compatible. BizTalk Server, and its mapping functionality in particular, can serve to reformat the output of the source document into the specification appropriate for the destination application.

- **Remote organization to remote organization** In this scenario, both the source and destination are remote organizations. Your BizTalk Server receives the document and processes and/or transforms it before ultimately routing it to the destination organization.

Organization Identifiers

Each organization can have one or more identifiers that serve to uniquely identify an organization on a BizTalk Server. Each organization can have more than one organization identifier, but no organization identifier can be shared across organizations. An organization identifier is made up of three components: a name, a qualifier, and a value. The name and qualifier serve to define the "type" of information the identifier defines. The qualifier is the real key for BizTalk to determine the meaning of the value field, and it is the qualifier and value fields that are included in the BizTalk envelope header of every document in transit, ready to be interpreted by the destination BizTalk Server. The name is nothing more than a friendly name to be used when designing your BizTalk applications; BizTalk Server 2000 uses only the qualifier and value fields when examining documents and routing them to the appropriate channels and ports.

By default, when organizations are created from within the BizTalk Messaging Manager, an organization identifier is created for you as shown in Figure 4.10.

Figure 4.10 Specifying Identifiers for an Organization

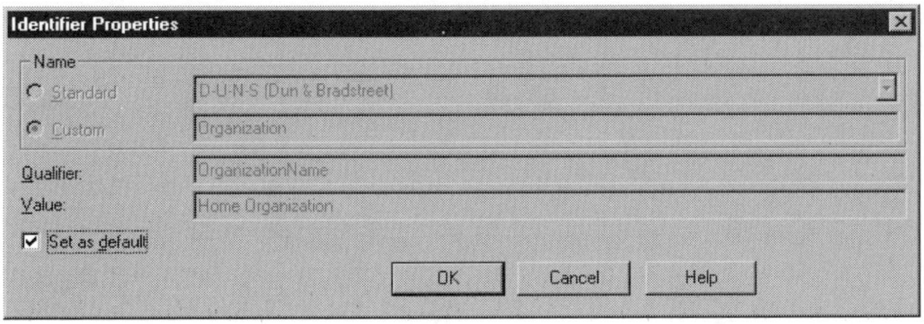

This default identifier's name is "OrganizationName," and its value is simply the name of the organization you specified when creating the organization. This organization identifier is also marked as the default identifier, meaning that if, in your application, no specific identifier is requested for document routing, this identifier will be used by default.

Channels

Channels are BizTalk Server objects that are responsible for receiving documents from the outside world. (In this context, the "outside world" could also mean an application in your enterprise that is not well integrated into your business processes.) The configuration of a channel determines several factors about whether a document is processed by the channel and where it is routed after processing. Channels act as a sink for source documents, process and/or transform them, and then route the resulting document to an associated messaging port or distribution list. Because a channel must have a messaging port or distribution list present to act as a document destination, any messaging port or list for a channel must be created and configured prior to creation of the channel itself. As such, the BizTalk Messaging Manager will not let you create a channel by itself—the menu option is grayed out unless a messaging port or distribution list is currently selected in the Messaging Manager. Creating a new channel while a messaging port is selected causes the new channel to have that messaging port configured as its document destination.

Channel Types

Channels can be configured to receive documents from an organization or an internal application (of the home organization). No functional difference exists between these options once a document arrives at the channel, but this configuration option affects which documents are routed into the channel.

Receipt Channels

Channels can also be configured as "receipt" channels. Certain BizTalk documents will require that the recipient provide a receipt on processing the document. When an ordinary, nonreceipt channel receives such a document, it must notify a receipt channel to initiate processing of the document receipt. These channels and their associated messaging ports exist solely to process receipts generated by another channel/port combination.

Receipt channels are configured using the Channel wizard, just as any other channel. Because of their restricted purpose, receipt channels have slightly fewer options available to them during configuration than do ordinary channels. First, you can neither expect nor generate a receipt from a receipt channel itself. Moreover, the "inbound document definition" is defaulted to "BizTalk Canonical Receipt." This is an internal document definition that is responsible for pulling the pertinent fields from the document envelope header and packaging them in a separate document. The document specification for the canonical receipt can be seen in the WebDAV repository on your BizTalk Server under the name "CanonicalReceipt.xml."

> **NOTE**
>
> When configuring an ordinary channel that processes a document requesting a receipt, you must provide details of the receipt channel that will handle the receipt. Therefore, you must configure the receipt channel and its associated messaging ports prior to configuring the ordinary channel that uses it.

User Defined Channels

User-defined channels are ordinary, non-receipt channels. They are created and configured to receive messages, process and/or transform the messages, and then deliver them to an associated messaging port. Channels also have the following properties:

- Channels can be configured to track specific fields from the document. This is similar in nature to global field tracking via the document definition. When channel-level tracking is enabled, however, the tracked fields replace any of those that would otherwise have been tracked according to the document definition.

- Channels can be configured to contain a filtering expression, which enables them to further restrict the types of documents that are accepted.

- Document logging can be enabled at the channel level. Logging can be configured to store the inbound and/or outbound documents either in the native document format or in the intermediate XML format. This information is logged to the document tracking database.

- Security can be enabled by using the channel's encryption and/or digital signature options.

Channel Filtering

Channel filtering is a way for a channel to further refine the types of instance documents that are accepted by the channel. A channel filter is represented by an XPath expression that returns a true/false value. If the expression evaluates to *true* for an instance document, then the instance document is accepted by the channel. If the expression evaluates to *false*, then the channel rejects the instance document. An example of selecting a filter is shown in Figure 4.11.

Figure 4.11 Applying a Filter to a Channel

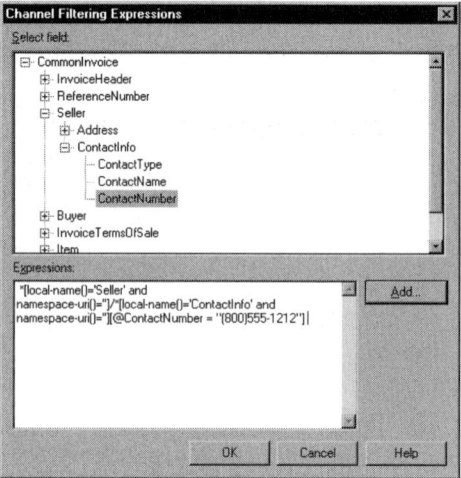

This example channel filter uses the CommonInvoice specification, and sets a filter that accepts only those documents where the Seller's contact information has the telephone number "(800)555-1212." All other documents will be rejected.

Using The Channel Wizard

The Channel wizard is the method of choice for creating a new channel from the BizTalk Messaging Manager user interface. There are several ways to initiate this wizard:

- Create a new messaging port, making sure the **Create a channel for this messaging port** check box is checked. If it is checked, the Channel wizard will be started immediately after the messaging port configuration is finished.

- Select an existing messaging port, and then right-click the port to get the pop-up context menu. Choose **New channel** from the menu, and then choose either **From an organization** or **From an application**.

- Select an existing distribution list and perform the same actions as above.

The Channel wizard appears the same regardless of whether you're creating a new channel for the first time or editing an existing channel, so it's always possible to go back and edit any configuration problems that you might accidentally introduce into a channel. You will not, however, be able to go back and change whether it's from an application or an organization. The initial screen of the Channel wizard allows you to set a friendly name and some comments for the new channel, as shown in Figure 4.12.

Figure 4.12 Creating a New Channel

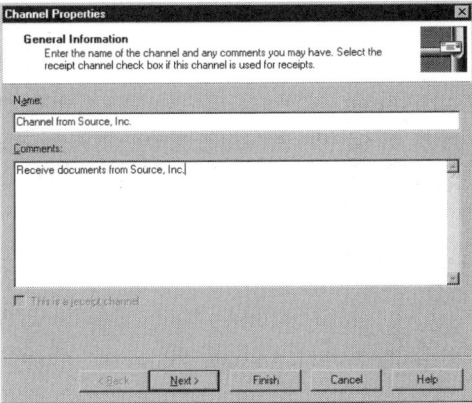

The next screen in the wizard allows you to configure the source organization (or specify "open source"), and specify whether to expect or generate receipts, as shown in Figure 4.13.

Figure 4.13 Setting the Channel's Source Properties

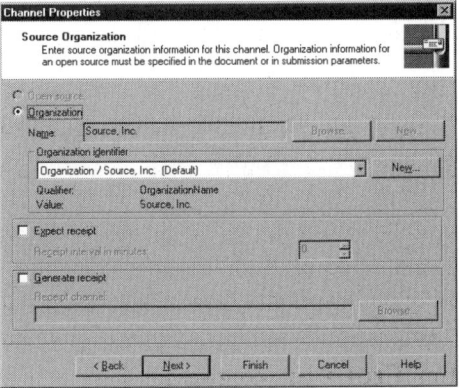

Specifying an organization name and an associated identifier in this screen allows the channel to receive only those documents that contain that organization's identifier in the BizTalk header. If "Open source" is selected, then other, dynamic criteria are used to decide if this channel should accept a particular instance document. In addition, "Expect receipt" signifies that our BizTalk Server will request that the destination server reply to this document with a receipt.

Finally, "Generate receipt" should be selected only if the type of document handled by this channel requires a receipt to be generated. If so, the corresponding, preconfigured receipt channel should also be selected here.

The next screen (Figure 4.14) acquires information about the inbound document. The inbound document definition is specified in the first text box, and the inbound instance document is validated against any document specification referenced by this definition. In addition, for any channels that are configured as open source, this document definition is used in part to help decide whether this channel is an acceptable target for this instance document. If the instance document is properly validated by the document definition, then this channel can be an acceptable target for the document. In addition, several security-related options are given, to decrypt the document content or verify its digital signature. Finally, both tracking and filtering options are given, as explained in the previous sections.

Figure 4.14 Configuring the Channel's Inbound Document Type

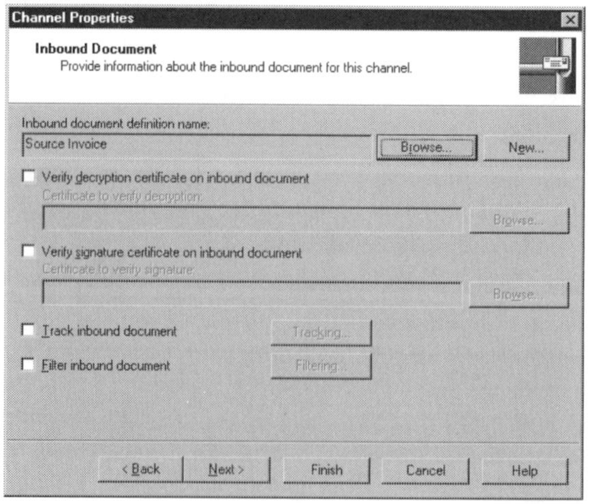

Similar to the inbound document page of the wizard, the next screen contains information pertaining to the destination document format (Figure 4.15). The outbound document definition is specified here. If the outbound definition and the inbound definition are not identical, then a mapping must be made between the two schemas. The "Map inbound document to outbound document" check box selects this, and the "Map reference" text box then contains a mapping file generated by the BizTalk Mapper. Finally, a digital signature can be applied to the outbound document here from a certificate store. This information informs the channel how to parse and treat the inbound document.

Figure 4.15 Configuring the Channel's Outbound Document Type

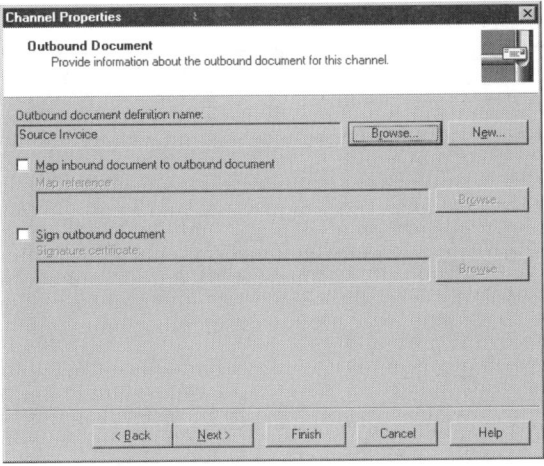

Next, the wizard accepts logging configuration information (Figure 4.16). As mentioned in the channel filtering section, you can opt to have the inbound and/or outbound documents saved to the tracking database in either the native format, the intermediate XML format, or both.

Figure 4.16 Configuring the Channel's Document-Level Logging Options

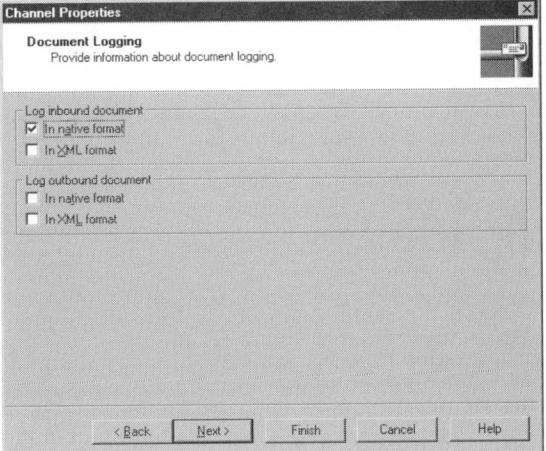

The final screen of the wizard (Figure 4.17) configures advanced properties of the channel, including the X.12/EDIFACT-specific group number, the number of document delivery retry attempts, and the retry interval.

Figure 4.17 Configuring Advanced Channel Properties

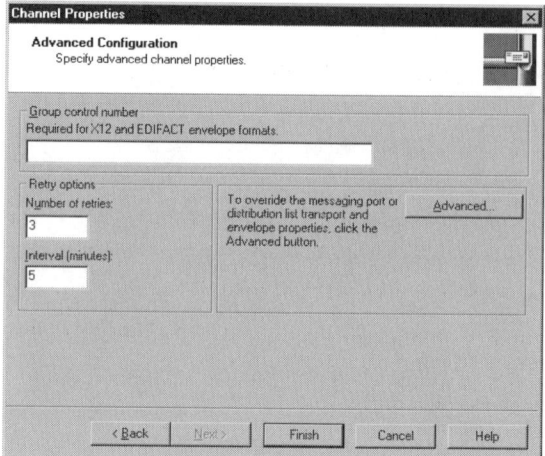

> **NOTE**
>
> If your BizTalk Server is under load, and a particular channel is receiving and processing a large amount of traffic, you might receive a number of BizTalk Server errors when you try to update the channel. These errors are caused by aborted transactions in the configuration database. This can be remedied by disabling the receive function associated with this channel while editing the channel.

Receipt Configuration

Receipt configuration consists of two separate tasks:

- Requesting that a destination system send a receipt back to your organization

- Generating and sending a receipt in response to a request by a trading partner's system

Both of these options are configured through the Channel wizard. The first option is accommodated by the "Expect receipt" check box. When requesting a receipt with this functionality, a document definition must be present in the system to handle the returned receipt. The second option requires a receipt channel/messaging port combination to be set up and referenced by the current channel in order for return receipts to be generated by your BizTalk Server. The internals of receipt processing are covered in detail in Chapter 6, "Tracking and Receipts."

Ports

While channels are used to configure a document's source and its subsequent processing, BizTalk messaging ports represent the configuration of a document's destination. Messaging ports allow you to specify the types of configuration important in packaging, securing, and transporting your document to its destination organization or application.

Static and Dynamic

Much like channels, messaging ports can be configured either to target a specific organization or application as the destination, or to specify an "open destination." Statically defined messaging ports specifically define the destination organization (or application) and the appropriate organization identifier for that organization. This enables BizTalk Messaging to directly include that transport information in the BizTalk envelope header. In some cases, however, you might not know exactly where your document should be sent immediately upon its arrival in the messaging port. In these situations, you would choose to make this an "open" or "dynamic" messaging port.

In open messaging ports, the document's destination must be specified in the document itself. The easiest way to accomplish this is to create a document specification that itself denotes the destination type and value, and then have your channel validate the document instance against that specification. An example of setting the destination routing parameters is shown in Figure 4.18.

In this example, a simple document structure was created that contains a "Routing" node. This node contains DestinationType (corresponding to the organization identifier type) and DestinationValue (the organization identifier value) fields. In Figure 4.18, the right pane on the Dictionary tab shows that beside the Destination Type and Value properties are XPath expressions describing where to find these values in the instance document. These XPath expressions are packaged into the document specification and subsequently packaged with the BizTalk envelope during transit so that the receiving messaging port can identify the transport information dynamically and apply the appropriate routing to the document.

Figure 4.18 Specifying Document Routing Information within BizTalk Editor

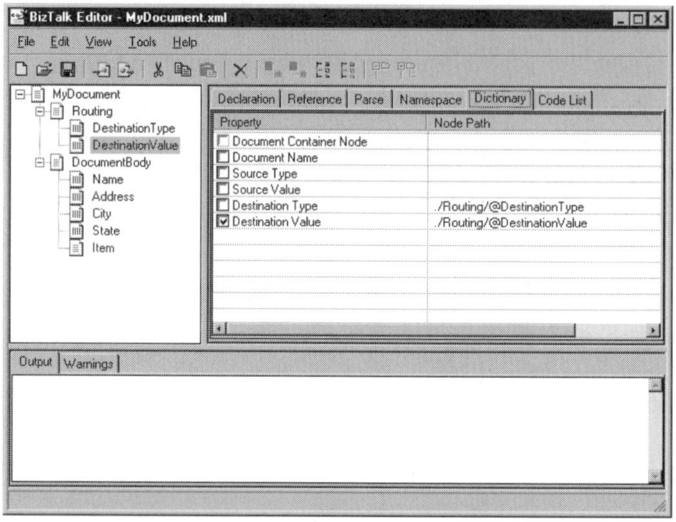

Using the Messaging Port Wizard

The first step in creating a messaging port is to decide whether the destination will be another organization or an application. Just as channels can accept documents submitted from a trading partner *or* a home application (but not specifically from remote applications or the generic home organization), a messaging port must send its document to a trading partner or a home application. This choice must be made initially before the wizard will appear, by choosing **File | New | Messaging Port** and then choosing either **To an organization** or **To an application**. After this step, the Messaging Port wizard appears.

The first screen of the wizard (Figure 4.19) looks a lot like that of the Channel wizard, asking for a messaging port name and some friendly comments.

The second screen provides information on the document's destination, and its appearance depends on whether you chose the destination to be an application or an organization. Let's look at the organization situation first (shown in Figure 4.20). The option is provided for you to choose between an "open destination" and a trading partner organization, as explained earlier. This example chooses an organization called "Destination, Inc." and subsequently identifies its primary transport as an HTTP URL. BizTalk Messaging allows messaging ports to choose one of several transport options, including HTTP, HTTPS, a file, a message queue, SMTP, and a custom application integration component. The target (a URL in this case) is specified along with the transport mechanism here. If, on the other hand, the destination is chosen as an application, the second screen looks like that in Figure 4.21. Instead of prompting for an open destination or organization, this screen gives you the option of choosing a new or running XLANG schedule (XLANG schedules are discussed further in Chapter 7, "BizTalk Orchestration Services") or an application of the home organization. In this example, an application was chosen. The same transport options are present for both application and organization document destinations.

Figure 4.19 Creating a New Messaging Port

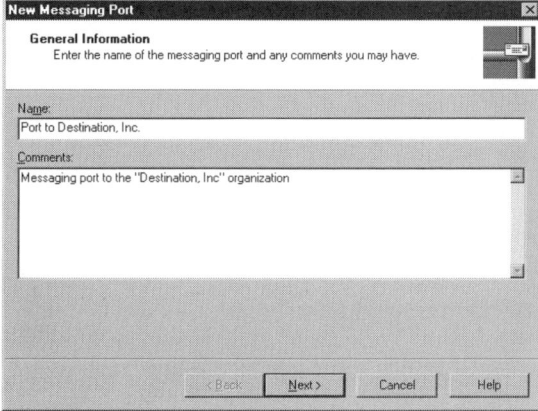

Figure 4.20 Configuring a Port for a Destination Organization

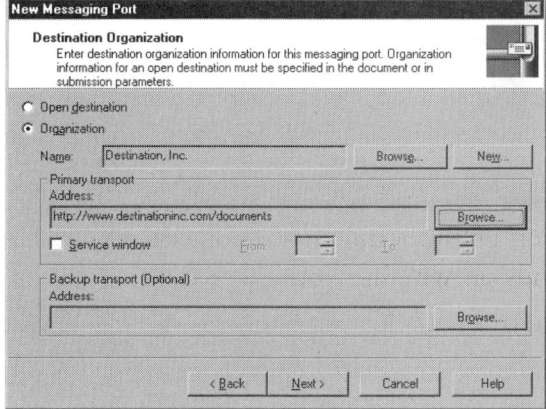

Figure 4.21 Configuring a Port for a Destination Application

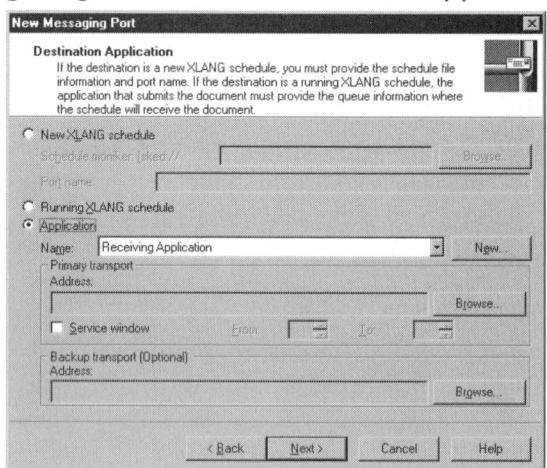

Figure 4.22 shows the next screen, which allows you to specify envelope information. Envelope information must be supplied if you must be able to handle outbound documents in a custom format. If you do not specify any envelope here, the document will be sent in XML format.

Figure 4.22 Configuring the Messaging Port Envelope

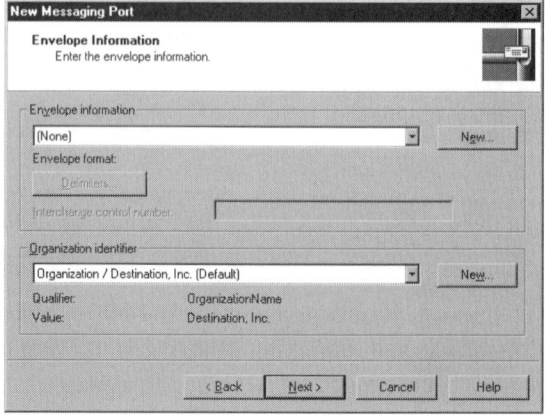

The final screen of the Messaging Port wizard enables you to specify security information as shown in Figure 4.23. MIME encoding and S/MIME encryption can be specified at this step. In addition, a digital signature can be applied in order to help your destination verify that the document has not been altered during transit. Finally, you're given the option to create a new channel based on this port. Since channels are inexorably attached to messaging ports, this option provides you with a convenient way to jump from messaging port configuration straight into configuring a channel that uses the port.

Figure 4.23 Configuring Messaging Port Security

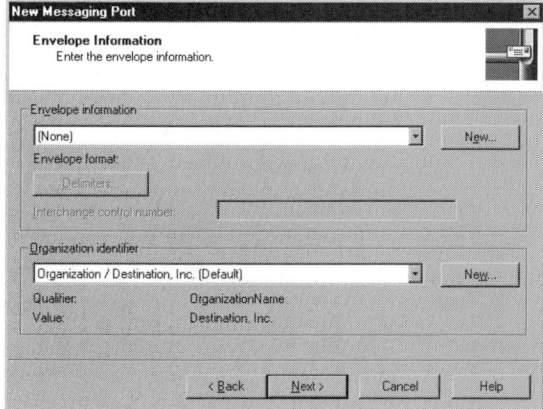

NOTE

Although the messaging port configuration dialog allows you to specify S/MIME encryption, it is not possible to alter the level of encryption from 40-bit to 128-bit encryption. To do this, you must access the messaging port via the BizTalk Messaging COM object model, which is discussed later in the chapter.

Distribution Lists

A distribution list is a simple way to associate multiple messaging ports for delivery of documents to each member of a list of trading partners. Distribution lists can be created from the Messaging Manager interface by choosing **File | New | Distribution list**. The New Distribution List interface is shown in Figure 4.24. It simply allows you to select from a list of all messaging ports on the left, and add the ports of interest to the list on the right. Distribution lists can be used just as messaging ports, in that a channel can be configured to use a distribution list as its document destination. The result is that an identical document is sent to each member of the list.

Figure 4.24 Creating a Distribution List

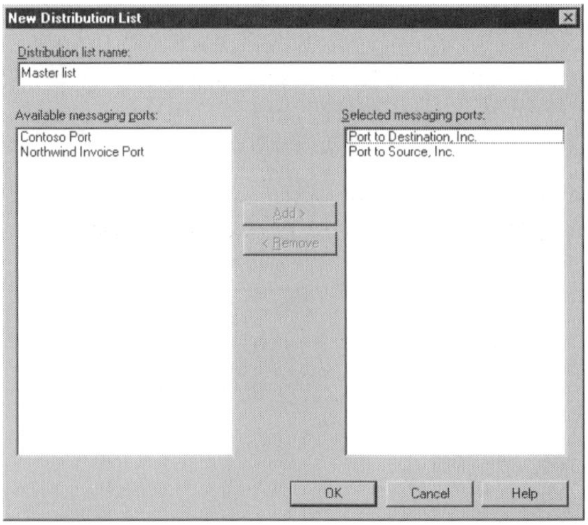

Debugging...

Using Receive Functions

Receive functions can provide an excellent tool to obtain a "snapshot" of your document transfer process through BizTalk Messaging. If you configure your messaging ports to save your documents to the file system rather than to an orchestration schedule or an HTTP resource, you will find it easier to examine those files as they are produced. If you have a more complex pipeline that your documents must traverse, you can use this technique to examine each step of the process. Use file receive functions to send documents to your channels, and then configure your ports to output your resulting documents to the file system. By building these units end-to-end and selectively disabling the receive functions from their property pages, you can examine a document's status at any point in the pipeline.

Messaging Services Object Model

The BizTalk Messaging Services object model is a full-featured interface to the capabilities of BizTalk Messaging, with capabilities surpassing even what is possible to do from the Messaging Manager interface. BizTalk exposes this functionality via a COM type library called the "Microsoft BizTalk Server Configuration Objects 1.0 Type Library," which enables you to use this object model from any COM-aware development language. In order to use this functionality from within Visual Basic, for example, simply set a project reference to the type library as shown in Figure 4.25

Figure 4.25 Adding a Project Reference to the BizTalk Configuration Objects

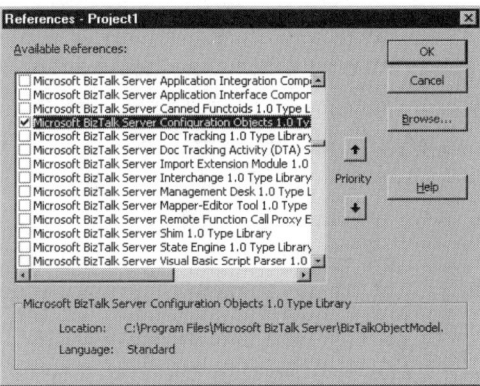

After the reference is created, you can access any of the interfaces shown in Figure 4.26.

Figure 4.26 The BizTalk Messaging Object Model

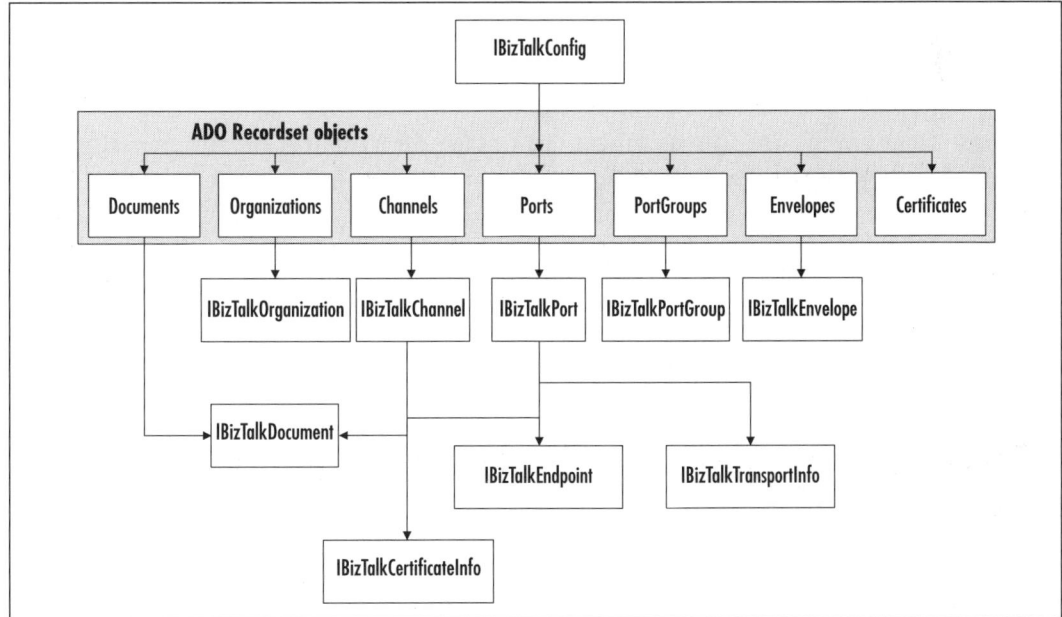

Although the interface names begin with "I" ("IBizTalkConfig" for example), when accessing them through Visual Basic, you'll directly access classes without the "I prefix (such as "BizTalkConfig"). The methods and properties of all these objects are too numerous to mention here, but are documented in the BizTalk Server 2000 documentation.

Any code written to use this object model must begin with the BizTalkConfig object. This object serves as the "parent" to all of the object collections that are stored in the configuration database, such as channels, ports, organizations, and so forth. BizTalkConfig objects have several properties—as shown in Figure 4.26—each of which represents one of these collections of messaging objects. In contrast to many object models that you might be familiar with in Visual Basic, these "collection" objects are not really Visual Basic collections at all. Rather, they are ADO Recordset objects, and must be accessed as such. This occasionally proves to be an awkward way to access the members of the collection, but it works. Depending on the specific type of object in the collection, the ADO Recordset contains different fields. For example, in the BizTalkConfig.Ports Recordset, you'll find "ID" (although the documentation will tell you "Handle"), "Name," and "DateModified." In a pattern common to all of these recordset/collections, in order to access an individual object represented by a row in the recordset, you must first obtain the ID of the object. Once you have the ID in hand, you can create an instance of the object by calling the BizTalkConfig.Create*XXX*() method, where *XXX* is one of Channel, Document, Envelope, Organization, Port, or PortGroup. These methods return an "empty" object of the appropriate type. The empty object shell can be populated with a real object from the system by calling its "Load" method, passing in the ID from the recordset. The following Visual Basic code demonstrates how to use this technique to obtain information on the messaging ports configured on the BizTalk Server.

```
Dim config As BTSObjectModelLib.BizTalkConfig
Dim rs As ADODB.Recordset
Dim port As BTSObjectModelLib.BizTalkPort

'Get a reference to a config object, the starting
'point to accessing all other BizTalk objects
Set config = New BizTalkConfig
```

```
'Get a list of configured ports
Set rs = config.Ports

'Loop through the recordset list of ports
Do While Not rs.EOF

    'Create a new "empty" port object
    Set port = config.CreatePort()

    'Load the port object with "real" data
    'based on the "id" handle in the recordset
    port.Load CLng(rs("id").Value)

    'Do useful work with the port... here we
    'merely print out some properties
    Debug.Print "Port name: " & port.Name
    Debug.Print "Port comments: " & port.Comments

    'Go to the next port in the list
    rs.MoveNext
Loop
```

This code simply creates a BizTalkConfig object, and then loops through the recordset obtained from its "Ports" property. For each row in the recordset, it creates an empty BizTalkPort object, and then loads the correct object from the database based on its ID handle. In this sample, we simply print the name and comments fields for each messaging port.

Not only can you merely read existing messaging configuration with this functionality, you can also create new messaging objects. The following Visual Basic code builds up a document path through BizTalk Server, first creating both source and destination organizations, then creating a document definition, and finally creating and configuring the messaging port and channel for the document exchange.

```
'Get a config object
Dim config As BTSObjectModelLib.BizTalkConfig
Set config = New BizTalkConfig
```

```
'Create a new source and destination organization
Dim org As BizTalkOrganization

'Get an empty organization
Set org = config.CreateOrganization

'Set its properties
org.Name = "Sad Clown Enterprises"
org.Comments = "Sad Clown is a sample source organization"

'Persist it to the configuration database
org.Create
Dim sadClownHandle As Long
sadClownHandle = org.Handle
```

First, we again acquire a BizTalkConfig object. We'll use this object repeatedly to create our helper objects along the way. Next, we create our source organization with the "CreateOrganization" method. We then set the properties, and then call "Create" on the organization object. "Create" causes the current data in the new object to be persisted to the configuration database. Similar steps are then taken to create a destination organization.

```
'Duplicate these steps for a new destination organization
Set org = config.CreateOrganization
org.Name = "Happy Clam, Inc."
org.Comments = "Happy Clam is a sample destination org"
org.Create
Dim happyClamHandle As Long
happyClamHandle = org.Handle



'Create a new document definition
Dim doc As BizTalkDocument
Set doc = config.CreateDocument
doc.Name = "Sad Clown Invoice"
```

```
doc.Reference = "http://CHRISF/BizTalkServerRepository/" & _
        "DocSpecs/Microsoft/CommonInvoice.xml"
doc.Create
```

A document definition is then created, referencing a file in the WebDAV repository, and persisted to the configuration database.

```
'Create a messaging port
Dim port As BizTalkPort
Set port = config.CreatePort
port.Name = "Port to Happy Clam"


'Set the port's endpoint information
Dim endpoint As BizTalkEndpoint
Set endpoint = port.DestinationEndpoint
endpoint.Openness = BIZTALK_OPENNESS_TYPE_EX_NOTOPEN
endpoint.Organization = happyClamHandle


'Set the port's transport information
Dim trans As BizTalkTransportInfo
Set trans = port.PrimaryTransport
trans.Type = BIZTALK_TRANSPORT_TYPE_HTTP
trans.Address = "http://www.happyclaminc.com/documents"


'Persist the port
port.Create
```

Next, the messaging port is created and configured. Note the two helper objects here of type BizTalkEndpoint and BizTalkTransportInfo. When you create a new BizTalkPort object, it is created with default representations of these objects as properties. These must be configured with the port itself in order to completely specify the port's properties. In our example, we specify that the destination is not open and that the document destination endpoint is the Happy Clam organization whose handle we stashed away earlier when creating the organizations. Similarly, we configured the transport to occur over HTTP, and we specified the destination URL to that endpoint. Finally, we persist the port to the database.

```
'Create a channel
Dim channel As BizTalkChannel
Set channel = config.CreateChannel
'Set the channel's name and documents
channel.Name = "Sad Clown Channel"
channel.InputDocument = doc.Handle
channel.OutputDocument = doc.Handle

'Point to the port we just created
channel.port = port.Handle

'Set the channel's source organization
Set endpoint = channel.SourceEndpoint
endpoint.Organization = sadClownHandle
endpoint.Openness = BIZTALK_OPENNESS_TYPE_EX_NOTOPEN

'Persist the channel
channel.Create
```

Finally, we create the channel that uses all of the previous objects. We configure the input and output documents, passing our document's handle to the channel properties. (If these documents had been different, a document mapping can be specified from the channel object.) We also set the destination port to that which we just created. Similar to the previous port example, we then set the source endpoint for the channel to point to our Sad Clown source organization. We end by saving the channel to the database.

Developing & Deploying...

Replicating Configuration Data

In many cases, you will be developing your applications on a development server, while your application will be targeted at a production server. Be careful about using the Messaging Manager to set up and configure a live BizTalk system. While the Messaging Manager provides

Continued

a clear and consistent interface, the many steps that are required to fully configure each object leave the door wide open to introducing bugs. Instead, look into using the BizTalk Server Configuration Assistant application (Figure 4.27). This is an officially unsupported application that is included with BizTalk Server 2000 and is located in the C:\Program Files\Microsoft BizTalk Server\SDK\Messaging Samples\ BTConfigAssistant\EXE directory. Source code is also available for this application, which will give you a head start on using the many features of the BizTalk messaging object model.

Figure 4.27 The BizTalk Configuration Assistant

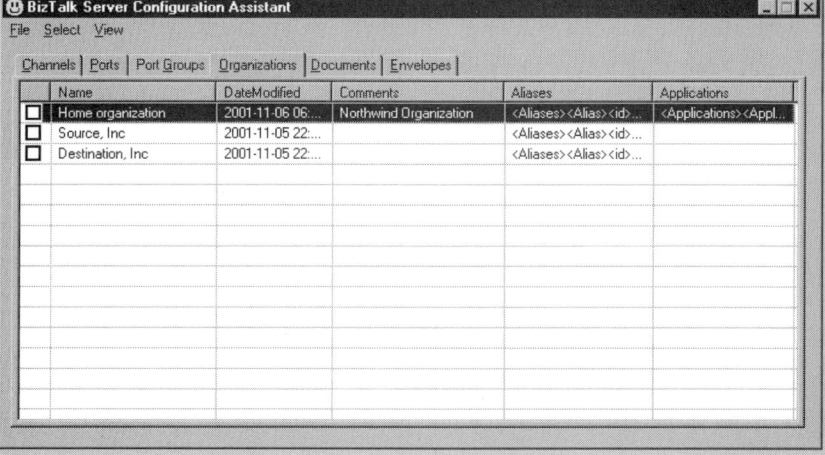

Summary

BizTalk Messaging Services is (along with BizTalk Orchestration) a core feature of BizTalk Server. Messaging Services represents the objects that participate in your business flow, and allow you to configure them through the BizTalk Messaging Manager. These objects are organizations, document definitions, document specifications, organizations, channels, messaging ports, and distribution lists. *Organizations* represent the logical endpoints—both source and destination—of the document exchange. *Document definitions* reference a specific document type and provide the ability to track and persist specific document fields to a database. *Document specifications* represent the schema/layout of the instance document, as well as specify any document routing information and any other transport-specific parameters that reside in the message envelope. *Channels* represent the document source. As the document is submitted to BizTalk Server, an appropriate channel will accept the document based on its configured source organization and/or document definition. *Messaging ports* represent the document destination, and must accept documents from channels, package them, and deliver the documents to the destination organization. Finally, *distribution lists* serve as convenient collections of messaging ports, allowing a channel to route its documents to multiple recipients at once.

In addition to its fundamental objects, BizTalk Messaging Services also specifies the path that a document must take through BizTalk Server. In summary, when a document is submitted to BizTalk Server, a channel picks up the document after recognizing it was sent from a particular source organization, then validates the document against a document definition/specification. The channel and/or the document definition can optionally save document tracking data to the tracking database. The channel then processes and/or transforms the document (based on a specified map between differing input and output document specifications) before passing it to an associated messaging port or distribution list. The messaging port then packages and optionally signs, encodes, and encrypts the document before sending it to the destination.

BizTalk Messaging can be configured via the BizTalk Messaging Manager application or a COM object model. The BizTalk Messaging object model contains classes representing each of the objects that are configurable from the Messaging Manager. The *BizTalkConfig* object represents the high-level parent and contains ADO recordset collections of *Channels*, *Ports*, *Organizations*, *Documents*, and *PortGroups* (distribution lists). The BizTalkConfig class also contains methods that create empty shell objects (e.g., CreatePort()), from which new messaging objects can be created and subsequently persisted to the configuration database.

Solutions Fast Track

BizTalk Messaging Services

☑ BizTalk Messaging Services is a core feature of BizTalk Server.

☑ Messaging Services is responsible for packaging and routing documents from source to destination.

☑ Messaging Services is configurable via the BizTalk Messaging Manager application and through a COM object model.

Document Definitions

☑ Document definitions represent a specific type of document that can arrive at your BizTalk Server.

☑ Global tracking fields can be defined that allow specific data from your instance documents to be persisted to the tracking database.

☑ You should always choose a document specification when creating a document definition—without it, you will see reduced functionality.

Specifications

☑ Specifications represent the schema of the instance documents and specify how to interpret non-XML instance documents.

☑ One can create specifications easily with the BizTalk Editor application.

☑ Mapping can be performed between different specifications using the BizTalk Mapper.

Organizations

☑ An organization represents your home organization as well as your trading partners with whom you exchange documents.

☑ Only a home (default) organization can be associated with applications.

☑ An organization can have any number of unique *organization identifiers* as long as the identifier's value uniquely describes a single organization.

Channels

☑ Channels serve as the "source" of document routing through BizTalk Server.

☑ Channels can be configured as a receipt channel, specifying that the channel is intended to send a document receipt to a trading partner.

☑ Channels can be configured to filter documents or track document fields based on XPath expressions.

Ports

☑ Ports serve as the "destination" of document routing through BizTalk Server.

☑ Ports receive documents from a channel, and then package, secure, sign, and deliver to the destination.

☑ Ports must be created before any associated channels.

Distribution Lists

☑ Distribution lists serve as lists of messaging ports.

☑ A channel can specify a distribution list as a target document destination to route the document to each of the list's members.

Messaging Services Object Model

☑ All messaging configuration objects can be accessed through methods and properties of the BizTalkConfig parent object.

☑ The BizTalkConfig object's "collection" properties are not really collections at all—they are ADO recordsets.

☑ The BizTalkConfig object can create an empty object shell with the Create*XXX* methods (CreatePort, for example), while the Create method on the object itself will persist the object to the configuration database.

Frequently Asked Questions

The following Frequently Asked Questions, answered by the authors of this book, are designed to both measure your understanding of the concepts presented in this chapter and to assist you with real-life implementation of these concepts. To have your questions about this chapter answered by the author, browse to **www.syngress.com/solutions** and click on the **"Ask the Author"** form.

Q: How can I create a document specification for a flat-file format?

A: Use the BizTalk Editor, just as if you were building a specification for an XML-based document. Build the desired hierarchy, and then change the root node's "Standard" property value to **CUSTOM**. Finally, specify the appropriate record and field delimiters and element cardinality. You can validate your specification against an instance document using the **Tools | Validate** instance menu option.

Q: How can I obtain a reference to a channel from the messaging object model?

A: First, create an object of type BizTalkConfig. From there, use its Channels property to obtain an ADO recordset containing one row for each channel on the server. Determine a record's value for the "ID" field to retrieve a "handle" to the individual channel. Obtain an empty "shell" channel using the BizTalkConfig's "CreateChannel" method, and then call that BizTalkChannel object's "Load" method, passing in the handle to the channel of interest. Your channel will now be populated with information from the configuration database.

Q: How can I narrow down the types of documents that a channel receives?

A: Each channel can specify a channel filter. This filter is based on the channel's document definition, and consists of various XPath expressions. If the expressions evaluate to true, then the document is accepted into the channel.

Chapter 5

Specifications and Mapping

Solutions in this chapter:

- **Creating and Using Specifications**
- **Mapping Data between Documents**
- **Functoids**
- **Using WebDAV**

☑ **Summary**

☑ **Solutions Fast Track**

☑ **Frequently Asked Questions**

Introduction

Having discussed the various properties and components of BizTalk Messaging Services, we'll now look at them in more detail. The complexity of today's business processes and transactions requires more than just getting a document to and from its destination. A common example is receiving a purchase order (PO) from one of your trading partners and, in return, sending them an invoice. BizTalk provides capabilities to define the document specifications, allows us to map common fields between documents, and perform inline operations on the incoming or outgoing documents.

We cover the process of designing and implementing specifications within this chapter. Examples are provided to help us understand the capabilities of functoids and other characteristics of specifications. We look at the low-level constructs of specifications and how/why they are used to provide the desired interoperability between heterogeneous systems. An overview of WebDAV is provided to assist us in organizing the many specifications that will arise within complex solutions.

Creating and Using Specifications

In this section, we begin to discuss the high- and low-level constructs of documents, specifications, and templates. We define the term *specifications* as BizTalk Server 2000-specific Extensible Markup Language (XML) schemas that you can create with a tool in BizTalk 2000 called the BizTalk Editor. The BizTalk Editor is introduced in the next section.

A user can create specifications that are based on the industry standards of XML, EDIFACT, or X12, or on nonindustry standards to include delimited flat files, positional flat files, delimited and positional flat files, blank specifications, or existing files. The BizTalk Editor tool is used to open and work with predefined or custom specification templates. We will look at how to work with both types. A specification created with the BizTalk Editor is considered well formed, and the actual structures can vary depending on how you choose to construct the specification. Let's look at how to create these specifications.

Using the BizTalk Editor

Within BizTalk 2000 is an incredibly useful tool, the BizTalk Editor. This tool provides a GUI-based look and feel for creating specifications and schemas. Document formats are viewed within the Editor in a tree-like view using a hierarchical XML-based schema based on BizTalk. Elements that contain data are *fields*, and elements that contain elements are *records*. Remember that BizTalk-based document specifications are shown in the BizTalk schema as part of the XML Data Reduced schema, more commonly known as the XDR schema. We will begin by creating a schema from scratch. In the following exercise, we will create a standard work form: a purchase order. For this exercise, you will need to work on a server with BizTalk 2000 properly installed.

Using the BizTalk Editor is not overly difficult. Fully understanding how BizTalk works as part of the .NET platform, and leveraging BizTalk in your organization is potentially more difficult. If you wanted to use industry standard-based EDIFACT or X12, you could use predefined specifications that are ready to be used as part of the BizTalk 2000 Server application. If you were interested in creating your own specification, you could use the BizTalk Editor to do so. We will look at using both a predefined and custom-made specification. First, let's look at what it takes to create a new specification, so that you will be familiar with what is involved in the process when you decide to use a predefined specification

To find the BizTalk Editor, go to **Start | Programs | Microsoft BizTalk Server 2000**, and then select the **BizTalk Editor**. You should see the screen shown in Figure 5.1.

Figure 5.1 The BizTalk Editor

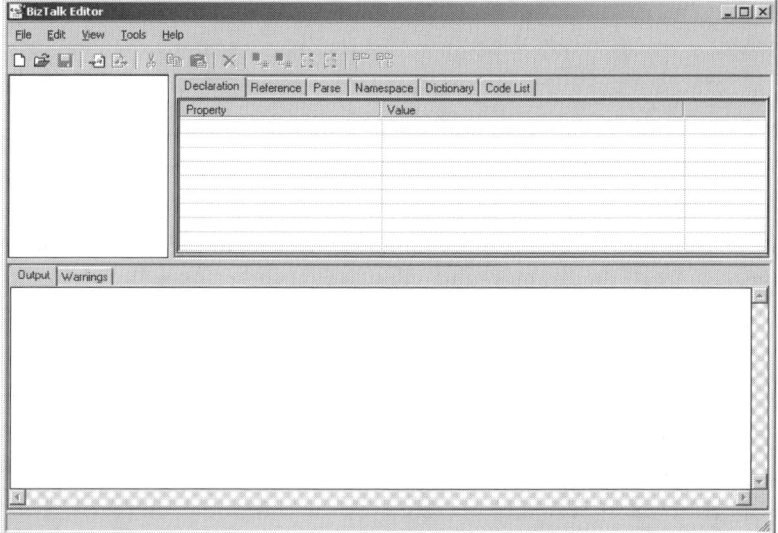

Upon opening the Editor, a blank dialog box appears. You need to either open a saved specification or create a new one either from a template or from

scratch. For this example, we will first work from a blank template and create our own specification. Before we actually create the specification, let's look at the internal workings and File menus that comprise the BizTalk Editor.

BizTalk Editor User Interface and Menu Structure

To work with the BizTalk Editor and learn all its complexities, we will examine the user interface in depth. Let's look at the functions of the User Interface tools available to us in both the Menu options and the Icon toolbar.

The menu and toolbar located directly below the BizTalk Editor dialog box contain many options that we need to discuss. Let's look at the options available to us in the menu bar at the top of Figure 5.1:

- **File** Used to save, open, and close a specification.

- **Edit** Used to copy, cut, insert, and work with fields and records in the specification.

- **View** Used to work with the panes (right, left, and bottom), such as changing text size, etc.

- **Tools** Used for validation, creating document instances, importing and exporting XDR schema.

- **Help** Used to search for help with the BizTalk Editor.

You can click the BizTalk Editor 2000 toolbar icons to quickly access certain options within the menu structure we just reviewed. The toolbar shown in Figure 5.1 directly under the title bar and File menu has a series of icons. From left to right, the first one is to open (thus creating) a new specification. The Open Folder icon depicts the action of opening a preexisting specification. The Diskette icon is for saving a specification you opened in the Editor. The next two icons are for retrieving from and storing to WebDAV (we discuss WebDAV in the last section of this chapter). The next four icons are for cutting, copying, pasting, and deleting specification nodes, respectively. The next four icons allow you to add a new record, add a new field, insert a new record, and insert a new field, respectively. We discuss what all these options do later in this section. The last two icons are used to collapse and expand data within the Editor. Table 5.1 lists the pre-established shortcut keystrokes to manipulate and maneuver through the Editor.

Table 5.1 BizTalk Editor Shortcut Keys

Key	Function
Ctrl+N	New specification
Ctrl+S	Save a specification
Ctrl+O	Open a specification
Ctrl+R	Add a new record
Ctrl+F	Add a new field
Ctrl+C	Copy
Ctrl+X	Cut
Ctrl+V	Paste
Shift+R	Insert a record
Shift+F	Insert a field
Shift+F6	Moves the focus of attention from pane to pane (counterclockwise)
F1	Help system
F2	Edit mode activation
F4	Highlight the next warning
F5	Schema validation
F6	Also moves focus of attention from pane to pane (only clockwise)
Alt + F4	Exit the program
Esc	Cancel editing

The user interface as seen in Figure 5.1 has three main window panes. Below the title bar, toolbar, and menu are three main working areas. We will be doing most of our work in the left pane. In this pane you will see a tree-like view of the root record and all the records and fields contained within the specification. Refer to Figure 5.2 for a complete view of what the tree looks like when occupied by records and fields.

Figure 5.2 The BizTalk Editor with a New Specification, BIZTALKPO

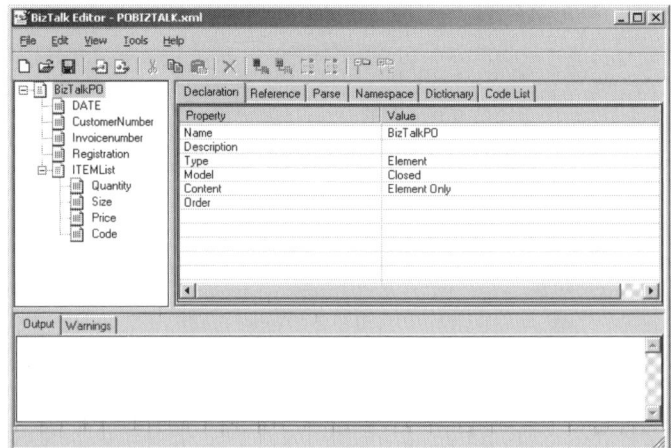

You can set property values for specification records and fields in the right pane. Let's briefly examine each tab:

- **Declaration** This view contains information based on what record or field you select within the left pane of the BizTalk Editor.

- **Reference** This view specifies specific things based on what context you are in. For example, if you select the **root record**, and then select the **Reference** tab, you will be able to modify the specification standard (XML to X12, for example). If you select a subrecord, you can specify how often there is an occurrence of referencing the element. A field will either be required or not, or you can clear the field by right-clicking it and selecting **Clear Property**.

- **Parse** This view contains information for serializers, as well as non-XML-based parsers.

- **Namespace** This view allows you to create custom namespaces not normally accepted by BizTalk Server. In this tab is the default namespace that cannot be altered by the Editor. You can, however, add a new custom namespace by typing a namespace prefix in the Prefix column, and a namespace in the Uniform Resource Name (URN) column of the Namespace tab. It is important to note that the BizTalk Editor will not validate the URN you just created.

- **Dictionary** This view helps you create channels for BizTalk to follow. Parsing will look for information found on the Dictionary tab. Consider a channel as a set of properties that designate the source of documents to the destination of documents using specific processing steps using Messaging Services. If you look at the root node record in Figure 5.2, which is **BIZTALKPO**, you can click on the **Dictionary** tab and select that as the **Document Container Node**. This will put a period "." in the Node Path field, which in turn designates it as the document container node. If you go to the first field below it, you can see that you cannot make this the root, but you can add mappings to types and values. Now, go down to **ITEMLIST**. If you try to make that record the root in the Dictionary tab, BizTalk will ask if this is what you want to do, because you can only have one root and it does not have to be the *root node* for the specification. You can also set Dictionary properties by right-clicking the field or record in the left pane and selecting **Set Routing Information**.

- **Code list** One aspect of the standardized specification of EDI is the ability to make constraints on code lists. You can view this by opening a predefined standards-based specification and looking at the fields within the Code List tab. You will learn how to open predefined standards-based specifications later in the chapter.

NOTE

Unicode is the *only* format you can use to save your document.

We now have a detailed understanding of the left pane, right pane, and menu systems of the BizTalk Editor. Next, let's examine the two tabs in the bottom pane:

- **Output** This tab is used to display XML as a "Document Instance" when you select to create the instance with the **Create XML Instance** command. Go to **Tools | Create XML Instance**. A dialog box opens to allow you to save this instance to a location specified by you (such as your hard disk). You can now use the Output tab to view this code.

- **Warning** A warning seen in the Warning tab is directly related to the validation and proven validity of a document instance against a specification. If you need to validate the document instance, go to **Tools | Validate Instance**. Open a dialog box that will allow you to browse to the document instance you want to validate. For this exercise, browse to the document you just saved. If you didn't save it, wait until the next exercise to create a new specification. Then, once you complete the exercise, create the instance, validate the document instance, and then use this tab to view generated warnings.

NOTE

BizTalk Editor *will not* provide a validation on a document instance with multiple documents contained within it.

Debugging...

XDR Limitations

XML document instances that contain XDR data types might have a problem validating against a specification. When performing this validation, make sure that XDR data types have Model Properties set as **Open**.

Creating a New Specification

Let's begin learning about specifications by creating one. We will then move right into working with a predefined specification. To access a blank template, go to the **File** menu and select **New**. This will open the New Document Specification dialog box, shown in Figure 5.3.

Figure 5.3 The New Document Specification Dialog Box

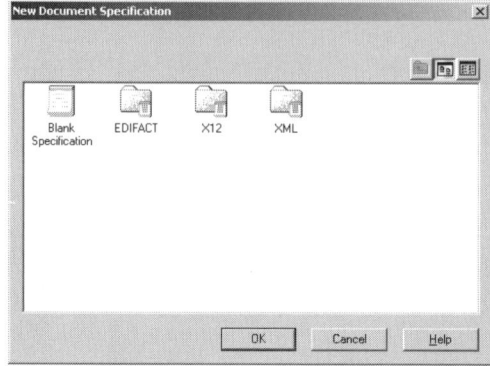

The New Document Specification dialog box contains a **Blank Specification** icon. Double-click this icon to begin creating a custom specification. (We will call this one PO, which is short for purchase order).

Now that we have begun making a brand new specification, you will see the BizTalk Editor create a new record as shown in Figure 5.2.

1. When you first open the Editor using a blank template, the specification in the left pane of the Editor will have a new record conveniently named **Blank Specification**. Right-click this document, and within the **Properties** menu, select **Rename**. Rename the root record **BIZTALKPO**. Please note that you cannot use spaces. Again, this record will act as the *root* of our document specification. (You may also edit the name right in the tree view of the left pane.)

2. Next, we can add some new fields and records to our new specification. Note in Figure 5.2 that we have already added quite a few records and fields for you. We will walk you through the process as shown in Figure 5.2. Right-click the new record named **BIZTALKPO**, and select **New Field** from the **Properties** menu. Create a new field titled **Date**. This will automatically create the Date field under the root of BIZTALKPO. You can continue to create the fields shown in Figure 5.2. Repeat these steps and create fields for the **CustomerNumber**, **InvoiceNumber**, and **Registration**. Note that you cannot skip spaces when creating records and fields.

3. Next, we will create another record under the root of BIZTALKPO. Right-click the **root document** and select **New Record** from the **Properties** menu. Name this record **ITEMLIST**. This will serve as a container for other fields within your specification. Once you have created the new record, follow the example described previously in step 2 and create fields for **Quantity**, **Size**, **Price**, and **Code**. You have now tackled the basics of creating your own specification.

Now, let's drill down a little further. When we made the record for ITEMLIST in step 3 of the previous example, we focused on the left pane of the Editor. Look at the right pane to see the effects of the changes you made to the properties and values of the records and fields. When you look at the record (left-click on **BIZTALKPO** once), look at the Type field in the right pane of the Editor in the **Declaration** tab. Notice that it is called an *element* (Figure 5.2). Now, if you do the same step and left-click on the **Date** field below it, you can see that it is classified as an *attribute* in the Type field.

Developing & Deploying…

XML with the BizTalk Editor

The BizTalk Editor might confuse those who are familiar with XML, because the Editor does not use the XML words *attribute* or *element*; it uses *records* and *fields*, as seen in Figure 5.2, which are more in tune with what database programmers are familiar with (records contain fields). Be aware of this to avoid confusion. To add even more confusion, you can create a field as an *element* and not an *attribute* by going to **Tools | Options** and checking the box to **Create a new field as an element**.

You can always view the actual underlying XML code that the Editor converts to by simply saving the specification and viewing it in Internet Explorer. To do this:

1. Save the specification as **BIZTALKPO.xml**. Go to the **File** menu within the **BizTalk Editor** and select **Save**. Save the document to your desktop.

2. Next, minimize the Editor. This will allow you to see the documents as XML attachments on your desktop.

3. Finally, view the XML code by right-clicking the new documents and selecting **Open With…**. This will open a dialog box for you to select a program with which to open the document. Select **Internet Explorer**. You can now view the code and it will appear within the browser. The file shown in Figure 5.4 will open, and will look similar to the code in Figure 5.5.

Figure 5.4 Saving a New PO on Your Desktop as an XML Attachment

Figure 5.5 Viewing the Saved XML Code within the Specification Using Internet Explorer

```xml
<?xml version="1.0" ?>
<!-- Generated by using BizTalk Editor on Wed, Oct 03 2001 10:19:32 PM  -->
<!-- Microsoft Corporation (c) 2000 (http://www.microsoft.com)  -->
- <Schema name="BizTalkPO" b:BizTalkServerEditorTool_Version="1.0" b:root_reference="BizTalkPO" b:standard="XML" xmlns="urn:schemas-microsoft-
  com:xml-data" xmlns:b="urn:schemas-microsoft-com:BizTalkServer" xmlns:d="urn:schemas-microsoft-com:datatypes">
    <b:SelectionFields />
  - <ElementType name="ITEMList" content="empty" model="closed">
      <b:RecordInfo />
    - <AttributeType name="Size">
        <b:FieldInfo />
      </AttributeType>
    - <AttributeType name="Quantity">
        <b:FieldInfo />
      </AttributeType>
    - <AttributeType name="Price">
        <b:FieldInfo />
      </AttributeType>
    + <AttributeType name="Code">
      <attribute type="Quantity" required="no" />
      <attribute type="Size" required="no" />
      <attribute type="Price" required="no" />
      <attribute type="Code" required="no" />
    </ElementType>
  - <ElementType name="BizTalkPO" content="eltOnly" model="closed">
      <b:RecordInfo />
    - <AttributeType name="Registration">
        <b:FieldInfo />
      </AttributeType>
    - <AttributeType name="Invoicenumber">
        <b:FieldInfo />
      </AttributeType>
    - <AttributeType name="DATE" d:type="number">
        <b:FieldInfo />
      </AttributeType>
    - <AttributeType name="CustomerNumber">
        <b:FieldInfo />
      </AttributeType>
      <attribute type="DATE" required="no" />
      <attribute type="CustomerNumber" required="no" />
      <attribute type="Invoicenumber" required="no" />
      <attribute type="Registration" required="no" />
      <element type="ITEMList" maxOccurs="1" minOccurs="0" />
    </ElementType>
  </Schema>
```

NOTE

Office XP will allow you to save documents as "XML attachments," and actually becomes a client for BizTalk Server 2000 in the respect that it has the functionality to save as XML documents.

Creating a New Specification from a Predefined Standard

Now that we have created a custom specification, let's move forward to editing a specification from a preexisting template based on one of the three standards contained within the New Document Specification dialog box. Refer back to Figure 5.3 to see the three predefined templates. For the purposes of the next exercise, we will select XML from the New Document Specification dialog box.

When you install BizTalk Server on the Windows 2000 server you are running, you can view the actual templates for predefined standards-based specifications by opening **Windows Explorer**, going to the drive on which you installed

BizTalk 2000, and going to **Program Files | Microsoft BizTalk Server | XML Tools | Templates | XML**. Here you will find the XML templates. You can find where the templates were installed during installation by looking at the path in Figure 5.6. Directly above them are the templates for EDI and X.12.

Figure 5.6 Explorer View and Location of Predefined Standards-Based Templates

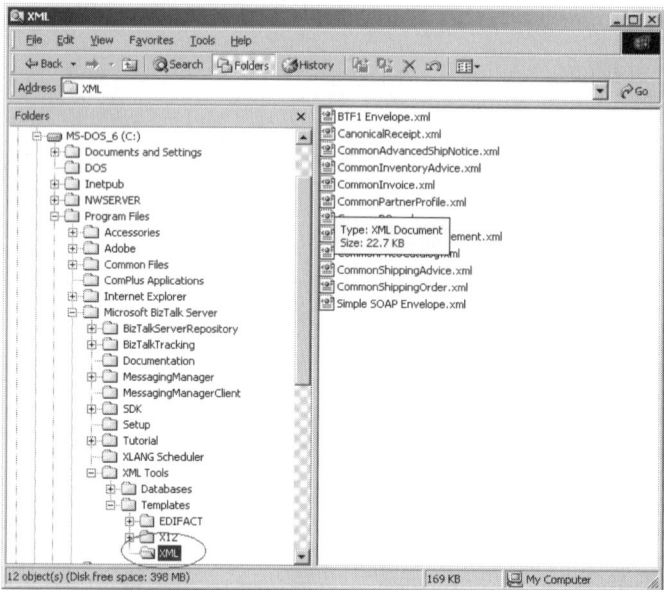

Now that we know where the templates are and why they are there, let's learn to work with them.

1. Go to the **File** menu, and select **New**.

2. The **New Document Specification** dialog box will open (Figure 5.3). Select **XML**.

3. Double-clicking on the XML template will open the list of XML templates within the XML Specification. Select the one named **CommonPO.xml**. If you cannot see this, select **List view** in the dialog box as shown in Figure 5.7. You can select this view by clicking on the **List** icon in the upper right of the dialog box. It will list all the templates and you will now be able to better read the XML documents.

4. Double-click on the **CommonPO.xml** template to open the BizTalk Editor with the predefined standard specification you just chose (Figure 5.8). We had you select the common PO to see what a professional PO

would look like within BizTalk 2000. We only made a very rough one here, because you would customize it based on your organizational and business needs. Remember, when working with BizTalk Server 2000, you also can wear the hat of a business analyst.

Figure 5.7 The New Document Specification Dialog Box in List View

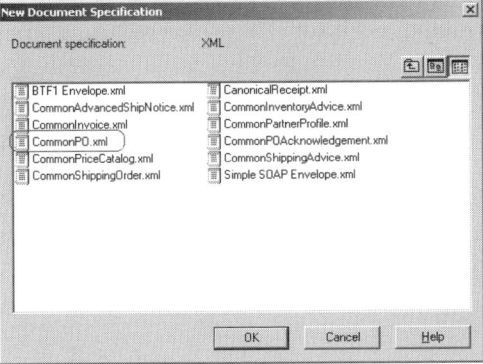

Figure 5.8 BizTalk Editor with the CommonPO.xml Template Selected and Opened

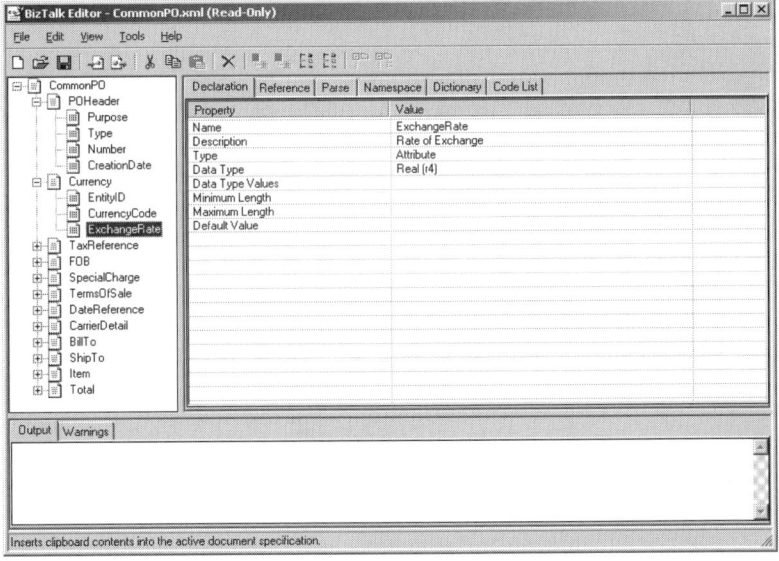

5. Referring back to the BizTalk Editor dialog box in Figure 5.8, you can see that we selected and highlighted the **ExchangeRate** field in the left pane, and we are viewing the field properties within the right pane.

6. Left-click on the **Description Value** and alter the description to **Rate Of Exchange 2001** to reference the year. You could make new fields under records to reference the month, or any other time the rate changes. This is, of course, a very simple change, and is only meant to show you that you could change it and how. Now, let's change the Data Type.

7. Left-click on the **Data Type** value and you will see a long list of values that you can change. The original setting is for Real (r4). Real (r4) means that this field contains a number that has a minimum value of 1.17549435E–38F and a maximum value of 3.40282347E+38F, meaning that a number within that range is acceptable. Let's change this Data Type.

8. Within the list, select **Number** from near the top of the list, and make that the new **Data Type**. Number suggests that the data contains digits and can have a leading sign, fractional digits, or exponents. An example could be number 1.

That's it! You just modified a preexisting specification. A template gives you a good framework from which to begin your work. You can always save your templates with another name and modify them later to suit your needs. Setting up specifications from scratch to fit particular situations can be very time consuming; modifying existing templates is a good alternative.

One other aspect of the BizTalk Editor we would like mention is its drag-and-drop functionality. As Figure 5.9 illustrates, all you need to do is left-click an item, hold down the mouse button, and drag it to a different Record container, or change its order within the current Record container, and then release the button to complete the move.

Figure 5.9 Alter a Specification by Dragging and Dropping Records and Fields in BizTalk Editor

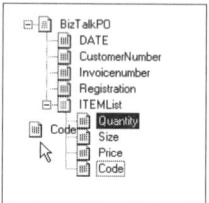

Importing/Exporting Specifications

Importing and exporting specifications is easy with the BizTalk Editor. Although the BizTalk schema is based on XDR, it does not mean that it is XDR compatible (hence, a weakness of XDR within BizTalk). This is easily solved by importing an XDR-compatible schema. This tool is crucial to place schema into ordinary XML documents. Let's import, export, and view the XDR schema.

> **NOTE**
>
> The main differences between XDR and XSD are that XSD is the schema that is currently being finalized as a W3C (World Wide Web Consortium) specification. XDR is Microsoft's release, and Microsoft has plans to release an XSD schema as soon as it is finalized with the W3C.

To import, and thus create, an XDR schema, you need to use the BizTalk Editor tool that comes with BizTalk 2000 Server.

1. Open the **BizTalk Editor** and go to the **Tools** menu. The full path is **Tools | Import**.

2. Once selected, you can now view the **Select Import Module** dialog box (Figure 5.10).

Figure 5.10 The Select Import Module Dialog Box

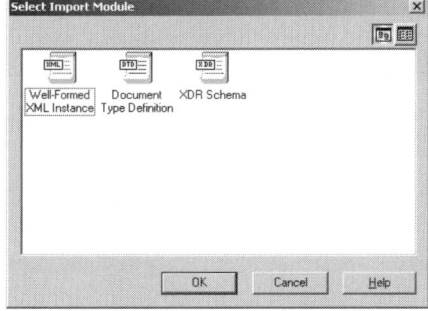

3. In the dialog box, double-click on the **XDR Schema** icon.

4. Next, you will be asked to select a file. If you wanted to select an XML document, you could do so to import the XDR schema into it, or, you could simply use the BIZTALKPO.xml document that we created in the previous exercise. For purposes of this exercise, browse to and open the PO we created earlier.

5. Now, when you open it, it will be part of the XDR schema.

Be aware that although the BizTalk Editor tool does a great job of importing an XDR schema into an ordinary XML document, you should never rely on any tool to be 100-percent foolproof. Make sure that any XML document you import XDR schema to is fully inspected for accuracy, since it could contain errors from translation.

To export, you will follow the same steps as you did when importing. When you export the schema, you will see the XML code as it looks in Figure 5.11. The reason to export would be to create an XDR schema from whatever schema type with which you are currently working with now. To view this, we will create a test file to work with so you can convert the schema to XDR, and then we will look at the difference.

1. Open the **BizTalk Editor**, go to **File | New**, and select **Document**. Open the **New Document Specification** dialog box, and select **EDI-FACT**. Again, we are starting this exercise by making a test file to export the XDR schema to.

2. After selecting **EDIFACT**, double-click **D98B**. Once **D98B** opens, open **SLSRPTSSchema.xml** at the bottom of the dialog box. Double-clicking this will open that template specification within the BizTalk Editor. Next, go to **File | Save As**, and save the XML file to your desktop as **EDIFACTTEST.xml**. We now have our test file, which was saved with the EDIFACT specification format. Next, let's create the XDR schema file.

3. With the **BizTalk Editor** still open, go to the **Tools | Export XDR Schema**, and select to **Export**. When you do, you will be asked where you want to export a file with the XDR schema to. Select to place this new file on the desktop with the filename **XDREXPORTTEST.xml**. You now have two test files on your desktop with which to work. Minimize all open windows so you can see both files saved to your desktop. With the files you just saved, right-click on them one at a time and select to open them with Internet Explorer. You will see the Code as labeled here:

- EDIFACT saved schema results within Internet Explorer:

```
<Schema name="EFACT_d98b_SLSRPT" b:BizTalkServerEditorTool_Version="1.0"
b:root_reference="EFACT_d98b_SLSRPT" b:schema_type="SLSRPT"
b:version="1.0" b:is_envelope="no"
```

```
b:standard="EDIFACT" b:standards_version="d98b" xmlns="urn:schemas-
microsoft-com:xml-data"
```

```
xmlns:b="urn:schemas-microsoft-com:BizTalkServer" xmlns:d="urn:schemas-
microsoft-com:datatypes"
```

■ XDR export schema saved schema results within Internet Explorer:

```
<Schema xmlns="urn:schemas-microsoft-com:xml-data"
name="EFACT_d98b_SLSRPT"
xmlns:d="urn:schemas-microsoft-com:datatypes">
```

As you can see, there are differences within the *schema* open tag. Now that we have viewed the two files, you should understand that with the Export function within the BizTalk Editor you are able to take a standard specification and export the file to a new saved file with the XDR schema. Let's move on to viewing the schemas.

To view the XDR schema, you need only a Web browser. We will use Internet Explorer for this exercise.

1. Right-click a saved file, and select **Open with…**.

2. When the dialog box opens, select to open the XML file with **Internet Explorer**. Make sure you do not have the **Always open with** box checked, or it might change the file's extension to HTML or HTM, which is not the same as XML, although they can both be opened with and viewed with a Web browser.

3. The other way to view the XDR schema is to just double-click the file itself, and it should open the file with your default Web browser. Either way, you should see the results as shown in Figure 5.11. One last note to mention is that there are Plus and Minus signs within the code in Figure 5.11. On the left side of the Web browser window you should see **(–)** and **(+)**. Clicking on these Plus and Minus signs has the same effect as expanding and collapsing menus within Windows Explorer as shown in Figure 5.6. You can use these items to condense or expand long lists of itemized code.

You should now be somewhat familiar with the basics of importing and exporting specifications, and how to view them. As with any file-based specification, you might have a need to convert this from one format to another. One way to convert to the XDR schema specification is to use the BizTalk Editor to import or export files with the XDR schema.

Figure 5.11 Viewing the Entire XDR Schema Exported from the BizTalk Editor

```
<?xml version="1.0" ?>
<!-- Generated by using BizTalk Editor on Wed, Oct 03 2001 10:45:39 PM   -->
<!-- Microsoft Corporation (c) 2000 (http://www.microsoft.com)   -->
- <Schema xmlns="urn:schemas-microsoft-com:xml-data" name="BizTalkPO" xmlns:d="urn:schemas-microsoft-com:datatypes">
- <ElementType name="ITEMList" content="empty" model="closed">
    <AttributeType name="Size" />
    <AttributeType name="Quantity" />
    <AttributeType name="Price" />
    <AttributeType name="Code" />
    <attribute type="Quantity" required="no" />
    <attribute type="Size" required="no" />
    <attribute type="Price" required="no" />
    <attribute type="Code" required="no" />
  </ElementType>
- <ElementType name="BizTalkPO" content="eltOnly" model="closed">
    <AttributeType name="Registration" />
    <AttributeType name="Invoicenumber" />
    <AttributeType name="DATE" d:type="number" />
    <AttributeType name="CustomerNumber" />
    <attribute type="DATE" required="no" />
    <attribute type="CustomerNumber" required="no" />
    <attribute type="Invoicenumber" required="no" />
    <attribute type="Registration" required="no" />
    <element type="ITEMList" maxOccurs="1" minOccurs="0" />
  </ElementType>
</Schema>
```

Property Configuration

To fully understand the properties, we need to discuss and work within records, fields, and their properties. Earlier in the chapter we discussed what a record is and what a field is—now, let's dig deeper into the development and modification of their actual properties in the BizTalk Editor. Let's look at how to change two types of properties before moving on to mapping the specifications we are making and altering:

■ Record-based properties

■ Field-based properties

Record-Based Properties

Record-based properties can be manipulated in many ways. You will have to work within these records to change many attributes and alter elements within them. We will go step by step through the processes involved in moving, editing, and manipulating the records within your working specification. Let's look at what we can change.

Adding Records to the Root Node, or Adding Records to Preexisting Records

1. To add a record to either the root node or to any other record within your specification, go to the menus in the BizTalk Editor and select **Edit | New Record**, or right-click the record that already exists and select

New Record from the **Properties** menu. You will now create a record under the record you right-clicked on.

2. You can now name this record and it will become a part of your specification when saved.

3. The **Insert** option found both in the **Properties** menu and in the **Edit** menu of the Editor will insert a new record as well, but it will go under the top-level record from which you are working under. This can be slightly confusing, so try to open a blank specification and make a few new records by selecting both **New Record** and **Insert Record**. You will immediately see the difference.

4. One last note to mention is that sibling records cannot have the same name, so make sure you name your records accurately and do a little preplanning before making your entire schema.

Moving and Copying Records within a Specification

1. You can easily move a record by dragging and dropping the record from its original location to a new one (see the section *Creating a New Specification from a Predefined Standard*).

2. Copying a file is not drag-and-drop friendly, nor is it an option within the Properties menu of the record itself. To copy a file, use **Edit | Copy**, or use the shortcut **Ctrl+C**.

Moving and Copying Records from One Specification to Another

1. This is very similar to the previous exercise, except that you need two instances of BizTalk Editor opened at the same time.

2. Open the first instance of **BizTalk Editor**, and open a **predefined specification**. Select one record within, and **Copy** it using the same procedures we just learned. You have just copied one record to memory, and there it will stay until pasted into **BIZTALKPO.xml**.

3. Open another instance (the second) of **BizTalk Editor** by going to **Start | Programs | Microsoft BizTalk Server 2000 | BizTalk Editor**.

4. Open the **BIZTALKPO.xml** file, which should still be on your desktop from a previous exercise, and let it open in the Editor. Highlight

the **root node** and go to the **Edit** menu. Select **Paste** and it will paste itself into the BIZTALKPO.xml specification. You can do the same for Copy or Move operations, and all the shortcut keys are operational in this format.

Field-Based Properties

Field-based properties are manipulated in exactly the same fashion as records are. Since they are nearly the same, we will only briefly go through the steps, highlighting any differences that are unique to fields. Creating new fields is almost identical to the creating records, with one major difference: fields are attributes and records are elements by default, although fields can also be turned into elements. This is by default, of course, and we already outlined earlier in the chapter that within the tools menu (**Tools | Options**) you can make fields into elements as well. We also mentioned in the last exercise that you cannot have duplicate records, nor could you have duplicate fields *except* when you use the option within the Tools menu to change a field into an element instead of an attribute. Now, you can have duplicate fields named identically if one is set to be element based and the other is set to be attribute based. The other way to change a field from an element to an attribute, and vice versa, is to highlight the field within the left pane of the Editor and alter the field in the Declaration tab located on the right side of the Editor. Go to the **Type** row and double-click the **Value** field. You can now select between the two (attribute or element).

Make sure you know how to manipulate the data within the BizTalk Editor. This means being able to make, move, alter, manipulate, import, and export the data within the BizTalk Editor.

Mapping Data between Documents

Now that we are comfortable with making and working with specifications, we will move on to working with them outside the BizTalk Editor. The whole point of specification creation and usage is the fact that you are going to eventually have to deal with dissimilar data specifications and standards. Remember that the whole basis and underlying functionality of BizTalk Server 2000 is to be able to transparently allow businesses to work seamlessly together and do business with dissimilar systems and infrastructures. BizTalk allows you to work with EDI and other standards between two companies that do not necessarily have the same standards, even over the Internet or Web with XML coding.

Once you have your specifications and your business partners are ready to connect and do business with you, the next step is to map their purchase orders to yours. You might work with five different companies that all use different purchase order formats. In this section of the chapter, we will look at creating two specifications and do a very simple mapping. We will describe the use of functoids and how they aid in the mapping of specifications. We will also describe how to map the specifications that already exist within BizTalk 2000 Server.

Creating the Specifications and Preparing the Mapping Tool

For this exercise, we will create two new specifications. The actual specifications used at this point are unimportant as we will work with real ones next, but it is easier to learn mapping when you are not concerned with what you are mapping. Let's use the knowledge you've picked up so far in the chapter to make the two specifications from scratch.

1. Open the **BizTalk Editor** and go to **File | New**. Note: Do *not* go to **File | Open. File | Open** will not allow you to follow the lab and create a map. It will allow you to open previous maps, not specifications that are not already mapped.

2. Select the **Blank Specification** option within the **New Document Specification** dialog box

3. Create a new record root node named **MySpec1**. Make a new record directly below that root node record called **Months**. Make 12 fields below that Month record for each month in the year, starting with January. You can keep the field names short because we are only setting up a test specification. You can refer to the map in Figure 5.12 to see how we named the records and fields.

4. Now that you have made the fields, save the new specification as **MySpec1** on your desktop.

5. Now, look at the BizTalk Editor and highlight the **Months** record. Go to **Edit | Copy** and copy the entire Months record with all the Month fields below it.

6. Go to **Start | Programs | Microsoft BizTalk Server 2000 | BizTalk Editor**, and open a second instance of the Editor. Follow steps 1 and 2 again, and when you create a new record root node, call it

MySpec2. Highlight the **new root node** by left-clicking on it once, and go to **Edit | Paste**. This will paste the Month record into the new specification, which eliminates having to type in all the fields again.

7. Go to **File | Save As** and save this new specification as **MySpec2** on your desktop. You should now have two new specifications saved on your desktop. These are the two specifications that you are going to use in the BizTalk Mapper.

8. Next, we need to open the **BizTalk Mapper** tool so we can set it up to learn about it. Go to **Start | Programs | Microsoft BizTalk Server 2000 | BizTalk Mapper** and select it. This will open the **Mapper** utility.

9. When you first open the BizTalk Mapper, it will be empty, as was the Editor the first time you opened it. Let's add the two specifications we made to it. Figure 5.12 shows what the BizTalk Mapper looks like.

10. Go to the **File** menu, and select **New**. A new dialog box appears, **Select Source Specification Type**, and asks you for the specification you want to select as the source, which will reside on the left side of the pane conveniently called the *Source specification pane*.

11. Select the **Local Files** icon, and browse to the desktop to select the **MySpec1** XML file.

12. After you add the Source specification, the prompt and dialog box for the destination will become the default so you will not have to go to **File | New** again. Instead, follow steps 10 and 11 again, except pick the **MySpec2** file for the Destination specification that will sit in the right-hand Destination Specification pane of the BizTalk Mapper.

Once you finish this last step, you will have a full view of both specifications loaded into the BizTalk Mapper, ready for you to begin mapping with as seen in Figure 5.12.

Now that we have set up the BizTalk Mapper as shown in Figure 5.12, we can map from source to destination and learn the fundamentals of mapping. Remember, mapping is used to identify how data in one format is translated to another; for example, from EDI to X.12.

Assume you are running one platform and your supplier of goods is running another. You communicate by creating maps, which give you an XML-based translation between the two specifications that can be held over the Internet or over dedicated lines.

Figure 5.12 The BizTalk Mapper with Source Showing Destination Specifications Ready to Map

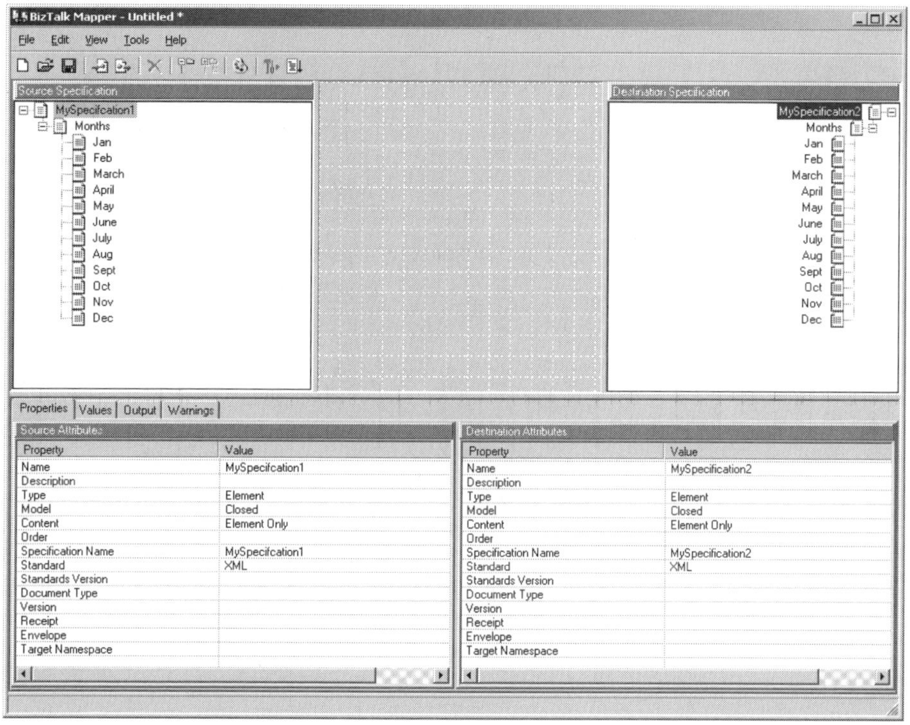

It is possible to have mapping across a WAN such as the Internet; we cover this in the section on WebDAV. Mapping data creates a translation process between records and fields from a source (perhaps you), to records and fields from a destination, which might be your supplier, shipper, or any entity you might be doing business with.

BizTalk Map Types

We would like to quickly explain the difference between map types that can be created with the BizTalk Mapper. There are two main map types: *specific* and *generic*. For our exercises, we will be creating specific maps, but you need to know the difference between the two types:

- Specific map types are designed to satisfy the needs of *one* partner.
- Generic map types are designed to satisfy the needs of *multiple* partners.

The main difference between the types is the number of people with whom you are doing business. Generic mapping is an ideal choice if you want to use one map for multiple partners.

Creating, Compiling, and Testing the Map

Now that we are familiar with the basics of what maps are and why you would use them, let's create a very simple one, compile it, and test it. This exercise will allow you to get the feel of the GUI that the BizTalk Mapper incorporates into its functionality, as well as gain some experience working within the tool itself. After completing the exercise, we will go through all the menus and items of the user interface to briefly discuss where things are and those items we did not use in the actual exercise.

Creating and Compiling the Map

Let's get started creating and compiling the map:

1. We need to have the BizTalk Mapper open. It should be in the same state as we left off from the last exercise. Both specifications should be loaded, and the Mapper should look similar to Figure 5.12.

2. We'll begin with basic mapping. Let's map October to October. Left-click October and hold the button down. Drag from the source (left side) to the destination (right side). A set of *sniper crosshairs* should appear in your Mapper utility. Drag the crosshairs all the way to the right side of the October field and release the button. It will connect, and you will have a mapping from one field to another. That's it! You created a mapping.

3. Now let's quickly learn how to "undo" a mapping. You can right-click the line that goes across the BizTalk Mapper to produce a Properties menu, but it is all relative to where you are in the Mapper. In other words, go to the left side of the Source Specification pane, and right-click the mapping line. You will see an option to **Replace the specification**, which we do not want to do (although this is how you can replace the specification with another if you need to).

4. Go to the Middle Grid pane and right-click the map line. Now you can see an option to delete the mapping. Select **Delete** and watch as the mapping line disappears. Now, repeat step 2 to recreate your mapping. In the menu option where you could delete the mapping is an option to "unselect." This is not to "unselect the mapping," but to unselect the line

you just clicked on. Left-clicking on the line once selects it and turns it blue.

5. You should now have October mapped to October, so let's map a few more items. Map August to August. Map the Source specification's December to the Destination specification's January. Map the Source specification's January to the Destination specification's December. You should have a mapping system that look like Figure 5.13. Now, we have four simple mappings.

Figure 5.13 Compiling a BizTalk 2000 Map and Viewing Output

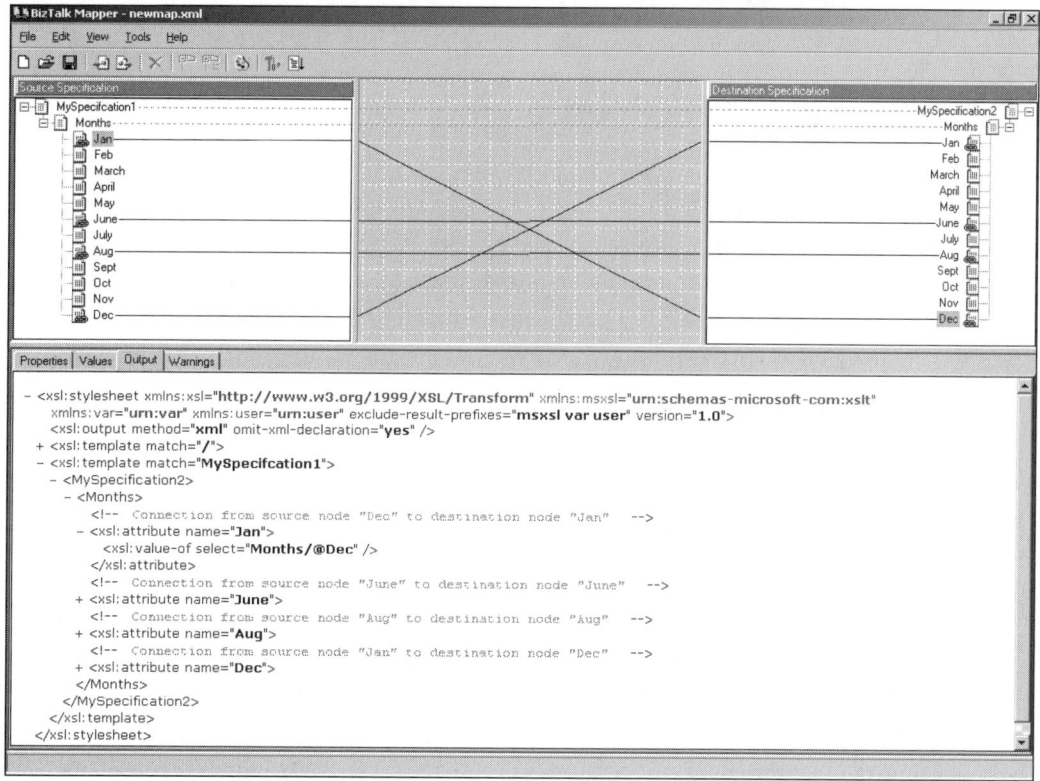

6. Let's finish this map by compiling it. Go to the **Tools** menu and select to **Compile map**. After you compile the code, look at the **Output** tab in Figure 5.13. You can see what we called XSL (Extensible Stylesheet Language), which we will cover next. With the compiling finished, let's move on to the testing and saving of the map we just made.

Debugging...

Mappings with Warnings

The BizTalk Mapper will generate a warning on the Warnings tab when the compiler creates the code compilation and gets incorrect results. A solid rule of thumb for any programmer or developer is that a map (or any program for that matter) should not generate any warnings; if it does, it should not be considered for a production environment. Go back and continue to test the mappings until they function properly.

Extensible Stylesheet Language

We mentioned XSL previously, but it warrants a good explanation for you to fully understand what the BizTalk Mapper is doing. The Extensible Stylesheet Language (XSL) is just like a cascading stylesheet (CSS) for HTML documents. The XSL language is used for expressing stylesheets with the underlying power to perform transformations. XSL Transformation (XSLT) is a subset of XSL that allows for transformation from one form to another. This is what the BizTalk Mapper was designed to do, transform one form to another using XML. Now when you look at the stylesheet in the Output tab shown in Figure 5.13, it should make more sense as to what the output really is.

Testing and Saving Your Map

Follow these steps to test and save the map:

1. To test the map, go to the **Tools | Test Map** option in the **Menu Tools** menu and select to test it.

2. When you test it, you will see the test results in the Output tab. Figure 5.14 shows that our mappings equal out and are correct. Any errors that occur pop up automatically in the Warnings tab, which will give you an idea on what the problem might be to guide you in the right direction to fix it. Now that it tests clean, let's save it!

3. To save the map, go to the **File** menu and open **File | Save As**, which will open the **Save Map Source As** dialog box.

4. Enter a name for the map you just created. Call it **MYSAVEDMAP**.

Figure 5.14 Testing a BizTalk 2000 Map and Viewing Output

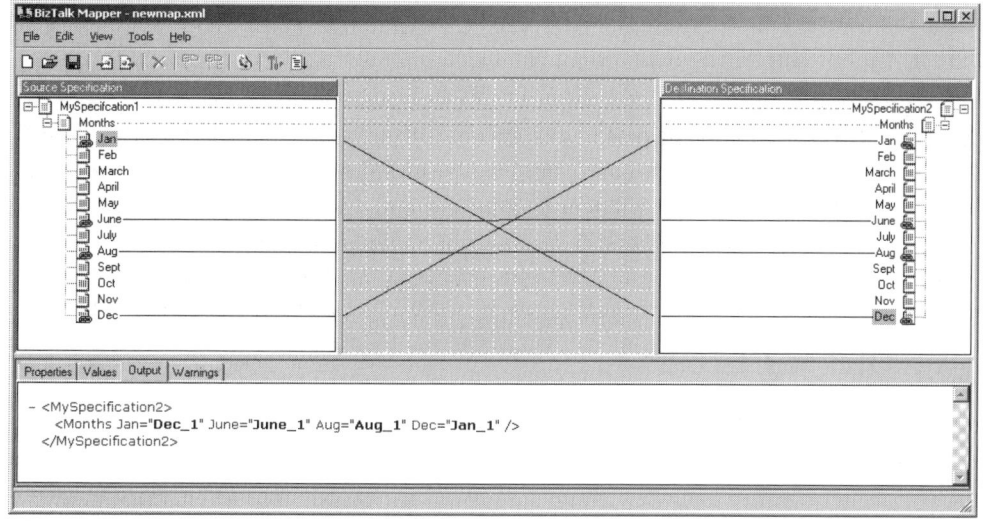

5. The map automatically compiles when you save it, so you don't need to specifically call on the BizTalk Mapper; it is set to do it by default.

6. Two important topics to mention are UTF-8 and Unicode encoding. If you select to save this as ASCII readable, choose **UTF-8**, which is the default. However, if you need to save the map as double-byte character sets, then you need to drop down the menu in the **Save As** dialog box and select **Unicode**.

7. If you want to compile it manually before saving, simply go to the **Tools** menu and select to **Compile Map** as we did in the previous exercise.

You have just created a map, tested it, compiled it, and saved it for future use. In the next section, we will look at altering the map using functoids, and in the last section, we will open and map two predefined specifications.

Functoids

Functoids are small programs that you can use to alter the mapping of records and fields within the BizTalk Mapper. We'll use the mathematical addition-based functoid to illustrate what a functoid does. For example, if you have a field that equals one from the source, and I have a field that equals two from the destination, essentially you could insert a function in the middle to add them. Now, what if you had a predefined script to do this? If you did, you could just drag and drop that code in between the specifications and it would handle the math for you. That coded function is a functoid, and that's what a functoid does. Another way to think of functoids is to consider how incompatible data specifications can be. Even if you were able to edit the XSLT stylesheet and tweak things not normally tweaked with the compiler, you still might run into computationally impossible incompatibilities. Functoids can help you achieve the impossible. We will look at all the predefined subsets of functoids contained within the Functoid palette, and look at the underlying script that finds its way into your stylesheet once compiled.

Functoid Palette

The BizTalk 2000 Mapper utility supports highly complex transformations from one tree to another (Source specification to Destination specification) in a drag-and-drop functionality. You can drag and drop functoids from the Functoid palette (Figure 5.15) to help in the creation of these mappings. There are many functoids from which to choose, so we will spend some time here detailing each.

Figure 5.15 The Functoid Palette

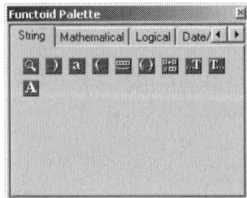

Adding a Simple Functoid to a Map

To learn how to manipulate the Functoid palette and create a simple mapping with a functoid, we will choose a functoid, place it on the map, and see how it alters the XSL stylesheet in the bottom pane of the BizTalk Mapper. We will look at where the functoid sits in the code, and once we perform the steps of adding this simple functoid, we will look at the rest of the palette. The last steps include opening two predefined specifications and looking at their mappings.

1. Open the **BizTalk Mapper** and let's make our final changes to the specifications we created on the Months of the year. You can follow along with Figure 5.16.

Figure 5.16 Using the BizTalk Mapper to Map Specifications with a Functoid

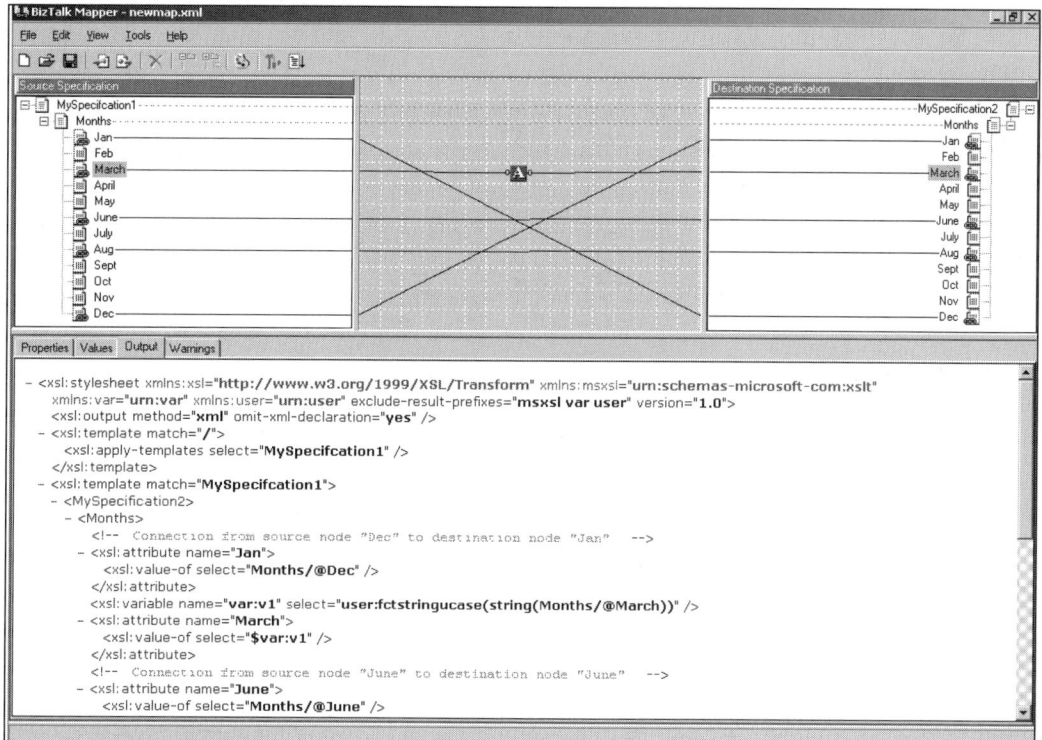

2. Next, go the **View** menu and select the **Functoid palette**. A dialog box will open as shown in Figure 5.15. You can also get to the palette by clicking the little artist's paint palette in the toolbar (Figure 5.16).

3. The Functoid palette contains many tabs. We will go through each tab in the next section of this chapter, but for this exercise, please focus your attention on the default tab called **String**.

4. On the String tab, you will see an **A**. Click on the **A** and hold your left mouse button. Drag that **A** to the center grid of the **BizTalk Mapper** and place it, by releasing the left button, in the center of both specifications' March fields as shown in Figure 5.16. Now you need to connect the two fields together with the functoid.

5. Left-click the **March Source specification field**, hold the button down, drag your mouse over to the **A** functoid, and then release it. Do the same from the **Destination specification March field** to the **A** functoid.

You just connected two fields with a functoid. Now, let's look at how it changed the output of the XSL stylesheet.

In the following code, note that placing a functoid into your map will add a function-based script. The output of this map was taken from the Output tab of the Mapper. The bold type shows where the functoid script is placed in the XSL stylesheet.

```
</MySpecification2>

</xsl:template>

<msxsl:script language="VBScript" implements-prefix="user">

<![CDATA[

Function FctStringUCase( p_strA )

    FctStringUCase = Ucase( p_strA )

End Function

  ]]>

</msxsl:script>

</xsl:stylesheet>
```

We are now going to show you exactly where this code in the XSL stylesheet comes from. In Figure 5.16, you will see the **A** functoid (which stands for uppercase and simply converts a text item to uppercase text). Right-click this **A** and go to **Properties**. Click on the **Script** tab and you will be able to match that script to what you see in the output we captured previously. This is what a functoid does; you put the icon in the grid and it puts the script you see here into the XSL stylesheet. That's it! Now that we understand the basics of functoids, let's dig into the palette as seen in Figure 5.15 and look at each tab's related function.

Working with Predefined Functoids in the Functoid Palette

Now that we know the basics of how to manipulate the data of a new set of specifications that we created, let's do a start-to-finish super lab using all the things we have learned up to now. We will open two predefined specifications, map them, and look at all the different functoids we can script with. We will finish with a look at the scripts and discuss WebDAV. As we move forward in our map development, we will have to use functoids. For a brief overview of all the predefined functoids, we have listed all of the functoids that exist in the palette, as shown in Figure 5.15. Within the palette are multiple tabs. They are listed here for you to reference.

- **String** The String tab contains functoids that manipulate data strings using *string* functions. To understand this, we could use the *find* string function to find data within another string of data.

- **Mathematical** The Mathematical tab contains functoids that use arguments to perform mathematical calculations. A good example is the multiplication functoid, which can multiply values of two or more fields.

- **Logical** The Logical tab contains functoids that perform logical testing. It works with logic that equates to True and False tables. These functoids can perform all logical needs relating to True and False-based equations.

- **Date/Time** The Date/Time tab contains functoids that are used to manipulate date- and time-based information and data.

- **Conversion** The Conversion tab contains functoids that convert ASCII to other forms, Base2 systems to Base16 systems, and so on. The functoids handle high-level conversion functions for data.

- **Scientific** The Scientific tab contains functoids that convert numeric-based data to scientific values, such as what would be needed to find angles and distances.

- **Cumulative** The Cumulative tab contains functoids that find sums, medians, and averages.

- **Database** The Database tab contains functoids that extract needed data from a database.

- **Advanced** The Advanced tab contains functoids that allow you to create custom VBScripts to create your own functoid functionality.

NOTE

You might never use all of the predefined functoids. Some are included for completeness, such as the Scientific tab. You will find that string, mathematical, and database are some of the most commonly used.

We will now look at some of the options you have when selecting functoids. From the preceding list, you can see that you have much to work with in terms of predefined scripts. You could script the stylesheet without the use of functoids and we will look at that last. Let's now work on creating a usable map with functoids.

Creating Predefined Specifications and Mapping Them with Functoids

In this section, we continue with the lab to create a map using functoids. We begin by making two predefined specifications from two different companies (two companies having different purchase orders are definitely very common these days). After the schemas are complete, we will move to creating a basic map. We will look at the dissimilar fields within the two specifications and devise a way to map them using basic techniques. Finally, we will discover that there are fields that might require a functoid, in which case we will add that functoid. We will compile and save our map and finish with a brief summary. This exercise will walk you through every aspect that has been covered thus far.

1. Open the **BizTalk Editor** by going to **Start | Programs | Microsoft BizTalk Server 2000 | BizTalk Editor**. Using the previous exercises in the chapter, we will create two predefined specifications based on purchase orders from two dissimilar systems from two different companies. We will make sure they are dissimilar by creating the specifications ourselves.

2. Once the Editor is open, start by creating your first new specification. Call the root node **CompanyOnePO**. This specification will have the root node named CompanyOnePO, and will have five fields under the root node. Note that as we make this, you can reference the specification as the source in the left pane of Figure 5.17. The fields will be titled from top to bottom: Date, Month, Year, Customer Name, Customer Phone, Supply Item, Price, and Quantity. As we create this schema, consider this Company One and this is how their systems define a purchase order. Remember, the whole point of BizTalk Server 2000 is to be able to do what we are doing right now!

3. Now, let's save this specification to the desktop and create another one.

4. Follow steps 2 and 3 again, but name the root node and save the PO as **CompanyTwoPO** with the fields, from top to bottom: Date, Customer Number, Name, Item, Price, Qty, and Total.

5. Now, with our specifications created, you can view the differences. Not all companies conform to the same systems or specifications, so we can use the BizTalk Server 2000 Editor and Mapper tools to manipulate and map the dissimilar schemas. Let's move to the Mapper.

Figure 5.17 BizTalk Mapper with Two New Specifications

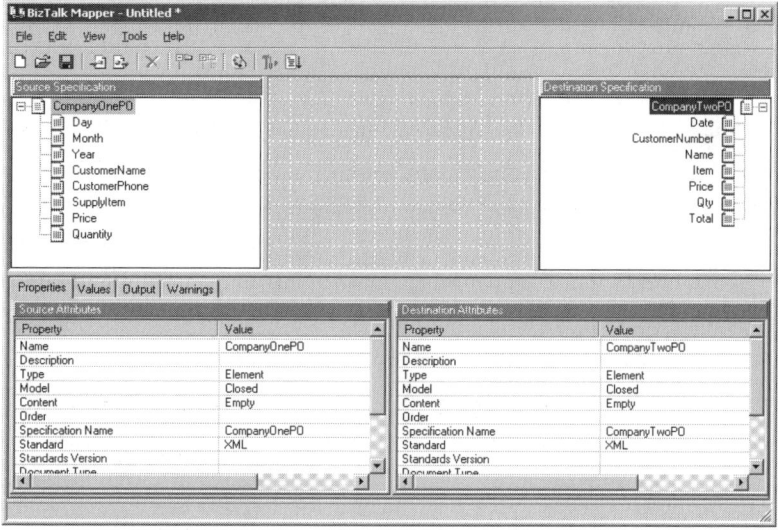

6. Open the BizTalk Mapper by going to **Start | Programs | Microsoft BizTalk Server 2000 | BizTalk Mapper**.

7. Next, go to the File menu or toolbar and select **New**, because we want to create a new map.

8. The appropriate dialog boxes will appear to ask you what specifications you want to map. Since you saved the two POs you just created to your desktop, we will select **Local Files** to browse to and find the documents we created. Select **CompanyOnePO** as the Source specification, and select **CompanyTwoPO** as the Destination PO. We will imagine that we are Company One and we want to map to the dissimilar purchase order of Company Two to make a transparent and seamless integration between document specifications.

9. With the Mapper open and ready to go as shown in Figure 5.17, we want to map the specifications. Let's map the common fields first without the use of any necessary functions. We will refer to Figure 5.18 for the rest of this exercise and review what we added to the map.

10. Let's map the obvious, and put in what needs to be added with functoids later. First, you can map the Customer Name from Company One to the Name field in Company Two. It is obvious that they are similar, but might have slightly different formats or naming conventions. We can also

map the Customer Phone field to the Name field in Company Two. In the Destination specification, we can map the Customer Number to the Customer Name field in Company One. We are linking the fields together because they might contain the same data. Finally, map the Price and Quantity fields from the Source specification to the Destination specification, as they are also very similar, if not identical. We have now mapped the obvious choices to one another for seamless transactions between the specifications.

Figure 5.18 BizTalk Map Using Functoids of Two Dissimilar Purchase Orders

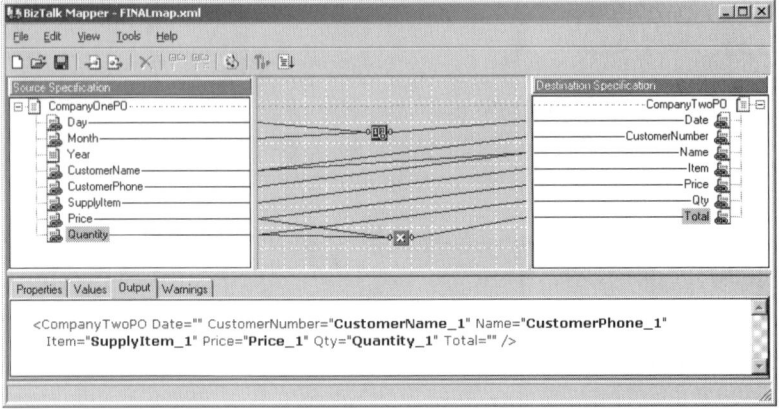

11. We do, however, have a few fields that have not been addressed because they either need a mathematical computation-based function run against them, or some other high-level function that one-to-one mapping will not solve. The first and easiest field is the Date, Month, and Year of the Source specification against the Date field of the Destination specification. We need to compute information that we received in advance. Wearing our business analyst hats, we asked Company Two what type of calendar system they use. For argument's sake, let's say they use a Julian date calendar. Therefore, we have to alter, manipulate, or change the amount of days in the calendar to be able to transparently map from one source to the other destination. We will add the Add Days functoid from the Functoid palette's Date/Time tab. This could be further altered, but it is just in place to give you an idea of how it might be seen or applied.

12. The other functoid we will add is from the Mathematical tab of the Functoid palette, the Multiplication functoid. As shown in Figure 5.18,

we were able to map the Price and Quantity fields pretty easily from Source specification to Destination specification directly, without any added functions. If you look closely at the Destination specification in the BizTalk Mapper in Figure 5.18, you can see that the Total field is only seen in the destination and not the source. So, how do we make this seamless and transparent and produce a total for the Destination specification's purchase order? By using a mathematical function, we will multiply the price and quantity to produce a total for the Destination specification. Again, this is just to show you how and why you would use the Functoid palette; there are virtually thousands of ways to use the functoids, and you always have the option to script your own functions into the XSLT stylesheet. We will look at that next.

13. Finally, we need to compile and save the map. Go to the **Tools** menu and select to **Compile** the map. Save the map to your desktop with a name of **FINALMAP.xml**; you just created two PO specifications and mapped them using functoids.

Scripting

The Scripting functoid is the most versatile tool in the Mapper. Nothing beats being able to apply your own script to work around any issues not solved with a ready-made tool. The functoid uses Visual Basic Scripting (or VBScript for short), and allows you to write your own functions. If you really want to excel at writing functional scripts, you need to know very basic, if not more advanced, VBScript and have an underlying idea of how the Mapper works with XML and XSLT stylesheets. If you do, then we will cover the basics of creating a VBScript-based function. However, if you are not a pro at scripting, don't worry, because this template is what you need to work with, and as long as you understand the basics, you could evolve to writing elaborate scripts with enough time and practice.

The most basic Scripting functoid you create is going to use ADO through COM. COM is Component Object Model (and is also distributed; hence, DCOM), and ADO is the acronym for ActiveX Data Objects. Remember that *all* functoids have an underlying script as we discussed earlier in the chapter. To view this again, do the following:

1. Open the **BizTalk Mapper** by going to **Start | Programs | Microsoft BizTalk Server 2000 | BizTalk Mapper**.

2. You can open the **FINALMAP.xml** map you saved to your desktop by going to the **File** menu and browsing to your desktop.

3. Once opened, you can have access to the Functoid palette. BizTalk Mapper will not allow you to open the palette without an open map. Now that the map is open as shown in Figure 5.18, look to the center of the Mapper, right-click the **Multiplication functoid**, and select **Properties**. You can see the Script tab in the dialog box. Selecting this will show you the underlying script as it is also seen in the compiled script of the XSLT stylesheet as seen in the Output tab of the Mapper itself. Go ahead and close that **Properties** box because we will look at the actual Scripting functoid.

4. Open the Functoid palette by selecting the easel on the toolbar, or go to **View | Functoid Palette**.

5. Click on the **Advanced** tab and you will see that the first icon is discolored from the rest of the icons in the dialog box (Figure 5.19). This yellowish icon with an "S" is the Scripting icon.

Figure 5.19 The Functoid Palette's Advanced Tab and Scripting Functoid

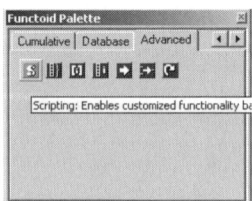

6. You can now drag and drop the Scripting functoid over to the grid within the BizTalk Mapper (in the center of the tool) and place it anywhere in the grid. Simply map two fields to it. Select **Price to Price** from the Source to the Destination specifications. Figure 5.20 shows the result.

Figure 5.20 The Script Functoid Placed on the BizTalk Map Grid

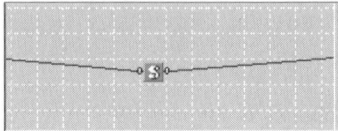

7. To edit the script in the Scripting functoid, simply right-click the **func-toid** as shown in Figure 5.20, and select **Properties** from the menu. In the dialog box is a Script tab. Select the Script tab and you will see a small VBScript as shown in Figure 5.21.

Figure 5.21 The Script Functoid Properties Sheet Scripting Tab

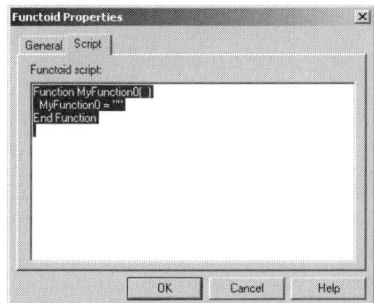

8. Our final task is to modify this script. We can make this script do simple addition by rewriting it as follows:

```
Function FctMathAdd0 (    )
    FctMathAdd0 = ""
End Function
```

That's it! You just created a functoid script. The level of your scripting is going to greatly depend on how much you know and understand about VB and scripting within it.

Now that we have created specifications, mapped them, and learned how to do both functions with the BizTalk Editor and BizTalk Mapper, we have one final topic to discuss: WebDAV.

Using WebDAV

WebDAV is short for World Wide Web Distributed Authoring and Versioning. It was created as a standard for collaboratively editing and managing Web documents, and is managed by the Internet Engineering Task Force (IETF). WebDAV is a set of extensions to HTTP that allow for the local and remote collaboration of Web documents. In BizTalk Server 2000, this is critical to mapping documents that are not local to your server. The World Wide Web Consortium (W3C) is highly involved with its development because WebDAV is an excellent Web-based remote collaboration tool. WebDAV has many general features, such as locking, which is important to erase the possibility of overwriting files. If you were remotely working on a file that others are collaborating on, you would need it locked while you were working on it so as not to confuse others. WebDAV is also based on XML, of course, and this is very important, as it is Web enabled, and XML allows for metadata, which allows for organization of data under data. WebDAV also has a subset of protocols to include DAV and DASL. DAV is used for retrieving, deleting, and setting properties, and the DASL protocol allows for searching and locating property values on the Web. You can find more information about WebDAV at www.webdav.org.

WebDAV is mapped to BizTalk Server 2000 under IIS. When you install BizTalk on your machine, the setup automatically creates a WebDAV storage facility (as a new virtual directory) within IIS, which is Windows Internet Information Server. This new default virtual directory is called BizTalkServerRepository and can be found on the default Web site within IIS.

NOTE

If you have a problem accessing and connecting to WebDAV, you might need to give a user access to the WebDAV repository. Make sure you configure IIS correctly with permissions to allow access to the WebDAV repository, as this can be a common mistake. Go to the **BizTalkServerRepositoryVirtual** virtual directory, click on the **Security** tab, and adjust the security accordingly.

You can access WebDAV in BizTalk Server by opening the **BizTalk Editor** and the **BizTalk Mapper** and going to **File | Retrieve from WebDAV**. You can store to WebDAV when you are finished working on the retrieved data from here as well, or you can use the **Retrieve from WebDAV** or **Store to WebDAV** icons on the toolbar to accomplish the same things.

Summary

At the beginning of this chapter, we talked about what a specification is. We discussed that in order for two or more organizations to do business together, a similar set of systems is needed to be able to transform information to and from each other (for example, EDI to XML). So, what happens when your business partners do not have similar systems? If this were the case (which it most often is), you would need to create specifications based on those differences that can be mapped and put together to make a seamless and transparent transaction of resources. You would need to implement Microsoft BizTalk Server 2000 and, more importantly, learn how to create those specifications and map them with the tools described in this chapter: the BizTalk Editor and the BizTalk Mapper. While learning these tools, we created new specifications and altered predefined templates. We worked at creating our own purchase orders and exporting data into an XDR schema. We also covered the details of records and fields, and how to work with and alter their properties. We then moved on to the BizTalk Mapper, where we learned how to add two specifications together to create a map. We learned how to use the Mapper tool and how to create basic mappings. We did an overview of creating specifications to be mapped and went through the entire process of creating schema data and mapping it together. We looked at mappings that were not simple in nature and required functions or *functoids* to be added to the script to provide the results needed. We then looked at the XSL stylesheet and how it is all tied together to achieve the end result. We finished the chapter with an explanation of WebDAV and how to access it. All in all, you should now have a good understanding of how to use the tools in this chapter to create a business solution with Microsoft BizTalk Server 2000 and the .NET platform.

Solutions Fast Track

Creating and Using Specifications

☑ To create and modify specifications, you need to use the Microsoft BizTalk Editor that comes bundled with BizTalk Server 2000. This product will allow you to change, modify, or detail all aspects of records and fields contained within each specification.

☑ You create records and fields within each specification. The top record is called the *root node*. Records are defined as *elements*, and fields are defined as *attributes*. You can changes settings to make fields as elements.

☑ Knowing how to export and import specifications is important because you might have to bring an EDI-based standard into your BizTalk Editor for editing, and export it as an XDR schema.

Mapping Data between Documents

☑ Mapping documents is critical to BizTalk Server 2000's functionality of interoperability. Mapping a document could entail taking an EDI-based document specification and mapping it to an XML-based specification to transparently allow two businesses with two different systems to work together regardless of their pre-established standards.

☑ The BizTalk Mapper is used to set up a Source and Destination specification to allow such mapping to take place. This tool supplies you with a GUI to map with and compile to an XSLT stylesheet.

☑ The BizTalk Mapper allows you to visually see what it is that you want to work with, and provides other tools (such as functoids) to make the mapping as simple as possible.

Functoids

☑ Functoids within the BizTalk Mapper allow you to perform certain functions to your mapped specifications without having to know advanced VB Scripting.

☑ There are 40+ functoids that allow you the functionality of performing math, scientific, string-based, and database querying functions as well as a host of others.

☑ If you can't find what you need within the Functoid palette, you can script your own functions into the BizTalk Mapper.

Using WebDAV

☑ WebDAV is the standard to allow for multiple party collaboration over local or remote means to access shared data.

☑ You can use WebDAV-based functionality within both the BizTalk Editor and the BizTalk Mapper (as well as other BizTalk components).

☑ Use WebDAV to upload information to a central repository for all to access for multipoint collaboration of projects.

Frequently Asked Questions

The following Frequently Asked Questions, answered by the authors of this book, are designed to both measure your understanding of the concepts presented in this chapter and to assist you with real-life implementation of these concepts. To have your questions about this chapter answered by the author, browse to **www.syngress.com/solutions** and click on the **"Ask the Author"** form.

Q: In a situation requiring the use of a functoid within mapping, which functoid should I select if none of the predefined functoids do what it is I need?

A: You can always script your own with the Scripting functoid. This functoid allows you to make your own script within it to make it a configurable option when mapping your specifications.

Q: As I use the BizTalk Editor, I find that none of the predefined specifications outlines exactly what it is I need. I need a custom PO (purchase order) defined specifically for my company. What should I do to find this PO?

A: If none of the predefined specifications for XML, EDI, or X.12 meets any of your needs, you can always create a custom specification. To do this, open the **BizTalk Editor**, select **New** from the **File** menu, and open a new specification from the **Blank Specification** template. Once you open it, name the root node, create your custom specification, and save it.

Q: Every time I try to retrieve from WebDAV when I click on the toolbar icon, the dialog box is empty. Am I doing something wrong?

A: No, you just need to configure directory browsing. This Internet Information Services (IIS) setting can be adjusted within the IIS Internet Services manager console. Simply enable directory browsing, and the dialog will not be empty.

Q: I created a field as an element and an attribute, so I actually have two fields with the same name. I thought that I could only create a record as an element and could not have duplicate fields. Is there a bug in BizTalk that allows me to do this?

A: No. The BizTalk Editor might confuse those who are familiar with XML, because the Editor does not use the XML words *attribute* or *element*; it uses *records* and *fields*. Be aware of this to avoid confusion. To add even more confusion, you can create a field as an element and not an attribute by going to **Tools | Options** and checking the box to **Create a new field as an element**. You can have two fields with the same name, but create one as an attribute, and then create one as an element. By default, fields are created as attributes.

Q: I have a document instance with multiple documents within it. I cannot get the BizTalk Editor to provide a validation on the document. I have tried everything I can think of; why does this not work?

A: Remember that the BizTalk Editor will not provide a validation on a document instance with multiple documents contained within it. There is no way around it, and you need to perform validation on a document without multiple document instances in it.

Chapter 6

Tracking and Receipts

Solutions in this chapter:

Introduction

Another one of the final capabilities that we will talk about for BizTalk 2000 Messaging Services is the ability to track documents and generate receipts. Document tracking has the capability to provide information on exchangeable documents down to the field level. This type of detail is helpful in recording and archiving physical characteristics of transactions for future audits, aids in troubleshooting both incoming and outgoing information, and can provide assistance in disputes that might arise during processing.

Working in conjunction with BizTalk Document Tracking are the receipt generation and acknowledgement functions. These provide what is known as reliable messaging that is supported under the BizTalk 2.0 Framework. Reliable messaging guarantees once-only delivery of documents and receipts via the Internet and other heterogeneous environments. This chapter covers the intricacies of these two features. We go into detail about configuration of channels to support user-defined field-level tracking of information and provide an outline on receipt generation. We finally touch on the schema of the Tracking database and talk about advanced capabilities of the tracking services in regard to XLANG schedules.

NOTE

If you have not already done so, consider upgrading your BizTalk Server 2000 installation to the most current service pack. Several key bug fixes have been made to BizTalk Server, and to document tracking in particular, that are included in the service packs.

BizTalk Document Tracking

Document tracking is a fundamental auditing mechanism in BizTalk Server 2000. Document tracking can be used to provide logging and verification of individual exchanges that occur on your BizTalk server. Depending on your particular business model, document tracking can be used to help maintain legal records of your business electronic transactions, help you respond to your customers' questions more quickly and easily, and also help in troubleshooting your document exchange configuration.

Document tracking can take several forms in BizTalk Server 2000. BizTalk Messaging Services allows you a lot of freedom to configure and customize document tracking to your particular needs. First, you can configure inbound and outbound documents to be logged in their entirety to the tracking database. The BizTalk Server Administration application allows you to configure this level of tracking from the property sheet of your BizTalk Server Group (Figure 6.1). In addition, field-level tracking can be enabled in several ways. First, a document definition can specify which fields in a document instance should be persisted to the database for each channel that references that document definition. These fields are known as *global tracking fields*. On a channel-by-channel basis, you can also configure field-level tracking by specifying fields defined in the referenced document specification. The topic of using BizTalk Messaging Services to configure these options is discussed in detail in Chapter 4, "Understanding BizTalk Messaging Services." In this chapter, we instead cover more of the underlying architecture of the document tracking system, and how we can use some of the more advanced features of the tracking system to query the database for information.

Figure 6.1 The BizTalk Server Group Properties

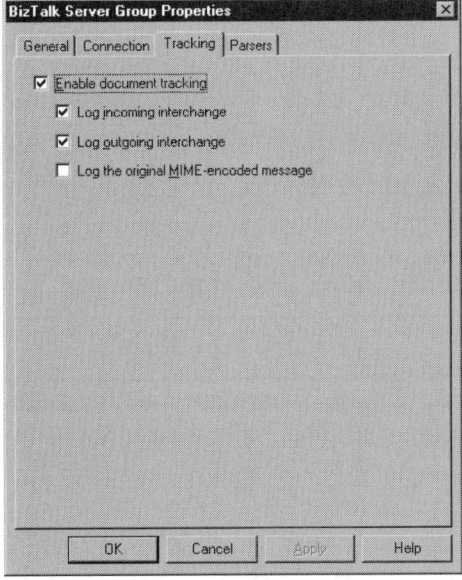

When documents or parts of documents are tracked in BizTalk Server 2000, the information is saved to a SQL Server database called "InterchangeDTA." If you installed the databases with your BizTalk Server configuration (rather than connecting to an existing BizTalk SQL Server database), this database was created for you. (Also installed were the InterchangeBTM database, which contains configuration information, and the InterchangeSQ database, which contains data for Orchestration queues.) The key elements of this database schema are shown in Figure 6.2. Only the primary and foreign key fields are shown for clarity.

Figure 6.2 Key Tables in the InterchangeDTA Database Schema

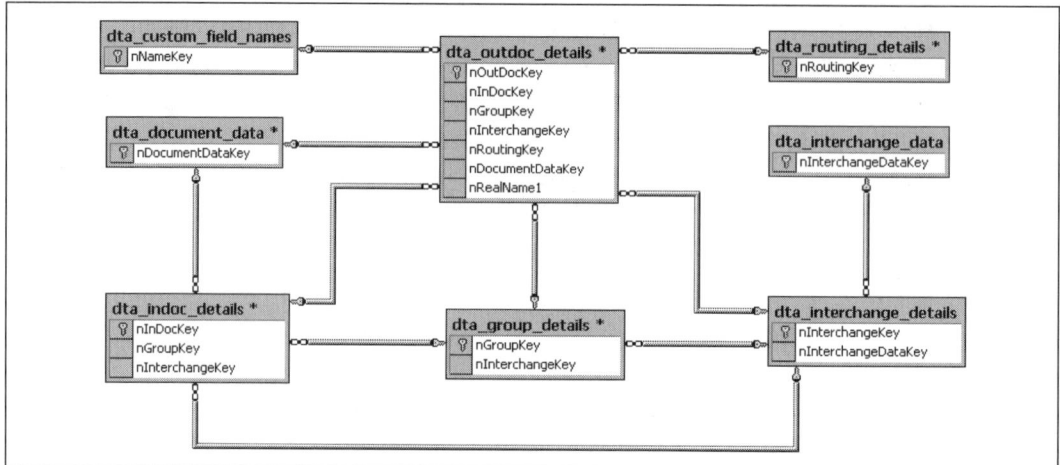

The most central and most frequently accessed tables in the schema are the dta_indoc_details, dta_outdoc_details, and dta_interchange_details tables. These tables contain core metadata about the specific interchanges and documents processed by BizTalk Server. A brief description of these tables and the data they contain is given in Table 6.1.

Table 6.1 InterchangeDTA Tables and Their Primary Function

Table Name	Primary Function
dta_indoc_details	Contains one row for each individual document that is submitted to BizTalk Server, and contains metadata linking it to its related interchange and document data.
dta_outdoc_details	Contains one row for each outbound document. Also contains tracked field data for each outbound document. Note that more than one outbound document can exist for each corresponding inbound document.

Continued

Table 6.1 Coninued

Table Name	Primary Function
dta_interchange_details	Contains one row per interchange processed by BizTalk Server. An interchange can contain multiple documents, as supported by the schema.
dta_document_data	Contains the actual data content of a document.
dta_interchange_data	Contains the actual data content of an entire interchange.
dta_group_details	Contains one row per functional group processed by extensibility components for EDI. This is populated only if the document definition supports functional groups.
dta_routing_details	Contains details of the source and destination organizations, or applications for a document transfer.
dta_custom_field_names	Contains field names and data types for tracked data fields that appear in dta_outdoc_details.

The dta_indoc_details table contains one record for each document that arrives at your server. Its fields are listed in the BizTalk documentation, so they are not duplicated here. We will instead concentrate on the important fields and relationships and how they model the document exchange process. The dta_indoc_details table has relationships with the dta_document_data, dta_group_details, dta_outdoc_details, and dta_interchange_details tables. The table itself contains fields representing data in the document's header, such as document type, document version, and document revision. It also contains information on whether this document was properly validated against its document specification. Finally, this table contains foreign key fields, which link it to tables containing associated document and interchange data.

The dta_outdoc_details table contains some similar information as that found in the inbound documents table. This table contains a single row for each outbound document. To help in correlating the inbound and outbound documents, a foreign key field exists in the outbound documents table that links it to the corresponding inbound document entry. Since an inbound document can be processed by a channel and then routed to a distribution list rather than a single port, this means that it's possible to have multiple rows in the outbound table for each row in the inbound table. In addition to the metadata and foreign key fields, this table also contains fields that persist any field values that are marked as globally tracked fields in the document definition or as tracked fields for the source channel. There are two fields for each of the real, integer, and string data types, and there is a separate field (nvcCustomSearch) that contains an XML representation of any additionally tracked custom type fields.

The dta_interchange_details table contains one row per interchange processed by BizTalk Server. According to the tracking database schema, an interchange can contain more than one document, although it is not possible to create a multi-document interchange with the current versions of the messaging tools. As such, there's a practical one-to-one relationship between the inbound/outbound document tables and the interchange details table. This table contains metadata about the document submission itself, such as the GUIDs that uniquely identify the interchange and the submission of the interchange, the source and destination organizations, the transport type and address, the handling BizTalk server name, size of the interchange, and number of transmit attempts.

The interchange-related data is horizontally partitioned into another table, dta_interchange_data. This table contains the actual data of the interchange, its type (i.e., XML or non-XML), whether the interchange was submitted as a file, and the UNC path to that file. Similarly, the document-related data is horizontally partitioned into dta_document_data, which contains a BLOB field with the actual document data. Both the inbound and outbound document details tables maintain a foreign key relationship to this dta_document_data table.

In certain cases, depending on the inbound document specification, multiple documents must be routed at the same time to the same destination organization. The dta_group_details table contains data pertinent to these functional groups. This table will not be populated unless the inbound document definition supports such groups.

The dta_routing_details table contains information about the source and destination organizations that are involved in the document transaction. The names of the organizations or applications involved are stored, as are the unique identifiers for the associated source channel and destination port.

Finally, the dta_custom_field_names table is used to manage the tracked fields that are persisted in the outbound document details table. For each tracked field, the name of the field is stored as an XPath expression here, uniquely describing the path to the specified field in an instance document. Also stored is the data type of this field. The outbound document details table maintains a foreign key relationship with dta_custom_field_names, storing only the ID and the field value for each of the tracked fields in the document.

Knowing the nuts and bolts of the tracking database schema is not strictly necessary to get what you need from BizTalk document tracking. A familiarity with it will help you greatly, however, if and when you find that the tracking application's Web interface presents some limitations. If you know the tracking database, then you will be able to more easily create your own tools to access this information in the way you choose.

Document and Interchange Queries

The Web-based document tracking system was introduced in Chapter 4. It allows users to view details about interchanges and documents that have passed through BizTalk Server. In this section, we'll discuss some of the intricacies of querying the tracking database and interpreting the resulting data.

Debugging…

Document Tracking

When first executing the document tracking application, depending on your browser settings, you might come across a JavaScript error that prohibits you from communicating with the tracking database. This error results from the browser's refusal to recognize a *.vb file as a VBScript source file. To remedy this problem, go into your BizTalk installation and into the BizTalkTracking folder. Change any instances of:

```
<script language="vbscript" src=
    "vbscripts\connection.vb"></script>
```

to:

```
<script language="vbscript" src=
    "vbscripts\connection.vbs"></script>
```

Also, rename connection.vb to connection.vbs. Your browser should now recognize this file as VBScript and be able to access your SQL Server. Also, recognize that Internet Explorer 4 or later must be used to access this application, since several ActiveX controls are used to provide functionality to the application.

Advanced Queries

The Advanced Queries section of the document tracking application is one of the most powerful features of document management in BizTalk Server. Within the Advanced Query interface, you can interactively build queries to extract only the data of interest to you. The Advanced Query Builder page is shown in Figure 6.3.

Figure 6.3 The Document Tracking Advanced Query Builder Page

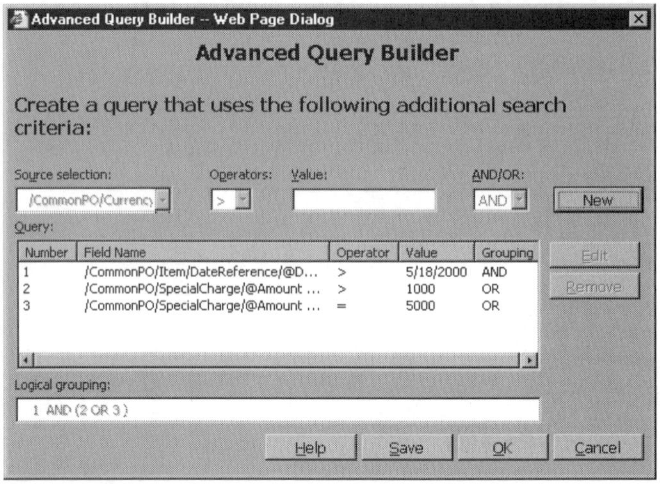

This first element on this page is the "Source selection" combo box. This drop-down is populated with a list of tracked fields from the dta_custom_field_names table, so each entry represents an XPath expression that points to a field in one or more corresponding instance documents. These represent all the unique field types from all the documents that your BizTalk Server has received, so this list could grow very large over time, depending on the number of different types of documents fields you choose to track. To begin entering a new search criterion, click **New**. (You will notice that the button's caption changes to **Done**.)

Once a source field is selected, you can choose a comparison operator and a value to compare to the source field. The final selection you need to make is in the **AND/OR** combo box, which allows you to specify the logical operator to combine this expression with the subsequent expression. The **Logical grouping** text box near the bottom shows how the accumulated criteria you have entered will be logically associated into a query. As you enter in each search criterion, it is simply added to the logical grouping in a left-to-right manner. Because of this, it is important to lay out your query carefully if it contains a mixture of ANDs and ORs. The query builder automatically associates consecutive entries that are separated by OR by surrounding them in parentheses, yet it does not provide any other mechanism to adjust the associativity of criteria after their initial entry. This results in a slightly limited functionality, but anything but the most complex queries can be created with a little planning. For anything more complicated, it is always possible to query the SQL Server database directly, either from query analyzer or from an independent application.

Developing & Deploying...

Persisting Advanced Queries

If you are building a complicated query and think you might want to use it again sometime, be sure to click **Save** before you click **OK**. Clicking **OK** first will indeed remember the query criteria for the current execution, but you will not be able to retrieve the same query for later use. If you first click **Save** and provide a name for the query you just built, it will be persisted in the configuration database and you will have the opportunity to retrieve the query from a list and execute the same query at any time in the future.

Reading the Results

Queries are executed and results are obtained by clicking **Query** on the Document Tracking application main page. When you do this, another Web page is created that contains the query results, as shown in Figure 6.4.

The first element on the result page is the "Search Parameters" node. The icon to the left of the "Search Parameters" heading represents a maximize/minimize symbol, and clicking it allows you to expand or contract the search parameters table that is visible in Figure 6.4. This is a handy table to help you distinguish between multiple search results, especially if you have many different results windows open. The table contains the search parameters that generated this result. One downside, however, is that you are not presented with the actual search criteria that make up any advanced queries that contributed to the search result. In this example, "Query 1" is the name of an advanced query. It remains up to you to remember what elements went into forming that query. The remainder of the fields in the table simply enumerate the selected values on the initial query page.

Figure 6.4 The Query Results Page of the Document Tracking Application

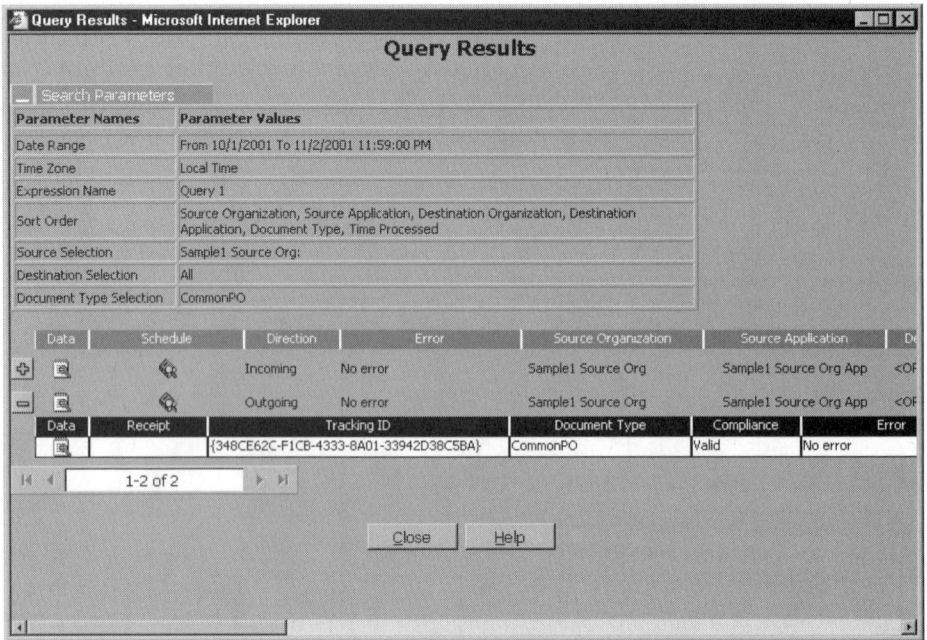

The main list of results is presented next. Each row in this list of results represents an individual interchange. The following columns are reported for each interchange in the search results:

- **Data** This icon, when clicked, launches another browser window that contains the full text of the interchange.

- **Schedule** This icon, when clicked, launches another browser window with information pertaining to any XLANG schedule that was a target of this interchange. Tracking information can be associated with any action elements in an XLANG Orchestration schedule, so you can follow the path of your document through your XLANG schedule.

- **Direction** Either "Incoming" or "Outgoing."

- **Error** Descriptive error text for any errors that occurred during processing.

- **Source Organization** The name of the source organization.

- **Source Application** The name of the source application, if the source organization is the default home organization; otherwise, blank.

- **Destination Organization** The name of the destination organization.

- **Destination Application** The name of the destination application, if the destination organization is the default home organization; otherwise, blank.

- **Document Type** The type of document that was contained in the interchange; i.e. the document definition.

- **Document Count** The count of documents within this interchange (usually one, since BizTalk Server is currently unable to produce multi-document interchanges, although such interchanges could be received).

- **Control ID** The EDI control number if this is an EDI exchange, or a unique identifier for reliable messaging.

- **Receipt Status** The status for the document's receipt. The possible choices are none, pending, overdue, accepted, accepted with errors, and rejected.

- **Time Processed** The server time when the interchange is first processed and this record created.

- **Time Sent** The server time when this interchange was sent. This value is empty if the interchange is an outbound interchange.

- **Source ID Qualifier** The organization identifier that qualifies the source organization for this interchange.

- **Source Identifier** The value of the source ID qualifier for this organization.

- **Destination Qualifier** The organization identifier that qualifies the destination organization for this interchange

- **Destination Identifier** The value of the destination ID qualifier for this organization.

If you expand the document(s) within a single interchange by clicking on the + icon, you will see an expanded list of documents that are contained within that interchange. The fields that are shown on a document-level basis are:

- **Data** If you have enabled document-level logging, clicking on this icon launches another browser window that contains the content of the document itself.

- **Receipt** Contains information pertaining to whether this document represents a receipt.

- **Tracking ID** The unique ID assigned to this document during submission to BizTalk Server.

- **Document Type** The document definition used to validate this document.

- **Compliance** Valid if the document was successfully validated against the document specification; invalid otherwise.

- **Error** Text description of any errors that occurred during processing of this document.

The following items are only present for outgoing documents and will not exist for incoming documents.

- **Receipt Status** Similar to the property of the same name for an interchange; acceptable values are none, pending, overdue, accepted, accepted with errors, and rejected.

- **Real 1** The first tracked field of type "real" for this document.

- **Real 2** The second tracked field of type "real" for this document.

- **Integer 1** The first tracked field of type "integer" for this document.

- **Integer 2** The second tracked field of type "integer" for this document.

- **Date 1** The first tracked field of type "date" for this document.

- **Date 2** The second tracked field of type "date" for this document.

- **String 1** The first tracked field of type "string" for this document.

- **String 2** The second tracked field of type "string" for this document.

- **Custom Search** The content of this field is structured XML representing the field names, data types, and values for any fields that were explicitly tracked as "custom" data. Since only two fields of any single data type can be stored directly in the database, any additional typed fields must be stored in this location.

While BizTalk Document Tracking can provide a wealth of information regarding individual interchanges that pass through your BizTalk Server, there are some limitations. First, you have seen that an extensive database schema exists to support the complex tracking capabilities in BizTalk Server. For each tracked document that enters or leaves your server, many rows are added to the tracking database. For a busy server, this could be detrimental in several ways. First, if your SQL Server and BizTalk Server reside on the same machine, the high level of database activity will cause a performance drag on your ability to effectively process documents. Even if your database resides on a different server, there are network bandwidth considerations to keep in mind. Furthermore, no out-of-the-box functionality exists to purge this database of old records when it becomes large, leaving the task up to your database administrator. Microsoft recommends that the tracking database not be cleared out manually, so you're on your own if available space starts to become an issue. Finally, there are known limitations associated with tracking large document interchanges. The moral of the story is that you should track only that information that you must, keeping the consequences in mind.

Receipts

Receipts are another integral aspect of the BizTalk Framework. Your business model might require receipts for the documents it sends to your trading partners, whether it be for auditing purposes, implementing subsequent business logic, or otherwise. BizTalk Server 2000 provides several ways to implement receipts, and also provides extensibility to allow you to implement receipts for your own custom data formats.

The process of transmitting and receiving receipts involves configuration for both the source and destination systems. An overview of the process is shown in Figure 6.5, and the steps are outlined here:

1. A business document is submitted to BizTalk Server at the source organization.

2. A channel on the source system accepts the document, and performs any configured document validation and/or transformation steps. This channel should be configured to "expect receipt." The channel then forwards the document to the associated messaging port that is configured to send the document to the destination organization. No special configuration is necessary here to enable the receipt.

3. A channel at the destination organization receives the transmitted document and begins interpreting it. This channel must be configured to "generate a receipt" and point to a related receipt channel. After passing on the receipt generation request to the receipt channel, ordinary document processing resumes.

4. The associated messaging port on the destination system handles the document. No special configuration is necessary on this messaging port to enable receipt processing, since the receipt processing is initially handled by the channel.

5. Information from the document headers is provided by the destination channel that originally received the document and is passed to the receipt channel.

6. The receipt channel uses the "BizTalk Canonical Receipt" document definition to interpret the incoming receipt information. This document definition contains information necessary for the destination organization to properly route the receipt document, and for the source organization to properly correlate the receipt with the original document. The channel can optionally map this to another outgoing document definition, provided that a suitable handler of that definition resides on the source system. Finally, the associated messaging port packages the receipt document and returns it to the source organization.

7. The source organization receives the receipt document and it is interpreted by an appropriate parser, based on a document definition appropriate for the receipt. Included parsers are the X.12 and EDIFACT parsers.

Figure 6.5 Overview of Receipt Processing

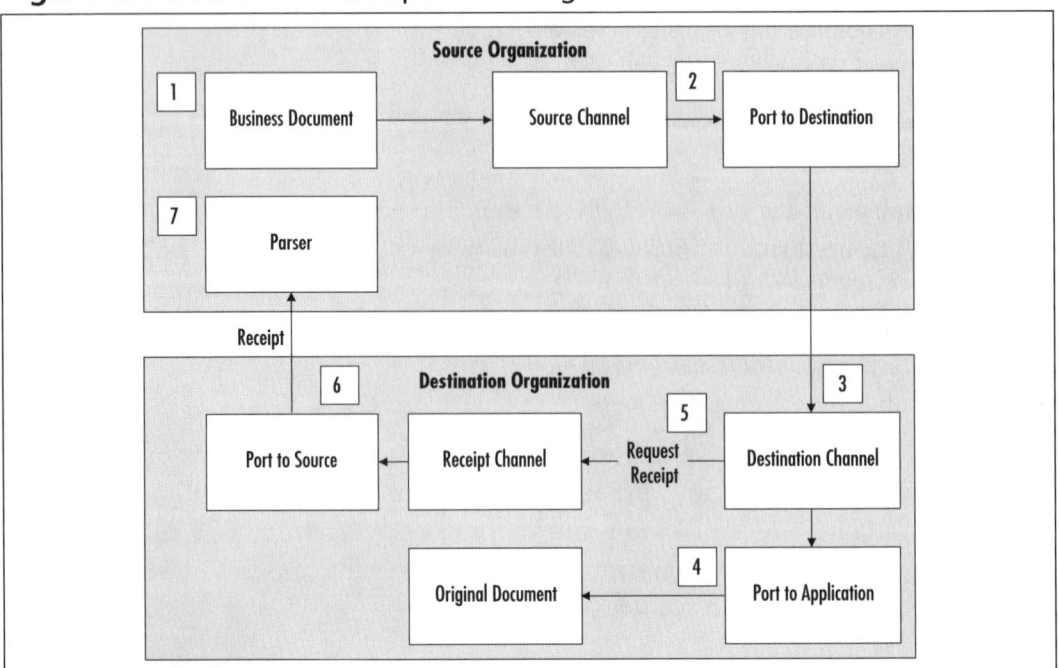

Configuration of channels and ports for receipt processing can be simplified by considering several basic rules. Channels that process *outbound* documents and require receipts should have their **Expect receipt** property set. Channels that receive *inbound* documents and want to send a receipt should have their **Generate receipt** property set. Finally, a *receipt channel* exists solely for the purpose of generating receipts. The destination of a messaging port bound to a receipt channel must match the source of the original document for which a receipt is requested. That is, the receipt must be sent back to the organization that sent the original document.

There are two main alternatives to generating and accepting receipts: *channel* processing and *reliable messaging* processing. Channel processing is designed primarily for X.12 and EDIFACT document formats, which include document routing information in their headers. This source and destination information includes the organization identifier type and value, enabling each system to uniquely identify both the source and destination. Also, a unique ID for the document itself is passed in the header, allowing the source and destination systems to agree on exactly which original document a particular receipt is associated with. Because receipt generation and acceptance are commonplace with EDIFACT and X.12 document exchange, parsers for these formats are included with BizTalk Server 2000. You can create additional parsers on your own, however, by implementing the *IBizTalkParserComponent* interface in C++. A custom parser is responsible for converting the instance document to an XML representation and routing it to an appropriate channel for subsequent processing.

Reliable Messaging Receipts

Reliable messaging is a feature of the BizTalk 2.0 Framework. It is intended to provide receipt functionality for XML-based instance documents. Reliable messaging works similarly to the channel method discussed previously. The channel method requires an X.12 or EDIFACT document, since those document formats are already configured to specify the source and destination routing information. In reliable messaging, a similar effect is obtained by specifying a "return address" in the header, known as a "reply-to URL." The reply-to URL must be specified in a document envelope, which is used to wrap the instance document in XML that describes the document's source and destination.

Let's go through the process of configuring reliable messaging and then configuring a messaging port to use reliable messaging. This process is used on the source system when a receipt is expected from the destination organization.

1. Launch the BizTalk Server Administration application. Choose **BizTalk Server Group** from the tree view on the left, and click **Properties**. You will see a property page similar to that shown in Figure 6.6. Enter a fully qualified URL to the resource you want to process any reliable messaging receipts. In this example, it is configured as an ASP page accessed via HTTP.

Figure 6.6 Configuring the Reply-to URL

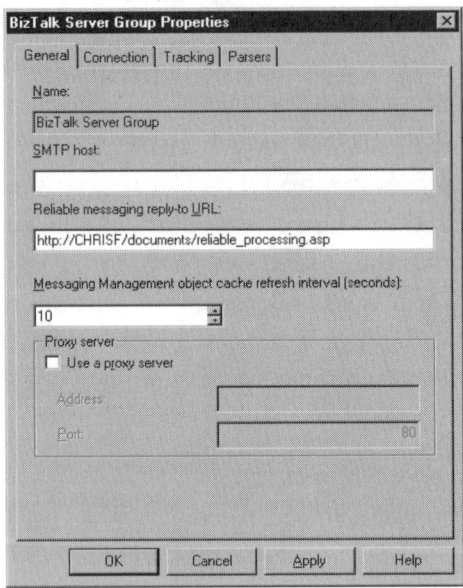

2. Now launch the BizTalk Messaging Manager application and create a new **Envelope**. Choose **RELIABLE** as the envelope format, as shown in Figure 6.7. Since you have specified RELIABLE in the format combo box, you will not have the option to specify an envelope document specification. If you choose one of the custom formats (CUSTOM, CUSTOM XML, or FLATFILE), you would have the option of specifying a document specification to tell the source and destination systems how to package and unpackage your document.

Figure 6.7 Creating an Envelope for Reliable Messaging

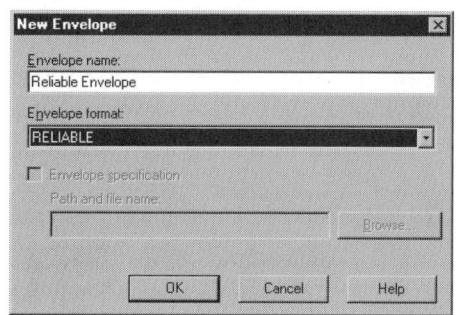

On the destination side, little configuration is necessary. In fact, in most cases, BizTalk Server 2000 requires no configuration on the destination server, and it will send a reply receipt to the source system automatically based on information found in the reliable messaging envelope that packages the document. The only case where modifications are required on the destination system is when an SMTP address is specified by the source system as the reply-to URL in the reliable messaging envelope. In this case, the destination system must identify itself to the SMTP mail service and provide a "from" address. Follow these steps to configure the destination system for replying to an SMTP address:

1. Launch the BizTalk Messaging Manager application on the destination system. Choose the **home organization** (the organization marked as "default"), and make note of its Properties. Choose the **Identifiers tab** (Figure 6.8), and then double-click the **Reliable Messaging Acknowledgement SMTP From Address** entry in the list box.

Figure 6.8 The Organization Identifiers Tab

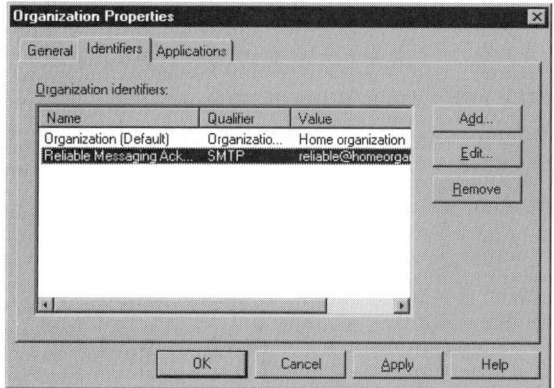

2. The Identifier Properties dialog box should appear. The custom name specified, "Reliable Messaging Acknowledgement SMTP From Address," is a special identifier included for the home organization to facilitate reliable messaging. Enter the e-mail address for your organization in the **Value** text box here. Any reliable messaging replies to SMTP sources will now include this as the From address.

Figure 6.9 Reliable Messaging "From" Address Configuration

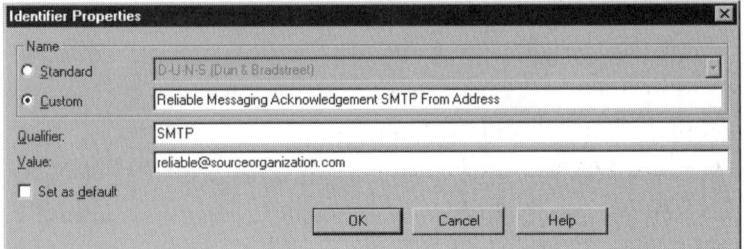

Parser Limitations

BizTalk Server 2000 comes with parsers to accommodate the vast majority of receipt-handling situations for most organizations. The included support for EDI-FACT and X.12, combined with the ease of use of reliable messaging for XML documents, means that few instance documents cannot benefit from this built-in support. Certain out-of-the-ordinary document formats, however, might require a custom parser (not only for receipt generation and acceptance, but for document parsing in general). For these situations, BizTalk Server 2000 provides you the ability to implement your own custom parser by implementing the IBizTalkParserComponent COM interface. These custom parser components must be written in a language such as Visual C++ using ATL, which supports the free- or both-threaded COM component creation demanded by the threading requirements of the parsing engine. Because Visual Basic 6.0 can only create apartment or single-threaded components, it is not suitable for the task. Custom parsers must process document instances and translate them into an XML document for internal use.

Summary

BizTalk Document Tracking offers powerful functionality for auditing or reporting on the documents exchanged by your business. BizTalk Messaging Services allow you to configure document-level tracking or field-level tracking of instance documents that are submitted to your BizTalk Server. Document-level tracking is configured via the BizTalk Server Administration application and is enabled at the server level. Field-level tracking is enabled at the document definition level, allowing you to choose specific fields to persist in the SQL Server tracking database. Configuration options for messaging channels allow you to override the behavior of field tracking in the document definition and specify tracked fields independent of the document definition.

The BizTalk Document Tracking feature of BizTalk Server 2000 provides the Document Tracking Web application to enable you to easily create simple queries to examine high-level details of targeted documents. The application also provides an "advanced query" functionality that allows you to drill down into the document itself, querying for values of specific fields in a single document. The tracking application is ideal for simple queries against the database, but for more substantial and complex queries, the SQL Server InterchangeDTA database can be queried directly using standard data access tools such as ADO with Visual Basic.

Receipts can be requested for any document that passes from a source system to a destination system. There are two basic methods for handling receipts in BizTalk Server: channel configuration and reliable messaging. Channel configuration is recommended for EDIFACT and X.12 interchanges for which the document routing information is encoded in the document itself, and for which BizTalk Server includes document parser functionality by default. Reliable messaging is fundamental to the BizTalk Framework 2.0 specification and is used when sending XML-based documents. Channel configuration involves creating a receipt channel on the destination system to create the receipt document and transport it back to the source. Reliable messaging is configured primarily on the source server, requiring destination system configuration only if the reply-to URL is an SMTP address.

Solutions Fast Track

BizTalk Document Tracking

☑ Document tracking data is stored in the SQL Server 2000 InterchangeDTA database.

☑ Document definitions and channel configurations provide the means for selecting individual document fields to persist to the database.

☑ The BizTalk Server Administrator allows you to configure the server to log all interchanges and document content to the tracking database.

Document and Interchange Queries

☑ The BizTalk Document Tracking Web application allows you to easily query the tracking database.

☑ Use the "advanced queries" functionality to query for specific document content.

☑ For queries requiring complex logic, query the database directly rather than using the tracking application.

Receipts

☑ Receipts can be configured to use channels or reliable messaging.

☑ Channel configuration is used mostly for EDIFACT and X.12 interchanges. Other document formats require a custom parser.

☑ Reliable messaging is well suited for XML-based documents and provides an easily configured method to request and create receipts.

Frequently Asked Questions

The following Frequently Asked Questions, answered by the authors of this book, are designed to both measure your understanding of the concepts presented in this chapter and to assist you with real-life implementation of these concepts. To have your questions about this chapter answered by the author, browse to **www.syngress.com/solutions** and click on the **"Ask the Author"** form.

Q: How can I track more than two document fields with the same data type?

A: The InterchangeDTA database contains only two fields for each data type in the dta_outdoc_details table, so the messaging manager wizards will not allow you to track more than two such fields for each type. In order to track more than two fields with any of the real, integer, date, or string data types, you need to track them as custom data. The custom data is saved with the other fields in dta_outdoc_details, but exists in the form of structured XML that contains the field names, data types, and field values. This custom data can be examined from the Document Tracking Web application.

Q: What is the difference between a document and an interchange in the Document Tracking application?

A: In theory, an interchange can consist of multiple documents. In practice, BizTalk Server 2000 can create only interchanges containing a single document (although it can receive documents from other BizTalk sources). Therefore, when you expand an interchange node in the tracking application, you will most likely see only one document. An interchange's record contains routing information, such as source and destination organization identifiers. A document's record contains document-specific data, such as data validity and tracked fields.

Q: How can I request a receipt for my XML document?

A: Use reliable messaging. Reliable messaging is independent of the XML document format itself, relying instead on an envelope that uses the reliable format. This envelope wraps your document instance and communicates with the destination system your requirements for a receipt and where to deliver that receipt.

Chapter 7

BizTalk Orchestration Services

Solutions in this chapter:

- Diagramming Business Processes
- BizTalk Orchestration Designer
- Flowchart, Communication, and Implementation Shapes
- Implementing a Business Process: An Example

☑ Summary

☑ Solutions Fast Track

☑ Frequently Asked Questions

Introduction

BizTalk Orchestration Services put the final piece into the puzzle. BizTalk Messaging Services provide a secure and robust set of capabilities that assist us with delivery and tracking of information through different interchanges. What these services do not cover is the ability to control the flow of information into or out of the various systems. Microsoft's .NET architecture provides a tier concept in which these business components would reside. With the aid of BizTalk Orchestration Services, we extend the n-tier concept into a more dynamic process in which components are provided the messaging subsystem, and are more autonomous in the functions they are designed to perform. Add in the BizTalk Orchestration Designer and we give a business analyst greater control over creating these business process definitions. To use BizTalk effectively, you must have a thorough understanding of workflows. This chapter discusses the fundamentals of business processes, with an overview of process integration between applications. We discuss how the business process definitions or XLANG schedules are designed and implemented in BizTalk 2000. We cover the integration of Orchestration and Messaging Services, and give an example of the complete solution. You will enable and configure your installation to handle long-running transactions, and to communicate between loosely coupled environments in a meaningful fashion.

Diagramming Business Processes

Before you start the BizTalk Orchestration Designer and start drawing flowcharts, take a step back and think about how to approach the task of building the business part of your application. Despite Microsoft's claim that the Orchestration Designer can be used by both business analysts and developers to realize a solution, it is an advanced development and implementation tool—no more, no less. We show you how to benefit from the features of the Orchestration Designer later in the book. For now, let's take a closer look at how you can go about putting the business processes you need to implement on paper.

The challenge with which you are faced is to model a dynamic situation into a static application. To achieve this, you can draw support from one of the many methodologies available. Perhaps you already use one with which you are comfortable, or perhaps you are still looking for one. Here, we will use ICONIX to show you how a proven methodology can help you model the dynamic world to a static application, and significantly speed the development/implementation tasks using BizTalk Orchestration Designer.

Avoiding the overhead you find in other methodologies, ICONIX (see www.iconixsw.com) is a Use Case driven method based on the Unified Modeling Language (UML). The minimal approach is suitable to use with BizTalk Orchestration Services, since it can progress into a XLANG schedule without significant modifications and without discarding unnecessary data.

We will not describe the ICONIX process in full, since there are numerous books on the market that are based on ICONIX or many other UML-based methodologies. What we will address is the way building a BizTalk Server-based application—in particular, an XLANG schedule—can originate from the results of a well-executed ICONIX process.

Documenting Requirements

Perhaps the biggest challenge you are faced with is to come up with requirements that are both complete and unambiguous. You will need to become involved with the stakeholders to get their views on the application-to-be. Stakeholders are those who are going to use the system, or have some interest in the application. In UML terminology, the users of an application are called *actors*, and can be users or other systems that interact with the system. Other significant terms in ICONIX are *Problem domain*, which is the part of the *dynamic* situation that you are trying to capture in a *static* application. The latter is related to the *Solution domain*. Remember that a BizTalk application is in essence an object-oriented application. Modeling within the premises of the domain should lead to a solution that meets all the demands. So, always keep your goal in sight, and do not be distracted by anything that can keep you from realizing that goal. This is one of the strong points of ICONIX, as it does not carry all of the "fat" that other methods tend to carry in a rigid process with a high level of detail. Every stage in a development process is organic. Never expect that every step along the way will be complete and detailed. Never think that you can only take a next step if the current one is perfect. It is better to revisit previous steps and refine them based on the knowledge you gather along the way. Draw on your experiences with previous projects, but do not let them lead you into making assumptions or premature conclusions.

The first step is to establish the set of requirements that will impact all future actions in the process. Draw from as many sources as possible. Remember that the users are possibly the most valuable, and at the same time, the most uncontrollable source available to you (see the sidebar "Users Hold the Key to the Requirements"). Once you have gathered all this information, you should start unifying it. Capture each requirement in a single sentence that explicitly phrases it. For example:

- The application must connect with the Database General Ledger.

- The application must provide user authentication.

- The application must print weekly statements.

- The application must log every transaction.

- The application will only accept money transfers over $5,000 if the user has at least an authentication level of "Department Manager."

Sort this list so that strongly coupled requirements are grouped together. Again, the list does not need to be perfect, but be sure that what is on the list is correct.

Developing & Deploying…

Users Hold the Key to the Requirements

You often come across developers who do not speak fondly of the users who are involved in the requirement phase—"They don't know what they want!" or "They always come up with new requirements!" or "Users just keep you from getting on with the development!" Although sometimes expressed in more subtle ways, there is a certain ring of truth to these statements. However, most developers are in the business for the technology, and forget that they develop for users, meaning that they are also in the "people business." Users often do not know exactly what they want, since they are not developers—this does not mean that they do not know what they need. They are perfectly capable of telling you what they expect from the application. It is the role of the developers, or business analysts for that matter, to coach them in formulating these expectations, which will then form the foundations of the requirements you are looking for. You can do this using a number of *interview techniques*, the number-one skill for a developer involved in establishing requirements.

A very productive way is the group session that is led by a moderator whose only task is to lead the group in getting the requirements on the whiteboard. The group must have a balanced composition to prevent

Continued

certain users from dominating. Begin with the question "what do *you* want the application to be able to do?" Give all the participants a number of cue cards—let's say five—and ask them to put down the five most important requirements for the new application, one on each card. After they are finished, the moderator collects all the cards and puts them on a board for everyone to see.

The next step is to let the group cluster these requirements, based on their relation to one another. It is very likely that most of these clusters will be too general, so ask the same sort of question focused on one cluster. Never go more than three levels deep per cluster, since you might exhaust the participants and lose their attention. The moderator should take time to discuss the results and make some objective conclusions, based on the information on the board. You may *have* to or *want* to do more than one group session, so there is no need to get a highly refined requirement package from the first session. Keep the participants motivated by keeping them involved!

A second interview technique that works for both a group and a one-on-one interview is, "Listen-Summarize-Continue asking" (LSC). This is an effective way of *requirement finding*, because you let the interviewee tell his story, you listen, make notes, and ask questions that make the interviewee refine his answer. You should have a list of questions—somewhere between five and ten—that need to be answered to your satisfaction. Even for the one-on-one interviews, multiple sessions might be needed.

Between group and individual interviews, it is up to you to analyze the results and start with the documentation of the requirements. This will bring new questions to the surface, or show areas for which you have insufficient information. Do not refrain from prototyping the user interface (UI), since visualization is a strong tool. Always start a new session/interview with the information from the previous one, and see if there is still a consensus on the conclusions. This interaction with the stakeholders/users is important; if you keep them involved and get their approval on the requirements, it is highly unlikely that they will complain about, or try to shoot down, the application you are building. You document the requirements both for you and the users. Requirements subsequently lead to Use Cases. Both are also used during the (functional) testing phase, since the test cases will (should!) be based on requirements and Use Cases. If both are not accessible to the people who make the test cases, you might end up with test cases that do not reflect the requirements—a major problem!

The next step might surprise you, but it makes a lot of sense if you take some time to think about it: "Start Building the Domain Model"(also known as *Domain modeling*), using a minimal set of the UML diagramming methods for Domain models. You are building an (object-oriented) application, meaning that you better start defining the boundaries of that application. The Domain model is part of the (static) Solution domain.

You can derive the Domain model from the requirements, assuming you have had prior experience in building Domain models. Do not overwhelm yourself with details; in fact, the Domain model has a strong resemblance to a simplified entity relationship diagram (ERD). During the next steps, you will very likely revisit the Domain model to make modifications, so the more details you put in it now, the more difficult it will be to complete the Domain model later. The details are left for the "Class diagram," which is based on the Domain model, and will turn up in your BizTalk Orchestration diagram (XLANG schedule diagram). Even if you are already familiar with making UML diagrams, here are some things you should take into account:

- Start identifying the core object, and from there, work to objects that are more specific and determine the relationship between these objects. This is also known as the "inside-out" approach.

- Use only *generalization* and *aggregation* relationships in the Domain model; other relationships in the UML model are left for the Class diagram, since they imply implementation assumptions.

- Focus on *object reusability* in your Domain model, since this is an important aspect of object modeling.

- Establish a naming convention that is accessible to everyone. Do not use "cTransAccntLog" if you can write "Transaction Log."

- Avoid data entities (*attributes*) and functions (*operations*) in the Domain model. Again, these obscure the Domain model and are left for the Class diagram.

- Avoid *design patterns* in your Domain model, since this is also an implementation aspect.

- Avoid n-to-m relationships (*multiplicities*) in your Domain model; again, this is an implementation aspect.

Figure 7.1 is a small example of what a Domain model in the ICONIX approach looks like. The Domain model is based on a person being able to make financial transactions on his bank account and create a new account.

Figure 7.1 A Bank Account Example for an ICONIX-Based Domain Model

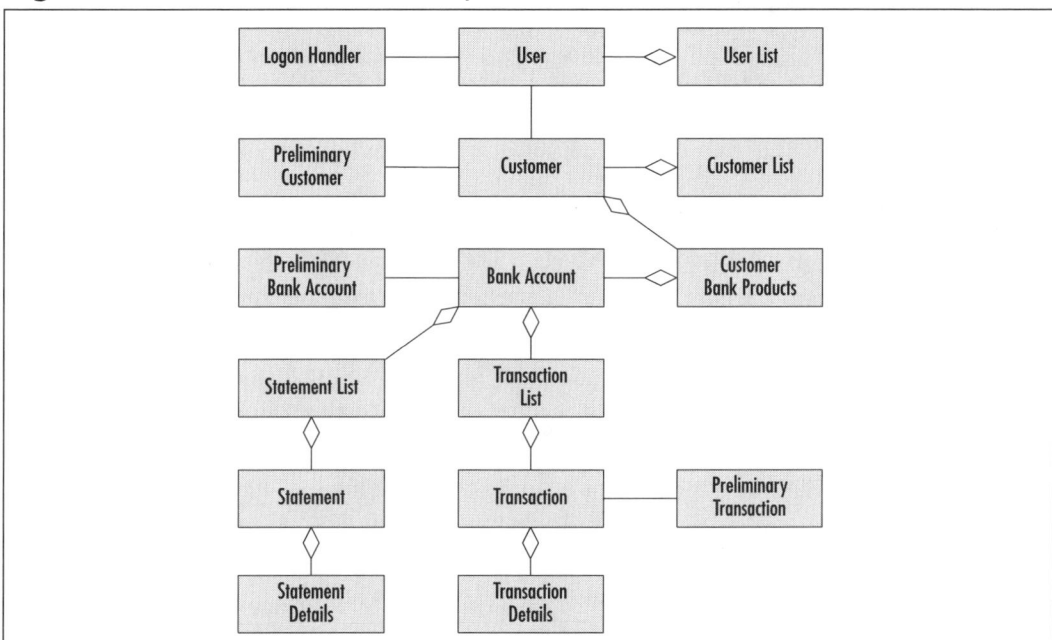

> **NOTE**
>
> The bank account example is meant for demonstration purposes. Although it is based on a real-life Problem domain, it is an excerpt edited for this chapter. Therefore, some details have been omitted to enhance the overview and thereby use it as an example. For example, we left out "Create User" and "Create Customer."

Once you have established this Domain model, review it with colleagues and employees from your client who are experienced in this business field. This way, you can establish that there are no misinterpretations in the Domain model. It needn't be complete; you can revisit and refine it as often as you like and make changes as the picture becomes more complete and transparent. As mentioned previously, you are in an organic improvement process where the results only get better by moving forward to gather more information.

> **NOTE**
>
> As you build your Domain model, you will come across a lot of information that is very useful in the application development, but should not appear in the Domain model; for example, attributes, operations, and design pattern. Instead of ignoring them, make a type of "scrapbook" Domain model and add this information. You will need this information eventually, and this can help you to jumpstart that step in the process.

Once you are comfortable with the Domain model, it is time for the next step: "Start Building the Use Case Model" (*Use Case modeling*). A Use Case describes a single interaction between a user (actor) and the application. It shows the boundaries of the system. In fact, all the Use Cases put together would make the foundation of a complete User's Guide. The Use Case model will show all Use Cases you can identify from the requirements and the User Interface prototype, by identifying the verbs in the requirements that connect two nouns. You will notice that of the two nouns, one will be related to the application—identifiable as an object from the Domain model you created in the previous step—and one will be an actor. When doing so, try to be as complete as possible, by going through the requirements and checking if you can identify every requirement in a Use Case. When this is completed, you should group the Use Cases based on their (logical) coherence to make it easier to divide the work among you and your colleagues, and to help you later in identifying subsystems or application modules. Using the analogy of the Use Case model being the User's Guide, a group of Use Cases can be seen as a subdivision of this User's Guide; for example, a chapter in the User's Guide. You need a Domain model to be able to determine the relevance of a Use Case, since it has to be based on the application you are building.

We mentioned earlier that the ICONIX process is Use Case driven, and in that respect, the Use Case model defines the boundaries of the Problem domain and drives the identification of the application's behavior. This behavior in turn will influence the Solution domain. We now have linked the Problem domain and Solution domain. You may have noticed that the Use Case model has an outside-in approach, going from the general requirements to specific application behavior—the opposite of the Domain model.

When you are satisfied with the Use Case model (Figure 7.2), it is time to describe the Use Cases that, according to the ICONIX process, should be kept simple without pre- and post-conditions, or goals. Again, pre- and post-conditions imply implementation aspects, and you are still some steps away from implementing. You can even argue that these extensive Use Case formats do not add significant value to the Use Case, but cost time to complete. Instead, the Use Case we promote consists of three parts: the "Use Case Name," the "Basic Course of Action," and the "Alternate Courses of Action." The Basic Course is what the Use Case is expected to do the majority of times that the Use Case is "executed." The Alternate Courses are all the other situations that can occur for the Use Case. A "Course" should be written from the actor's perspective, and from thereon follow the course of events that happen. The course should be written in the following structure: "The actor does this, then the application does that, followed by … and then …." Be explicit when naming the objects involved in the Use Case. Use the Domain model *and* identify the objects with which the actors interact, called *Boundary objects*; for example, "Login Page," "Bank Account Details Page," or "Error Page." Do not overwhelm the Use Case and yourself with details, since these are very likely implementation aspects and not relevant at this point. This does not mean that you should ignore them—remember your scrapbook! By the way, you can also make a copy of your Domain model and start adding attributes to the objects, instead of cluttering the Use Case with them. Since you identify the object involved, you ensure yourself that there is a reference to the attributes.

Do not try to convince yourself that you captured all possible Use Cases, but be sure you have identified the Use Cases based on the requirements that are known. You can do this by continuously cross-referencing the material you have and modifying it if needed. You will be surprised by the things you catch in this early stage. If you are convinced that you identified and described all the Use Cases, based on the information at hand, you can move to the next step. Do not lose time (and sleep) trying to be complete the first time around. If the different something does not match up, go back and fix it. Do not hesitate to call on a colleague or expert for a second opinion; peer review is a very useful instrument during the entire process. Remember that if you are able to explain your work to colleagues and the clients (users), without them staring glassy-eyed at you, it is more than likely that you did it correctly. Tables 7.1 and 7.2 show two of the Use Cases from Figure 7.2.

Figure 7.2 The Use Case Model for the Bank Account Example

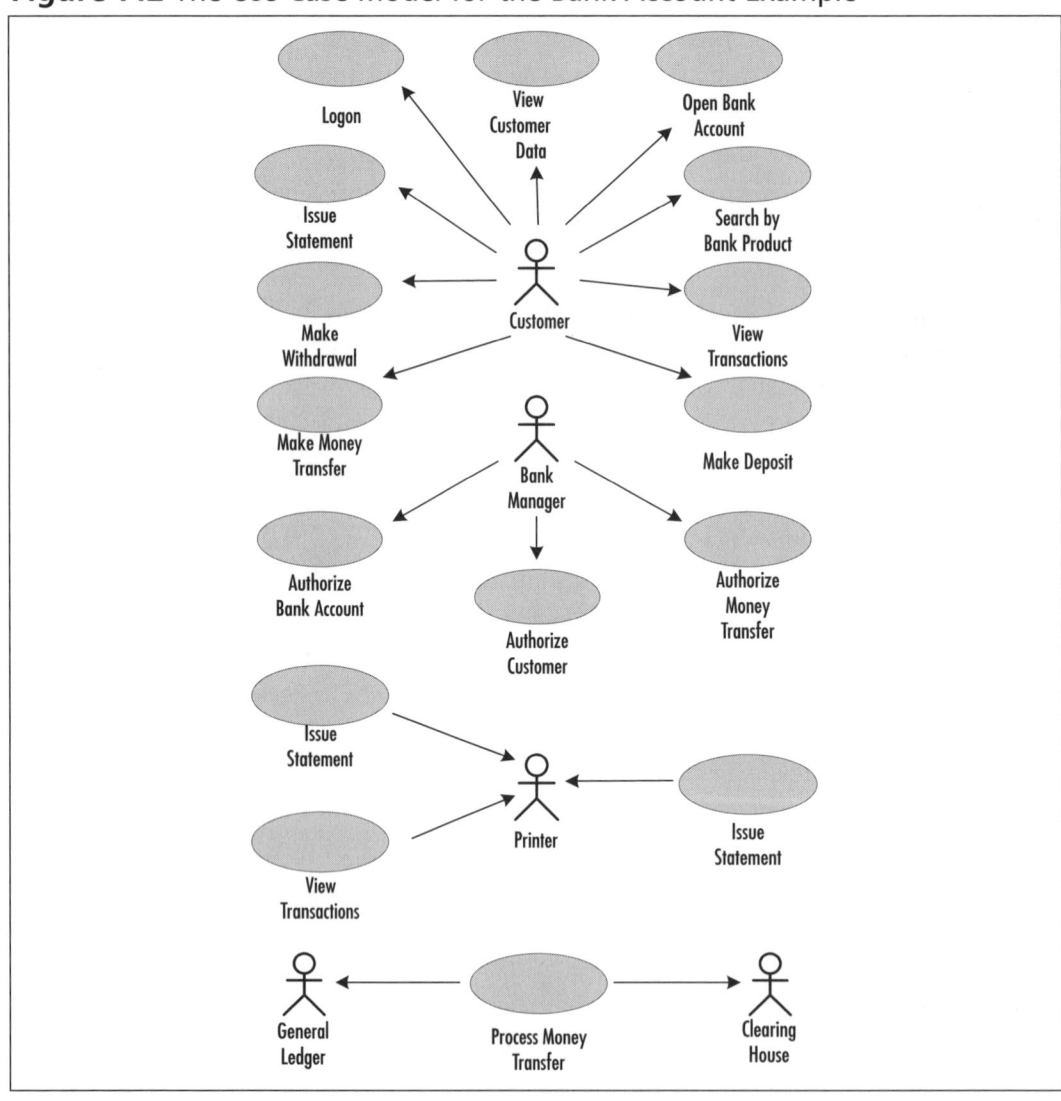

Table 7.1 The Make Money Transfer Use Case

Basic Course

---

1   The **Application** *shows* the **Money Transfer page**.

2   The **Application** *retrieves* the **Open Bank Accounts List** *associated* with the **Customer**.

Continued

Table 7.1 Continued

Basic Course

---

3   The **Customer** *selects* one account in the **Open Bank Accounts List** from where the money must be transferred, *fills out* the recipient data with account number, recipient name, and address information, *fills in* the amount of money on the **Money Transfer page**, and then *clicks* OK.

4   The **Application** *validates* the recipient data from the **Money Transfer page** to ensure that all fields are correctly filled (e.g., correct bank account number and ZIP code).

5   The **Application** *retrieves* the **Bank Account Details** *associated* with the selected **Bank Account**, and *validates* the entered amount of money against the customer's **Bank Account** holds.

6   The **Application** *creates* a **Preliminary Transaction** and *copies* the customer's bank account, name, and address data to the **Preliminary Transaction**.

7   Then the **Application** *retrieves* the **Customer Address** *associated* with the **Customer**.

8   Then the **Application** *copies* the recipient data to the **Preliminary Transaction**.

9   The **Application** *copies* the amount of money to the **Preliminary Transaction**.

10   The **Application** *displays* the **Preliminary Transaction** on the **Confirm Money Transfer page**.

11   The **Customer** *clicks* OK on the **Confirm Money Transfer page**.

12   The **Application** *calls* the **Process Debit Transaction Use Case**.

13   The **Application** *returns* to the **Customer's Home Page** and *returns* control to the **Use Case that called Make Money Transfer**.

Alternate Courses

---

14   If the **Open Bank Account List** is empty, *display* a "No Account Available" message on the **Error Page**, and *return control* to the **Use Case that called Make Money Transfer**.

15   If the recipient data is incomplete or incorrect, *display* an "Incorrect Recipient Data" message on the **Error Page**, and the **Application** *returns* to the **Make Money Transfer page**.

16   If the amount of money in the **Bank Account Details** is not sufficient, *display* an "Insufficient Funds" message on the **Error Page**, and the **Application** *returns* to the **Money Transfer page**.

Continued

Table 7.1 Continued

Alternate Courses

---

17 If the **Customer** *clicks* Cancel on the **Money Transfer page**, the **Application** *returns control* to the **Use Case that called Make Money Transfer**.

18 If the **Customer** *clicks* Cancel on the **Confirm Money Transfer Page**, the **Preliminary Transaction** is removed and **Application** *returns* to the **Money Transfer Page**.

Table 7.2 The Process Debit Transaction Use Case

Basic Course

---

1 The **Application** *retrieves* **Bank Account Details** *associated* with the **Transaction**.

2 The **Application** *validates* the Recipient Bank Account Number associated with the **Transaction** against the bank's **Bank Account List**.

3 The **Application** *validates* the amount of money on the **Preliminary Transaction**.

4 The **Application** *creates* a **Transaction** and *copies* the data from the **Preliminary Transaction**.

5 The **Application** *decreases* the **Bank Account balance** *associated* with the **Transaction** with the amount of the **Transaction**.

6 If the recipient Bank Account Number is also of the same bank, the **Application** *calls* the **Process Credit Transaction Use Case**.

7 The **Application** *sends* the **Transaction** to the **General Ledger**.

8 The **Application** *changes* the status of the **Transaction** to "Completed."

9 The **Application** *returns control* to the **Use Case that called Process Debit Transaction**.

Alternate Courses

---

10 If the amount of money exceeds the thresholds, the **Application** *changes* the status of the **Transaction** to "To Be Authorized" and *returns control* to the **Use Case that called Process Debit Transaction**.

11 If the recipient Bank Account Number is not of the same bank, the **Application** *sends* the **Transaction** to the **Clearinghouse** and *changes* the status of the **Transaction** to "Pending."

Before you go to the next phase of the process ("Modeling the Interactions"), it is important that you consolidate your results so far: the Domain model and the Use Case model. Figure 7.3 shows what parts of the Problem domain and Solution domain we have already filled in, as well as the blank spots that we still need to cover. This consolidation, called the *Requirements Review*, is the first milestone of the project. You do this review with both your colleagues and the customers (stakeholders). Ask everyone involved: "Do we all agree that these are the requirements we have identified for the application?" You should only proceed if the response is a firm "Yes."

Figure 7.3 The Requirement Steps in the ICONIX Process

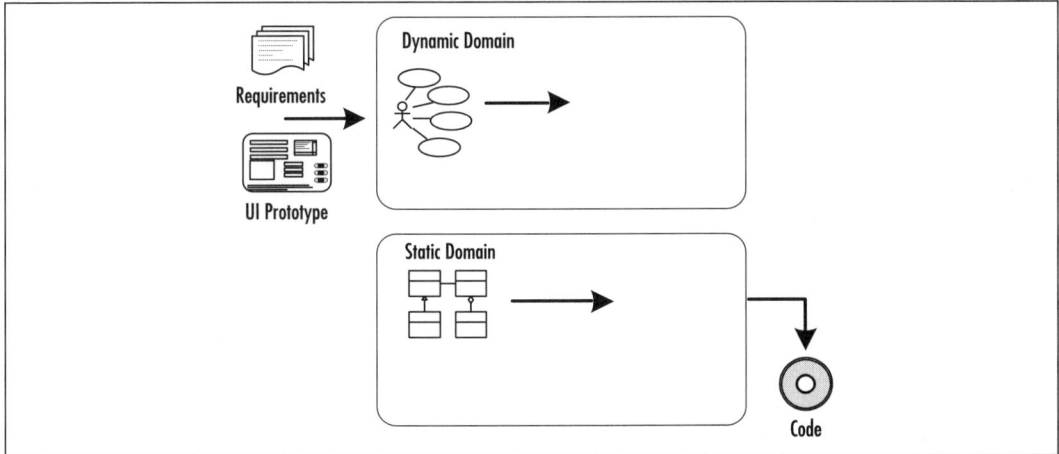

Most projects are of such a size that you will most likely divide the Use Case groups between you and one or more colleagues. If this is the case, before you can present the results to the customer, you should bring it all together, review it, and check to make sure the results match up and nothing is omitted. In case there are some unanswered issues, take care of them. While you do the collegial review, you must ensure that:

- All requirements can be traced back to one or more Use Cases.

- Every Use Case can be traced back to a requirement.

- The objects that are referenced in a Use Case must be part of the Domain model.

- Every object in the Domain model must be referenced by at least one Use Case.

- You have captured all alternate courses within every Use Case.

NOTE

If your client requests major changes, you have done something wrong. You can avoid this by keeping in touch with the client, especially in an informal way. Take the time to contact different stakeholders to show them what you have up until that point, and ask for their opinion. Never surprise the client with a "This is it!" result, since this may very well trigger a reaction of disapproval. Keeping the client "in the loop" and keeping them informed is known as "expectations management."

Modeling the Interactions

Now that you have reached your first milestone and everyone is convinced that the requirements are solid, it is time to start fleshing out the Use Case model and the Domain model by performing the next step: *"Robustness Analysis."* What this means is that you create a robustness diagram for every Use Case, which is similar to a UML collaboration diagram.

Since you still want to build an object-oriented application, you need to close the void between the Problem domain and the Solution domain (Figure 7.3). We already established that our Domain model was created using an inside-out approach, and our Use Case model was created using an outside-in approach. If you did this right, they should meet somewhere in the middle, so you need to check if both are robust enough to do so. You do this by "dissecting" each Use Case in terms of objects, and determining how these interact with each other. The robustness diagram uses three types of objects, each with its own icon (Figure 7.4):

- **Boundary object** A Boundary object lets an actor interface with the application. This object is not part of the Domain model, but will eventually show up in the final Class diagram. A boundary object can, for example, be an ASP page, dialog window, or component.

- **Control object** A Control object enables the coupling of Boundary objects and Entity objects. This is factually not an object, but performs validation of the relationships between objects. A controller will not be part of the Class diagram. A controller will be part of the application logic and will surface as part of the business process flow.

- **Entity object** An Entity object is an object that is part of the Domain model, with a sporadic exception, and will be part of the final Class diagram. An entity object can be a part of a database, but can also be an XML document that is exchanged between two (or more) BizTalk XLANG schedules.

Figure 7.4 The Robustness Diagram Icons

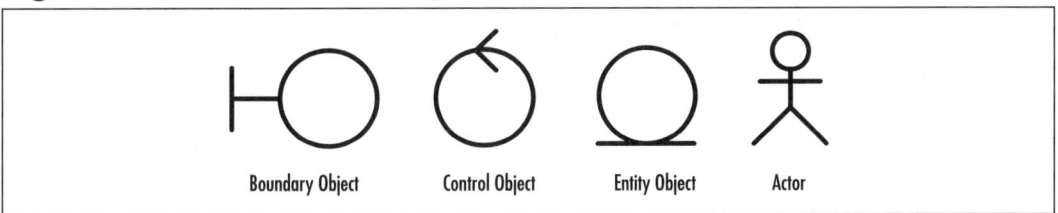

When you start drawing the Robustness diagram for every Use Case, read the Use Case carefully and start adding the corresponding objects and/or actors to the diagram, connecting them using associations. A Use Case matches a Robustness diagram if you can follow the diagram while reading the Use Case. Only developers with prior ICONIX experience will very likely have phrased their Use Cases in a way that matches up with the Robustness diagrams. You will not only fine-tune your Use Cases, but also your Domain model, discovering new objects, adding new attributes to the objects in your Domain model, or changing relationships between objects.

When the Use Case model, Robustness diagrams, and Domain model are in full balance, aligning with one another 100 percent, you have reached an important point in the process: the start of the design phase. As you will notice, the Robustness diagrams do look a lot like flowcharts, or, we should say, you remodeled the Use Cases into abstract processes. This is no small achievement! Remember that these robustness diagrams are fully based on the user requirements without the need for implementation assumptions; and you are already turning a problem in the direction of a solution. Again, you are encouraged to revisit the results of previous steps and modify them as more information becomes known. You improve the results of previous steps by moving forward, due to the self-correcting behavior of this process. Of course, ICONIX is not unique as a development methodology, and other methodologies deliver equal results. However, by its concept of "the minimal approach," it shows that the *developer* is in control, not the *method*.

Now you know what robustness analysis is about, but we still have not discussed how you draft these diagrams. With just four icons, there are not many variations available. The noun-verb-noun relationship, as mentioned in the Use Case model step, returns in the Robustness diagram where the controller (Control object) represents the verb, and the noun becomes an Entity object or a Boundary object. Obey the following guidelines when drawing the diagram:

- An actor can only interact with a Boundary object.

- A controller connects with at least one other controller, Boundary object, or Entity object.

- A Boundary object always interacts with one actor and connects to at least one controller.

- An Entity object connects with at least one controller.

- The relation between two icons is drawn using an arrow based on the direction in which the data flows

Figure 7.5 shows the Robustness diagrams based on the Use Cases described in Table 7.1. To understand the relationship between the Use Case and the Robustness diagram, read the Use Case and use a pencil, finger, or any other pointing device to follow the diagram, and notice the one-on-one relationship between the two representations. Arrows can carry an annotation regarding the data that is carried over the relationship, which can be useful to distinguish between basic courses and alternate courses.

You are now at a crucial point in the project: you are about to go from the *analysis* to the actual *design*. This is your second milestone that you and your team must use to synchronize with your customer, before embarking on the second leg of the journey. It is likely that, as a developer, this is the moment you have been waiting for. This is also an important moment for the customer, since it is their last opportunity to match the results on paper with the ideas they have about the application. If the customer signs off, they give their approval to the design and development—make sure the customer is aware of this. In this "Preliminary Design Review," you meet with the same group as in the "Requirements Review." If you kept the customers in the loop, used them as a resource, and interacted with them, chances are that this review is an open-and-shut case. Nevertheless, before you meet with the customer, the development team should review each other's work (*peer review*); integrate the work of all team members, align them, and check for overlaps (*white spots*) and for forgotten requirements (*black spots*). It might seem boring to go over the same details again, but it will pay off in the end. You get a much better understanding of the requirements and what the application entails, and prevent a "back to the drawing board" situation. Try to imagine what it means when the development is halted due to a serious design flaw. If you haven't experienced that yet, talk to your senior developers!

Figure 7.5 A Robustness Diagram Based on the Make Money Transfer Use Case

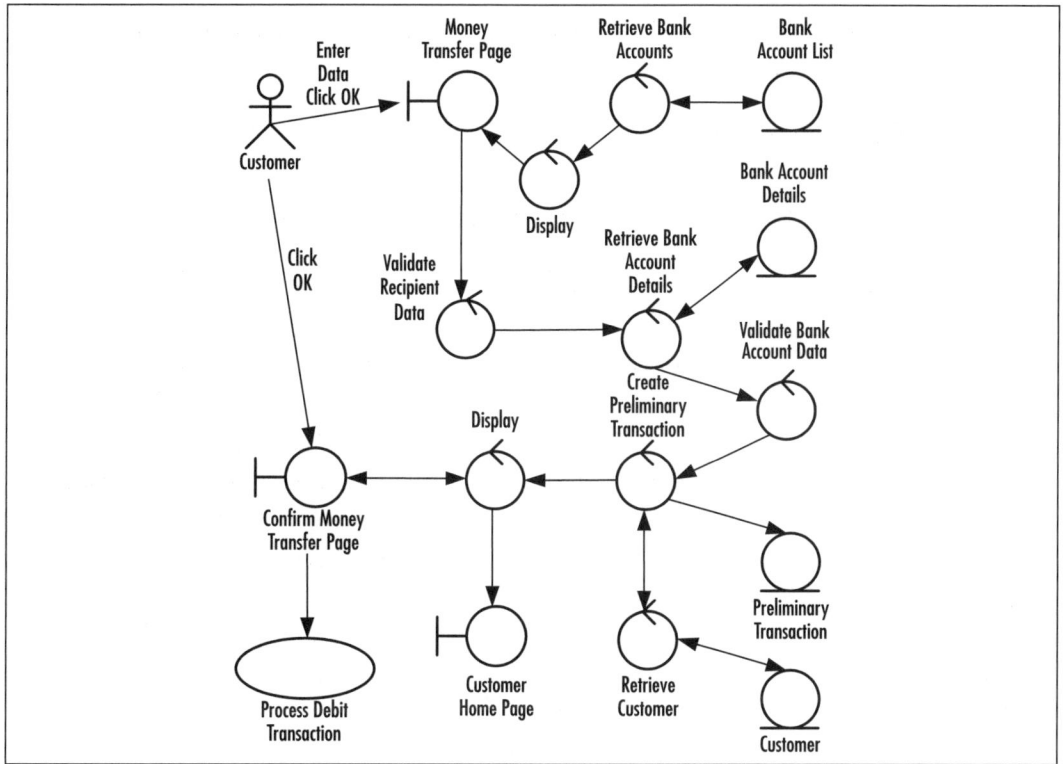

Once you pass this point, you can look to the robustness diagrams and Use Cases with the eyes of a designer/developer. Which technologies you are going to use, how will the application architecture look, and how is it going to match up with the technical infrastructure? Sure, you will be using BizTalk Server 2000 and the technologies aligned with it, but how about lining up the different tiers, scalability and reliability, performance and security? There are many things to consider. You do not need to have all the answers right away, but before you really start developing/implementing, you should know in which direction you're headed!

Get your scrapbook on the table, start thinking in patterns and looking for them in the diagrams, populate the Domain classes, and then adapt the Domain model to your new discoveries. Always expect to come across "lost objects" and new detailed insights. When you do, go back to your original Use Cases and

Robustness diagrams to make sure you are not drifting away from the requirements. In this stage, you can develop a close relationship with your whiteboard—
nothing is permanent, yet.

It gets more serious in the next step, "Sequence Diagramming," in which you
do the real design work and can show your design skills. The sequence diagrams
will embody the behavior of the application and will be the Dynamic
Application model, with your Class diagrams as the Static Class model. Since this
will become your application blueprint, it needs to reflect the level of detail that
ensures this role. You should be thinking in terms of COM components,
methods, properties, and so on. This does not mean you should riddle the diagrams with details that do not reflect application behavior. It *does* mean making
use of well-established design patterns, or even building one of your own.

Sequence diagrams are comprised of:

- **Use Case text** The complete Use Case, basic course and alternate
  courses, are placed on the left side of the page. Assuming you did a
  serious job in getting the Use Case text broken down into sentences
  (the noun-verb-noun composition) that you already used in the
  Robustness diagrams, you white space these sentences, grouped under
  "Basic Course" and "Alternate Courses." This way, you can correlate the
  Sequence diagrams directly with the Use Cases, ensuring that you covered the entire Use Case.

- **Actor, Boundary, and Entity objects** are placed at the top of the
  page, in that order. You take them directly from the Robustness diagrams.
  It is a good idea to use both the name and the icon, so you can correlate
  them to the Robustness diagrams as needed. Draw a vertical line from
  the object to the bottom of the page. They will serve as the object's
  placeholder when interaction between objects is visualized, based on the
  Use Case. Note that controllers, thus Control objects, are not placed at
  the top of the page; we use them to glue the other components.
  Nevertheless, they will reappear in the form of one or more messages.

- **Messages** Represented as arrows between objects, and are accompanied
  by a function-like name, expressing the purpose of the message.

- **Methods** Used as the "Focus of Control" of objects. A method is
  depicted as a rectangle, overlaying the placeholder line, starting from the
  first message entering the object and ending when it returns with a
  result. The latter is not always indicative within a Sequence diagram,

since we decided to leave out insignificant behavior. For a COM+ component, you can state that it has focus of control from the moment it gets instantiated until the moment it is released. However, with a mix of synchronous and asynchronous methods and different type of components, it is not always easy to get the focus of control in the diagram. Leaving it out does *not* render the diagram useless. In fact, if you cannot get the methods in correctly, leaving them out is the best choice.

NOTE

Design Patterns from E. Gamma, R. Helm, R. Johnson, and J. Vlissides (Addison-Wesley) is considered the "bible" on design patterns. By the way, these authors are also known as the "Gang of Four."

Once you have your empty sequence diagrams, comprised of Use Case text, actors, Boundary objects, and Entity objects, it is time to start filling them with messages. The controllers (Control objects) from the Robustness diagram are your guides in doing this:

- Read the Use Case text sentence by sentence.
- Identify the part of the Robustness diagram that captures the sentence.
- Determine the controllers and the objects it binds.
- Draw one or more messages that correspond with this.

Chances are you will occasionally run into a hidden object; correct it where necessary before continuing. After you create a Sequence diagram for every Use Case (see Figure 7.6 for a Sequence diagram for the bank account example), you can build and finalize the Static Class diagram (see Figure 7.7 for the Static Class diagram for the bank account example).

Figure 7.6 The Sequence Diagram Based on the Make Money Transfer Use Case Example

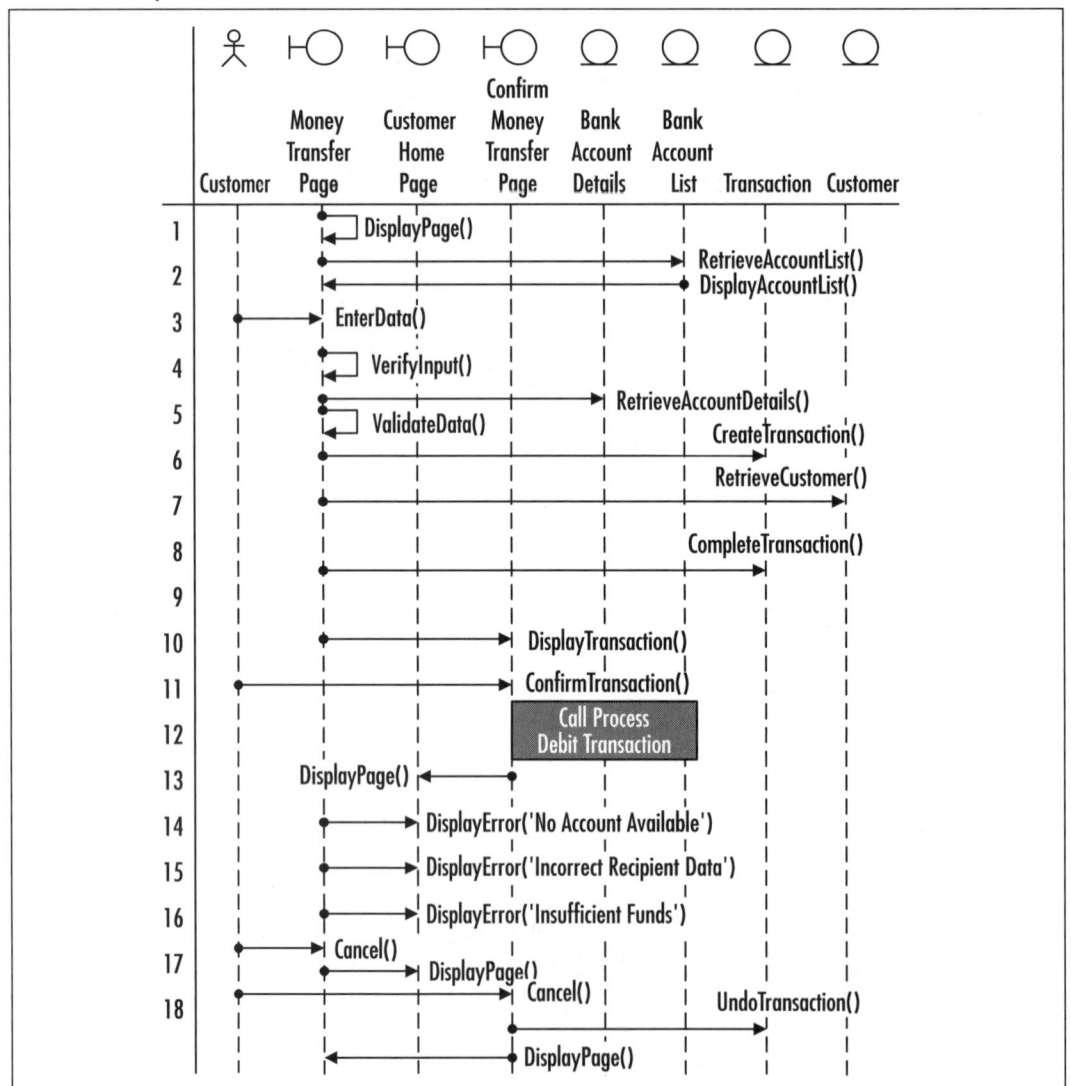

Figure 7.7 The Class Diagram Based on the Make Money Transfer Use Case Example

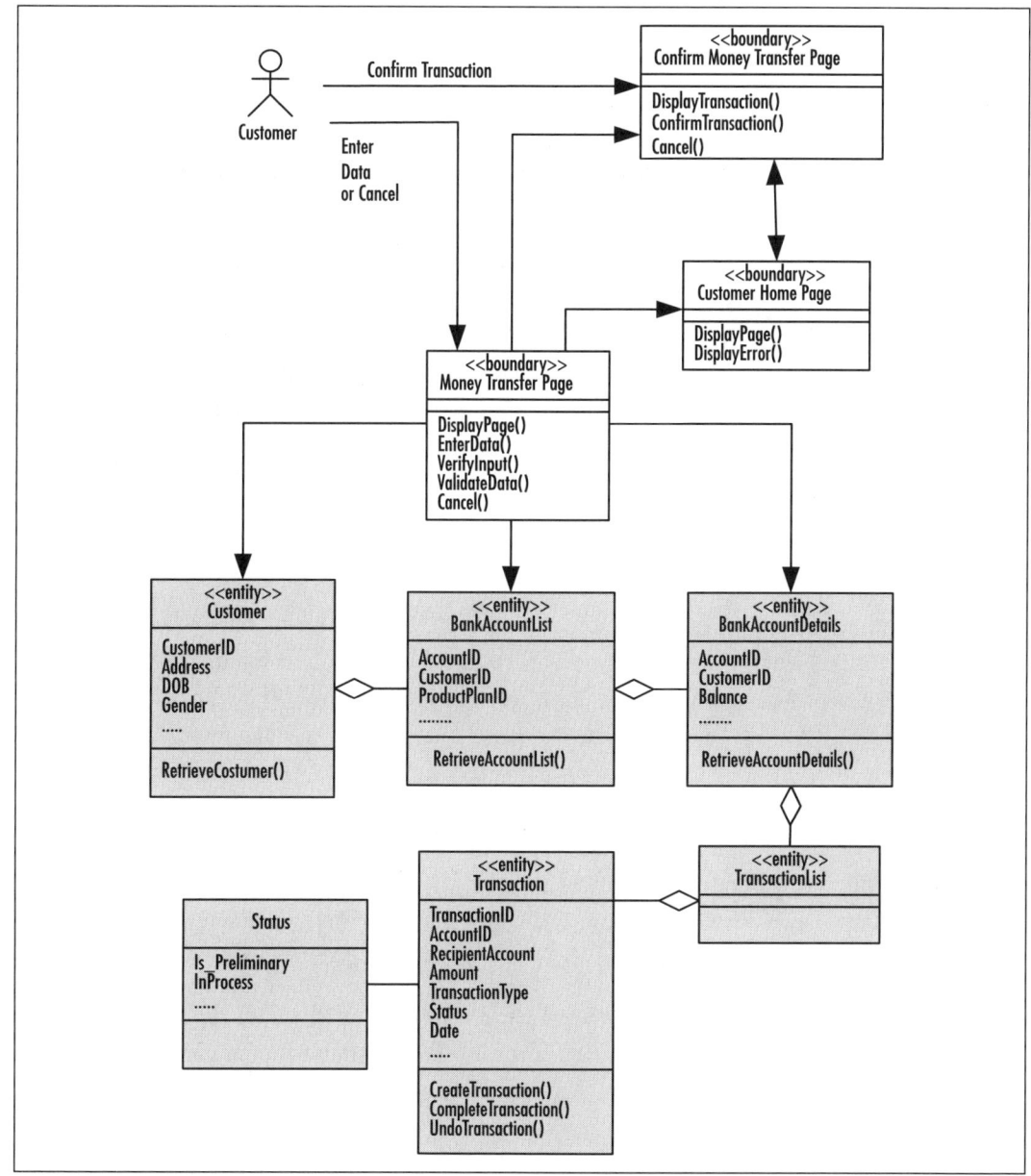

Before you start coding, you have to finish the design phase with the "Critical Design Review," which is the third milestone. Again, there should be peer review of all Sequence diagrams. Once it has been established that they are all okay, they have to be integrated and aligned, to assure that no white and black spots exist. Now the team can review the complete static Class diagram. Make sure you take the following into account:

- **Cohesion of classes** Make sure that the attributes and methods that are grouped within a class can all relate to each other, and do not need another class to do so.

- **Uncoupling of classes** Make sure that classes can live independently from each other. Of course, there is likely some coupling with a few directly related classes, but this should be very limited. If classes rely very strongly on each other, they are not meant to be separate, and you should make them into one class.

- **Complexity** The complexity of a method is a good indicator if it is assigned to the correct class. If you can build the same method more easily by assigning it to another class, do so.

- **Reusability of classes** This is one of the primary goals of object-oriented development. Reusability can be increased by using as many design patterns as possible. Theoretically, this is also true by applying "primitiveness." Simply put, "primitiveness" means chopping up classes to a level at which you have a limited number of methods (the less, the better) and attributes, needed by the methods, within a class. These small classes can be used to build larger ones. For example, a component is an empty wrapper for persisting a database row. Practically, this introduces a lot of system overhead and, consequently, performance degradation. Therefore, reusability is important, but not a goal in and of itself.

Do not try to overanalyze the Sequence diagrams and Class diagrams; keep things practical but discrete. Now that the design is finished, you can begin the coding/implementation of the application. Rounding out the Analysis and Design steps and adding the Iteration steps to Figure 7.3, you get the complete overview of the ICONIX steps in Figure 7.8.

Figure 7.8 The Requirement and Iteration Steps of the ICONIX Method

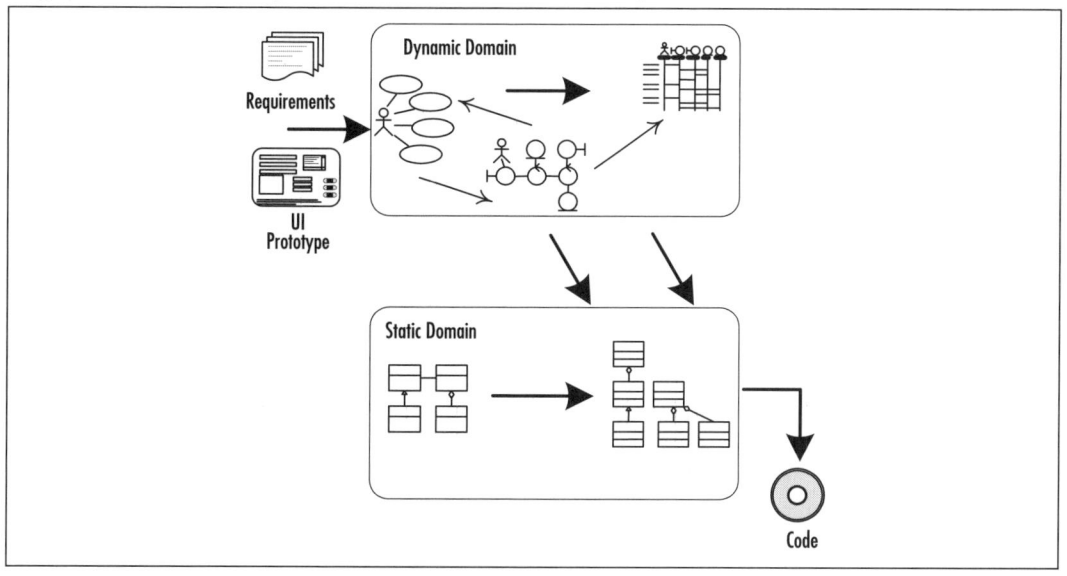

Reviewing Current Practices

While you are implementing the application, the business analysts can also resume working. Introducing a new application to the organization will most likely require a review of current practices to make any adaptations necessary to incorporate the application into the organization. In business analyst terms, this is called *business process redesign/reengineering* (BPR). Depending on the size of the new applications, or the number of business processes it affects, BPR can vary from little change to significant change. The reason for introducing a new application to a business it to improve their business and efficiency. Since the new application will incorporate part of the existing business processes, if not take over a number of them, it is sure to impact the current organization.

Change can be very threatening to some employees, so a business analyst should take this into consideration when introducing a new way of conducting business. The introduction of a new application, especially a big one, is a very delicate process. Do not call it redesigning or reengineering, since this is often interpreted as "we are doing things wrong, and some outsider is going to tell us how we should do our work." Refer to it instead as a "business process adaptation/evolvement," and get the employees directly involved. One of the reasons in getting stakeholders directly involved, besides the fact that they are good sources of information, is that by making them part of the "team," they will accept the solution more readily if it is seen as being partly their solution. It is inevitable that processes have to be adapted and the employees directly involved with the new application will have to do new things. However, by making them part of that process, by inviting them to help think of the best solution, it is unlikely they will not accept working with the new application. Here are some guidelines for this review process:

- Take inventory of the current business processes that will be embedded in the new application, partially or totally. Make a detailed description of how these processes currently work and interact with other processes.

- Take inventory of the processes that interact with the processes that are going to be (partially) embedded in the new application. Make a detailed description of how these processes interact with the processes that are going to be part of the new application.

- Make an initial assessment on how both groups of processes are going to be changed.

- Take inventory of the employees involved in these processes and the roles they currently play.

- Talk to these employees and explain the situation. Encourage them to help you come up with solutions to embed the new application in the organization. You can use the same group technique discussed previously in the sidebar "Users Hold the Key to the Requirements."

- Important goals are (1) the way the application is going to interact with current processes; (2) the roles involved with the new application; and (3) the new tasks the new application introduces.

- Assess how these new roles and tasks should be divided among the employees. Make it known to them and ask for their cooperation.

- Provide adequate training for using the new application.

Of course, it is more complex than this, but we are writing a developer's guide about BizTalk Server 2000, not a book on BPR. We want to make sure that you understand that this part of the development process is as important as the actual building of the application, if not more so. Again, you are working with people. The application you helped build can be perfect for its task, but if it is not used correctly, it will be rated a failure. The history of IT projects is riddled with failures, not necessarily because the applications themselves were poorly designed, but because employees were left out of the equation.

BizTalk Orchestration Designer

The BizTalk Orchestration Designer plays a pivotal role in getting a BizTalk application to work, since it enables you to create the core of the application, based on process flows. You use the Orchestration Designer to create XLANG schedule drawings; these drawings are compiled to an XML-coded XLANG schedule that can be run by an XLANG scheduler engine, also called a COM+ application that hosts XLANG schedules. Did we already lose you? Probably, since putting the principal terminology surrounding BizTalk Orchestration Services into one sentence is highly confusing. It is clear that Microsoft had a hard time finding distinctive terminology within BizTalk Server. Do not worry! The Orchestration Designer in itself is very clear, straightforward, and easy to use. This will become apparent the first time you start BizTalk Orchestration and see something similar to Figure 7.9.

Figure 7.9 The BizTalk Orchestration Designer

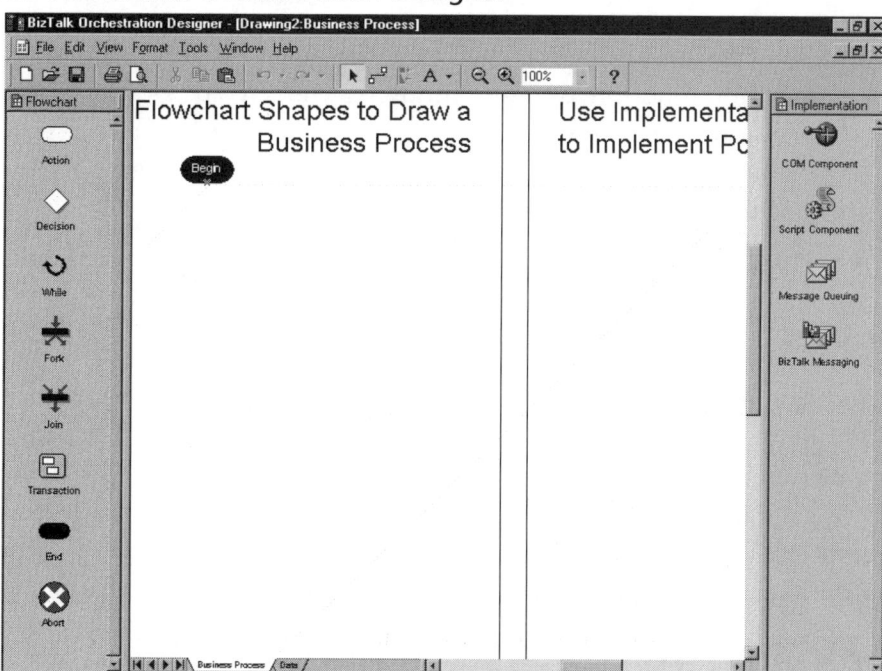

The default layout of the Orchestration Designer consists of:

- Two windows, called *stencils*, with a green background. The one on the left is called *Flowchart*; the one on the right is called *Implementation*.

The stencils contain the shapes that can be used within the drawing. We discuss these in detail in the section *Flowchart and Implementation Shapes*.

■ A drawing window that has two pages: *Business Process* and *Data*. The Business Process page is shown with a divider in the middle. In the section *Business Process Drawings*, the Business Process page is detailed. The section *Data Flow Definition* discusses the Data page.

You can use the **View** menu to modify the layout of the screen. It is also possible to have more than one open drawing visible at the same time, although this will limit the view of the drawings. To enlarge the drawing window, without zooming out, you can close a stencil. You can open or close a stencil through **View | Stencils**. When you reopen a stencil, you need to resize it since it does not return to its original width. There is a better way to create more room for the drawing without closing a stencil, however: by overlaying the stencils. Suppose you want both stencils on the left-hand side of the screen. You need to move the Implementation Stencil to the left. This can be done in two ways:

■ Point to the title of the Implementation stencil and, while holding the left mouse button, drag the mouse to the left side of the screen and position it just below the title bar of the flowchart stencil. As you let go of the mouse button, the Implementation stencil is docked on the left, and the Flowchart stencil is collapsed.

■ Point to the title of the Implementation stencil, and right-click it. Choose **Position | Docked to Left** and the stencil is also moved to the left, collapsing the Flowchart stencil.

You can now open the stencil you want to use. As you develop your drawing, it is not likely you will need to have both stencils open at the same time. The View menu lets you also switch the **Grid** on and off, while **Page Breaks** shows you the page margins the printer leaves blank. The part of the shape that occupies this unprintable zone will not appear on the printout. Before getting further into what the Orchestration Designer is all about, we will first look at the result.

Compiling the XLANG Schedule Drawing

In previous chapters, you learned about what comprises BizTalk Server 2000. To understand where the Orchestration Services fits into this picture you need to know what the Orchestration Designer delivers as a product to fit the solution.

All your efforts put into the use of the Designer can be put to work after you compile the drawing you created by calling the **File | Make XLANG Drawing Name.skx**. The extension "skx" refers to the XMLized schedule, as opposed to the extension "skv" that is used for the schedule drawing, with the "**v**" reflecting the use of Visio as the basis for the Orchestration Designer.

WARNING

Do not use any release other than Visio 2000 SR-1A, or you will not be able to work with BizTalk Orchestration Designer. If you currently have Visio 2000 installed, your BizTalk installation will abort until the proper version (Visio 2000 SR-1A) is installed. However, if you are working with a system without Visio, you should be able to complete the installation, and install Visio 2000 SR-1A at a later date.

To get a better understanding of what a compiled drawing looks like, you can open a "skx" file with Internet Explorer, or any other Web browser that can parse XML:

1.   Open Windows Explorer.

2.   Expand to the folder **Program Files | Microsoft BizTalk Server | Tutorial | Schedule | Solution**. In case BizTalk Server is not installed under Program Files, go to the appropriate folder.

3.   You will see two "skx" files: Buyer1 and Buyer2. Select one of them, right-click it, and select **Open With**.

4.   Select **Internet Explorer**. Be sure the option **Always use this program to open these files** is not checked.

5.   Click **OK**.

If you are familiar with XML, it is all very recognizable, but nowhere near an executable program—it is a schedule in need of an interpreter, like the music rolls for a player piano. The XLANG schedule engine is the default interpreter, but you can build your own.

The compilation process checks the syntax and semantics of the drawing and returns an error with any inconsistencies, which you have to correct before an XLANG schedule is generated. Once the drawing compiles without errors, you can run it. However, this does not mean that it always work flawlessly. More information on XLANG schedules and debugging them can be found in the next chapter. Here, we will focus on how to create a drawing that will compile into a XLANG schedule.

Business Process Drawings

Upon opening the BizTalk Orchestration Designer, you get a blank Business Process page (Figure 7.9) that is comprised of three areas. This division of the page becomes more apparent when you open an existing drawing; for example, Buyer2.skv from the tutorial (Figure 7.10). If you zoom out you will see that the vertical lines on the page divide the page in two-thirds for the Flowchart shapes (the left side), and one-third for the Implementation shapes (the right side). You can convince yourself that these vertical lines indeed represent a separator of the page by trying to move an Implementation shape to the left of the lines and/or a Flowchart shape to the right side—not possible! Another way to view this division is to select one of the following filtering options in the **View** menu:

- Flowchart Shapes
- Flowchart and Communication Shapes
- Flowchart, Communication, and Implementation Shapes

Figure 7.10 A BizTalk Business Process, Buyer2

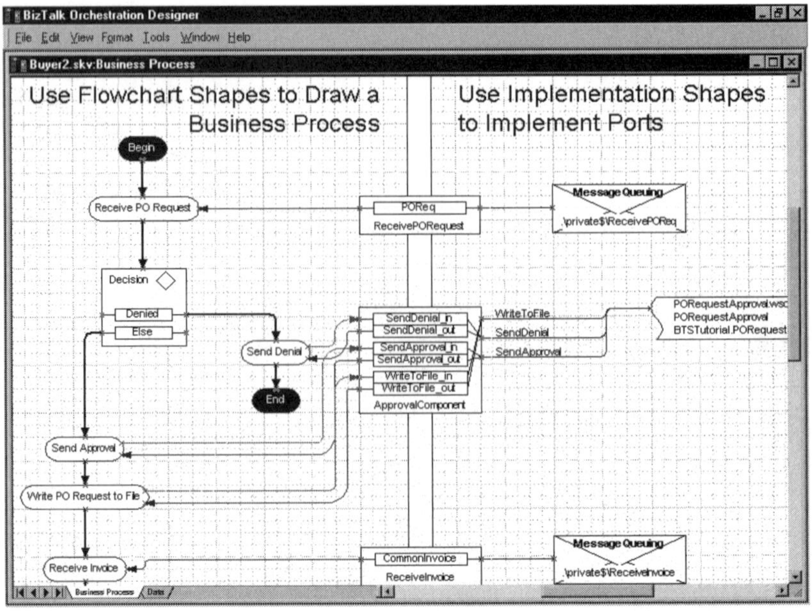

The last filtering option is the default selection, and will show all shapes on the Business Process page. The second option shows only the Flowchart shapes on the left side of the page and the Communication shapes on the separator. The first option will, of course, only show the shapes at the left side of the page. Those who have worked with Visio before will recognize that this is done through layers.

The rectangle shapes overlaying the separator line are called *ports* and are categorized under "Communication Shapes." When you drag an Implementation shape onto the page, a wizard will start that automatically creates a port. You can also manually create a port by right-clicking the **separator** and selecting **Add New Port**. Since the port is not connected to an Implementation shape, it is called *unbound*. The meaning of this will become clearer later in this section.

Let's go back to the left side of the Business Process page. Here is where you draw a flowchart representing the business process, or any other type of data-driven flow. It is likely that you cut up a business process in smaller parts and make a XLANG schedule for each part that is connected during runtime. However, for the sake of this discussion, we will use "Business Process," as Microsoft calls it.

The flowchart represents a business process, and the flow of your application. It has one, and only one, *Begin* point that anchors the flow, so when the schedule is run, the schedule engine knows where it should start. The flow can have as many *End* points as is needed for the flow. The flow can be controlled by an *If-Then-Else* construction, called *Decision*, or a *While*. The rest of the flow is comprised of *actions* that are responsible for sending (the red arrows) or receiving (the blue arrows) data, which is all they do. You need to connect the Flowchart shapes to create the flow. These black arrows always go from the bottom of the shape to the top of another shape. With *Decision* and *While* shapes, the arrows go out from the side. This is what you do to connect two shapes:

1. Select a **shape**, or in case of a *Decision* or *While*, select the required named rectangle within the shape. One or two blue crosses of the shape turn into little green squares.

2. Select the desired **green square** and keep the left mouse button pressed while you drag the pointer to the shape it is meant to connect with. While you drag the pointer. a connection line is shown.

3. When the pointer is on the top blue cross of the Destination shape, a red box is shown; as you release the mouse button, a black arrow is drawn between the two connection points.

4. Even if you move the shapes, the arrow stays connected, and will be redrawn so that it does not cross another shape. Try it! Add an Action shape to the drawing and release it over a connection arrow. You will see that the arrow is moved!

It is important to understand that these arrows only show the flow and do not carry data across. An Action shape can only receive or send data from and to a port. Note that the left side of the business dataflow process only controls the decision making in the flow, and does not actually handle the message data. That is done by the right side (implementation side) of the business process.

As mentioned earlier, an action can only exchange data with an Implementation shape using a port that functions as a pickup and/or drop-off point for data. The Implementation shape can be either a component or a Messaging Service. In case a port is connected by:

- A **component**, the port has for each component method both a drop-off (in) and pickup (out) point. The data exchanged is defined by the method. The component can be a *COM component* or a *Windows Scripting component*. Although their implementation is different, they are handled similarly in a business process diagram.

- A **BizTalk Messaging Service**, the port has one connection point per action. The port is either a send or a receive port connecting to the channel.

- A **Message Queuing Service**, the port has one send or receive point per action. The port connects to a queue.

The previous chapter discussed the Messaging Services in detail, so here we are more concerned that you connect the workflow action in the right way to the ports of a messaging service. In doing so, you need to know what is connected to the other side of the queue or channel. If this does not match up, your application will produce errors during runtime or stall. It is quite easy to send the incorrect data, or to receive data that is different from what is sent by the other party. The compilation process is not able to check the content format on either side of the channel or queue, since it does not have the information to do so.

So, what is the use of an unbound port? The only benefit it has is that you can create your flowchart and link every action with a port without having to know to what Messaging Service it is going to connect; for example, because you are only doing the flowchart development. Unbound ports cannot be used if you later need to connect a component to the port. Before you start compiling the XLANG schedule drawing, all ports need to be connected to an Implementation shape; otherwise, the compilation process will prematurely exit with an error message. You can find detailed information on all available shapes in the section "Flowchart, Communication, and Implementation Shapes."

Data Flow Definition

On the second page of the XLANG schedule diagram, called *Data*, there is not much going on if the Business Process page is still empty. In fact, the Data page fills up only if you add and implement ports to the business process. You can access the Data page by clicking on the **Data** tab at the bottom of the BizTalk Orchestration Designer window. You are not able to make any changes to the data entities on this page, except for the *Constants*. If you want to make changes, you need to modify the port properties. The Data page must be used to define the flow of data from one message to one or more other messages. This data flow information is needed to correctly populate messages during the execution of the business process flow. As mentioned earlier, the flowchart itself does not carry any data, so if you want an action to send out data, you have to "tell" BizTalk where to get if from. This is where the Data page comes into play; from here, you can draw arrows indicating the source of a message. When you look at a data page of an existing drawing (Figure 7.11), you see a number of Communication shapes that represent ports and the message the data page will exchange. In Figure 7.11, you see that the document that is received over port POReq is used as input ("populates") for the ports SendDenial, SendApproval, and WriteToFile. The compiler will report an error if you want to send a message that has no origin. However, if you remove the arrows and recompile the drawing, you will receive no error message, because the compiler does not check component parameters. Always draw population arrows and double-check them so that you will not be surprised by runtime errors. The same is true for the parameter *WriteToFile_In.FileName*. The only reason that the tutorial runs is that the scripting component assigns a default value to FileName.

The relevance of the population connections is checked during compilation, based on the flowchart. A connection is relevant if the source exists prior to the moment the message is populated. If this is not the case, an error message will occur. The compilation will only check to see if the message is populated, it does not check to see if the content or message types correspond. All in all, you need to pay a lot of attention to the data flow, not only based on the way you populate messages, but also on the way you integrate it with the Messaging Services.

We detail the different Communication shapes on the Data page in the section "Flowchart, Communication, and Implementation Shapes."

Figure 7.11 A BizTalk Data Flow Definition, Buyer2

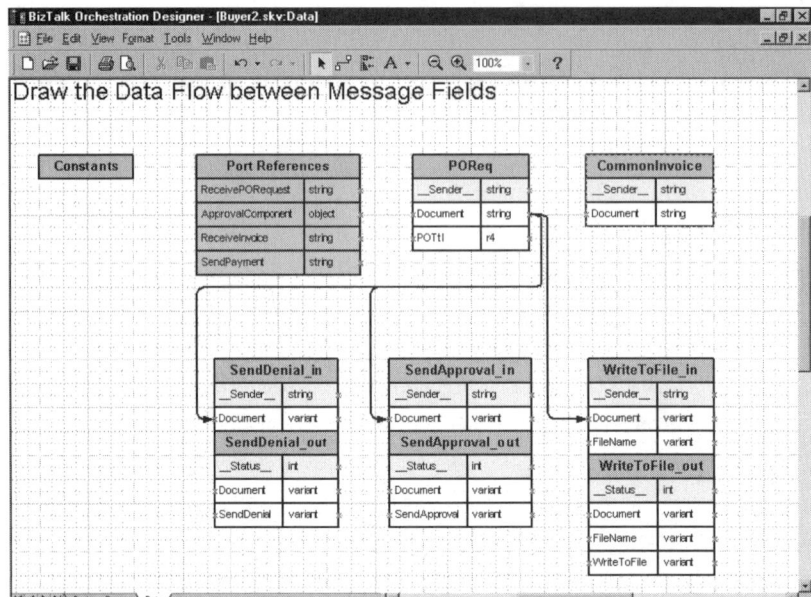

Transactions

One of the most important aspects of the BizTalk Orchestration Server is *transactions*, not only because a XLANG schedule can activate updates to one or more databases, but also because of the different ways transactions can be implemented. Figure 7.12 gives an example of what a nested transaction looks like; this figure has no value as a business process.

The first step in using transactions is deciding what controls the transaction, which can be the XLANG schedule or the XLANG schedule engine. You can control this through the **Begin Properties** dialog (Figure 7.13), by right-clicking **Begin shape** on the **Business Process** page.

Figure 7.12 An Example of a Nested Transaction

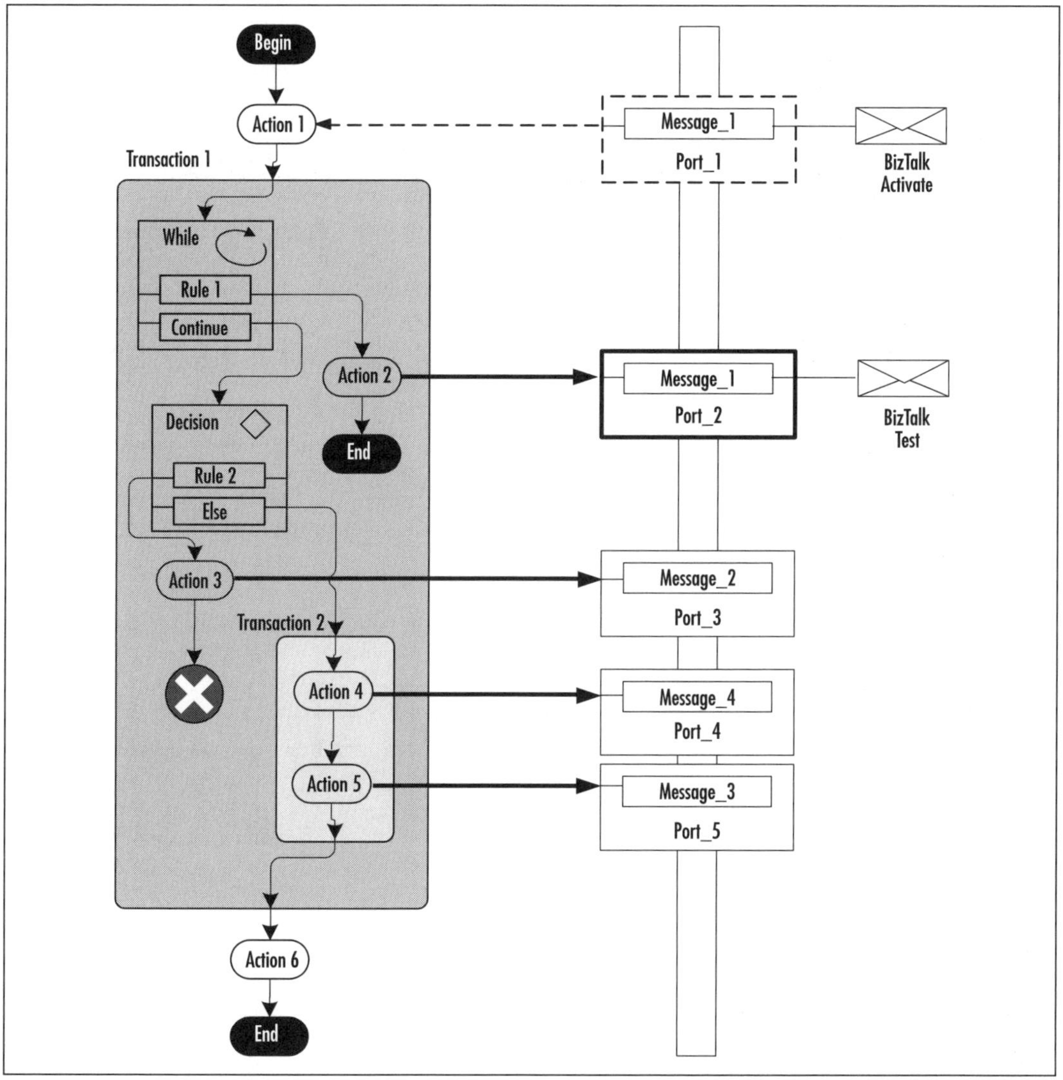

Begin

Action 1 ← ----------------- Message_1 / Port_1 — BizTalk Activate

Transaction 1

While
Rule 1
Continue

Action 2 → Message_1 / Port_2 — BizTalk Test

End

Decision
Rule 2
Else

Action 3 → Message_2 / Port_3

Transaction 2

Action 4 → Message_4 / Port_4

Action 5 → Message_3 / Port_5

Action 6

End

Figure 7.13 Begin Properties Dialog

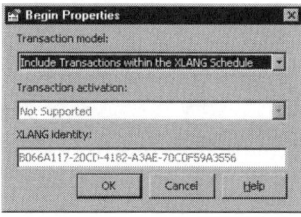

The dialog shows the following fields:

- **Transaction Model** This field can have two values:
    - **Include Transaction within XLANG Schedule**, meaning that the XLANG schedule controls the use of transactions.
    - **Treat the XLANG Schedule as a COM+ Component**; or the XLANG schedule engine. Since an instance of a schedule is hosted by a COM+ application, also referred to as the schedule engine, the execution of the schedule takes place within the context of this COM+ application.

- **Transaction activation** This field is only active if you choose **Treat the XLANG Schedule as a COM+ Component** as a transaction model. The values are:
    - **Not supported** The XLANG schedule will never run as a COM+ transaction.
    - **Supported** The XLANG schedule will only run as a transaction if the COM+ component that activated the schedule runs within a transaction.
    - **Required** The XLANG schedule needs to run in a COM+ transaction. If the COM+ component that activated the schedule does not run within a transaction a new transaction is created. In case a transaction is already active, the XLANG schedule will run in that transaction context.
    - **Requires New** The COM+ component will start a new transaction in which the XLANG schedule will run, even if the COM+ component is already running in a transaction.

- **XLANG Identity** This is a read-only field that displays the unique identifier of the current XLANG schedule drawing. Every time you save the drawing, a new identifier is generated. This enables you to match the drawing version with a compiled version of the schedule. If these do not match, the compiled version is based on another version of the XLANG schedule drawing.

When you decide to use the COM+ transaction mode, you can no longer use transactions within your XLANG schedule drawings. You can draw them, but the drawing will not compile.

Developing & Deploying...

The Meaning of Transactions and the DTC

When working with databases, you know that applications need to modify data in different databases or database tables in an "all or nothing" manner. Because these multiple database actions are part of one (business) transaction, it would render the database inconsistent if only a part of these actions were executed. Therefore, in case one of the modifications fails, the others need to be undone (rolled back). This is the only way to keep the database(s) consistent. This is the classic way of a transaction that is defined by the ACID attributes:

- **Atomicity** Stands for the "all or nothing" approach of the transaction. It has to be guaranteed that all modifications are committed or that all the modifications made during the transaction are undone.

- **Consistency** When a transaction starts, the database is in a consistent state, and as the transaction is committed or rolled back, the database is left in a consistent state.

- **Isolation** When more than one transaction is running concurrently, their modifications to the database are isolated from each other, as long as they are not committed. From the viewpoint of the transaction, it is the only one using the database. Concurrently running transactions leave the database in the same state as if they where running one after the other, also called *serialization*.

- **Durability** The modifications to the database made by the transaction are permanent once the transaction is committed. Even a database failure cannot result in a modification becoming lost.

The database logs play an important role in enforcing ACID. For example if a severe database failure occurs and an older (consistent) version of the database has to be restored, the database logs can be used to replay the transactions, bringing the database to a consistent state just before the failure occurred. This replay is also called *"roll-forward."*

Within BizTalk Server, only the "short-lived, DTC-style" transaction has all these attributes. The long-running transaction fails to comply with any of the four attributes, especially isolation.

Continued

A good rule of thumb is that the longer a transaction takes to finish, the less likely it is that it can persist ACIDity, without locking out other applications/transactions. Why? Because once a database modification is used by another application/transaction, it cannot be rolled back.

The database transaction coordinator (DTC) always sits in between the application and the database(s), thus coordinating reads and writes to a database by multiple transactions, *and* coordinating reads and writes to more databases by one transaction, thereby enforcing ACID. In the latter situation, it will take care that on a rollback of a transaction, all modifications made to the databases involved are undone. *Isolation* is an attribute that the DTC supports at different levels. Let's first look at the different levels, and then explain what they are about:

- **Read Uncommitted** A DTC transaction running at this isolation level is able to read all records in a database even if those records are written to by other transactions and these writes are not yet committed. This is the lowest level of isolation possible by the DTC.

- **Read Committed** A transaction running at this isolation level is able to read only records that are not written to, thus where the writes are already committed. After the transaction has read the record, another is allowed to change it. This is the default isolation level of SQL Server 2000.

- **Repeatable Read** A read committed, but now no record that is read by the transaction can be changed by another transaction, until the first transaction finishes. This is done to guarantee that when the record is read more than once by the transaction, it will return the same result.

- **Serializable** A repeatable read, but extended to the level that when a query is run multiple times within the same transaction, it must return the same result. This can be the best explained by the following example: You perform a query on a bank account table to determine the total number of bank accounts that are held by the customers from the state of Massachusetts, and what their total balance is. If you ran this query twice within the same transaction, it must return the same result. Therefore, not only can the read records not be changed, but any bank account of Massachusetts customers can be added or removed.

Continued

Only *serializable* is the thorough level of isolation; exactly what you want in a transaction. So, why the other isolation levels? Because serialization prevents other transactions from accessing these records, so they have to wait for the transaction to end, before it is their turn to access the records. This affects the performance of applications. Isolation is directly related to the locking mechanism of the database, but explaining that goes way beyond the scope of this book. However, if you get increasingly involved in application development projects, you should read into the more technical details of the databases. A good source is *Designing SQL Server 2000 Databases for .NET Enterprise Servers* (Syngress Publishing, ISBN: 1-928994-19-9).

Let's get back to the subject. To increase performance, you need to increase concurrency, thus more transactions having access to the same records. You do this by claiming the lowest isolation necessary for your transaction, since many transactions do not need *serializable* isolation. Second, you release your claim (lock) on records as soon as you do not need them anymore. If every transaction adheres to these two points— lowest necessary isolation and minimizing claim on records—every transaction, thus application, will benefit.

Serializable isolation is also about locking records you want to read, and every lock that a database has to set costs time. So, why bother about a lock if the chance that a change takes place is minimal (read uncommitted)? Or, you can accept the fact that records can change, except while you want to read that record a single time (read committed).

However, as the results of queries become more important, you need to isolate data records from other transactions and accept less performance. Repeatable read will lock larger numbers of records for longer periods, using *page locks*, which is more efficient than locking individual records; hence, less performance loss. Serializable will use index locking, or when the number of records becomes so large, it will lock the whole table.

With the setting of the isolation level, you can influence the efficiency with which your XLANG schedule short-lived transaction uses databases.

In the rest of the section, we will discuss the different transaction types that the XLANG schedule supports in more detail. The sidebar "The Meaning of Transactions and the DTC" explains what transactions are about and which role the *distributed transaction controller* (DTC) plays. We encourage you to read it, since this information enhances the understanding of the discussion of XLANG schedule transactions. Placing the transaction on your Business Process page is easy, and tying a part of the flow to the transaction is straightforward. However, using the transaction in a proper manner, especially if you are using a nested transaction, requires an understanding of what the transaction does during runtime. Let us first look at placing part of your flow in a transaction:

1. Start with an empty drawing, and drag an **Action** and **End** shape onto the page. Connect **Begin** with **Action1**, and **Action1** with **End**. This drawing will not compile because there is no connection with an Implementation shape; that's OK, we do not want to compile it anyway.

2. Drag the **Transaction** shape onto the page, overlaying **Action1**. As you will notice, Action1 will be placed on top of the Transaction shape, together with the connection arrows. If you compiled now, you would get an error message telling you that the transaction is not properly connected.

3. Notice that there is a connection point (a blue cross) at the top and bottom of the Transaction shape, meaning that it has one entry and one exit point. This means that:

   ■ The connection arrow of the shape before the transaction has to be connected to the transaction entry point.

   ■ A connection has to be made from the transaction entry point to the first shape inside the transaction.

   ■ The connection of the last shape within the transaction has to be connected to the transaction exit point.

   ■ A connection has to be made from the transaction exit point to the first shape outside the transaction.

4. Before you do this, first select the **Transaction1** and move it to another position on the page, keeping it to the left of the separator. Notice that every object enclosed by the Transaction shape also moves! Why? Because BizTalk Schedule Designer already made the assumption that every object within the transaction enclosure will be part of the transaction. Only the compiler needs these explicit connection points.

5. Because the compiler always wins, we will satisfy its needs. Select the connection arrow between **Begin** and **Action1**. Move the mouse pointer over connection point of **Action1** (now represented by a red solid box). As the mouse pointer changes to a crossed arrow, press the left

mouse button and keep it pressed while you move the mouse to the entry point of **Transaction1**, as it turns into a red square, release the mouse button. Connection made, just as you expected! Do the same with the other connection arrow. Now **Action1** is 'floating' within the transaction, so you need to connect it with the beginning and end of the connection.

NOTE

If you choose to use the transaction model **Treat the XLANG Schedule as a COM+ Component**, you might want to change the transaction support of the XLANG Schedule Engine component. By default, the transaction support of the *WkFlow.SysMgr* component is disabled. Therefore, if you select **Supported** for the Transaction activation, the schedule will still not run under a COM+ component. This will only be the case if you choose **Required** or **Requires New**. You are advised to select **Required** for the Transaction activation, so you do not have to change the transport support for the COM+ component. This is important to understand, since the XLANG schedule engine can run different XLANG schedules with different transaction settings.

We discussed how to connect shapes earlier in the chapter; however, there is a second way: the Connector tool. If you are familiar with Visio, you may already have noticed it. It is on the toolbar, and is the icon depicted by two white solid boxes with a line connecting them. The advantage of the Connector tool is that you do not need to select a shape first and grab a connector point. To use it:

1. Select the **Connector** tool and move the mouse pointer over the entry point of **Transaction1**. It will automatically change to a red square.

2. Press the left mouse button and move the mouse pointer to the connection point at the top of **Action1**. Again, as the mouse pointer touches this point, it turns into a red square. Release the mouse button and the connection is made. Do the same to connect **Action1** to the exit point of **Transaction1**. Now the compiler stops complaining—at least on this issue.

You can rename the shapes according to their meaning within the flow. You do this by right-clicking the shape, selecting **Properties**, and changing the value of the **Name** field. In the **Properties** dialog of **Transaction1** (Figure 7.14), you can change more than just the name; you can also change the following:

- **Type** Determines which of the three possible transaction types you want to use. We discuss their characteristics in the following sections. For now, we will just mention them:

  - **Timed Transaction** The Transaction shape is *blue* colored.

  - **Short-lived, DTC Style** This is the default transaction type, and is *gray* colored.

  - **Long-running** The Transaction shape is *beige* colored.

- **Transaction options:**

  - **Timeout (seconds)** The number of seconds after which the transaction will abort, if the transaction is still not completed. This is to prevent transactions from existing forever, or until the next system reboot. The minimal value is zero seconds; the maximum is 50,000,000 (nearly 579 days); and the default value is 60 seconds. This option is not valid for the long-running transaction type.

  - **Retry count** The number of times the transaction will be retried in case it ends prematurely; for example, if the transaction times out.

  - **Backoff time (seconds)** The number of seconds waited before retrying the transaction in case it ended prematurely. The time that is actually calculated is based on the formula Backoff_time ^ Current_Retry_Count ("^" means "raised to the power of"). This formula is also known as "Exponential Backoff." With a default value of 20 seconds and a retry count of 3, the backoff periods are 20, 400 (20★20) and 8000 (20★20★20).

  - **Isolation level** Only available for short-lived (DTC-style) transactions. For the meaning of the isolation value levels, see the sidebar "The Meaning of Transactions and the DTC."

  - **On Failure** Gives you the opportunity to run a business process after the transaction has failed. To use this option, click Add Code; the button changes to Delete Code. Clicking Add Code activates the Enabled check box. Only when you check this option will the business process actually be executed if the transaction fails. The use of Enabled comes in handy if you temporarily want to disable your

"On Failure" procedure so you can better inspect the type of failure. What the business process is that can be executed on a failure becomes apparent when you click OK. A third page, On Failure of Transaction, is added to your schedule drawing. *Transaction* is the name of the transaction, in case you did not change it to **Transaction1**.

Figure 7.14 Transaction Properties Dialog

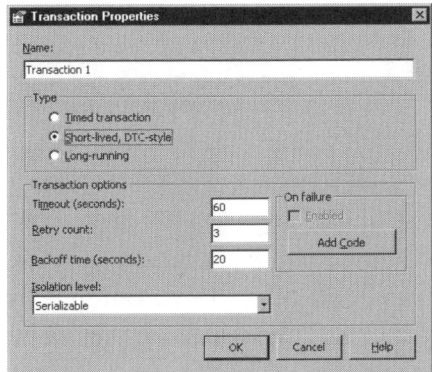

NOTE

To be able to retry a transaction, the XLANG schedule engine will save the status of the business process in the XLANG database.

You can access the **On Failure of Transaction1** page by clicking on the tab at the bottom of the BizTalk Orchestration Designer window. When you do so, you will see at least the **Begin** shape, anchoring the beginning of the process flow. If you already have Implementation and Communication shapes on the Business Process page, they will also appear on the **On Failure of Transaction1** page. In fact, if you add Implementation and Communication shapes to the **On Failure of Transaction1** page, these will also appear on the Business Process. You can have an **On Failure of Transaction** page for every Transaction shape, and for a Transaction shape that appears on an **On Failure of Transaction** page. Be careful not to go overboard with this type of page cascading; you might create more problems than you solve. The **On Failure of Transaction** page is only reached when:

- The transaction hits an abort situation, due to:

  - A timeout of the transaction (not valid for long-running transaction).

  - An Abort shape within the transaction is reached.

  - A port returns a failure it received from as Implementation shape to which it is bound.

  - A technical failure occurred.

- The transaction is retried for the specified Retry Count and still is not able to successfully finish.

After the *On Failure of Transaction* process is finished, control is handed back to the business process and it will exit the transaction, as if nothing had happened. Once the transaction is finished, the rest of the business process has no way of knowing if it succeeded or failed; only the transaction or the On Failure of *Transaction* business process can leave information behind that indicates the result of the transaction. Let's now look at the three different transaction types, when to use them, and what their special considerations are. We added a fourth special situation as well: *nested transactions*.

NOTE

When you remove a transaction from your Business Process, *On Failure of Transaction*, and *Compensation for Transaction* page, everything within the transaction is also removed, including On Failure of *Transaction* and Compensation for Transaction pages. To prevent this from happening, you need to drag all the shapes out of the (outer) transaction, delete the (outer) transaction, and reconnect the shapes in the existing flow.

Timed

A *timed* transaction is a long-running transaction that you want to end sometime in the future. This type of transaction is useful if you send out a message and wait for the response. However, since it requires human intervention to get the response, you are not sure this response will come. The transaction is aborted after the timeout period you specify in the Properties dialog, to prevent the transaction from existing indefinitely, or until the next reboot.

Long-running business processes, having at least one long-running transaction, have a mechanism that prevents the business process from occupying system resources while they are waiting for a response. This is called *dehydration*. After the response is received, the business process is *rehydrated*. Dehydration isn't useful if you have just one XLANG schedule waiting, but if you have tens or hundreds, you will understand the issue.

Dehydration takes place when a schedule is in a wait state for more than 180 seconds. Here is where the XLANG database, connected to the XLANG schedule engine, comes into play. This is called the *persistence database*, and all state information of the business process that is dehydrated is saved to this database. After that, the resources are released. The state of the business process is restored if a message arrives on a port where a response is expected, and the business process can continue executing. Since this is a timed transaction, the business process is also rehydrated if it times out. Depending on the number of retries, the transaction is retried or an abort event is raised.

NOTE

If you have never developed or administered COM components, you might wonder why dehydration takes place after 180 seconds (three minutes). Well, a COM application is allowed to be idle for three minutes (default value) before it is shut down to save system resources.

Now comes the "but"—dehydration is not always possible! This is very important to understand and to act upon, since it is technically possible that long-running transactions that cannot be dehydrated will drain the resources of the system. The following are the exceptions where dehydration is not possible:

- One or more *short-lived* (DTC-style) transactions are active. This is possible since a business process can have concurrent flows, which we discuss in the section "Flowchart, Communication, and Implementation Shapes." This is also true if a long-running transaction contains one or more DTC-style transactions.

- A component that is bound to a port is nonpersistent. A component is persistent if it holds state and supports the *IPersist* interface that enables the XLANG schedule engine to retrieve the state of the component and save it in its database. If you are not a component developer, this might seem to be a trivial remark, but Microsoft's component development guidelines always discourage the use of stateful components because of the negative impact on performance and scalability.

■ The business process is not in a full wait state. As mentioned, if you have concurrent flows in your business process, they all need to be in the same "Wait for response" state for the scheduler engine to dehydrate.

The second and third exceptions are issues that you need to address during the development process. The first exception is in most cases a temporary run-time issue.

Keep in mind that when the long-running transaction fails, committed database changes are not automatically rolled back. This is only possible with DTC-style transactions. The On Failure of Transaction page should be used to compensate eventual database changes. This touches on a very important issue: if you change database rows that are used by other applications, or worse, also *changed* by other applications, you cannot restore the "old" values without bringing the database into an inconsistent status.

Short-Lived, DTC-Style

The short-lived transaction is the "traditional" transaction (see the sidebar "The Meaning of Transactions and the DTC"), and is used to assure that tightly coupled updates of database rows are performed together or not at all. For example, say you have a banking application that processes financial transactions, among other tasks. The results of a financial transaction (e.g., a deposit) are recorded in the Transaction database and as a result, the bank's Ledger database is updated. Since both updates are directly linked, both have to be committed. In case one update fails, the other update should not take place or be rolled back. This can be accomplished by placing them in the same DTC-style transaction.

The default timeout of a short-lived transaction is 60 seconds; the same default timeout as is used by the DTC. Most DTC-style transactions are likely to be finished within this period. However, it is theoretically possible that a transaction might need nearly a minute to finish, so if the short-lived transaction period starts a few seconds earlier than the DTC transaction, you could miss a successful DTC transaction. You can prevent this from happening by setting the short-lived transaction time to, for example, 70 seconds.

Long-Running

Since a long-running transaction is the same as a timed transaction, but without the timeout, there is not much left to say about this type of transaction. You use this transaction type if you are sure a response will come; you're just not exactly sure when. For example, your business process communicates with another application over a message queue. Since both sides of the queue operate according to a predetermined protocol ,assuring a response, you do not need a timeout. You can set the retry count and backoff time for a long-running transaction because a technical failure—for example, the message queue not accepting the message— might stop the transaction from retrying.

Nested Transactions

By using nested transactions (as depicted in Figure 7.12), you create a situation that deviates at some points from the default workings of the transaction described previously. The inner transaction can finish before the outer transaction fails, thus making an automatic rollback of the inner transaction impossible. To give you the opportunity to correct this situation, you can add a **Compensation for** *Transaction* business process for the inner transaction. You can do this from the **Transaction Properties** dialog (Figure 7.15).

1. Click **Add Code** in the **Compensation** frame.
2. Toggle the **Enabled** check box.
3. Click **OK**; the Compensation for Transaction2 page is now added.

Figure 7.15 Transaction Properties Dialog for the Inner Transaction

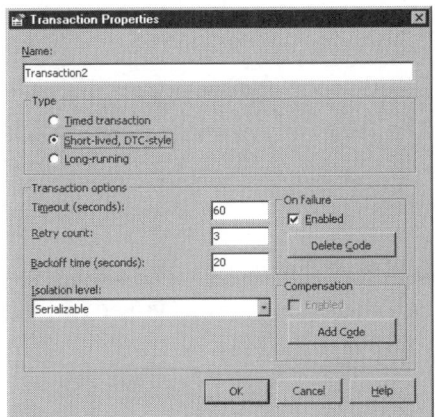

As you can see in Figure 7.15, all transaction types are enabled. You must be careful, since BizTalk Orchestration Designer allows you to make the outer transaction timed and the inner transaction long-running. If you do so, you are destined for trouble. The Transaction Properties dialog for the outer transaction (Figure 7.16) also shows some changes. First, you can no longer make use of the Short-lived, DTC-style transaction. Remember that a nested transaction cannot be rolled back after it is committed, and since that is exactly what a DTC-style is, it is ruled out as an outer transaction. Second, you can no longer retry an outer transaction, for the same reason. Retrying the outer transaction also means that you will retry the inner transaction, and since that transaction ended successfully, it should not be redone. The only way to prevent the inner transaction from being redone is not retrying the outer transaction in case of a failure. Therefore, you should not set the retry count for a transaction when it contains a nested transaction.

Figure 7.16 Transaction Properties Dialog for the Outer Transaction

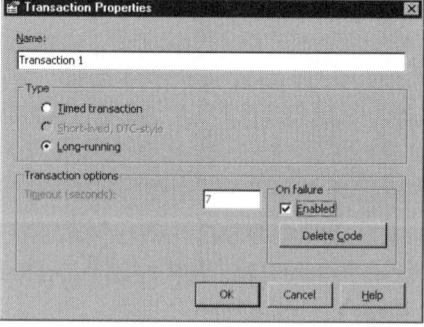

Even if the inner transaction fails, this will not automatically lead to the abortion of the outer transaction. If this is your intention, you should use the On Failure of Transaction page of the inner transaction to set a message field. After the inner transaction returns the outer transaction, it should flow in a decision that can act on the value in this message field. Let's end the discussion on transactions with a few remarks:

- A component that is instantiated within a transaction will not be available outside the transaction. In case you need the component to be available after a transaction—for example, you need to retain processing results—you must instantiate the component, using the Initialize method, before the flow goes into the transaction.

- Messages that are created in a While loop on an On Failure of *Transaction* or Compensation on *Transaction* page will not be available outside the While loop. To retain the results, you need an empty message before going into the While loop.

Flowchart, Communication, and Implementation Shapes

It is now time to discuss all the available shapes. We need to do this because we have to discuss the integration of the Orchestration Services with the Messaging Services. This process is controlled by five wizards, which are activated when you drag one of the four Implementation shapes onto the Business Process page or when you connect an Action shape with a Port shape. We discuss the wizards in the section following the *Shapes* section.

Shapes

As you go through the BizTalk Server documentation—in particular, the part that discusses the Orchestration Services—you will notice that a distinction is made between the flowchart of the Business Process page and the implementation part on that same page. The former is regarded as the domain of the business analyst, and the latter is the domain of the developer. We will follow this split, because this enables you to cross-reference this book with the BizTalk Server documentation.

Shapes from a Developer's Perspective

Since it is the responsibility of the development team to implement the business logic and link it into the business flow, the developers will work with the following shapes:

- **COM component** Links to a COM+ component and enables you to make the methods of the exposed interfaces available to the flow. Dragging this shape to the page will start the COM Component Binding Wizard. This wizard will also be started when you open the Properties dialog (right-click the Components shape, and select **Properties**). A COM Component shape can be placed on the implementation (right) side of the Business Process, and On Failure of Transaction and Compensation for Transaction pages. COM components are used to implement business logic or to be able to persist data. Especially during development, it is possible that the parameters of a component's method are modified. You need to make the schedule aware of this, by refreshing the *method signatures*. This is done by running the tool **Refreshing Method Signatures** (under **Tools**) that checks all method parameters in the schedule and applies changes to the parameters. A refresh is performed every time you compile an XLANG schedule. If you need to modify a COM component on a schedule while there are instances of that schedule still running, you need to shut down these instances before you can apply the modifications. You can perform the shutdown using the **Shut Down All Running Schedule Instances** tool (under **Tools**).

- **Script component** Links to a Windows Script component and makes all the script's methods available to the flow. Dragging this shape to the implementation side of the page starts the Script Component Binding Wizard. The same wizard will start if you open the **Properties** dialog of the Script Component shape. A Script Component shape can be placed on every page but the Data page. You can use Script components to implement business logic and persist data. You are advised not to do, so since scripts need to be interpreted during runtime, which can have a significant performance impact. Since scripts are by default nonpersistent, you should not use them in long-running transactions. However, a Script component is very useful as a mock COM component. During development, COM components will be developed parallel to the implementation of the business process. To test the flow without the COM component being available, a Script component can be made with the same methods, but these will only return a fabricated result. The sidebar "Creating Windows Script Components" describes how you can create a Script component to use with the Script Component shape.

- **Message queuing** Links to a message queue, that must exist during runtime, and makes the queue available to the process flow. Dragging the shape onto the page starts the Message Queue Binding Wizard. Opening the **Properties** dialog will also start this wizard. This shape is available on all pages, except for the Data page. Message queuing enables the business process to communicate asynchronously with other (local) applications. Message queues can be managed by the administrative tools *Computer Management* for the local server, or *Active Directory Users and Computers* for a domain.

- **BizTalk messaging** Links to a BizTalk channel that must exist during runtime, and makes the channel available to the flow. Putting the BizTalk Messaging shape on the page will start the BizTalk Messaging Binding Wizard. Opening the Properties dialog of the BizTalk Messaging shape will also start this wizard. The use of BizTalk messaging—hence, a BizTalk channel—enables the XLANG schedule to communicate, synchronously and asynchronously, with another XLANG schedule, local or remote application. See Chapter 4, "Understanding BizTalk Messaging Services" on how to manage channels.

- **Port** Used to link an Implementation shape to an action. In fact, after the binding wizard (from one of the previous four shapes) finishes, a Port shape is added to all the Business Process, On Failure of Transaction, and Compensation for Transaction pages. The port that is connected to a messaging technology contains the message that can be exchanged between the implementation technology and the action. If the port is connected to a component, it contains two messages, one for input and one for output, for every exposed method. You can also create a port that is not directly related to an Implementation shape. These unbound ports can only be connected to a messaging technology.

- **Message** Contains the definition of the message that is exchanged between an action and an implementation technology. The Message shape is only available on the Data page and cannot be removed. Message shapes are automatically added when a port is created, and automatically removed if a port is deleted. For a messaging technology, the message consists of the document and a field holding the sender of the message. This __Sender__ system field is null when a message is sent, and will contain the sender's name if the message is received. Additionally, you can specify a separate field from the document. For the component technology, you have two messages, one inbound the component and one outbound the component. The inbound message consists of the sender and the method parameters; the outbound consists of a __Status__ system field that will hold the HRESULT value of the method, the method parameters, and a field that holds the exit value of the method.

- **Port references (Data page)** This is a special type of message that contains an entry for every port on the business process page. It holds the location of the port, and when a message has to be sent to a specific port, the value of this field is used. You can also use it to populate a field—like "Reply-To"—in a message. When a port is configured for a dynamic channel or queue, you need to populate the port reference for this channel/queue. In fact, you need to draw an arrow on the reference page, to indicate which field will be used to populate it. Notice that dynamic ports—the ports that are dynamically bound to an implementation technology—have an exiting connection point (at the right side) and an incoming connection point. In fact, before you can successfully compile your schedule drawing, you have to draw a data flow arrow to that incoming connection point, so it is known which message field should be used to populate this port reference.

- **Constants** The only message on the Data page where fields can be added, deleted, or modified. As the message name already indicates, it can be used in case you need fixed values to be used in populating specific fields in outgoing messages. Here is how it works:

1. Right-click the **Constants** message, and select **Properties**. The Constant Message Properties dialog (Figure 7.17) appears. All present constants are listed.

Figure 7.17 The Constants Messages Properties Dialog

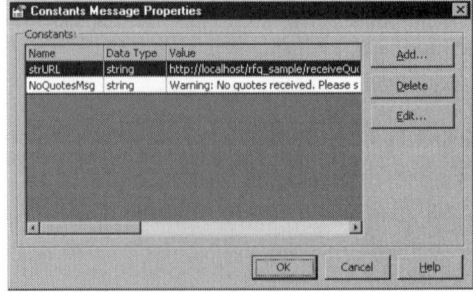

2. Click **Add** to add a constant, and **Edit** to modify the selected constant.

3. Suppose you want to edit the constant *strURL*. Select this row, click **Edit**, and the Constant Properties dialog (Figure 7.18) appears.

4. You can rename the **Name**, as long as it remains unique; change the **Data type** to one of the data types that are allowed in XML messages; and modify the **Value** of the constant. Of course, the data type and value must be in agreement with each other.

Figure 7.18 The Constant Properties Dialog

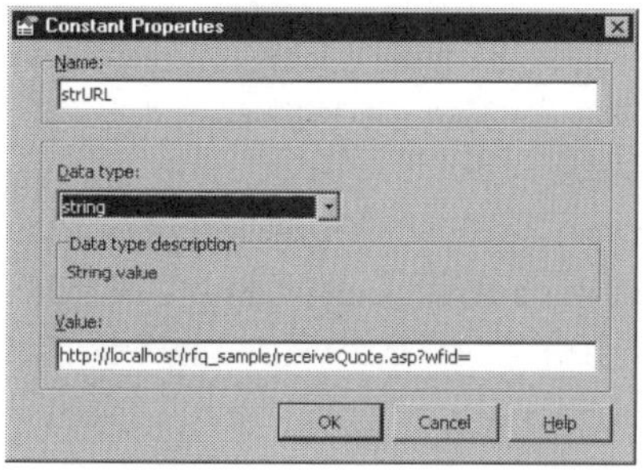

As mentioned previously, a Constants message only appears on the Data tab, and is different from the other messages. Not only is there just one Constants message, the value of every field cannot be populated by a field of any other message.

Developing & Deploying…

Creating Windows Script Components

Using Windows Script components in an XLANG schedule enables you to develop the process flow without having to wait for the necessary COM components to be available, thereby shortening the development time. By creating a Script component with the same exposed methods and parameters, you can simulate the working of a COM component.

Writing these Script components is straightforward; however, there are some rules that you must follow. The most important rule is that the script needs to be wrapped in an XML message. Microsoft has released a Windows Script Component Wizard that can create this XML wrapper in just six steps. In case you do not have this wizard yet, you can download it from msdn.Microsoft.com/scripting. Go to **Windows Scripting Components | Downloads**, and click on **Windows Script Component Wizard released**. Once you installed the wizard, you can run it from **Start | Programs | Microsoft Windows Script | Windows Script Component Wizard**. After running the wizard, a script is generated that looks similar to the following code. All you need to do is complete the function highlighted in bold. Register the Script component, and it is up and able to run!

Continued

```xml
<?xml version="1.0"?>
<component>
<?component error="true" debug="true"?>
<registration
    description="Script_Component"
    progid="ScriptComponent.WSC"
    version="1.00"
    classid="{7000a3c9-d646-4e5d-9084-d6cd4cdc1ba8}"
>
</registration>
<public>
    <method name="Method_1">
        <PARAMETER name="strDocument"/>
    </method>
</public>
<script language="VBScript">
<![CDATA[

function Method_1(strDocument)
    Dim xmldoc
    Set xmldoc = createObject("MSXML2.DOMDocument")
    xmldoc.loadXML(strDocument)
    ' The rest of the function comes here
    Method_1 = xmldoc.xml
end function

]]>
</script>
</component>
```

The value of a constant is entered during the creation of the business flow, before compiling, and will never change after compiling, unless you manually change it and recompile the XLANG schedule diagram. What, then, is the function of constants? You can use them for fixed values like a business address, the base address of your Web site, or the URL where the Active Server Pages are located. In many cases, these constants are used as part of a message value. For example, you send a message to a trading party that needs to hold a response address. This return address is an ASP page that needs to be called together with a parameter. The parameter is unique per message, and the ASP address is always the same; hence, suitable to be saved in a Constants field. To concatenate the unique parameter with the fixed ASP address, you can create a Windows Script component and populate the input parameters of the method with these two values. The output parameter contains the concatenated field.

Shapes from a Business Analyst Perspective

It is the responsibility of the business analysts to implement the business process flow. To do so analysts will work with the following shapes:

- **Begin** This shape is available on all pages that can hold a process flow; it is not available on the Flowchart stencil and cannot be deleted from the page. It is used to assure that there is only one point where a flow begins. In fact, a flow is regarded complete if it starts with a Begin and finishes with at least one End. If you do just this and compile the flow, you will create an "empty" XLANG schedule.

- **Action** This shape always needs to be bound to a port in order to receive or send a message. Since a schedule has to receive a message/document first before it can process it and send a message, the first Action shape will always receive a message and will also be the first shape that follows the Begin.

- **Decision** We referred to this shape earlier in the chapter as the *If-Then-Else* construction. This was not completely correct, since its structure is in fact:

```
If <script expression 1> Then <Start subflow 1>
If <script expression 2> Then <Start subflow 2>
If <script expression n> Then <Start subflow n>
Else <Start subflow m>
```

Every If statement is called a rule; we discuss the construction of rules in the section *Defining Rules*. To determine which sub flow to choose, the rules are evaluated, starting at the top. The sub flow of the first "script expression" that evaluates to TRUE is the one that is going to be followed. The Else flow is mandatory, as it is some kind of "Flow of Last Resort," and that flow will be followed when all other Rules evaluate to FALSE. In the script expressions, you can evaluate message fields and you are free to evaluate different fields in each script expression; there does not need to be any relations between the rules, aside from the fact that they belong to the same Decision shape. You can add rules by right-clicking the Decision shape and selecting **Add Rule**, or you can select **Properties**. The former will bring you directly to the **Rules Properties** dialog. The latter will open the **Decision Properties** dialog (Figure 7.19) first. Here you can add, delete, and edit rules, as well as change the order of rules. Since the first rule that evaluates TRUE will take the flow, the order of rules is very important.

Figure 7.19 The Decision Properties Dialog Can Be Used to Reorder Rules

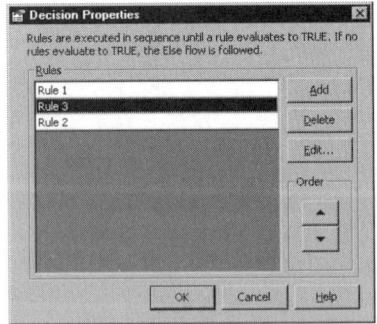

- **While** This is the only shape with loop capability. You can add one rule to the While shape; in fact, it is mandatory that you do so. If the rule evaluates to TRUE, the flow attached to the rule is followed. When the end of the flow is reached, the rule is reevaluated and so on, until the rule evaluates FALSE. In that case, the While shape is exited through the Continue and will follow that flow. To add a rule, right-click the **While** shape and select **Add Rule**. If the While shape already has a rule attached to it, instead of Add Rule, the option will be Delete Rule.

  When you want to modify the rule, right-click the rule in the **While** shape and select **Properties**. This will take you to the **Rule Properties** dialog. Now, right-click the **While** shape, select **Properties**, and the **While Properties** dialog opens. It contains one option labeled **State persistence**. By default, it is set on **No**, which is fine unless the While is part of a transaction. In that case, you might consider setting it to **Yes**. With State persistence active, the messages that are referenced in the loop are also saved in the XLANG Persistence database. If the transaction fails, the On Failure on *Transaction* flow is called for every time the loop is traversed, even if the loop is completed. If this While is part of the inner transaction of a nested transaction, and the outer transaction fails, the Compensation for *Transaction* flow is called for every time that While loop is traversed. As you will find out, all rules in While and Decision shapes are centrally stored. This means that the same rule can be used by the different shapes. This will come in handy, since processing messages will often result in performing the same check at different stages in the process. Of course, the chances are that during the development, rules may become obsolete. Without going through the hassle of removing the rules manually, you can always use the **Delete Unused Rules** utility (under **Tools**).

- **Fork** This shape can be used if you need the business process to split into two or more independent flows that will be executed concurrently. As many as 64 flows can start from a Fork, and they have to finish in an End or come together in a Join. Flows that originate from different Forks cannot come together in the same Join. Since concurrent flows run independently from each other, they cannot exchange messages or other information.

- **Join** This shape can be used to let concurrent flows that originated from the same Fork flow together into one flow. As you drag a Join on the page, you will notice that it contains the word *AND*. This is a Join type. When you right-click the **Join** shape and select **Properties**, the **Join Properties** dialog will open. It holds the Join Type as the sole property of this shape. The two values it can have are *AND* or *OR*. The default value is *AND*, which means that the flow leaving the Join will start, as soon as all incoming flows have finished. When you select *OR*, the flow that leaves the Join will be started as soon as one of the incoming flows reaches the Join. All the other concurrent flows will continue until they finish in the Join.

- **Transaction** This shape enables you to group other shapes into a transaction. We discussed this issue previously, so there is not much left to say about it, except that a transaction is not allowed to contain an AND shape. Be careful when drawing nested transactions, since only shapes that are fully within the inner transaction are regarded as part of this transaction. In the situation that a shape is not fully within the inner transaction, it will be regarded as part of the outer transaction, which can be determined by the fact that the inner Transaction shape will overlay that shape.

- **End** This shape determines the end of a flow. Every flow must have an end, which means that every business flow will have at least one End shape; unless you use the Decision, While, and/or Fork shape, you can have more than one End shape within your flowchart.

- **Abort** This shape can only be used as an end of a flow *within* a transaction. It forces the transaction to abort and to be retried, if the transaction did not reach its retry count. Abort can only be used in conjunction with a Decision and/or While shape. Although it is possible to use an Abort together with a Fork, this is not logical since it will always abort a transaction.

- **Port** This Port shape is the same one as addressed in the section *Shapes from a Developer's Perspective*. In this situation, an action will be connected to a port, which will open the XML Communication Wizard, when the port is bound to a messaging technology or it is unbound. This wizard allows you to define the message definition in that port. In case of component technology, the Component Communication Wizard will start and let you choose one of the available methods. You can connect more than one action to the same port. For a port bound to a messaging technology, it is possible to share the same message with more actions, but also have each action have its own message in that port. Ports bound to component technology can also have more actions connected to that port, only now for each action, a *Message_In* and *Message_Out* is created, even if these actions use the same Method.

  This brings us to a similar situation. When using the Orchestration Designer, notice that the ports appear on all Business Process, On Failure of *Transaction*, and Compensation On *Transaction* pages; however, the messages do not.

- **Message** This shape is created in the port after the XML Communication Wizard is finished. It represents the data that is exchanged between the action and the Implementation shape. As you right-click the **Message** shape in the port and select **Properties**, the Communication Wizard is started. Note the second option **View Message on Data Page**. If you choose this option, Orchestration Designer switches to the Data page, selects the message, and positions the page so the message is visible.

As you develop your schedule, it is likely that there will be ports and messages on the pages that you will no longer need. Instead of deleting them manually—running the risk of deleting one accidentally—you can use the utility **Delete Unused Ports and Messages** (under **Tools**). It will remove all ports that are not connected to an action and Implementation shape. If a port has more messages and at least one has a action and an Implementation shape connected to it, only the message that lacks one of the two connections is deleted. The messages are also removed from the Data page, including the data flow arrows that enter and/or exit these messages.

As mentioned under Fork and Join, more flows can run concurrently between these shapes both in your XLANG schedule diagram and in your machine. The XLANG schedule engine will instantiate a new component for each concurrent flow so it can run independently from others. In addition, since there is no provision made that lets these instantiations directly communicate with each other, they cannot exchange any messages directly. Moreover, since you are nearly never allowed to read messages from a queue, or other Implementation shapes within a concurrent flow, you also are not able to exchange messages via a queue. The reason not to allow reading messages by an Action shape within a concurrent flow is that there is no way to guarantee that a message is or will become available. This will block the concurrent flow from continuing. If you would use an OR-Join, the XLANG schedule can reach the End shape, as long as one of the concurrent flows reaches the Join. However, it will only finish if all concurrent flows have ended. If this is not the case, the schedule will not release its resources. You can imagine what this would mean for your system if this continues over time. This behavior is called "memory leak," and can slow your system or, eventually, bring it to a halt. If you are lucky, the schedule gets at least dehydrated. For example you are waiting for a message that never comes…the reason this could happen is because you had an AND-Join and one of the concurrent flows was not able to end. You will never reach the flow beyond the Join; thus, the XLANG schedule will never finish.

You will use concurrent flows to speed processing, by executing independent actions simultaneously. Of course, these actions will be based on the same input message. We discuss concurrent flows in the section *Concurrent Actions*.

Binding and Communication Wizards

The six wizards help you to easily connect your process flow to one of the four implementation technologies. We will walk through all six wizards, and show you what needs to be done to successfully put an Implementation shape on the page and connect an action to a port. These wizards are:

- COM Component Binding Wizard

- Script Component Binding Wizard

- Message Queuing Binding Wizard

- BizTalk Messaging Binding Wizard

- XML Communication Wizard

- Component Communication Wizard

COM Component Binding Wizard

Dragging the **COM Component** shape to the implementation part of the Business Process page launches the COM Component Binding Wizard:

1. The Welcome screen will prompt you to **Create a new port** and you can enter an appropriate name. Going through these wizards we keep the default name, this is **Port_*number*** (where number starts with 1 and is always the last used number plus one). In our case *Port_1*, as we start with an empty XLANG Schedule drawing.

2. Click **Next** and you will be brought to the page **Static or Dynamic Communication** (Figure 7.20). You can choose from three options:

   - **Static** The default value, meaning that the component is instantiated (started) by the XLANG Scheduler Engine on behalf of the schedule. Therefore, you will need to provide the exact component you need to be instantiated.

   - **Dynamic** The component is already instantiated at the time the schedule needs it. This is done by another schedule or application. In order to access that component, the schedule/application that instantiated the component needs to send you a message containing the address (moniker) of that component. You can recognize a dynamic component in your drawing by the gray shadow around the rectangle.

- **No instantiation** Allows another application to send this schedule instance a message, without the need for a component to be instantiated. At the end of this section is an example of a noninstantiation component. You can recognize a dynamic component in your drawing by the black shadow around the rectangle.

Figure 7.20 Choosing Static or Dynamic Communication for a COM Component Binding

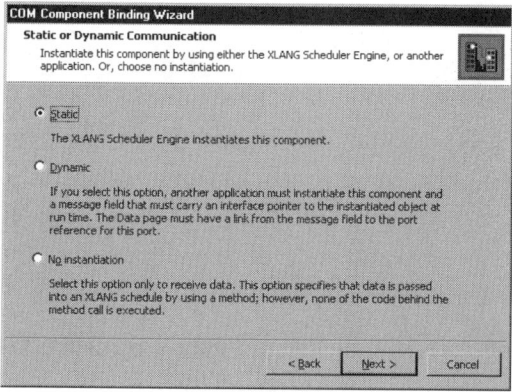

3. Click **Next**, and you are prompted to select a COM component interface. Depending on your previous choice of static or dynamic, the dialog differs slightly:

- For **Static**, you need to select class **From a registered component** or **From a moniker**. The latter is the address (pathname) of the component, which does not need to be on the local computer. Proceed to step 4.

- For **Dynamic** and **No instantiation**, you need to directly select an **Interface** from a Component class. This means that this component needs to be known to the local machine. Proceed to step 5.

4. Click **Next**, and if the selected class has more than one interface, the wizard will present you a list of available interfaces. You need to select one before you can continue.

5. Click **Next**, and if the interface has more than one method, you can select all the methods you want to use in your schedule (Figure 7.21).

Figure 7.21 Select the Component's Methods for Use in the Schedule

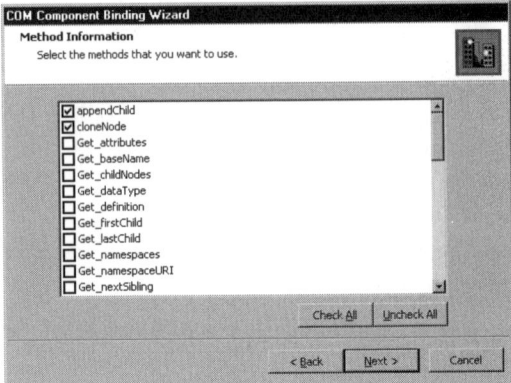

6. Click **Next**, and the **Advanced Port Properties** page appears (Figure 7.22). These settings must correspond to the properties/characteristics of the selected component. If they do not, you will be confronted by run-time errors, since the schedule will use the component incorrectly. The page has the following frames:

- **Security** If it is *Not required*, the XLANG scheduler engine will make no attempt to get a confirmation on the sender's identity. The __Sender__ will remain empty. If you select **Optional** or **Required**, the scheduler engine will attempt to get a confirmation of the sender's identity. In the former situation, the method call will go through, while in the latter situation, the call is rejected. If the identity is established, the sender's identity will be put in __Sender__.

- **Transaction Support** This setting must agree with the transaction support of the component. By default, the transaction support value of the component is selected. The possible settings are:

  a. Disabled Indicates that the component is "mute" for anything that is related to transactions. The sole benefit is that this cuts down on system overhead. It is not advisable to use this setting unless the component has transaction support disabled, or unexpected runtime errors can occur.

b. Not Supported Indicates that the component can be run from a transaction, but will not participate in a transaction or start one on its own. This value is the default setting for transaction support.

c. Supported Indicates that the transaction can participate in a transaction, but will not start one on its own.

d. Required Indicates that the component needs to be part of a transaction. In the case that it is not started from inside a transaction, it will start a transaction on its own.

e. Required New Indicates that the component always starts a new transaction, since it wants to control its own transaction context.

- **State management support** This setting tells the XLANG scheduler engine what to do with the component when it dehydrates the schedule. There are three options:

   a. Holds no state In this case, the scheduler engine can shut down the component and instantiate it when the schedule is rehydrated.

   b. Holds State, but doesn't support persistence Since the component is stateful, the scheduler engine cannot shut it down as it dehydrates the schedule, without causing the state of the component to be lost. Moreover, since it is not persistence, the component cannot be saved to disk. Therefore, the component is kept running, in the hope that it is still alive when the schedule is rehydrated.

   c. Holds State, and does support persistence This stateful component has a IPersist interface implemented, enabling the scheduler engine to write the component to persistent storage (disk) and bring the component back in memory as the schedule gets rehydrated.

- **Error Handling** This setting determines what the XLANG scheduler engine must do with a transaction as the component returns an error. The option *Abort the transaction if the method returns a failure HRESULT* can only be used if the component is part of a transaction. When you select this option without the component being part of a transaction, the compiler will report an error. The meaning of this option is clear; if the component is not able to successfully complete the method call, thus returning a failure HRESULT in the __Status__ of the *Message_Out*, the scheduler engine will abort the transaction.

Figure 7.22 Set the Advanced Port Properties Reflecting the Component Characteristics

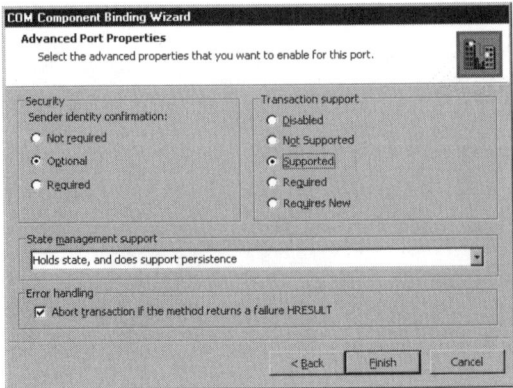

7. You have reached the end of the wizard, and by clicking **Finish**, the wizard will create a port and a COM Component shape that can be used in the business flow. Remember, the port is still empty, since the XML Communication Wizard has not been run.

Now we get back to the noninstantiating COM component. Suppose you send out a message and the recipient of the message needs to send you a response. The question is, where should this message be dropped off? There are some issues: first, the recipient lives somewhere on the Internet; second, the communication is asynchronous and you expect a response somewhere down the flow; and third, this response should be delivered to this specific instance of the XLANG schedule instance, although more instances of the same XLANG schedule can exist at the same time.

The solution sounds simple: you tell the recipient the exact location that they can deliver the response. But how? This is where the fun part comes in.

■ You create a port in your XLANG schedule drawing, where you expect the documents to be delivered.

■ You make the schedule instance identifier (GUID) part of the //Reply-to field in the message. Remember, this GUID is part of every port reference.

■ You create an Active Server Page on your Web server that can intercept the reply and transfer it to the port. This means that the //Reply-to field also has to hold the HTTP address of this ASP—although HTTPS is better, security wise. The Reply-to might look something like this: https://www.company.com/pickupdoc.asp?InstanceId=sked:// host1!groupmgr1/{4CCA62DA-00ED-4418-8CE6- 9ED3BDBDF3DC}. Note: The part to the right of "InstanceID=" is a moniker.

- To do this, you need to create a component with a method that the ASP can call to hand over the moniker (InstanceId) and the document. Let's call this method *HandOver*.

- Up to this point, it has been straightforward, but now we have to address the noninstantiated component. To do this, you create an empty method that has one string parameter that can be used to pass the document. Lets call this empty method *ReceiverPort*.

- In the XLANG schedule drawing, you create a COM component port that has *ReceiverPort* selected as the method. Of course, before this, you have to register the component on your local system.

- The method *HandOver* does the actual trick. Since *ReceiverPort* is a method turned port, you can address it by adding "/ReceiverPort" to the *InstanceID*, making it into the moniker of the port. *HandOver* can now access the port by calling:

```
oRcvPort = GetObject(InstanceID & "/ReceiverPort")
oRcvPort.ReceiverPort(sDocument) 'passing the document.
```

This works, even though there is no code in the *ReceiverPort* function, and it does not have to be instantiated to be active. Two final remarks:

- A port on a XLANG schedule diagram is in fact an interface to a component, which means that COM+ components can reference ports on your diagram directly.

- In the preceding example, we used an ASP page, but there are more ways you can use this same technique of noninstantiated components; for example, using ISAPI, IBM MQSeries, or any other solution that can make a call to the noninstantiated component.

NOTE

You may not know what is meant by the term *moniker*, so let's take a quick look at what a moniker entails. Basically, a moniker is the name of an instantiated component. In most cases, a component that can be called through a moniker is persistent. It is explicitly stated that the component is instantiated, which implies that each instantiation of the same component has its own unique moniker. The moniker is an indirect way of calling the component, since there is a process that needs to bind the actual component instance based on the moniker. The advantage is that you do not need to know what kind of class type the component is; this is handled by the binding process. There are different types of monikers; for example, file and URL. Another advantage of a moniker is that the component does not has to be on the local machine, as is mandatory with calling registered components.

A little further on you will see an example of a moniker, and in Figure 7.25 you see that the moniker of a Windows Script component is the path and filename of the script.

Script Component Binding Wizard

The Script Component Binding Wizard is very similar to the COM Component Binding Wizard—which makes sense, since they act similarly. Nevertheless, we will go through the wizard step by step:

1. First, **Create a new port**; again, use a name that fits its functions. In our case *Port_2*, is suggested, since we used Port_1 in the previous wizard.

2. Click **Next**, and you will be asked to choose Static or Dynamic communication. This is the same as with the COM Component Binding Wizard.

3. Click **Next**, and supply the name of the Windows Script component (Figure 7.23). You can click **Browse** to find the file to use. If you chose Dynamic or Noninstantiation in the previous step, you can go to step 5. Note that noninstantiation is also a form of dynamic communication.

4. Click **Next**. If you chose Static Communication in step 2, you have to make a choice in the way you want to instantiate the Script component. You have two options (Figure 7.24):

- **Use a moniker of the script file** The default moniker is the name of the file. If you use a moniker, you do not need to register the component.

- **Use the ProgID** This option is selected by default.

Figure 7.23 Select the File with the Windows Script Component

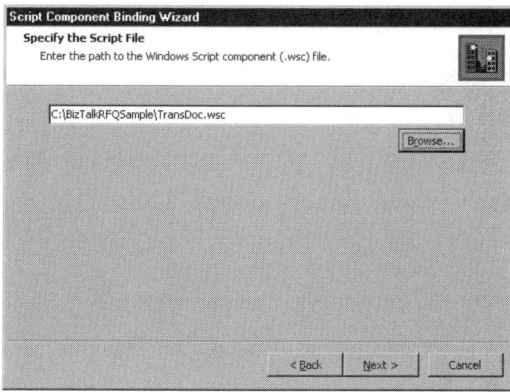

Figure 7.24 Select the Way in Which the Script Component Must Be Instantiated

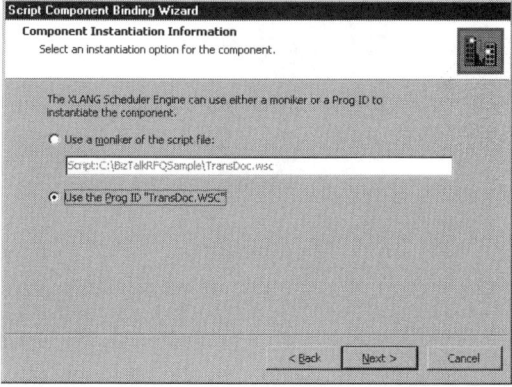

5. Click **Next**, and if the interface has more than one method, you can select all the methods you want to use in your schedule (see Figure 7.21 for a similar screen representation).

6. Click **Next**, and you will enter the **Advanced Port Properties** page. This screen is the same as the COM Component page (Figure 7.22), except for the State Management Support option. For an explanation of

Security, Transaction Support, and Error Handling, see the section "COM Component Binding Wizard."

7. Clicking **Finish**, and the wizard will create a port and a Script Component shape that can be used in the business flow. Again, the port is still empty, since the XML Communication Wizard has not been run.

Message Queuing Binding Wizard

Dragging the Message Queuing shape onto the Business Process page will launch the Message Queuing Binding Wizard. It will create a port that enables you to access a message queue. The wizard goes through the following steps:

1. As with the Component Binding Wizard, you are asked for a port name; only now, you are presented with an option. Besides the option to **Create a new port**, you can also use an **Existing unbound port** (Figure 7.25). As discussed earlier in this chapter, if you create an unbound port you can only bind it to a messaging technology.

Figure 7.25 Select the Port for the Message Queue

2. Click **Next**, and you must choose from the following options (Figure 7.26):

   ▪ **Static queue** This queue must exist during runtime. An additional limitation is that BizTalk Server does not support access to a queue on another computer. This is not a serious problem, since you can use a local queue to forward the messages to the desired remote queue. How this is done is beyond the scope of this chapter.

- **Dynamic queue** The queue name can only be known during runtime, since the schedule must first get a message that informs which queue must be used. Therefore, is it necessary that you get to the Data page and draw a data flow arrow between the field that will hold the queue name and the port reference for this port. You can recognize a dynamic message queue in your drawing by the gray shadow around the rectangle and the word *Dynamic*, instead of the queue name. If you choose **Dynamic Queue**, you can skip step 3.

Figure 7.26 Selecting a Static or Dynamic Queue

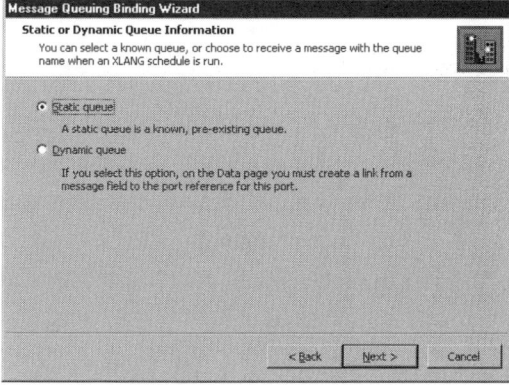

NOTE

Although mentioned previously in this chapter, the following is so important that we restate it here:

As you use dynamic queues, channels, or components, you must indicate during development how its location can be determined. You do this on the Data page by connecting the message field that is expected to carry this information to the Port Reference field. The compiler checks if this is a feasible connection. If it is, the schedule drawing compiles nicely. However, during runtime, things can still go wrong if the queue name, channel name or moniker is incorrect; hence, not referencing an existing object. A way to prevent this is to add a component that can validate this value before you use it. In case it does not correlate to an existing queue, channel, or component, you can take control of the situation, without your XLANG schedule crashing because of the incorrect data.

3. Click **Next**, and you are prompted for a choice of queue (Figure 7.27):

- **Create a new queue for every instance** The XLANG scheduler engine creates a new queue for every instance of this schedule. As the schedule ends, the scheduler engine removes the queue. When you choose this option, you have to enter the queue prefix that is made up out of the folder where the queues have to be created. By default, this is *.\private$*. This folder is a relative path from the directory where all the queues are stored. The queue name prefix is by default the port name. The XLANG scheduler will tag a unique identifier to it.

   You want to choose this option if the schedule engine has to communicate with another application, where you send a message to the other application, or schedule informing it what queue to use. If the other party is also a schedule, it will have a dynamic queue port defined to use for this communication. For example, your schedule receives orders and has to check if the items are in stock. Therefore, it communicates with another schedule that can query the stock database. Since you want that "stock" schedule to send the information to the correct instance, it has to send it to a queue that is unique to this instance.

- **Use a known queue for all instances** An existing queue, at least during runtime, is used and shared by all instances. If you select this option, you have to enter the full queue name; for example, .\public$\collectorqueue. Again, the compiler does not check if this is an existing queue. Double check for typos, or you might experience unexpected runtime errors.

   There are two types of situation in which you can use a shared queue. Take the situation of a banking application, where the schedule has to process a money transfer. One action for all transfers is to update the bank's ledger. This is a central application, so each instance sends a message to the ledger's queue, and that application will take care of it. In the second situation, you have all the bank's branch offices make use of the same central application in the main office. Therefore, they all send their transaction messages to a central queue. You constructed a component to monitor the queue, and if the number of messages reaches preset thresholds, it will instantiate a new schedule to process the transactions. The processing XLANG schedule instantiations use a *decision* to keep reading messages from the queue, until it is empty. Once the queue is empty, the instance will end itself. In this case, you want the instances to also share a queue.

Figure 7.27 Choose Whether a Schedule Instance Needs a Private or Shared Queue

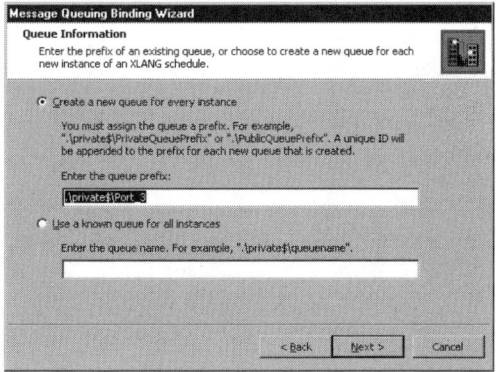

4. Click **Next**, which will bring you to the **Advanced Port Properties** page (Figure 7.28). It consists of two frames:

   - **Security** This has one or two options. The second option, **Use a Windows Group or User Name to control the queue**, is only presented if you defined this queue as static. It gives you the opportunity to determine which user or group is allowed to enter messages in the queue. So, what user/group should you enter? The most obvious choice is the user who runs the XLANG scheduler engine, since he owns the process that runs your schedule instances. Remember, the XLANG scheduler engine is a COM+ application, and every COM+ application is started under the security context of an existing user. Therefore, if you want to restrict access to the queue, you should enter the user that starts the XLANG scheduler engine, or in case you have more applications that host XLANG schedules, you can create a group for these users and enter the group's name. Be careful, since you have to enter the name manually and the compiler does not check if this is a valid name. Therefore, if you make a typo, no one is allowed to enter messages in the queue and the schedule will probably abort. If this happens, check the event log, and you should see an error message that explains your misfortune.

     The other option, **Sender identity conformation**, is one we also saw in the other two wizards. It tells the scheduler engine how to handle sender identity:

a. **Not required** The XLANG scheduler engine will not attempt to establish the sender's identity, and the __**Sender**__ field will remain empty.

b. **Optional** The scheduler engine attempts to get a conformation on the sender's identity. In case it does, the identity is put in the __Sender__ field. If the identity could not be established, the __Sender__ field remains empty, but the message is allowed through.

- **Required** The scheduler engine must to be able to get a confirmation on the sender's identity. If it does, the identity is put in the __Sender__ field. However, if it is not possible to get that confirmation the message is not allowed through and the message is put in the queue .\private$\xlang scheduler.deadletter.

- **Transaction Support** Has one option: **Transactions are required with this queue.** This option is directly related to the *transactional* setting of the queue. In fact, if the setting of both does not agree, it will result in a runtime error. You should use this option if the queue is part of a transaction. The scheduler engine will address the queue in a different way if it is transactional. Since it also means more overhead, it should only be used if necessary. Remember that an aborted transaction results in a rollback, meaning that the message in a transactional queue will be retracted. Indeed, it means that a message is only released by the queue if the transaction succeeds.

Figure 7.28 Set the Advanced Port Properties of the Queue

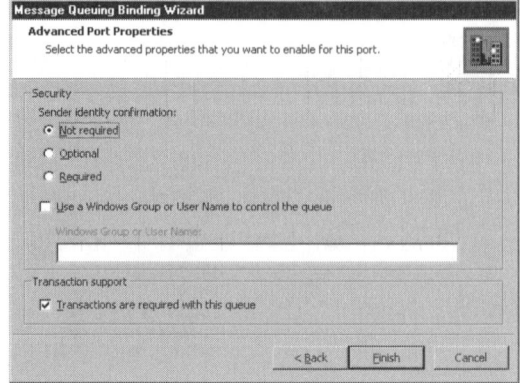

BizTalk Messaging Binding Wizard

The BizTalk Messaging Binding Wizard is the last of the implementation technology wizards. It helps you create a port that is connected to a channel.

1. This step is the same as with message queuing; you can **Create a new port** or use an **Existing unbound port**.

2. Click **Next**, and you are prompted for the **Communication Direction**: **Send** or **Receive**. Note the remark "This Wizard only enables receive through HTTP URLs." If you choose **Receive**, go to step 4. If you choose **Send**, proceed to the next step.

3. Click **Next**; this will bring you to the **Static or Dynamic Channel Information** page. When selecting the **Static channel**, you need to enter an existing channel. Remember, the existence of the channel is not checked, but needs to exist during runtime or the instance will fail, so again, check for typos. If you choose the **Dynamic Channel**, make sure that you go to the Data page to indicate which field is going to populate the Port Reference for this channel, and proceed to step 6.

4. Since you have chosen to receive messages over a channel, you are shown the **XLANG Schedule Activation Information** page. It prompts you with the sentence "Confirm whether the BizTalk Messaging channel is configured to activate a new schedule instance upon message arrival." You use this if a message that arrives through this type of channel will start the business flow. You will use this option frequently to start a schedule. Every message will create a new instance of the XLANG schedule. If this is what you want, select the **Yes** radio button. This choice is only allowed for the first action after the Begin. If you use it somewhere else in the flow, the compiler will generate an error dialog. Note that the sentence "This port cannot be used in multiple receive actions or within a single receive action in a loop" is related to the **Yes** option. However, if you want or need to receive more messages over this BizTalk channel, since it is going to be used for a regular exchange of messages between your XLANG schedule and another application or schedule, choose the **No** radio button. If you selected **Yes**, go to step 6.

5. You now have to enter the **Channel name** and **The HTTP URL address where the BizTalk Messaging Service receives documents**. Of course, both need to exist during runtime, or the schedule will abort.

6. Click **Finish**, and a channel port is created. Notice that if you selected **Yes** in step 4, the shape on the page will state "Activate."

XML Communication Wizard

The XML Communication Wizard helps you in connecting the action to a port and defining the message structure that goes in and out of the port. Since there is little difference between a port connected to the Message Queuing technology and BizTalk, we will walk the wizard for both of them at the same time:

1. As you connect an action with a Messaging port, the Welcome page will prompt you for the direction the message will be flowing; if it will **Send** or **Receive** a message. For a BizTalk messaging queue, this option is disabled because when you defined the port, you already decided on send or receive. When you choose **Send** the message will be put in the queue and the flow will continue. If you choose **Receive**, the action will read a message out of the queue, or wait until one arrives. To prevent the flow from waiting indefinitely for a message, you can enter a time period for the flow to wait for a message. By default, it does not wait (zero seconds), and it will continue even if there is no message. You should take notice of this, especially if other messages, or even port references, depend on this message. If the period you entered is longer than 180 seconds, the XLANG scheduler engine will dehydrate the instance, assuming you did not change the default dehydration threshold. You will use this timeout option only when the message does not come in on a regular basis, the flow incorporates the control on the availability of the message, and the flow can proceed even without the message. If you do not take care of the situation in which no message is available, the schedule instance will exit with a runtime exception.

2. Click **Next**, and you enter the next page that prompts you for **Message Information** (Figure 7.29). At this point, you can **Create a new message** for that port, or **Add a reference to an existing message**. In the former, a new message will be created on the Data page. In the latter, an existing message is used. This should be used if you want to send out the same message (document) as you received.

3. Click **Next**. This will bring you to the **XML Transformation** page, which deals with transforming XML documents to strings, and vice versa. Remember, the messages/documents within BizTalk are in XML format,

which is not necessarily the case for the applications that exchange data with your schedule. Here you have to decide if the document you send needs to be stripped of its XML format—also called its *wrapper*—or whether you have to add an XML wrapper in case you receive a document in string format. If you are sending a message to the queue, you have to choose between **Send XML messages to the queue** and **Send messages to the queue as string**. For receiving messages, the choices are **Receive XML messages from the queue** or **Receive string messages from the queue**. When you select to use string messages, a field called **StringData** is added to the message. It will hold the document that is stripped from its XML wrapper. The field Document is still in the message and holds the XML version of the message.

Figure 7.29 Choose between Creating a New Message or Referencing an Existing One

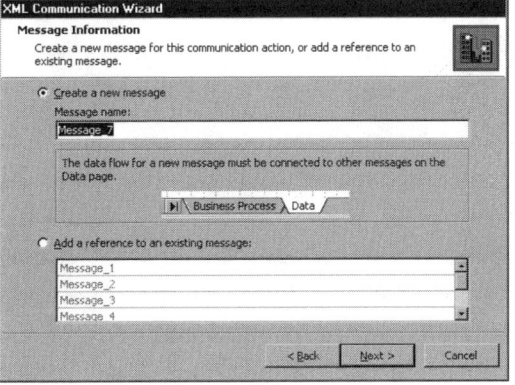

4. Click **Next** to go to the **Message Type Information** page. Here you have to enter a message type, which is a label that is tagged at the front of the message when you send a message, or is used to verify an incoming message. How exactly do you use this? Let's go back to our financial transaction application. The branch offices are still sending their transactions to the main office. We decided that internal money transfers, or those that travel between accounts within the bank, and external transfers, which come or go to an account of another bank, will be handled by different schedules. Since we do not want to change the infrastructure and we just want to keep that one queue, we use different message types: "Internal" for internal transfers, and "External" for external transfers—not very original, but effective. The application (schedule) that is running at

the branch office can distinguish between the two types, and uses two different message contents on the same queue port. The message with the content for the internal money transfers will be tagged with the type "Internal," and the message content for the external money transfers carry the "External" tag. Now both types of transfers are received at the main office where the two different schedules are running. One schedule will look for messages with the type "Internal," and the other for those with "External" as the message type.

This example shows the benefit of using message types; the drawback is that this is a mandatory field. What if the application we are talking to is unaware of message labels? If the scheduler engine is unable to match the message label with the message type, it will verify if the root element of the XML message is equal to the message type, and when it does, you also have a match. The advice is to use the XML root element name as the message type, which is easier to correlate anyway. Remember, messages that cannot be matched remain in the queue. If you selected **Send messages to the queue as string** or **Receive string messages from the queue** in the previous step, you can skip step 5.

5. As you click **Next** you enter the last page in the XML Communication Wizard, in which you can specify the **Message Specification Information** (Figure 7.30). Initially, the **Message specification** field is empty, the **Validate messages against the specification** is disabled, but will be enabled as a message specification is selected, and the **Message fields** list holds by default two fields __**Sender**__ and **Document**. This page is the same for sending and receiving messages. You do not need to select a message specification; however, if you do, you can then do the following:

- Validate incoming messages on their correct specification.

- Single out fields that can be used in decisions or other data processing. To fully benefit from the use of a specification option, you need to select a XML specification file that is made by the BizTalk Editor. If you do not have one, you can create it by clicking **Add**, or if you have a sample message, you can import that in the BizTalk Editor and then save it. More information on the BizTalk Editor can be found in Chapter 5 "Specifications and Mapping." Use the Browse option to select the specification file that should be used for this port. Once you select the specification file:

- The **Add** button becomes the **Edit** button. Note that if the selected file is not a specification file that is created with the BizTalk Editor, you will receive an error message.

- The **Validate messages against the specification** option is enabled.

- The **Add** in the Message fields is enabled. When you select the check box **Validate messages against this specification**, all incoming messages on this port are checked against this specification. Only messages that conform to this specification are allowed in; all other messages will be put in the dead-letter queue. This option is not used for outgoing messages. The **Message fields** frame lets you **Add** fields (nodes) from the XML specification to your message definition. Fields that are not part of the specification structure cannot be added or edited. Only the fields you added to the Message fields can be removed. **Document** and __**Sender**__ can never be removed from the list. The fields are addressed by their node path, and the syntax of the node path conforms to the XPath standard. Singling out fields has the following benefits:

- If you are receiving a message, you can use these fields in Rules for a Decision and While shape.

- If you are sending a message, you can fill these fields with values from other messages. You do this by data flow arrows on the Data page. When you click **Add** for Message fields, the **Field Selection** Dialog (Figure 7.31) appears and shows you the XML structure from the specification file. Once a node is selected, its node path will appear in that field. Click **OK** to add it to the list.

6. Click **Finish**, and a message, together with a connection between an action and a port, is created.

Figure 7.30 Selecting a Message Specification that Can Be Used to Access Message Fields

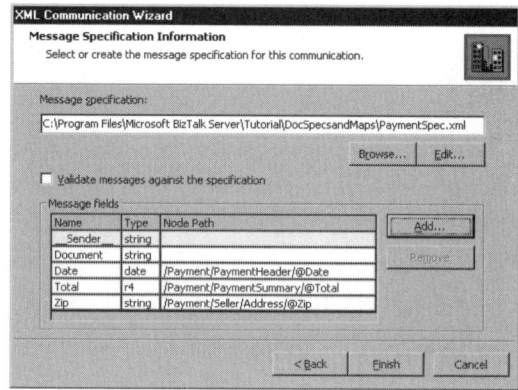

Figure 7.31 Select a Field in the Field Selection Dialog to Add to the Message

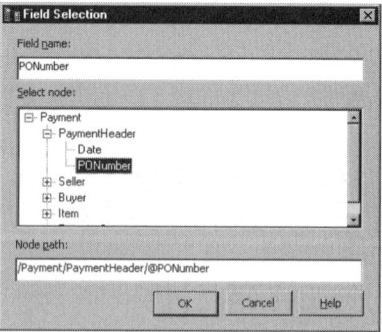

Component Communication Wizard

The Component Communication Wizard, used for both the COM component and the Script component, resembles the XML Communication Wizard; however, it is limited by the fact that you can only select an available method. Let's walk through this wizard:

1. At the Welcome page you are prompted whether the action will **Initiate a synchronous method call** or if it will **Wait for a synchronous method call**. The former means that the XLANG scheduler engine will make that method call on behalf of the schedule and then wait for the response. In the latter, it will wait for another application to make the call and relay the response to the action. When using the noninstantiated component, you make use of this way of interacting with the

schedule. To prevent the schedule from waiting forever, you can enter a wait period. By default, this is zero, which means that you expect that the method call has already been made when you arrive at that point in the schedule. A period longer than 180 seconds will force the schedule to be dehydrated.

2. Click **Next**, and you will go to the **Message Information** page (Figure 7.32). Here you can choose to **Create a new message** for the method call, or **Add a reference to an existing synchronous message pair**. The latter is useful if you want to make a method call for which a message already exists, although you can make a new message pair for a call to the same method. If you choose **Add a reference to an existing synchronous message pair**, go to step 4.

Figure 7.32 Select to Create a New Message, or Use an Existing One for a Method Call

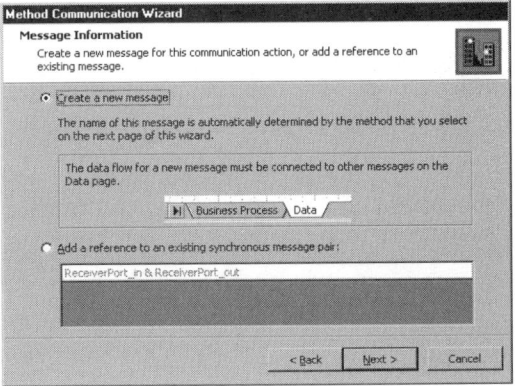

Note that the Component Communication Wizard explicitly mentioned synchronous method calls. You may or may not know that there are also *asynchronous* method calls. Why you cannot use asynchronous method calls within XLANG scheduler will be addressed shortly, but first we will discuss what you need to know about synchronous calls.

The only thing important to remember is that a synchronous method call will only return when the component returns with a result or an error. This means that the processing of the XLANG schedule only continues after the method call returns. Asynchronous method calls directly return without waiting for the result. If you used asynchronous method calls in your code, it would continue executing, without the delay of waiting. Of course, this assumes that the code does not directly need the result to continue. Once the called component has finished and has something to return, be it a result or an error, it will make a "callback." Therefore, the calling component has a callback function that is called to hand over the result. An example of the use of asynchronous functions is a main program requesting information, like status info, from different services on the same or on other systems. It needs this information for logging or processing information, but the processing will only start after the information is returned. Moreover, since you do not know how much time it takes for the component to return, you can "poll" one after the other component and process the information as is comes in. Technically, this will mean that after the asynchronous component calls the callback function; this function needs to save the returned information in a place—for example, in a object queue—that the main procedure can regularly check to see if a result has arrived, and if so, take it from the queue and process it.

So, why is it not possible to use asynchronous method calls in XLANG schedules? First, since the flow would not wait for the result, the schedule can end before the result is returned. Second, if the result is returned, it is not clear how the XLANG schedule has to handle it. Remember, the result is returned through a callback function, which works differently than a component that makes a synchronous call to a port, where the in- and out-result are bound together in one port. Asynchronous communication can be easily achieved through messaging, so there is no need to make complex provisions to be able to handle asynchronous method calls.

3. Click **Next** to arrive at the last page, **Message Specification Information** (Figure 7.33). Here, you can select one of the available methods. Below this field are two lists: **IN Fields** and **OUT Fields**. The IN lists the __Sender__, which may hold the identity of the caller, and the method's parameters. The OUT lists the __Status__, which will hold the HRESULT, the parameters, and the method (function) result, if relevant. You are not able to modify the fields, and you need to populate the parameters on the Data page.

4. Click **Finish** and the connection is added. Notice that on the Data page, the IN and OUT messages are fused together and act as a single unit.

Figure 7.33 Select One of the Available Methods for the Component

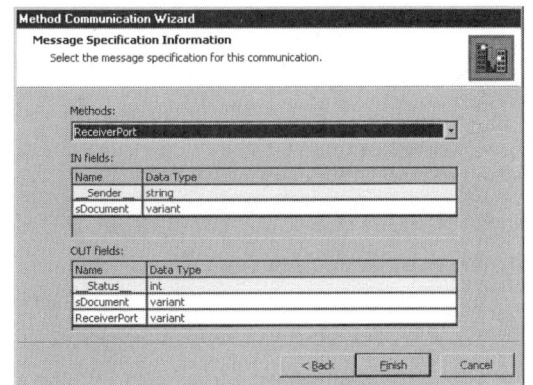

Defining Rules

Earlier in this chapter, we discussed the Decision and While shapes, and mentioned that both use rules. We mentioned how you can add rules, but not how to define them. Before we do this, let's quickly review how you can add and access rules for a Decision and While shape.

After you drag the Decision shape onto the page, it only has an **Else** exit from the shape. You can add rules to the shape by right-clicking the shape and selecting **Add Rule** that will open the **Add Rule** dialog (Figure 7.35), or you can select **Properties** instead—of course, after right-clicking the Decision shape. In this case, the **Decision Properties** dialog appears (Figure 7.34) and you can click **Add** to go to the **Add Rule** dialog. If you need to reorder the rules, you need to open the **Decision Properties** dialog to do so.

Figure 7.34 Manage Rules from the Decision Properties Dialog

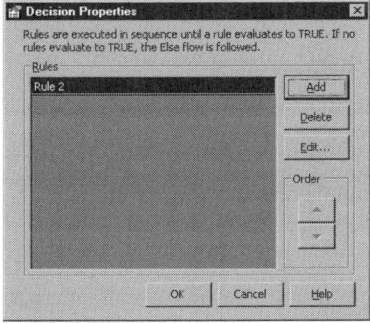

Figure 7.35 Create a New Rule, or Select an Existing One for a *While* or *Decision* Shape

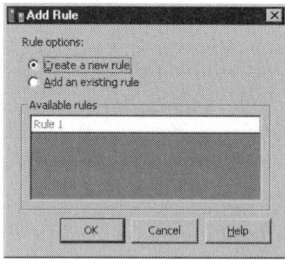

Once you are in the **Add Rule** dialog, you have the option to **Create a new rule** or **Add an existing rule**. The latter means rules that are defined for other Decision and While shapes and not yet used for this Decision.

For the While it is a little different, since it can only have one rule, but as you first drag it on the page, it only has the mandatory **Continue** exit. When you right-click the shape, you can select **Add Rule**, which presents the **Add Rule** dialog (Figure 7.35). Once you have a rule in place, you can only replace it by first deleting the current one by right-clicking the **While** and selecting **Delete Rule**.

The quickest way to edit a rule is to double-click it, or right-click it and select **Properties**. With the Decision shape, you can also do this using the **Decision Properties** dialog.

Now that we have this out of the way, we can focus on defining rules. Let's first look at what comprises a rule. Open the **Rule Properties** dialog (Figure 7.36). Select **Create a new rule** from the **Add Rule** dialog, and click **OK**.

Figure 7.36 Use the Rule Properties Dialog to Enter the Script Expression of the Rule

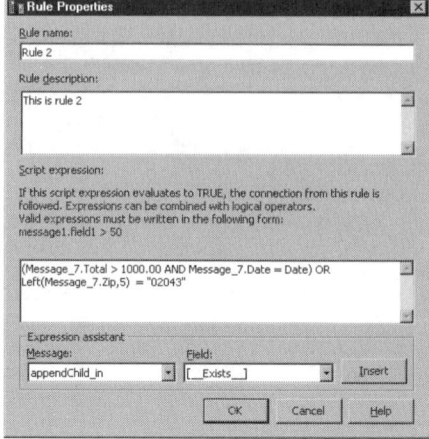

The first field is Rule name; use a name that is no longer than 32 characters and tells you what the rule does. Since the whole rule name is placed in the shape, the shape can become very wide! The **Rule description** leaves you much more room to explain what the rule is about. Of course, a real IT professional will leave it blank! The second part of the dialog is the most interesting: the **Script Expression** and its **Expression assistant**. The Expression assistant is initially disabled, but will be enabled as soon as the cursor is placed in the **Script Expression** window. The Expression assistant is a convenience that helps you limit the chances of a typographical error, and saves you a great deal of frustration. It lists all messages that are available from the Data page, and all the available fields for each message. Single out the field you want to use, click **Insert**, and it is placed in your script expression.

The Script expression is any correct VBScript expression that:

- Evaluates the value of message fields; for example, *Message_7.Total > 1000.00, Left(Message_7.Zip, 5) = "02043"*, or *Message.[__Sender__] = "administrator"*. Notice the use of the square brackets for system fields starting with an underscore. Remember, **Constants** is also a message that can be used in an expression.

- Evaluates the existence of a message; for example, *Message_7 .[__Exists__]*. Notice that __Exists__ does not appear as a field in a message, and is in fact not an existing system field.

- Uses built-in VBScript functions; for example, *Date, Time* or *Left*.

- Can be evaluated to TRUE or FALSE.

When you compile the drawing, the Script expression is checked and an error will be generated if:

- The expression is empty.

- The general syntax is incorrect; for example, if you missed a bracket or mistyped AND or OR.

However, you will get no errors if:

- There are misspelled message and/or field names. For example, *Messgae_7.[Exists]* has two spelling errors, but will not result in a compile error.

- It uses different data types on both sides of an equation; for example, *Message_7.Total = "ABCD"*; *Message_7.Total* has data type "r4" (Real), and *"ABCD"* is obvious a string.

If, during the execution of the XLANG schedule in the evaluation of the VBScript expression, an error is encountered, it will not able to successfully complete. Therefore, double-check the script expressions on this type of mistake.

Concurrent Actions

Previously, we discussed the Fork and Join shape and the possibilities of flows that run parallel to one another. What we did not discuss are the rules that you have to obey so your flows make it through the compile phase. A quick recap: the Fork lets you split a single stream into a maximum of 64 concurrent flows. This is more than enough—why? Try putting 64 concurrent flows on one page! The Join brings the concurrent flows back together and can do this in two ways:

- **AND** The Join waits for all concurrent flows to finish before continuing the flow.

- **OR** The Join waits for the first concurrent flow to reach the Join before continuing. The other flows will finish.

To make a concurrency successful, the schedule needs to conform to the following guidelines:

- Only flows that originated from the same Fork can come together in a Join. Figure 7.37 shows a valid Fork-Join construction, and Figure 7.38 shows an invalid Fork-Join construction.

- A flow that originates from a Fork must end in a Join or an End shape.

- Concurrent flows are not allowed to communicate or share messages with each other.

- Flows entering an OR-Join can have no more than one action.

- Concurrent flows can contain Decision and While flows.

- Concurrent flows can contain transactions, and a transaction can hold a Fork-Join construct.

- Concurrent flows that enter an OR-Join are not allowed to have more than one action.

Figure 7.37 A Valid Join-Fork Construction

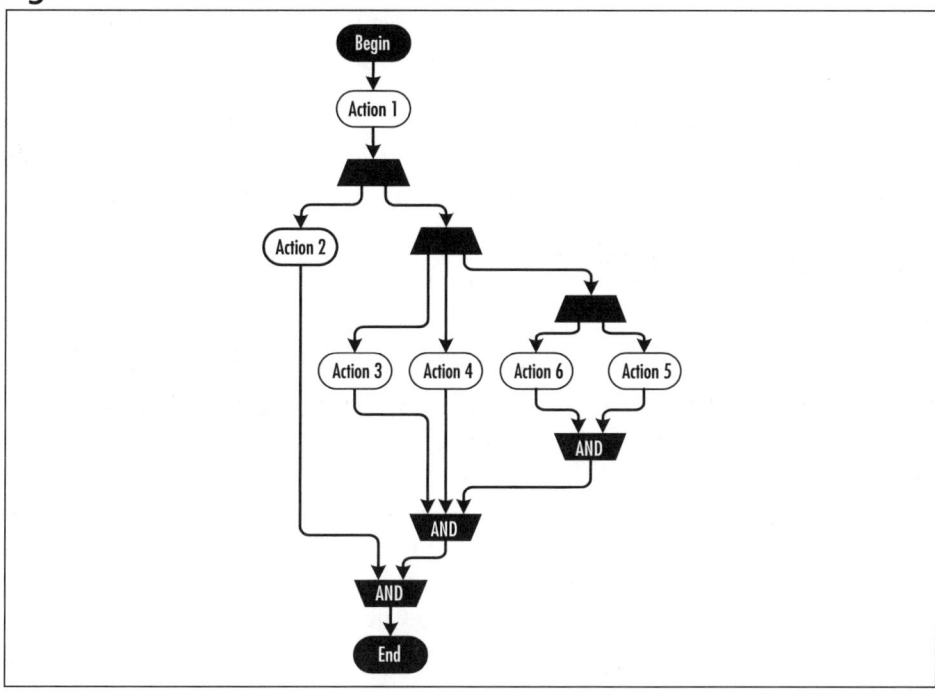

Figure 7.38 An Invalid Join-Fork Construction

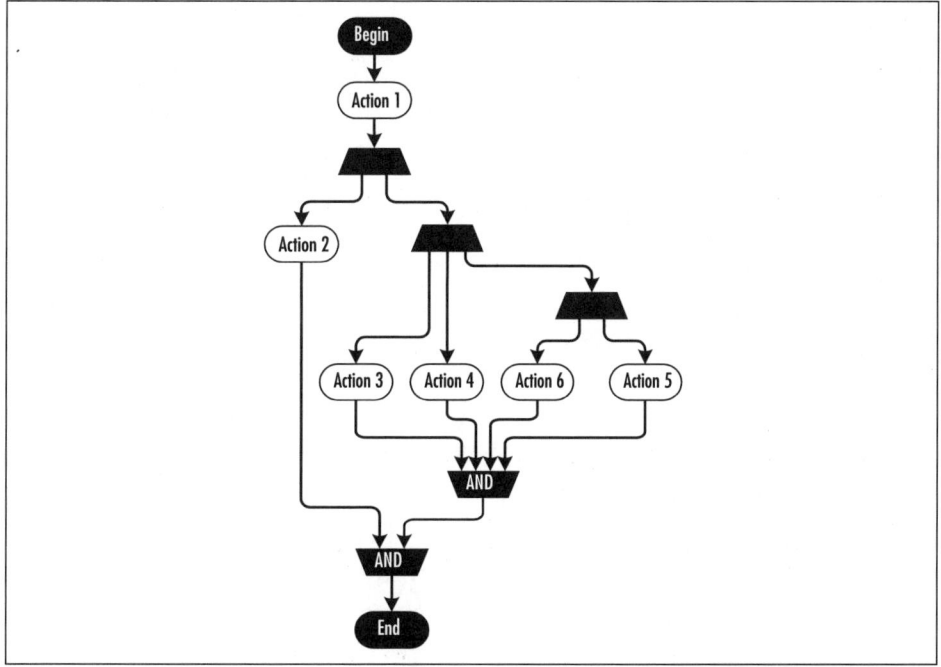

■ The flow exiting the OR-Join is not allowed to make use of data that becomes available through an action in one of the concurrent flows. This is to prevent a situation where the data is not available at the time the main flow reaches that action.

As you can see from these guidelines, the OR-Join is far more restrictive than the AND-Join. The reason for this is technical, and related to the way it is implemented. What it comes down to is that the OR is not a real synchronization point, and the AND is. Therefore, the schedule loses control of the "pending" concurrent flows, while the main flow finds it way to the end. However, the XLANG schedule can only finish if all concurrent flows finish. In a way, they can hold the schedule hostage from exiting and releasing its resources. Since the business flow is finished, it cannot be dehydrated. This would be a classic example of "*memory leakage.*" The compiler wants to be positive that the design of the business process does not create such a situation. Remember, you do not have this problem with the AND-Join; since the business process is stuck at this Join, and the Schedule will not finish, you will notice right away you have a problem.

Instead of relying on the compiler, try to think ahead when designing concurrent flows. First, use an OR-Join only in situations where the business flow can benefit from it, by improving performance. Second, determine under which circumstances a concurrent flow can be delayed (indefinitely). Third, prevent these situations from happening; for example, if you are not sure when a synchronous method call will return, place it in a timed transaction so you are sure it will be aborted if things take too long. Another example: if an action waits, in a Receive, for a message or method call, use the wait period to curtail the waiting.

The last question that remains is when to use the OR-Join and when to use the AND-Join? You will use concurrent actions to speed the execution of the business process, by doing actions at the same time independently from one another. Let's look at an example. A request comes in to open a bank account. Before this can be done, the data in the request has to be checked against different data sources; for example, "is the requester already a customer," "can the provided address information be correlated," and "is this person blacklisted?" When these answers are in, the business flow can make a decision. This is an example of an AND-Join, since the flow can only proceed if all the information is collected. An Or-Join can be used in a situation where the business flow has to perform an action if at least one of a number of actions is performed. For example, the request for a new bank account is authorized; therefore, the customer data has to be saved in the main customer database and the branch office database. This is done since these databases are only synchronized during the weekends. Therefore, it is sufficient that this information is saved in at least one database before continuing the business flow.

The Fork itself can be used if there are some spin-off actions that have to be performed. For example, after the customer information is saved in at least one database, a welcome package has to be sent to the customer, and the branch office gets an e-mail informing them of the new customer. These spin-off actions can be done independently from the main flow and are therefore forked.

Implementing a Business Process: An Example

Earlier in this chapter, we looked at a UML-based method that helps us in analysis and design of our Problem domain. We used a Bank Account example—in particular, the Make Money Transfer Use Case—to show what the different ICONIX steps are in the analysis and design phase of a project. It is true that such an example has a limited value, and the advantage of a method such as ICONIX will only manifest itself in larger projects. Hopefully, you already see its value and haves plans to start reading books on UML—after you finish this book, of course. If you have already used UML, you may have gotten a different look on how a minimal UML also works. In this chapter, we set out to show you what BizTalk Orchestration Services is all about. You have seen what you can accomplish with the BizTalk Orchestration Designer, but now it is time to see how you go from the ICONIX results—for which we use our Make Money Transfer—to a working business process in Orchestration Designer. Let us walk through our example and see how we can make it work. Afterward, we will try to make some generalizations that can help you as guidelines for bridging the gap between the design and implementation. (The source code for this example is available at www.syngress.com/solutions.) Take the following into account:

- Since our BizTalk business process is not involved in any user interface interaction, some other application needs to take care of that. A good option is Active Server Pages.

- We have to decide what instantiates our schedule. We have two options: (1) when the customer clicks the "Make Money Transfer" button; or (2) when the customer clicks OK to shoot out the money transfer transaction. For our schedule, we will choose the former, so we keep the Use

Case as it is designed. Since we need to make the instantiation for this customer, the instantiating message just needs to contain the customer credentials.

- The first real action is to retrieve a list of bank account numbers that the customer owns. This can be done to make a call to a component that we develop to do so. In our schedule, we will use a Script component for quick development.

- We will choose to send the message over a queue that is created for every schedule instance, and will use this queue throughout the rest of the schedule to communicate with the Active Server Pages that wrap the user interface.

- The next step is to wait until the customer sends his or her transaction data. For security reasons, we decide not to wait longer than five minutes; after that, we end the schedule. Whether the ending is an End or Abort will depend on the use of a long-running transaction.

- Once the data comes in, we can start validating it. However, one of our alternate courses is that the customer can cancel the transaction. We assume that, either way, we get a message that has the transaction data, and a Status field. This field can be used to transmit the cancellation.

- So, we have a three-way decision: abort, timeout, or OK. The latter will be wrapped in the Continue rule of the Decision.

- The next thing to do is start validating the recipient data. We use a Script component to do so.

- If the data is not OK, we need to return an error message and wait on new data. In real-life application data, you will see that this validation is performed into the first tier; this can be the Web site or even an ActiveX Control on the customer's system. In our example, we keep it in the schedule. Again, we need a Decision.

- The next actions are Retrieve Bank Account Details, Retrieve Customer, and Validate Bank Account Data. For convenience and because they handle the same data, we do all in the same Script component.

- If the bank account data does not validate, we return an error, or we create a preliminary transaction, followed by a request for a confirmation.

- Now we must wait for a response—again, for five minutes max—and we can get an OK or Cancel back.

- If we get the Conformation, we can shoot a message to the Process Debit Transaction Schedule. Whether this message instantiates this Schedule or if it is continuously running to process all transaction is a decision you can make yourself. It will work either way. In this example, we use a Channel. Since we do not know if or when the transaction actually is processed, we will not wait for it and finish the Make Money Transfer schedule.

Now we have completed the draft of our Use Case business process, we can decide on the use of a transaction. There are indicators that make it worth considering the use of one or more transactions:

- We using a five-minute waiting period and since dehydration starts after 180 seconds, we must be sure that we do not need to persist any data. However, we do not want the timeout period to abort the transaction and retry it, since we timed out for security reasons.

- In case we receive invalid recipient data, we have to wait for a new response. If we want to use a transaction, we can just abort it and start again.

For the sake of the example, we will use a long-running transaction. Figure 7.39 shows the flow before the transaction, and Figure 7.40 shows the flow after the transaction. One thing to notice is that even with a simple Use Case, the page is being filled quickly, which can be a serious handicap. (We had to heavily edit the flowchart to get it on one page in this book!) Figure 7.41 shows the action port setup, which also had to be edited to fit in the book. Figure 7.42 shows you the data flow that corresponds to Figure 7.39. Lastly, Figure 7.43 shows the partial data flow page.

Figure 7.39 The Make Money Transfer Schedule Business Flow without Transaction

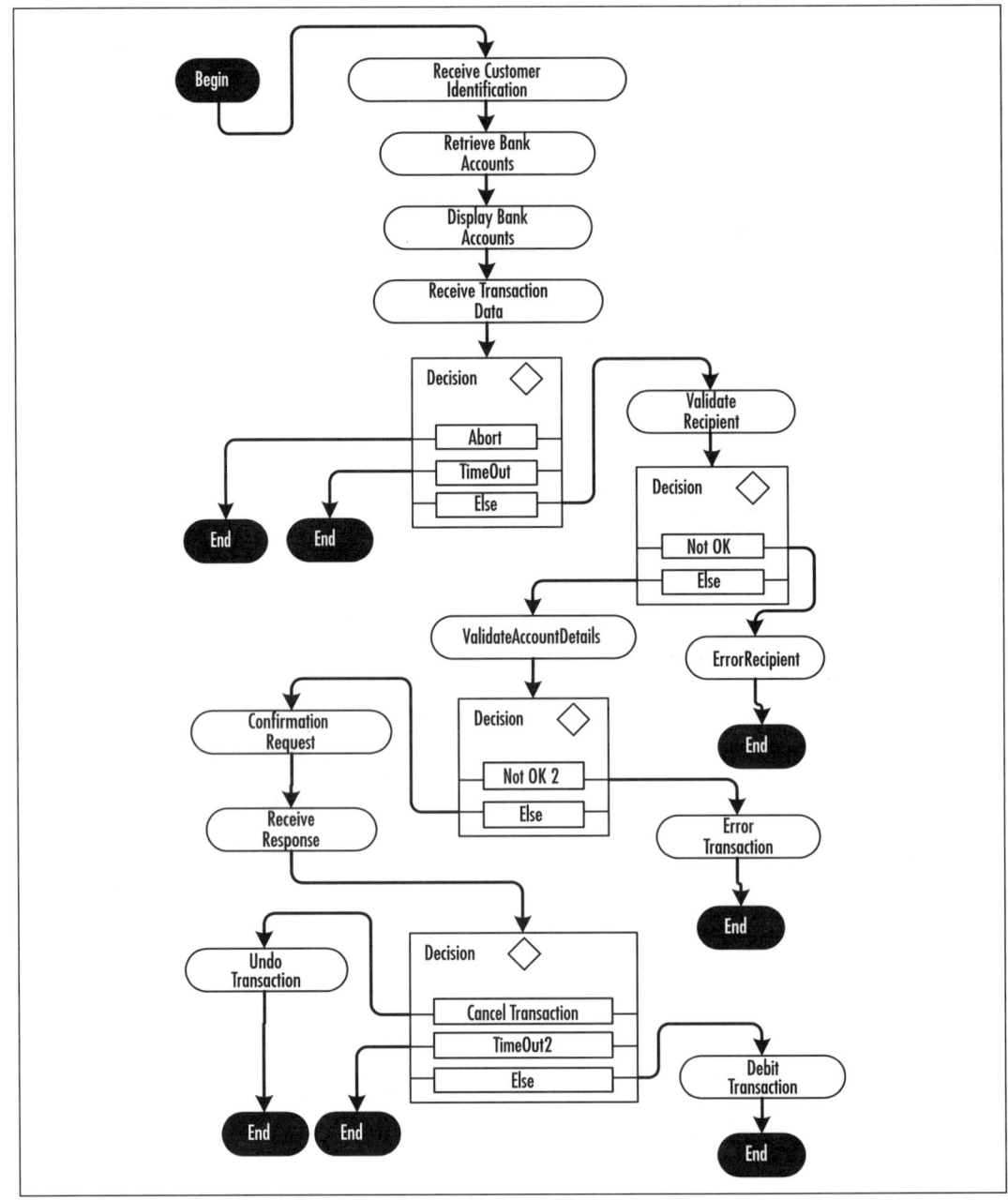

Figure 7.40 The Make Money Transfer Schedule Showing Transaction Modifications

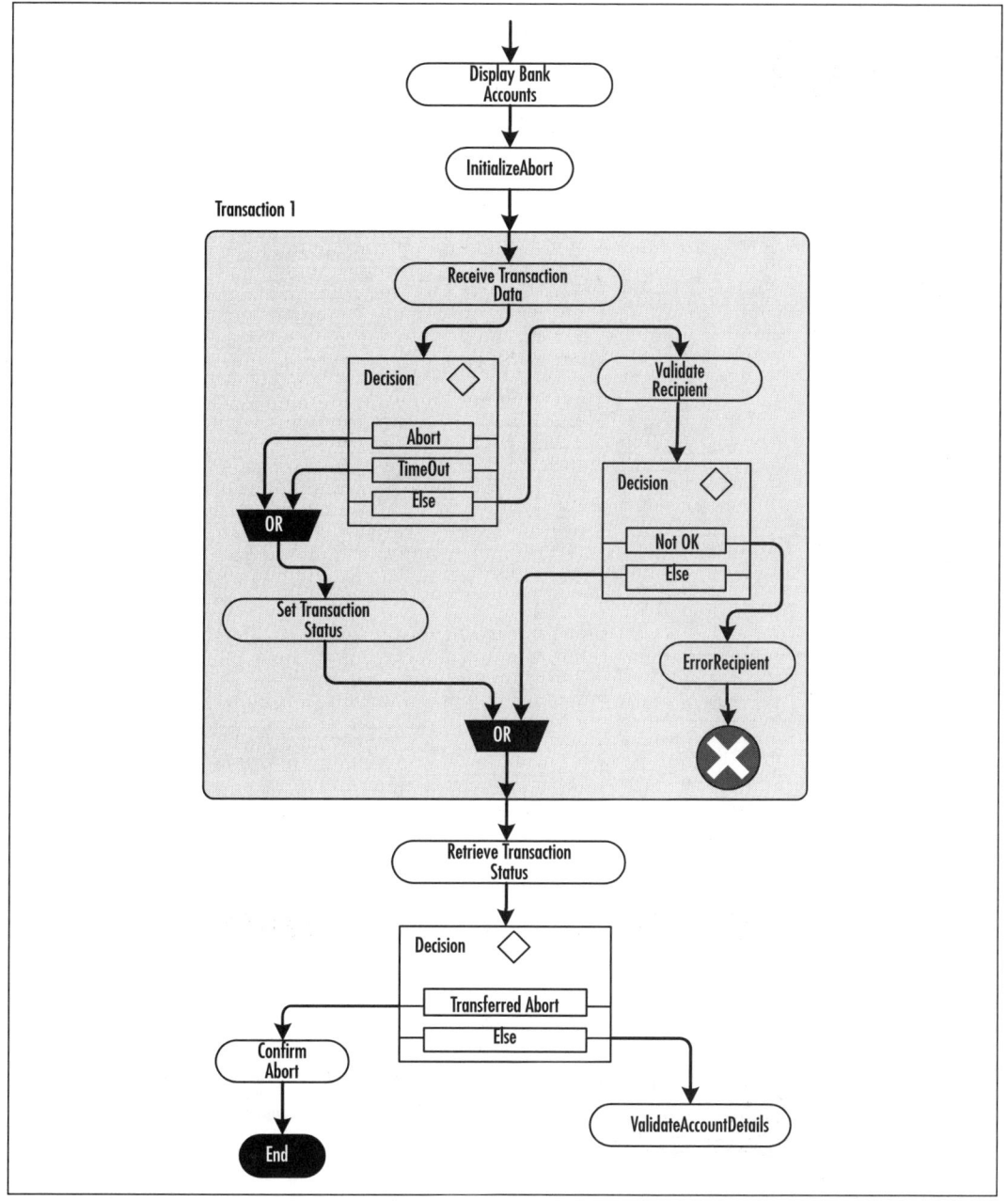

Figure 7.41 The Action-Port Setup and Interaction for the Make Money Transaction Example

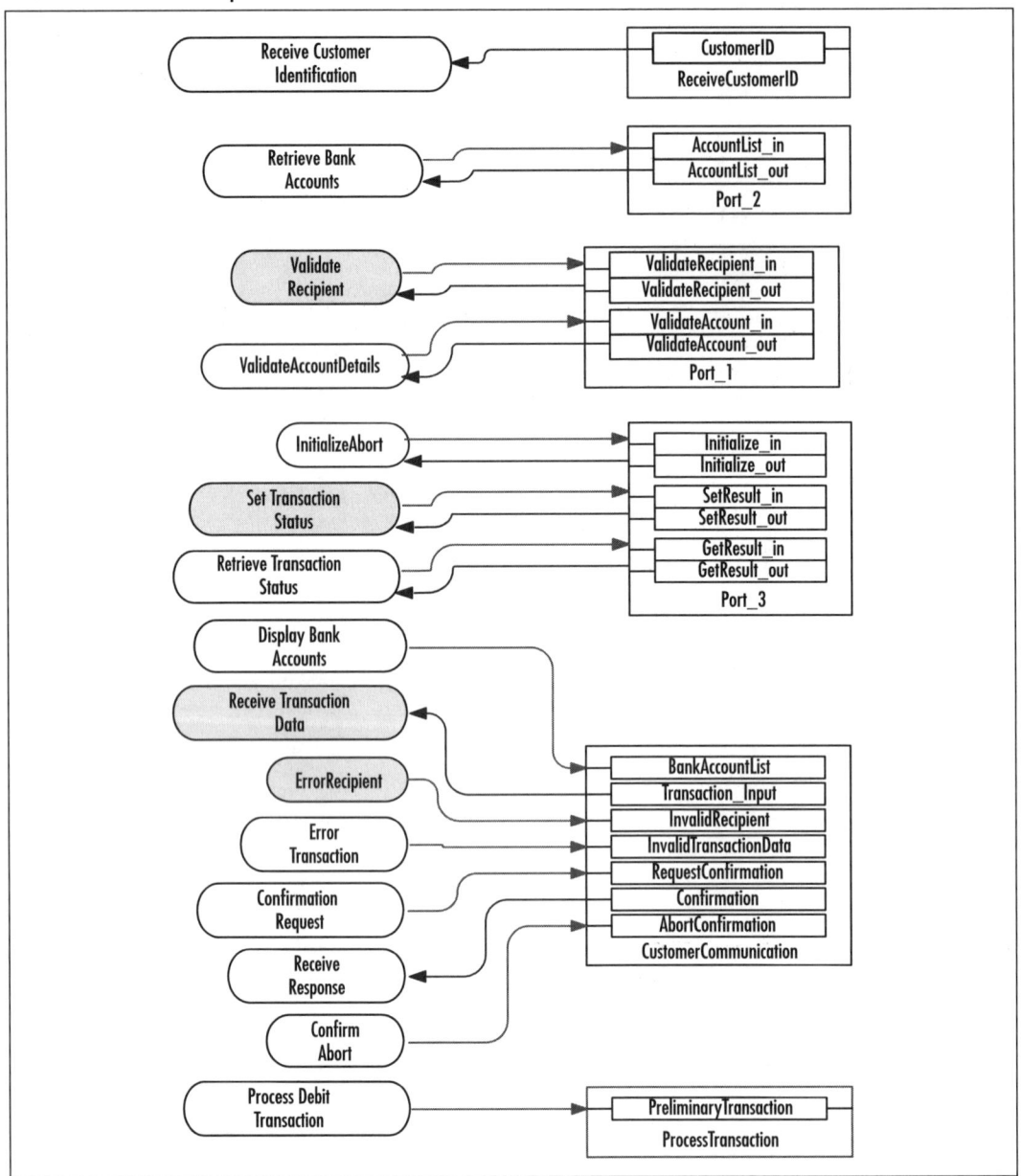

Figure 7.42 The Implementation Shapes Side of the Make Money Transfer Example

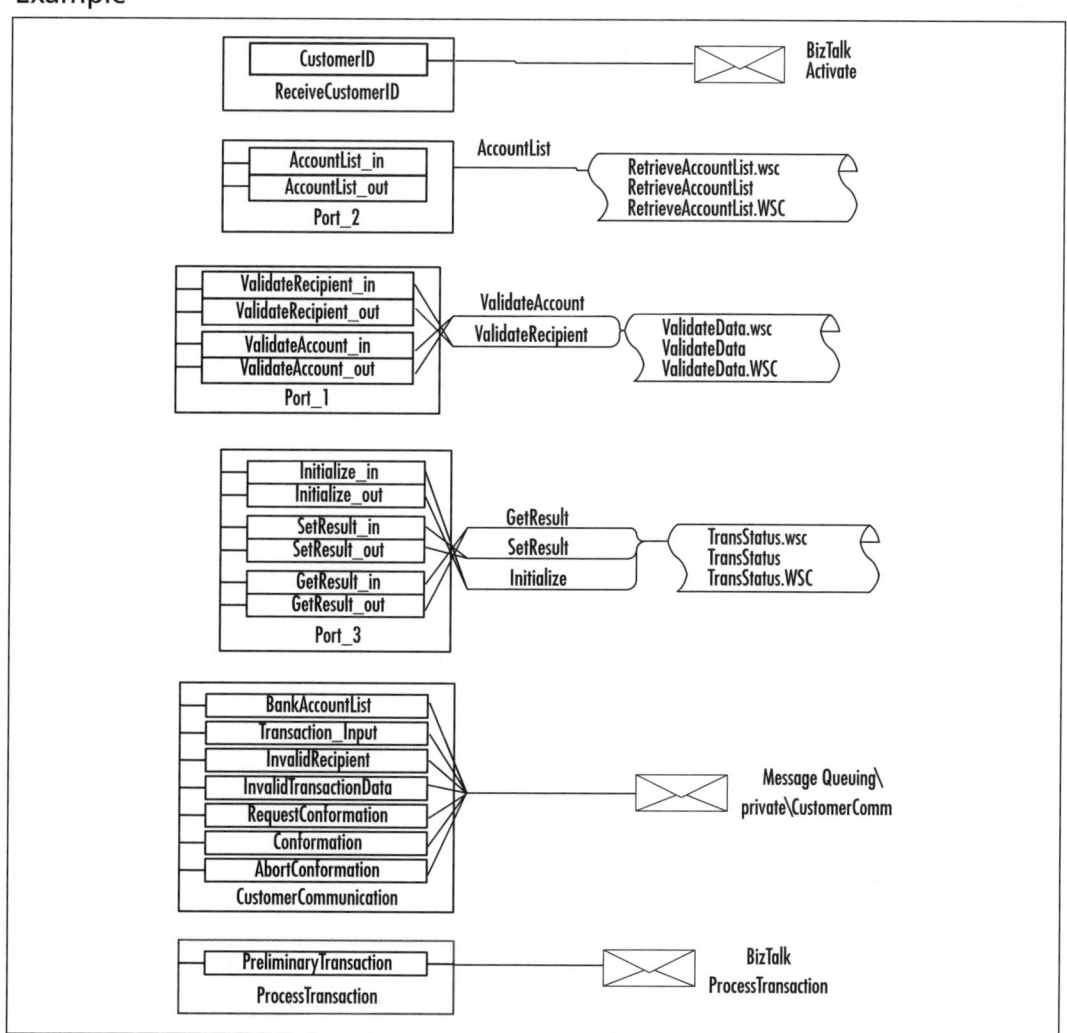

Figure 7.43 The Partial Data Flow Page of the Make Money Transfer Example

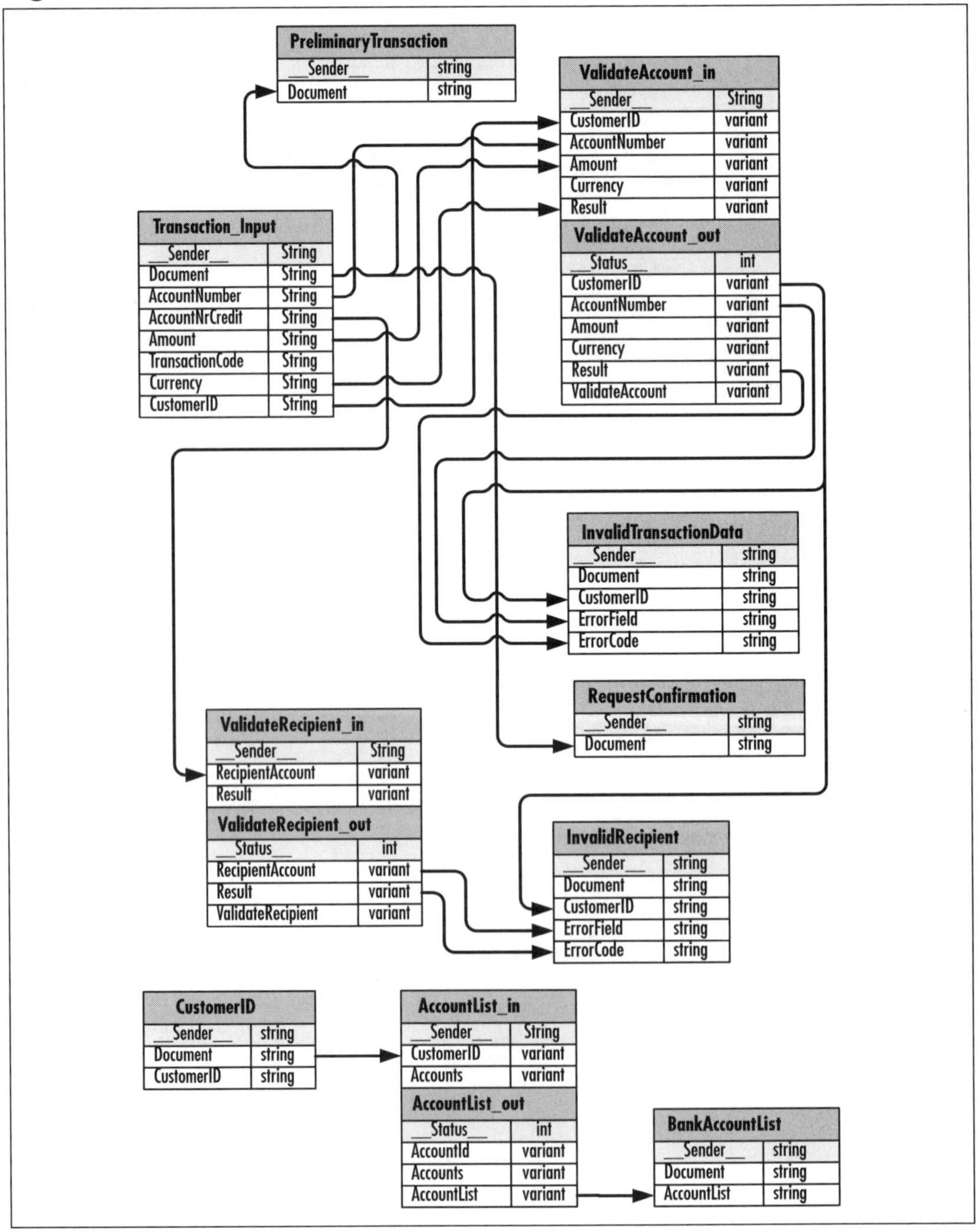

Let's summarize what general guidelines we can derive from this example:

- Choosing the proper activation of the schedule is important. Do not instantiate a schedule if there is a chance that the schedule is ended before doing anything significant. In our example, there is a chance that after retrieving the bank account numbers, the customer does not continue. It would make more sense if sending the transaction data would instantiate the schedule, but we dared to take that risk.

- Using the Robustness diagram makes it easy to determine the actions in your schedule. Nearly every controller (Control object) translates to an Action shape.

- The sequence diagrams show you when which data has to be exchanged, and in what format.

- Retrieving and storing persistent data is best done through method calls. You can group a number of methods in one component, which can also be derived from the Class diagram.

- Use transactions where they are really needed. In our example, we "forced in" a transaction for demonstration purposes. However, in the Use Case Process Debit Transaction (Table 7.2), you see that there is a possibility that the transfer goes to a recipient account of the same bank; therefore, the transaction is completed at that moment. This is a good example of using a short-lived (DTC-style) transaction to ensure that reducing one account balance and adding it to the other account balance happens atomically; thus, both balance updates are performed together or neither of the balances is updated. Of course, you can do both actions in the same method, but then the method needs to run in a transaction (Requires New).

- Make schedules independent and do not rely on the interaction. One of the reasons we used a five-minute timeout is to prevent the schedule from never finishing. The flow continues anyhow, even if the customer does not respond at all. That is why you should put components in transactions, since that ensures you that the DTC will time it out after 60 seconds. If the progress of a flow is not controlled with the schedule, it can become unpredictable.

Summary

The BizTalk Orchestration Services hold a pivotal role within BizTalk Server 2000, since this part will run the XLANG schedules that will be responsible for the data flow of your BizTalk application. You will use the BizTalk Orchestration Designer to implement your business processes and link them to the BizTalk Messaging Services or COM+ and Windows Scripting components. Before you start drawing diagrams, you need to have a firm picture of which business processes you need to implement, and you must know what the information is that will populate this application. Without the use of a design methodology, you will never be able to get a complete picture of the business process and information involved. The applications you build with BizTalk Server are object oriented, so using a methodology that is based on UML (Unified Modeling Language) is a good choice. For the purpose of example, we use ICONIX in this chapter to demonstrate the use of a good design method. The most prominent benefit of using a UML method is that at the end of the design process, you have all the information you need to start the implementation, and in a format that speeds the implementation. The same information can be used by all members of the development team, each doing his or her part of the puzzle. The person responsible for diagramming the business processes will use the BizTalk Orchestration Designer.

The BizTalk Orchestration Designer lets you create XLANG schedule diagrams in which the business process flow is linked to messaging or component implementation object. The business flow itself does not handle any data; it only controls how the data, wrapped in XML messages, flow from one implementation object to another. As you open an empty diagram stencil, you will see that it is divided in two parts: the left side can be used to draw the business process flow, and the right side holds the implementation objects. Only the Action shape, which is one of the available Flowchart shapes, in the business process diagram can be, or better to say "must be," linked to an Implementation shape at the right side. The Divider bar not only separates both sides of the stencil, it also forms an abstraction layer, by means of ports. These ports do the actual binding between an Action shape and Implementation shape, by means of defining the messages that are available at the port.

To be able to populate the messages, you must use the Data Flow stencil that every XLANG schedule diagram has. Since you need a message to populate another message, the schedule will most of the time start with receiving a message that is the trigger to start a business process. The Data Flow stencil holds all messages that are defined on the Business Process stencil. By drawing data flow arrows from one message field to a field in another message, you are able to populate new messages.

An important implementation aspect that needs to be addressed in the business process diagram is "transactions." This is so important because it is able to influence the business process flow. The purpose of a transaction is to group a part of the diagram that holds more than one Action shape in such a way that it acts as one shape. Therefore, if one of the actions fails to complete or produces an error, the entire transaction fails and needs to undo all actions it performed before the failure. If such a transaction has only performed updates on a database, it is easy to automatically undo the transaction, since the SQL server has the capability to take care of that. However, if the transaction communicates with other applications—for example, through messaging—undoing an action is not trivial. In these cases, you can create separate flowcharts that take care of the undo or compensate for the failure. These Compensation flowcharts become an integral part of the business process, since compensation might imply sending a message to the other application (or trading party) to inform them of the compensation action you take. It is obvious that the other party needs to understand these messages and know how to handle them.

Once you have the XLANG schedule diagram ready, you have to compile it to an XLANG schedule, which is a diagram translated to a BizTalk XML file that can be run by the XLANG scheduler engine. The compilation also checks the diagram for correctness and completeness. The correctness has more to do with restrictions that are imposed on the implementation of XLANG schedules than errors in the diagram. The restrictions are there to minimize the chance that a schedule encounters an unexpected runtime error and crashes.

This chapter uses a simple banking example to show how to go through the ICONIX design process and eventually implement it in BizTalk Orchestration Designer. It demonstrates the usefulness of an object-oriented design methodology, and how the design result can easily be turned into a BizTalk XLANG schedule implementation.

Solutions Fast Track

Diagramming Business Processes

☑ The basis for using BizTalk Server is to diagram business processes, and since the resulting BizTalk application is an object-oriented application, it is advisable to use an object modeling methodology such as UML. For the purpose of the example, the ICONIX method is use to explain business process modeling with the purpose of creating a BizTalk Server application. ICONIX has all the strength of UML, but is easier to work with since the iterative nature of the methodology does not force you to have it right at the first go.

☑ The ICONIX methodology is based on Use Cases, which sequences the interaction between an Actor and the System in basis and alternate courses. Every task or activity that has to be performed by the application has at least one Use Case. In its turn, a Use Case can be described by at least one business process. Since Business Process diagrams within BizTalk Server can only hold a limited diagram, breaking down the Use Case into smaller business processes can benefit the implementation.

☑ The ICONIX method takes seven steps and three milestones to produce a complete design. First, the user requirements have to be determined, which is perhaps the most important of all, since the rest of the process is based on those requirements. Second, the initial domain model has to be determined, which will give you the extent of the application you need to build. After this, you reach the first milestone, the "Requirements Review."

☑ In order to reach ICONIX's second milestone, the "Preliminary Design Review," you need to identify and describe all Use Cases that will make up the application. Next, you have to perform a Robustness analysis of the Use Case descriptions. Before you can complete the second milestone, review everything you have and update the data of previous steps, if needed. This is the iteration part of the methodology by going back to further detail, add, and complement the results you already achieved.

☑ The third milestone, the "Critical Design Review," is reached after turning the information from the Use Cases and Robustness diagrams into Sequence diagrams, this will likely have you going back to previous results to complete these. At this point, you must have all the necessary information to draw the Class Model diagram on which the object-oriented implementation will be based.

BizTalk Orchestration Designer

☑ The BizTalk Orchestration Designer lets you create XLANG Schedule diagrams that form the heart of the BizTalk applications. Once compiled, these schedules take care of the message flow of the application, although the business process flow that is implemented in the schedule itself does not handle the data.

☑ The XLANG Schedule diagram stencil is divided into two parts. In the left part of the stencil, you can create the Business Process diagram, using the Flowchart shapes. The right side is used for the Implementation shapes that represent COM and Windows Scripting components or the MSMQ and BizTalk Messaging Services. The two parts are separated by a Divider bar that will hold ports that bind an Action shape with an Implementation shape. The port also holds the message definition that flows into and/or out of an Implementation shape.

☑ Besides the Business Process stencil, the XLANG Schedule diagram has a Data Flow stencil that holds all messages that are defined on the Business Process stencil. The Data Flow stencil is used to show how fields from one message populates (flows into) the fields of other messages. Two additional messages always appear on the Data Flow stencil: the Constants and Port References. The former can be used to hold fields that have a fixed value throughout the execution of the XLANG schedule. The latter holds the unique port name of every port. A port reference name is a moniker that can be used in a message to supply a reply address to the recipient of the message. Note that "unique" means that the port name will be different for every instance of the same schedule.

☑ Within the Business Process diagram, you can group part of the flowchart within a transaction. If one of the Action shapes fails, it will let the entire transaction fail, or it will force the transaction to be redone. Since a failed transaction means undoing the complete transaction, it has to provide a mechanism to signal this undo to other applications/trading parties with which the BizTalk application is communicating. As you can create a transaction that can also be nested, you have the capability to create new stencils, called "On Failure of Transaction" and "Compensation for Transaction." The former can be created for every transaction; the latter is only available for nested transactions, to compensate for a completed inner transaction at the moment the outer transaction fails.

☑ A finished XLANG Schedule diagram needs to be compiled to create the XLANG schedule, which is a file in XML format. These XML files can be read by the XLANG scheduler engine. The compilation process transforms the diagram to a flat file, and does extensive checking on the diagram and data flow to minimize the chance of unexpected runtime errors.

Flowchart and Implementation Shapes

☑ The Business Process, On Failure of Transaction, and Compensation for Transaction stencils all have the same division of Flowchart and Implementation, so you have the availability of two groups of Implementation shapes. The Flowchart shapes can only be used in the left part of the stencil, where the Business Process diagram resides, and the Implementation shapes can only reside on the right side of the stencil. If you try to move the shape to the other side, it will automatically be moved back.

☑ A Port shape is created on the Divider bar for every Implementation shape you put on the stencil. In addition, both the Implementation shape and Port shape (which is actually also an Implementation shape) are placed on every On Failure of Transaction and Compensation for Transaction stencil. By means of the Implementation shape wizards you use, each port will have a message defined. These messages will automatically appear on the Data Flow stencil.

☑ The Flowchart shapes are also a limited set of shapes, of which only the Action shape can be used to interact with a Port shape. The Decision and While shapes add flow control, while the Fork and Join enable you to create concurrent flows and join them again. The Transaction shape is a special Flowchart shape, as it will automatically capture all Flowchart shapes on the stencil that are fully enclosed by the transaction rectangle. Transactions can be nested; thus, you can place a Transaction shape within a transaction. If you delete a Transaction shape, it will delete everything within the transaction, no questions asked.

☑ The Message Implementation shapes on the Data Flow stencil need to be linked so the BizTalk Schedule knows how to populate the fields in a message. This is done by drawing connections (arrows) out of a field into a field in another message. Of course, these message fields need to have the same type. In drawing these data flow arrows, they leave the right side of a field and enter the left side of another field.

☑ The Data Flow stencil, by default, always contains two specific messages. In the Constants message, fields with fixed values can be inserted; these fields accept no input from other fields, and can only be used to populate other fields. The Port Reference message contains one field for every port that appears on the Business Process stencil (or the other stencils that can contain ports). Since you have static and dynamic ports, these Port Reference fields can slightly differ. Static ports are known during compile time, so they can only be used to populate fields in messages. A dynamic port gets its identifying name (moniker) during execution; therefore, it is necessary to populate this field with the field value of a received message.

Implementing a Business Process: An Example

☑ This simple example shows how the results of the ICONIX design process can be used to create a XLANG schedule diagram.

☑ From the example, general guidelines are distilled on how to use the design diagrams for your BizTalk XLANG schedule. It is clear that in complex business processes—thus, Use Cases—the available space to create a Business Process diagram may be too small, forcing you to cut the Use Case into smaller pieces.

Frequently Asked Questions

The following Frequently Asked Questions, answered by the authors of this book, are designed to both measure your understanding of the concepts presented in this chapter and to assist you with real-life implementation of these concepts. To have your questions about this chapter answered by the author, browse to **www.syngress.com/solutions** and click on the **"Ask the Author"** form.

Q: Why do I need to go through extensive analysis and design before I can use BizTalk Server? Can't I design the business process directly in my BizTalk schedule?

A: Developing applications starts with little concrete information to go on. It is a creative process of discovery and analysis; sitting behind a monitor won't do the trick, a whiteboard is far more effective. Developing an application can only be successful if it is done with dedication, persistence, and small, well-defined steps. In fact, in the early days of software engineering, design methods where developed using only a pencil, ruler, and paper. Today, we have great applications that help us in the analysis and design process, from simple drawing tools to extensive Computer Aided Software Engineering (CASE) applications. Unfortunately, this version (1.0 SP1) of BizTalk Server is far from being a design applications, no matter what Microsoft says. Here's why!

We used ICONIX as an object-oriented analysis and design method to show that this part of the development process is very important for a smooth implementation. Of course, you can use any method you wish, as long as it supports a successful development project. The Unified Modeling Language (UML) has proven to be a very good method for object-oriented development. ICONIX is based on UML, but is much more pragmatic because it uses less diagramming overhead than UML does. This method, as any UML method, is based on a dynamic part (the sequence diagrams) and a static part (the Class Domain). You need an application such as Rational Rose (www.rational.com/products/rose) to support your analysis and design phase. As you look to BizTalk Server Orchestration design, you are able to draw a business process, but you cannot do any kind of modeling. The business process part, of what Microsoft claims to be the "domain" for the business analyst, can be derived from the Sequence and Robustness diagrams, but is very implementation driven. For example, the use of short-lived (DTC-style) transactions in the business process is a good choice when implementing an application, but is never found in a pure business process, simply because a business analyst is unaware of any database structure, let alone database-related transactions. Another example is the need for adding actions to the flow to bring component results out of a transaction. You need to add a component instantiation action before entering the transaction. This type of process modification to ensure a solid implementation can bring a process flow far from its original business process. The business process within BizTalk has the function to glue your processing of documents together. Is BizTalk Server therefore less valuable? Absolutely not! It is a great implementation platform that speeds your application development, and is in that regard more a rapid application development (RAD) tool.

Q: What is the best approach in creating a BizTalk schedule?

A: There is no such thing as "the best approach." Every approach is good as long as it enables you to go from user requirements to implementation. Moreover, you have to be comfortable with the method; never use a method you do not like, as this will show in the result. This starts out with an object-oriented analysis and design method, UML has a proven track record, and ICONIX is a UML-based method that is so simplified that is very pragmatically and even for developers who have strong dislikes for using design methods it is highly usable. A note to those who even dislike ICONIX: your only other choice is eXtreme Programming (XP).

Once you have taken the seven steps of the ICONIX method, you have a solid base to start coding. The Robustness diagrams and the Sequence diagrams define the business process flow, and the Class diagram determines the data exchange and persistence. Do not add transactions to the business flow until you are confident that it is complete, because only with a complete flow can you make a correct assessment about shapes embedded in the transaction. Second, you might need to add additional actions to initialize messages or instantiate components, so their results will also persist outside the transaction. Third, reshuffling shapes and transactions can be a hassle, especially if the page is full. Fourth, you need to design on failure and/or compensation flows, so you need to know what is in the transaction to determine any type of countermeasure.

Another decision you have to make before you begin coding is whether you are going to make a schedule for every Use Case, or group a number of Use Cases together in one schedule. The latter is preferable from a performance perspective; the former probably has better maintainability. Every time you start a schedule, it creates an instance that uses resources. Therefore, many small Use Cases—thus, schedules—can put a significant load on the system. Grouping a number of Use Cases in one schedule is only useful if it is likely that they will be used in the same session. Another performance enhancement is to create schedules that are so generalized that they can handle a mix of messages, through one Use Case or a group of Use Cases. For example, with the bank account example in this chapter, the Use Case "Process Transaction" can be started every time a transaction is made. However, you can also put in a loop and let the same instance handle all transaction processing. Therefore, this schedule only needs to be instantiated once. If you don't feel this is a viable solution, you can also add the Process Transaction Use Case, together with the Make Money Transfer Use Case in one schedule, thereby at least saving one instantiation per money transfer transaction. However, the latter is more practical than object oriented.

Security

Solutions in this chapter:

- **Defining Your Security Policy**
- **Physical Security Considerations**
- **Securing XLANG Schedules**
- **Component-Level Security**
- **Database Security**
- **Certificates and the CryptoAPI**

☑ **Summary**

☑ **Solutions Fast Track**

☑ **Frequently Asked Question**

Introduction

Every implementation of a business application involves security issues. The two main questions any business must ask are, "What do we regard as security issues?" and "What are we going to do about these issues?" You will find the answer to the first question in the following paragraph. The second question will take rest of the chapter to answer.

Applying security to a business application of BizTalk Server means preventing any situation that would result in disruption of the application, the data involved, or the infrastructure the application uses. A disruption can originate either from the technology involved or from human behavior. This chapter does not give you a summation of all possible scenarios that could arise and the solutions to counter them. Instead, it gives you a broad grounding in security that will enable you to limit the chances of a disruption occurring, be it your BizTalk server going down, a disgruntled employee who wants to sabotage the system, or a script kiddie trying to find a way into your network. Although the latter is not likely if your company is not as high profile as Microsoft or Yahoo!, such intrusions do occur, especially when such persons are in it for the notoriety and fame it will potentially bring them.

Having said this, it is time to look at the first step in setting up a secured BizTalk Server environment; namely, defining the company's security policy.

Defining Your Security Policy

In developing a secure BizTalk Server solution, or any other Information Technology (IT) solution for the organization/company for which you work, you need a framework for realizing a security level with which the organization is comfortable. This framework is your *security policy*, and it needs to be business driven instead of technology driven. Too many organizations lack a security policy as a whole, and others leave it up to the IT department. However, working on an overall security policy for your business/organization is beyond the realm of this chapter. Instead, let us focus on a security policy dealing with the development and deployment of a BizTalk solution.

WARNING

Do not wait until the BizTalk solution is deployed to develop a security policy—the sooner you start, the better. Be sure that your policy is in place before you take the BizTalk solution into its testing phase. The

---

necessary security infrastructure can have implications for the BizTalk architecture. Making unexpected last-minute changes to the BizTalk architecture can be very unpleasant.

Awareness

Any type of plan or policy is only as strong as the weakest link. The best example of this is passwords. You can find them everywhere—on the back of employees' keyboards, in the top drawers of their desks, or on Post-Its that always seem to be stuck on their monitors. Often this is done not because employees are unable to remember them, but because nobody told them just how important passwords are. They only know that they need them to get into their computers. Sometimes they have more than one password because they also have to access other systems, which they might see as even more reason to make a list of them. Often, when employees do know enough not to write their passwords down for security reasons, they select passwords that are easy to remember instead. Some examples are the name of a spouse, child, dog, or favorite goldfish. For a person with malicious intent, these passwords are relatively easy to discover, by using *social engineering*.

More and more organizations are realizing that security is not only about technology, but also about people. They are beginning to understand that security awareness is an important part of the introduction of new employees to the organization, and integral to the training programs for existing employees.

The introduction of BizTalk in your infrastructure is a good reason to put a security awareness program in place. Because BizTalk not only automates business processes, but also integrates individual information systems, or at least connects them, it will make it easier for misuse to propagate without being noticed. This is especially true if BizTalk is directly connected to the outside world. If this is the case, things can get nasty.

Risk Analysis and Risk Management

The next step in creating your security policy is to take a good look at the risks you are facing. Ask yourself the following questions:

- What can go wrong?
- What is the chance of this happening?
- What will be the consequence(s)?

This should be done throughout the entire organization, but first, start by listing the big risks, and then work your way down to the smaller ones. You should consider both malicious intent and accidental mishaps. Rate all the risks as low, medium, or high, depending on their chance of happening and the consequences thereof. Two real-world examples follow.

A small business had Internet access through an ISDN connection. A firewall/router box was used to protect their network, and since the vendor configured it, they thought they were safe. When the configuration was audited, however, it turned out that the box allowed someone to establish a connection if he or she called in on the ISDN line, and get unlimited access to the network. In this case, "incomplete configuration" was the problem. Since configuring is the work of imperfect human beings, the chance of this happening is realistic (medium risk). The consequences were that someone with malicious intent could have brought the entire network down with relative ease. The company was lucky that this had not happened.

A system administrator team of two persons, swamped with work, was often forced to cut corners. There was a lack of electrical outlets in the computer room. Instead of adding additional outlets, they strung an extension cord to solve this problem. This was an accident waiting to happen, and it did. One system administrator, running around solving problems, tripped over the extension cord, bringing all three servers down. The result was that 28 employees had to wait an hour to regain access to the network. In this case, "someone accidentally interrupted the power supply," due to the extension cord lying in the way. The chance of someone pulling the cord is very real (high risk). The consequence was the loss of an hour of productivity.

Calculating the Cost of Risks

An important aspect of risk analysis is considering the monetary losses that a security disruption might cost the business or organization. This is not always as obvious as it might appear to be. Sit down with a few colleagues and try to calculate what it will cost if the BizTalk solution in full production is not available for one complete day. You might be surprised at how expensive this turns out to be, especially if all the hidden costs are uncovered! Think about the following:

- The number of employees who are unable to work, times the personnel cost for one day.

- The number of employees who have to work overtime to get things running again, multiplied by the overtime wages.

- The loss in production, orders, and so forth.

- The unhappy customers and suppliers, since bad news travels fast and has a tendency to linger.

Another point to consider is to estimate how much time it will take to replace the BizTalk server from the moment it goes down and you find that there is no way to reboot it. You might be surprised how fast time goes! Think about the time it will take to do the following:

- Get a replacement server in place.

- Install the bare system.

- Restore the latest version of the BizTalk solution.

- Determine if information is lost.

- Synchronize all systems involved.

- Test that the whole system is running correctly.

Once the initial risk analysis is complete, your work is by no means done. Risk analysis is an ongoing process that must be audited periodically. After the analysis, it is time to start managing the risks, since that is what security is all about. Focus first on the high and medium risks, and ask yourself, "What needs to be done to reduce or eliminate these risks?" Often, multiple solutions will spring to mind. Make a fair estimate of the cost these security solutions will entail. Take the initial cost for purchase and installation into account, and determine what the operational costs entail, such as maintenance and service agreements. After that, it is simple economics: A security solution that costs less to implement and maintain than the cost involved if the problem it is supposed to protect against occurs is worth implementing. This does not mean that you should always implement solutions that eliminate a risk. Reducing a risk from high to low is, in most cases, sufficient, especially if the cost to do so are small compared to the cost of eliminating the risk.

Eliminating the possibility of some potential problems is often simply not feasible or possible. In cases like this, monitoring the situation is usually the best bet. For example, the chance that someone will try to break into the BizTalk server from inside or outside is slim, but realistic. Trying to eliminate this risk is an uphill battle. However, by using monitoring tools for intrusion detection and log analysis, you will, in most cases, be warned of a break-in attempt before it succeeds.

In the previous two real-world examples, using risk management would easily have curbed the risks. In the first example, a simple audit on the configuration (see the next section, *Auditing*) would have revealed the incomplete configuration. It would have cost a few hundred dollars at most to address this risk, much less than what it would have cost if someone had actually breached this security hole. In the second example, using a longer extension cord and taking 10 minutes to guide the cable along the walls would have significantly reduced the risk of pulling out the cord, and would have only cost a few dollars. For about $500, the company could have installed uninterruptible power supplies (UPSs) that would have allowed the administrator enough time to put the cord back into the power outlet, without the servers going down.

Auditing

Putting a security policy in place and applying security measures takes some effort, but is relative easy compared to keeping the security at the same level. You need procedures to check if the measures you have taken to curtail risks are fully implemented and maintained. This is where auditing comes into play. There are several different types of auditing:

- **Collegial review** Colleagues can check each other's work; for example, with XLANG schedule diagrams. This should not be used to place blame for making mistakes, but instead to catch errors while they are still at an early stage. This saves money and raises the quality of work. Another example is that after a BizTalk server is fully installed and tuned, another system engineer could check the server to see if the configuration is complete according to the security standards set in the security policy.

- **Internal audit** The IT department, with outside expertise if necessary, runs a full check of the complete BizTalk infrastructure, both the technical issues and the procedures. To enhance the value of the internal audit, you can run tests to determine if these procedures, like full BizTalk server recovery, actually work. You can also check if backup tapes are useable and complete. This is something we will discuss in more detail later. Another example is to check if the XLANG schedules running on the BizTalk server are the correct ones, and see who has access to these files. Perform an internal audit at least once a year. An even better policy is to run two partial audits, in which you revisit the shortcomings of the previous audit.

- **External audit** This is also called the *independent audit*. You hire an IT audit organization to run a full audit. They deliver a report with all the plusses and minuses, in addition to a large bill. Perform an external audit at least once every two years.

The dynamics of the organization or business will quickly bring the security level down. Audits are the perfect way of improving your security of the BizTalk infrastructure. Remember, security policies are never perfect in any organization, but through critical review and auditing, you can bring them to a higher level.

Contingency Plan

The best security policy and most advanced risk management cannot guarantee protection against major failures, such as fire or flooding. Large businesses can afford to duplicate their IT infrastructure in a different geographical location. Most companies cannot afford such a luxury, so they need to have a contingency plan to cope with these types of situations. Suppose you are the manager of the IT department and receive a telephone call in the middle of the night telling you that there was a fire on the floor on which the computer room is located, and there is substantial water damage to the equipment. That is enough to get you awake and reaching for the contingency plan that you (hopefully) always have within arm's length. The plan tells you exactly what has to be done to get the information systems running again, and who needs to be involved. Chances are you will have to set up the system from the ground up. Important factors to keep in mind when doing so include:

- What type of hardware is needed?

- What software versions and builds are used for production?

- Who is going to deliver the replacement hardware?

- Which backup tapes (which should have been stored offsite) are going to be needed?

- If the temporary BizTalk environment has to be set up offsite, what needs to be done to hook up this environment with the network at the main location?

Overall, you write the contingency plan for the BizTalk environment as a guidebook to help you to act quickly in case of disaster. For major disasters (also called *Force Majeur*) such as the entire building burning down, even the average contingency plan can fall short. In these cases, decisions at a tactical level need to be made that might put the execution of the contingency plan out of your hands.

Designing & Planning…

IT Security Policy Is a Business Affair

Over the years, I have had many discussions with my clients regarding security and establishing a security policy. Usually, these discussions always went the same way. The business management was under the impression that security meant keeping hackers out of the network, and that a firewall accomplished this. That's all there was to it, as far as they were concerned. When asked what if one of their own employees wanted to do any harm, the default answer was that their personnel would never do this. My default response was always the same: research of misuse and fraud of IT facilities consistently has shown that 75 percent of the time, either current or former employees are to blame. It is an unfortunate fact that most organizations think that threats come only from the outside. Often, healthy business protection is confused with mistrust of personnel.

At this point, I usually ask them when, and for how long, it would be acceptable for a particular business application to be down and unusable. Nine times out of 10, the answer is a resounding "Never!" Next, I inquire as to whether this risk should be eliminated, regardless of the cost. Again, the answer is usually "No, obviously cost has to be taken into account." Going back and forth about what is the acceptable time for a business application to be offline, and what it might cost to minimize the risk of this happening, we end up talking about risk management.

Talking about risk management is talking about IT security policy. Discuss what security measures you need to reduce the risk that the availability of a business application might be disrupted. If management has set these security goals, the IT department can then fill in the technical details.

So, what has this discussion to do with a book about developing BizTalk Server solutions? Everything! Depending on the level of use, BizTalk Server can grow to become the proverbial spider in your information Web. Disruptions or misuse of a BizTalk solution can have severe consequences, such as bringing parts of the company to a standstill or losing both reputation and the goodwill of customers and suppliers. By implementing a security policy and spending money to realize a reliable BizTalk solution, you in fact take out insurance on the continuity of your business processes.

Testing

Making errors is human, so it would be wise to assume that while developing your BizTalk solution and implementing the BizTalk environment, there will be slip-ups, inconsistencies, or errors that make your solution prone to disruptions. When developing applications, it is important to put them through a rigorous functionality and user acceptance test. It is a good practice to draft thick test plans and form test teams to achieve this. However, many organizations fail to fully implement structured security testing. You might ask yourself why so few organizations perform security testing. The two main reasons:

- It's expensive, since you need to build a test environment that is a copy of the production environment. You cannot get away with just a few servers and a switch, because security testing is not only based on the exact configuration of a server, firewall, or network switch. Most of these tests need to be performed on complete communication paths, a process known as *end-to-end testing*.

- Most IT departments work in a reactive way and are organized to *solve* problems, not *prevent* problems. This means that they seldom have time to make security test plans and execute them, as there are too many problems in need of solutions.

It only makes sense to take measures to limit risks. An IT department must be proactive, using security and infrastructure test plans to solve problems before they become out of control. In fact, every change on the production IT infrastructure must be preceded with thorough testing to confirm that the change has the anticipated effect and does not disrupt other functions.

I have witnessed too many instances where changes in the infrastructure left users unable to access the applications they needed. One example was a router table that was modified incorrectly, disabling a remote location from accessing the main network. Another example was a library (DLL file) on a Windows NT server that was replaced with the newest version, instantly killing the MSMQ service. Both problems could have been avoided, or at least minimized, by proper planning and testing.

Roles and Access Levels

As mentioned previously, people are the weakest link in the security chain. The best security measure is to keep them away from your BizTalk application. Unfortunately, this is not a very realistic solution. Instead, try to limit the people who have access to the BizTalk application, and limit the level of access these people have.

Employees who will have access to the BizTalk application should have a legitimate need to do so before they are granted access. Perform the following steps to assess the roles of employees who will be working with the BizTalk application:

1. Make an overview of all the roles and put them in groups, based on the type of use they will make of the application. Try to minimize the number of groups—the more groups, the more administration involved, and the greater the chance of error.

2. Determine for each group which parts of the BizTalk solution they will need to use, and what type, or level, of access this will require. Be very strict about this. If users only need read-only access, that should be all they get.

3. Add only the usernames of the employees you have identified as needing access to the BizTalk solution to the groups. Review these group members at least twice a year, since employees have a tendency to change jobs.

4. *Never* give access rights at user level, as this only complicates the system administration tasks.

During the installation of BizTalk, only two groups are created: BizTalk Server Administrators and BizTalk Server Report Users, which might be enough for most solutions. Remember that with BizTalk Server, you create multitier solutions in which nearly all users will only need to have access to the outer tier.

For the XLANG Scheduler, four roles are created: Creator, User, Administrator, and Application. Except for the Administrator role, everyone has default membership in these roles. This needs some adjustment, which we discuss later.

Security Patches

You will probably hear from time to time that a security bug was detected in a Microsoft product that you use. Most of the times, a fix/patch is released within a few days of its discovery. Do not install any of these patches before doing extensive testing. Often, these bugs will have little or no effect on your BizTalk solution, and since Microsoft rarely does regression testing on their patches, they can often do more harm than good.

Keep your ear to the ground in the weeks following the release of a patch. If the signals are OK and you are convinced that you need to install the patch, install it on the test environment, do the necessary regression testing, and if no problems occur, you can release it to the production environment. You should accompany every patch with a protocol that should at least describe:

- What the patch is about.

- On which servers it needs to be installed.

- How the patch should be installed.

- What tests should be performed to confirm that the patch is installed properly.

- How the patch can be uninstalled in case it causes problems.

You can find information on Windows-related updates, patches, and service packs at http://windowsupdate.microsoft.com. Every Windows version comes with a Windows Update utility that helps to automatically detect which available updates are not installed on your system. Never use this utility directly on the production servers, and never do any type of product update over the Internet from them. Additionally, Microsoft delivers a tool called "Windows Critical Update Notification" that checks frequently if there are new updates available. This is a handy tool, but again, never install it on production servers. Avoid any circumstance that can change the installation of the production servers. Instead, place an "Update" server in the demilitarized zone that has all applications in use installed on it. Let this server run the Update Notification programs to keep you informed about the available updates.

Physical Security Considerations

Physical security issues are an important aspect of the overall implementation of the security policy. These can range from very simple considerations, such as not using extension cords, to complex considerations such as what type of security infrastructure your BizTalk environment is embedded in. We will look at some of the measures you can take to prevent the most common disruptions.

Your BizTalk environment might consist of one server that holds all components necessary to run BizTalk Server, or a number of servers with different tasks and functionalities. If you subsequently bring in security measures, an extensive infrastructure will begin to emerge. Figure 8.1 shows three levels of security as applied to a BizTalk infrastructure. We will be referring back to this figure several times in the following discussion. For more architectural solutions for a BizTalk Server 2000 environment, see the Microsoft document *Microsoft BizTalk Server 2000 Deployment Considerations* (located in the MSDN Library under **Technical Articles | Microsoft .NET Development | Microsoft .Net Enterprise Servers | BizTalk Server 2000**).

Figure 8.1 Three Levels of Security Measures for the BizTalk Environment

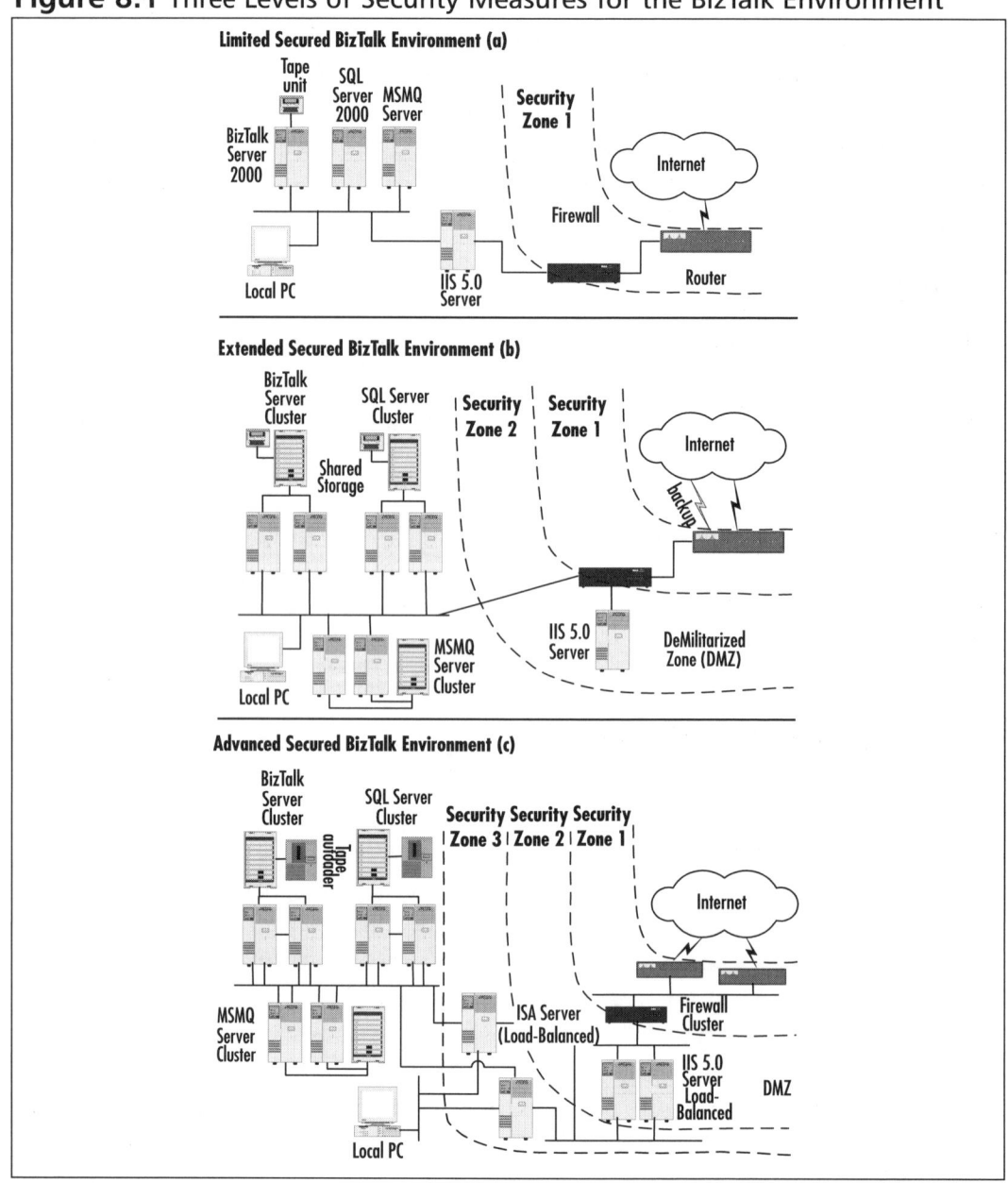

Routers, Firewalls, and Proxies

In designing the BizTalk infrastructure, use the multitier character of the BizTalk architecture to put defense lines between the tiers. To make this type of security effective, you must prevent using synchronous communication between tiers. Unfortunately, this is not possible between the client and the Web site, since a connection between the two remains open until the Active Server Page (ASP) script is running. At a programming level, you should take care that the time these connections remain open is as short as possible, or that they time out within a reasonable amount of time. The Web site is technically vulnerable to a distributed denial of service (DDoS) attack, something that is hard to protect against, especially if you allow users to enter your Web site at an anonymous level. Now, let us look at the different security components.

Routers

The *router* is the device that actually connects your local infrastructure to the outside world. In our example, this "outside world" is the Internet. Depending on how you use it, this can be a dial-up or permanent connection. Let us assume this is a permanent line, a leased line, a Frame Relay, or an xDSL connection. The router can have an abundance of functionalities or hardly any, so first determine what functionality you need and which router fits the budget. In most cases, you do not need more than a router that routes; the firewall will handle other functions such as filtering and address translation. Performing the same functions at two places will only complicate administration, and has a negative effect on performance. However, if the router is used to connect more than just the BizTalk infrastructure to the Internet, packet filtering on the router might be useful for traffic separation. This is the case when you connect more than one network segment to the router, and the router then determines what data from the Internet is allowed to go to which network segment, or even what data can be exchanged between the segments. This implies that each segment has its own firewall. Extensive filtering can drastically decrease the router performance. In this book, we see security as protecting ourselves against disruptions in the BizTalk infrastructure; therefore, special attention must be given to how you want to protect yourself from losing the Internet connection if the router fails, or if the line to the Internet goes down. Remember, we are talking about "risk management." If Internet connectivity is important to your business or organization (and when is it not?), you definitely need a backup solution for the loss of the Internet connection. Drawing from experience, the chance that the line will go down is greater than that of the router failing. Let us assume that you have a leased line going from your router to your ISP. You will need a secondary line between the router and ISP in case your primary goes down. However, a second leased line can be an expensive solution. Instead, you can decide to use a standard ISDN line, also called Basic Rate ISDN, or BRI. Be sure to buy a router that has a BRI interface. Let the ISP deliver your connections for leased line and standard ISDN. You have to configure the router so that when the leased line goes down, the router automatically brings up the ISDN interface. Test to see if the ISP can transparently route traffic over both connections.

Having a second line will not solve the problem of a failed router; in this case, only a second router will do the trick. This will only happen transparently if the router supports fail-over configuration. Let's take a Cisco router as an example. Cisco routers, in general, support fail-over configuration by using the Hot-Standby Routing Protocol (HSRP). You can take two routers, activate HSRP, create a group that holds both routers, and make sure they share an HSRP group IP address. Although this is an original IP address, it does not specifically belong to any of the routers, as only the active router holds it to route traffic. It is important to remember that the group has at least two Cisco routers, one of which is active and the other which is on standby, waiting for the active router to go down so it can step in. When the standby router steps in, it takes over the HSRP group IP address and starts routing accordingly. The group can hold more than two routers; however, an HSRP protocol is used to decide which router becomes active, which are on standby, and which "stay in the wings." Without going into detail, it is only when both the active and the standby router are both offline that the additional routers in the wings will negotiate who becomes active and who will remain on standby. One strength of this protocol is that it does not require additional hardware or software.

The three different levels of security depicted in Figure 8.1 also show three different setups for the router. In the "Limited" (a) configuration, there are no special security measures taken for the router. In case of a line or router failure, you are left without an Internet connection. The next level, "Extended" (b), makes use of a backup Internet connection, so in case the line fails we have a second way of automatically connecting to the Internet. Be sure that your ISP connects this backup line to its network in a way that circumvents the situation in which a hardware failure at the ISP's end prevents the backup connection from coming online. The "Advanced" (c) security setup uses two routers, where each is a separate connection to the Internet. To enhance this setup it makes sense also to use different ISPs for each router, so in case one ISP runs into serious problems, the other router will be operational.

Firewalls

The next device in line is the *firewall*, which is the gatekeeper of your BizTalk infrastructure. Firewalls come in all types of forms and shapes, from a homegrown Linux box turned firewall to a plug-and-play firewall. You have a number of options for supplying the functions of firewall, each with its own pros and cons:

- **Microsoft ISA Server** The Internet Security and Accelerator Server is more than just firewall software; it also contains Proxy Server software, Web-cache server, and Voice-over-IP (VoIP) server. In other words, it is packed with functionalities. The pros are that you can do a lot with this software. It can be managed from the Active Directory, and if your IT department only has Windows NT/2000 Server experience, you might feel inclined to use this software. The downside is that Windows 2000 Server is generally regarded as a platform vulnerable to attacks, and it takes a lot of tuning to harden the platform. Placing it at the edge of your environment poses risks. By placing the firewall in a Windows 2000 domain, you run the risk that if the ISA server is compromised, the attack might find its way into the domain using the same type of attack; hence, getting access to other servers in the domain, possibly including your BizTalk server. Security experts consider a firewall with no more than the basic firewall functionality a high security risk, since is it is then more difficult to harden the platform against attacks.

- **Windows 2000-based firewall application** There are a number of firewall applications available that run on a Windows 2000 platform; for example, Symantec (AXENT) Raptor and Check Point FireWall-1. The pros are that they run on Windows 2000, so you probably will not need extra knowledge and experience to run the firewall software. Second, it is a pure firewall application, with no additional functionality. Third, you are able to manage the firewall server from the Active Directory, although keeping the server stand-alone and not letting it join a domain is more secure. Cons are that Windows 2000 Server is generally regarded as a vulnerable OS, and placing it on the edge of your infrastructure poses additional risks to your infrastructure for being compromised.

- **Unix-based firewall software** This is a Unix system/server on which a firewall application is installed. Examples are Check Point Firewall-1 and Symantec/AXENT Raptor. The pros are that Unix can be hardened at installation time, since you have more control over what is installed on the system. For example, you will not be installing a Windows system, but stick instead to command-line interface. Second, Unix is a more open and simpler operating system, so turning it into a bastion server is easier. Third, even if the Unix firewall is compromised, the attacker needs another type of attack to force his or her way into the Windows 2000 server. Generally, a firewall running on a UNIX platform has better performance than an ISA Server, if both are running on the same type of hardware platform. The cons are that you need UNIX experience within your IT department, and if the firewall is going to be the only UNIX system, this may be a problem to acquire.

- **Internet-appliance firewall** Also called a "plug-and-play" firewall, this is a hardware platform with a hardened (embedded) operating system, nowadays often based on Linux, and with a tailor-made firewall application preinstalled. The pro side is that you only need to know how to work with the firewall application, so it does not take special knowledge. These platforms are much harder to compromise because the operating system has been stripped of all unnecessary code. Even when it is compromised, attackers are not able to access your Windows 2000 servers. On the negative side, it might be the odd system in your infrastructure, and not all Internet-appliance firewalls can be placed in a fail-over configuration.

- **Homegrown firewall** This is an Intel-based platform on which you install a Linux-flavor or BSD (OpenBSD/FreeBSD), harden it, and use the filtering tools that come with the OS to build a firewall. The real plus in this option is that it is the cheapest firewall solution possible, with all the firewall functionality you need. Additionally, if it is compromised, your Windows 2000 server will be protected until the attacker can come up with another method of attack. Linux and OpenBSD are open source operating systems, meaning that the code is freely available, so the security of the code is under a lot of scrutiny and vulnerabilities are quickly solved. The biggest drawback is that you need sufficient knowledge of Linux or OpenBSD to harden it and manage it. There also is no administration tool to manage the firewall.

Configuring & Implementing...

Bastion Servers

Security experts will advise you to install the ISA Server as a stand-alone server, just as you would do with a firewall that runs on a UNIX-based platform. Firewalls especially, but also proxy servers, are the barriers to protect you from attacks from the outside. As depicted in Figure 8.1, the outside is not only the Internet but also the parts of the local network where the users access the network. For reasons of additional security, firewalls and proxy servers should be installed as bastion servers. When installing a server as a bastion server, remember:

- The system should be fully operational as a stand-alone server, and not part of a distributed system.
- When installing the operating system, you must only install the core components.
- Only install additional software when necessary, like the ISA server software.
- All certified security fixes and patches must be installed.
- All Windows services or Unix daemons that are active but do not need to be used must be permanently disabled and preferably removed from the system.
- Deactivate all well-known IP ports.
- Remove all users from the system that are not used, and do not allow anonymous login.
- Restrict user access to an absolute minimum.
- Use security analysis tools—for example, ISS System Scanner—to determine if all security leaks are closed and all known vulnerabilities have been eliminated.

Before you make a decision on the firewall solution you will implement, weigh the pros and cons. Let security prevail, but always feel comfortable with your choice. In a majority of the situations, use an Internet-appliance firewall. In case you choose to use a Windows 2000 Server platform, try to avoid placing it in a domain by installing it standalone. Be careful with placing two-way trust between this server and other Windows servers. These can become an easy path for malicious attacks traversing from the firewall into your protected network. Since your BizTalk environment is based on Microsoft technology, it would be a good decision to choose a different operating system for this outer firewall, preferably a Unix-based OS.

Whatever type of firewall you choose, its function is to let in "good data" and keep out "bad data" by using *data filtering*. You enter rules into the firewall software that tell the firewall what to do with packets entering the firewall.

The first firewall rule should be something like: "ANY data from ANY source to ANY destination is DROPPED," meaning that the firewall by default denies all access. From that position, you start inserting rules that let specific data through. In our example, this would mean data that is addressed to the IIS server, SMTP server, or FTP server. Actually, you need to be more specific. For the IIS server, this means that only data is let through the firewall if it complies with the following criteria:

- You should only accept HTTPS connections, which respectively communicate by default over IP port 443. HTTP connection uses IP port 80.

- The destination can only be the outside IP address of the IIS server.

- The source can only be the IP addresses that originate from the customer sites.

Since you have decided that you only accept HTTPS connections from known sites, it is strongly recommended not to use the default port, but choose a unique port number, from 2000 and up, for each site. Now you will only accept a connection if the IP address *and* IP port match. For the customer, this means that the Web address looks like https://order.company.com:8080.

This is not viable if you have a Web site that allows users in on an anonymous basis. In this case, you cannot filter based on the IP address of the client, and therefore, you cannot assign a special port, especially if the number of possible customers is unlimited. In this case, you need to accept all HTTP traffic to your Web site using default port 80.

For the SMTP server you can keep using the default ports. This is port 25 to retrieve mail from a mail server on the Internet, and port 110 to send mail to the mail server. Since your mail server sets up the connection, the firewall rule should be "IP data over ports 25 and 110 with source IP address is the external IP address of the local mail server, and destination is the IP address of the remote mail drop is ACCEPTED." In the case of the FTP server, that uses IP ports 20 and 21, you can also choose to change these port numbers. For both the SMTP and FTP server, you have to tell your customers on which ports they have to communicate.

There is a second important function for the firewall in protecting your BizTalk infrastructure, Network Address and Port Translation (NAPT). You have probably heard of Network Address Translation, or NAT. The principle of NAT and NAPT is that the firewall substitutes the original IP address of a system with another IP address that is physically not in your network. Using this, you can obscure the IP addressing structure of your local network and make it difficult for direct attacks on your servers. It has also another function; namely, the number of IP addresses that you get from an ISP is very limited, so you need to share these limited IP addresses, say six, with all the systems that need Internet access.

In the case of the firewall, you are faced with the question of what to do if the firewall goes on the blink. The type of firewall is important, since most firewalls retain information regarding connections that are allowed to pass the firewall. This session information is part of what is called *stateful inspection*. Some firewalls can be set up in a load-balancing configuration, and some in active-passive fail-over configuration. The latter means that one firewall is actually doing the work, and the passive one checks frequently to ensure the other one is still alive. If the active firewall no longer responds, the passive firewall takes over. To do this, the active firewall sends session information to the passive firewall so it is synchronized at all times. In case of load-balancing firewalls, the sessions are divided between the firewalls, which synchronize with the session information of the other firewall.

Again, three different firewall configurations are depicted in Figure 8.1. The "Limited" (a) configuration connects the internal network to the router (external network). Although you only let traffic destined for the Web server through, you enable direct contact between the internal and external network. The "Extended" (b) configuration uses a third leg of the firewall as a "demilitarized zone," where the Web server is residing. In this setup, only the Web server has contact with the internal network. The "Advanced" (c) solution is a firewall in fail-over mode, and creates a double-firewalled DMZ. For the internal firewall, the Microsoft ISA server is depicted, although this could be any other firewall. The strength of this solution is that if the outer firewall is compromised, there is still no direct access to the internal network.

Proxies

The next line of defense can be formed by the Internet Security and Accelerator Server (ISA Server), the successor of MS Proxy Server 2.0. Although you could decide to substitute it with a Unix-based firewall, the advantage of the ISA server is the proxy component. Instead of the IIS server setting up a connection with the MSMQ server, it sets up a connection with the ISA server, and the ISA server sets up a connection with the MSMQ server. This has a slight negative effect on performance, but enhances security. The network between the firewall and the ISA server is a demilitarized zone, a neutral zone that forms a buffer between your company network; in this case, the BizTalk environment and the outside world. Nobody can have direct access to your servers in the DMZ. Besides proxying, the ISA server also does data filtering, since all you need is access to the MSMQ server, which uses IP port 1801.

The ISA server runs on a Microsoft Windows 2000 platform, so it can make use of the load balancing or Cluster Services of Windows 2000. For you to use the Cluster Service, you need to have Windows 2000 Advanced Server installed.

Only the "Advanced" (c) solution in Figure 8.1 makes use of a proxy server; annex firewall, in this case. Since the ISA server can do both proxying and fire-walling, it is a budget-friendly solution. Symantec Enterprise Firewall (formerly known as AXENT Raptor) is a firewall that does application proxying. The strength of the proxy is that it is not transparent to the connection. In fact, the connection ends in the proxy server, and a new connection—in this case, to the MSMQ Server—is set up. Depending on the implementation, the proxy can also directly contact the BizTalk server. Take notice of the fact that the proxy server should always have at least two network connections, one for the internal network and one for the external network. It works with one network card, but this is considered less secure. A nice feature of the Microsoft Proxy Server is *reverse proxying*, also called *reverse hosting*. If you really want to protect your Web server, you could place a proxy between the firewall and the Web server. By reverse proxying, you advertise to the world that the proxy server is your Web server when in fact, IIS is running on the proxy server. However, the proxy indeed acts like a Web server, only it redirects the requests through the backdoor to the actual Web server. This gives you an additional barrier between an attacker and the information on the Web server.

There is no actual defense line between the BizTalk server and the SQL server, although you can add another firewall or ISA server. You can also rely on network security, assuming that the risk of somebody forcing access to the SQL server is low.

Server Configurations

Microsoft recommends that you use three servers for optimal performance of BizTalk Server 2000: one for BizTalk Server 2000, one for the Tracking database, and one for BizTalk Messaging Management and Share Queue Databases. Additionally, Microsoft makes recommendations for the BizTalk infrastructure in regard to horizontal and vertical scalability. Horizontal scalability is adding CPUs, memory, and storage to a server—also called "in-the-box" scalability—which gives the server the capability to handle an increase of work. Vertical scalability has to do with adding additional servers to the infrastructure, and is called "out-the-box" scalability. Here, the load is spread over the available servers. However, the recommendations are all based on increasing performance. Sadly enough, Microsoft makes no recommendations regarding securing this Web of servers from disruptions, let alone how to recover from disruptions.

Independent from the number of servers your BizTalk infrastructure holds and the complexity of your BizTalk solution, the main focus in regard to possible disruptions is prevention of data loss. Data sits mainly in three places:

- A database
- A message queue
- A process

You can minimize the loss of data by:

- Enhancing the server so the failure of a component does not bring the entire server down
- Using modular hardware solutions
- Enforcing asynchronous communication between tiers where possible, which makes restoring and rebuilding of the data easier
- Backing up data in such a way that restoring data does not imply loss of data (see subsection "Safeguarding Installations")

By now, you might wonder what considerations there are in the hardware configuration of Windows 2000 Server in your BizTalk infrastructure. Keep the following points in mind:

- Choose a scalable server platform, and configure it in that way, with at least two processors and preferably room for two more. Start out with enough memory, but use as few banks as possible. One 512MB memory module is better than two 256MB modules.

- Make sure it has a RAID controller, and put in two internal SCSI II disks in a RAID-1 or RAID-10 configuration. These RAID configurations always go in sets of two, in which one is an exact copy of the other. This internal storage should be used for the operating system and other system software.

- Put in at least two of the same network interface cards (NICs) and configure them as load balancing using Windows Load Balancing Services (WLBS), which is part of the Windows 2000 Clustering Services. For security reasons, use different NICs to connect the server with different tiers. In Figure 8.1, the IIS server connects with one interface to the network with the firewall. This NIC is called the *external interface*. The other interface connects to the network with the ISA server, the *internal interface*. This is the same for the ISA server, MSMQ server, and the BizTalk server. By forcing data to enter over a specific NIC, you have better control over the way servers are accessed and therefore enhance the security. You can take this a step further and add a third NIC that is only in use for administration purposes.

- Fit the server platform with at least two power supply units (PSUs), hook both PSUs up to a different UPSs, and make sure both UPSs are on different power groups. Be sure that you check the UPSs on a yearly basis.

- Use a separate storage system that connects to the server with one link, but preferably use a second fail-over/standby link. Again, you should connect these links to separate adapters in the server platform. Depending on your budget and preference, this can be a SCSI or Fiber Channel. These storage systems should be used for the application data or, if you put the server in a Microsoft Cluster, all "shared" data.

- For the storage system, take the same configuration considerations into account, such as RAID-1 or RAID-10 configuration, two RAID controllers, and two PSUs.

- Use autoloader tape units. Be sure that every tier in your BizTalk infrastructure is equipped with at least one, to ensure the independence of a tier and the ability to restore a tier more easily. Autoloaders prevent backups from being interrupted if the end of the cartridge is reached sooner than the end of the backup cycle. Remember that with some SQL Server 2000 backup schemes, it is essential that the tape unit is directly attached to the server. In other cases, or if you use third-party backup or archiving software, you can make use of tape units that are attached to other servers.

Figure 8.1 showed a number of configuration possibilities, from simple (three servers) to complex (10 servers). This is clearly also a budgetary issue. If we first look to the "Limited" (a) configuration, there are three BizTalk-related servers: the BizTalk server, the SQL server, and the MSMQ server. The latter is introduced to prevent direct contact between the Web server and the BizTalk server, a pure security decision. It also gives you other application-related advantages, such as asynchronous request processing and prioritizing. It is your choice to make use of the MSMQ server, but it also follows Microsoft's .NET Architecture guidelines. In fact, technically, you are able to integrate the BizTalk and SQL servers on one server platform.

The server hardware is straightforward, although be sure you are able to easily add memory and storage to the server. For the BizTalk server with two CPUs, and 512MB memory, 18GB RAID-1 storage is sufficient for an average BizTalk application. An important factor in the performance of the BizTalk server is the number of COM processes, thus the more worker threads that are concurrently running. As every thread needs to be serviced, the system has to switch between threads, known as *context switching*. This intensive CPU activity can result in performance degradation.

The platform you need for the SQL Server depends on the load the BizTalk Application will put on the SQL Server. This load is primarily related to the use of Stored Procedures, the type of database access these Stored Procedures deploy and the size of the database.

An SQL server needs two to four CPUs, 512 to 1024MB memory, and 18 to 36GB RAID-1 storage. The way you divide the storage is an important performance issue; separating SQL logs and DTC logs and databases can provide an noticeable performance increase since these are all I/O-bound services. The MSMQ server and IIS server can use the same specifications as the BizTalk server. Again, depending on the load and the accepted response times, these numbers must be adapted. Remember: Adding memory will not automatically improve performance, and too little memory slows your entire system and can even introduce instability of the server.

Technically, one backup unit can service all servers in a domain, provided you use backup software that supports this. If you want to make full use of the backup functionality of the SQL server, you need to directly attach a tape unit to this server.

The "Extended" (b) configuration in Figure 8.1 already makes use of Windows Clustering Services. This is necessary for the SQL and MSMQ servers, since the SQL and MSMQ services are not able to share their persistent data. For the BizTalk server, you can also choose load balancing in conjunction with Microsoft Application Center 2000. A cluster needs a separate storage device that can be shared between the cluster servers.

NOTE

The storage device is shared; the data on the device cannot be shared!

Although not necessary, we strongly recommend that the servers in a cluster have identical hardware. Doing so makes life easier for the administrator, and leaves you with the ability to switch hardware around in case of a small disaster.

An additional tape unit has been added in the "Extended" (b) configuration, not just so the backup load can be balanced, but also so that in the case of a tape unit failure, the other can take over. The Web server is not load balanced or clustered, since it is not supposed to hold important (and persistent) data.

The "Advanced" (c) configuration in Figure 8.1 adds more fail-over capabilities to the servers, and a load-balanced ISA server to the environment. As noted earlier, the ISA server adds firewall and proxy protection to the BizTalk environment. In addition, two network cards are used in the ISA server, so the internal and external network can be separated.

All servers are load balanced or clustered to increase the availability and, when necessary, spread the load of increased utilization. Doubling the number of server network connections can add load balancing over the cards, and fail-over in case of a defective network card.

NOTE

Do not use network cards with two network connections; this will not help you if the card fails. Instead, use two cards.

Using tape units with an autoloader can prevent the backup from stalling if it reaches the end of the tape. It will load a new tape and finish the backup process.

The most interesting point is that local PCs no longer directly connect to the LAN with the BizTalk, SQL. and MSMQ servers—any access to these servers will be proxied. This is a security measure that ensures that users no longer have uncontrolled access to the network where the servers reside. In case the local users need to make use of a Web server to access the BizTalk application, it is advisable to place a Web server on the segment where the users reside, making full use of the ISA server.

Figure 8.1 also showed that increasing security measures also increases the number of security zones. Each zone adds hurdles to the infrastructure that attackers have to overcome to ultimately be able to reach the servers in the internal network, where all the important business data is stored.

A last remark: The necessary UPSs have been left out of Figure 8.1. It is strongly advised to use UPSs for all servers, not only for catching power failures and doing a safe and graceful shutdown of the servers, but also to level out any fluctuations in the power supply.

Designing & Planning...

Windows 2000 Versions and Clustering Services

When implementing a secured BizTalk Server 2000 solution, you will use clustering or load-balancing at the network operating system level. These functionalities are only available in the Windows 2000 Advanced Server and DataCenter Server. If you want to go for a server with more than four CPUs you need to use the DataCenter Server version of Windows 2000.

It is good practice to limit the number of different configurations, which makes system administration tasks more transparent. Install the same OS version/build on all servers, including service packs and patches. If possible, when buying or leasing the servers, make sure they consist of the same hardware (up to the same revision numbers) and use the same firmware.

With network load balancing (NLB), all incoming traffic is divided over the participating network interfaces, on one or more servers. All interfaces share the same load balancing IP address, in addition to a

Continued

unique IP address. Server clustering is different; one server is put in standby (inactive mode) waiting to take over for the active server. Only one of the servers can be active, since only one can have ownership of the cluster storage. The servers in the cluster share a heartbeat network that signals if a server is still up. A big drawback is that individual services can "die" without the other server taking over, since there is still a heartbeat.

Microsoft now has an application called Application Center 2000 that can be used to perform component load balancing (CLB). CLB also uses the term *cluster*; only it carries a different meaning than that for server cluster. Servers that are part of a CLB cluster do not share storage or a heartbeat network. The server must have the same COM+ applications installed, so calls to COM+ components are round-robin distributed over the servers in the CLB cluster, based on a response-time table. Therefore, if a server goes down, it will have no response time and will be excluded from the list. Application Center 2000 is a good solution to use between your Web server(s) and the BizTalk application. Please take note, however, that COM+ components *must* be cluster aware.

Installing the Servers

You considered all the options, selected the proper configurations, and are now ready to install the servers, thereby introducing the next phase in securing Windows 2000 servers. Before you put the CD-ROM in the server and start booting the machine, consider the following:

- Make sure that you have all the necessary software, the correct versions, and corresponding licenses.

- Make sure that the servers you have are complete and diagnostically working.

- Define an Active Directory (AD) structure, first deciding if the BizTalk environment will have its own domain, or will be part of an existing domain. Let's assume you make a special BizTalk domain, with its own AD forest. You need a server that will become the domain controller (DC), so you must install an additional server for this purpose. If your AD structure contains security vulnerabilities, you run the risk that someone who "hijacks" one server can use these vulnerabilities to gain control over other servers. Adding a server to an AD domain has many advantages over installing it as a stand–alone server.

- Check Microsoft TechNet for possible "Known Issues" before starting the installation.

- Check the website of the server manufacturer for known issues with the firmware and device drivers, and download the latest Windows 2000 certified versions. Note that the latest version of drivers are not always certified, so only get those that are W2K certified.

- Make sure all the servers have access to the Internet, so you can confirm that you have applied all available updates, and because many Microsoft products need to be activated after installation.

- Make an installation plan and protocol. The plan describes the sequence in which you want to install the servers. My suggestion is to go one by one or by cluster; finish the complete installation, do thorough testing, make a full backup, and go on to the next server. The protocol is the checklist of what you have to install and in what sequence. Do not install Windows 2000 components if the server does not need them. Be extra careful with components such as Windows Scripting Host (WSH) and Collaboration Data Objects (CDO), as these can be a recipe for disaster if your server is compromised. For example, e-mail viruses such as "ILOVEYOU" could only run on systems with these components installed.

- Make a logbook of every server, starting with the installation. This is not the most fun part of system administration, but it might hold valuable information in case you run into problems further down the road.

- After each step in the installation process, check the event log for possible errors. In case there are unexpected errors, be sure to fix them before continuing.

- In case of load balancing or clustering, test to make sure everything is working properly. The setting up and configuring of a cluster with, for example, SQL Server 2000, can be tricky. Therefore, make sure you test that the active server fails over correctly.

- Set up your BizTalk environment tier by tier. Make sure that communication between servers works correctly.

The last step in securing server configurations is the one we can call *access restriction*. Much can be said about securing the Windows platform, so much so that you could write a complete book about it. This chapter only touches on several of these aspects, so for more in-depth information you can read *Hack Proofing Windows 2000 Server* (ISBN 1-931836-49-3), also from Syngress Publishing. As you read under "Roles and Access Levels," your main targets are to:

- Limit the users who have direct access to the server.

- Restrict users' access to only those parts of the server they need.

- Limit access to the lowest access rights possible.

WARNING

The sequence in which you install software can be crucial for the proper working of your system. History has shown that certain applications install different versions of DLL files over existing ones without asking, or they may ask "Replace with a newer version?" implying that you should answer "Yes." The result is often that an application that had been working without a flaw suddenly ceases to do so. This is the reason that on Windows NT 4 systems, the service packs had to be reinstalled after you installed a new piece of software.

Much like we did with the firewall, begin by disallowing access to the server altogether, and then add groups and users to the system one by one. Within Windows 2000, the security of users, groups, and computers are managed through different tools. Instead of using these separate management tools, you can group them using Microsoft Management Console (MMC) shown in Figure 8.2. To do so:

1. Go to **Start | Run**, enter **mmc**, and press **OK**.

2. Within MMC, go to **Console | Add/Remove Snap-in…**.

3. On the **Standalone** tab, press **Add…**.

4. A list of available snap-ins is shown in Figure 8.3. Select an appropriate snap-in, press **Add…**, and choose any others you will need.

5. Now press **Close**, and when you get back in the Add/Remove Snap-in dialog press **OK**.

6. Save the console through **Console | Save** or **Save As…**. This saved MCC configuration is added to the list of Administrative Tools.

Figure 8.2 Using the Microsoft Management Console for Security Management

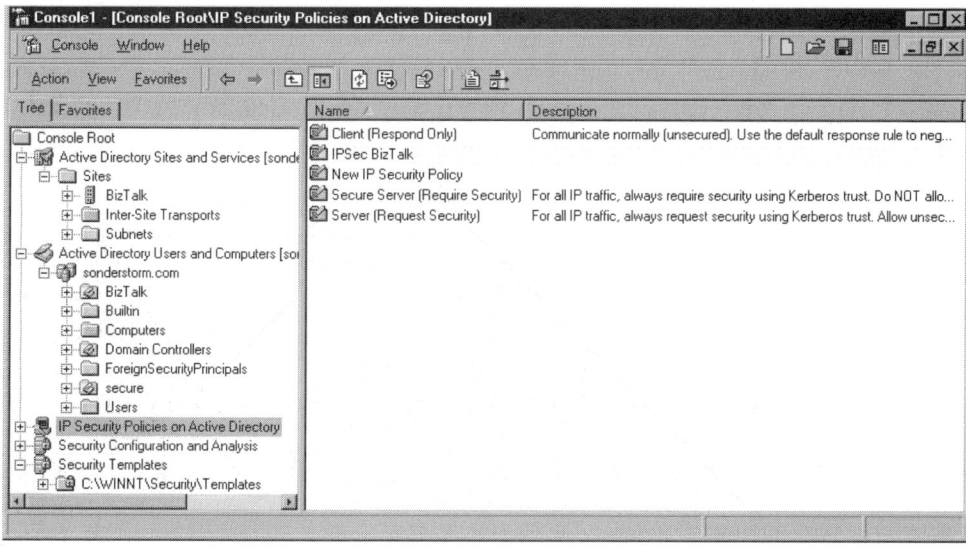

Figure 8.3 Select the Appropriate Security Management Snap-Ins

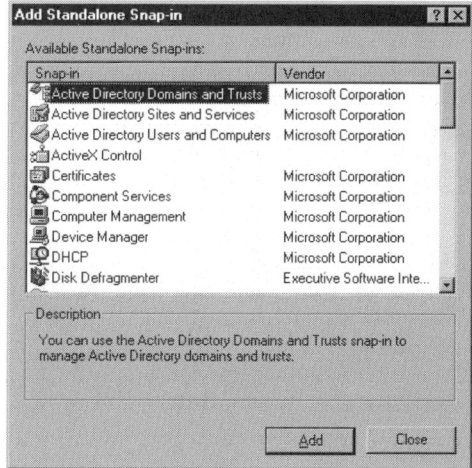

It is virtually impossible to give you all the details on securing your BizTalk servers in one chapter. Nevertheless, here are some practical recommendations on configuring Windows 2000 security that you can use as pointers in establishing a more secure configuration:

- Never use anonymous logons, not even on the IIS server. Each person who needs access to a server has to log on with his or her own account.

- Use group policies to maintain control over the computer and user configuration of a group.

- Remove any type of application on the production servers that can influence the BizTalk runtime environment or easily modify BizTalk files. Be careful with the WHS component!

- Make sure that you can trace the use of the system through the event log. You can control the auditing settings in Group Policy. We recommend that you turn on as much auditing as possible during the first month of production. This first month is the life "shake down" of the system, and the event log can provide you with a wealth of information. After this initial period, you can reduce the level of editing. Be sure to analyze the event logs on a daily basis, and after analyzing them, make a backup copy.

- Create an account for every BizTalk Server-related service. This account has some differences in user rights from that of an interactive user. These specific user rights for the service account should negate the rights of the interactive user. To do so:

  1. Enable **Act as part of the operating system**.

  2. Disable **Deny logon as a service**.

  3. Disable **Shutdown the system**.

- Defuse the system/domain-managed group "Everyone." Everyone is a group that roams around your system and can be granted access to parts of your server without you knowing it. The best approach is to take all the rights away from Everyone. You do this in two areas. First, eliminate any risks in accessing sites by adding Everyone explicitly to the Security list and allow them read-only access. Second, check all COM+ applications and remove Everyone from the user list of the roles (see the section "Securing XLANG Schedules" later in the chapter).

- Do not use the Administrator account. Instead, make an identifiable account with administrator rights for every employee who needs administrator access. Sharing administrative accounts makes it harder to trace system-related issues.

- Do not use REGEDIT.EXE, but rather use the administrative tools. Registry values can be reset when you install additional system software, or apply a service pack or security patch. Of course, there are times when you have no choice but to use REGEDIT. Before doing so, make certain that this is necessary and if there is no other way to accomplish the same. If you do so, enter these changes in the logbook, and make before and after copies of the Registry's subtree.

Safeguarding Installations

As mentioned earlier, it is a good practice to make backups of your system after installation. It would be even better to make a full system backup every few weeks and after every significant configuration change. Backups are a safety net in the event something goes terribly wrong, like a burned-out server. The system you put on tape never represents the exact situation at the moment the system fails. Again, here is where the logbook comes into play. Other points of attention include:

- Never store tapes in or close to the computer room; in case of disaster, you might not be able to retrieve the tapes.

- Always put tapes directly into the data vault after the backup.

- Periodically test the tapes to confirm that you can restore the data from tape.

- Periodically perform a full restore of a server.

- Replace tape cartridges after a year to lower the risk of read/write failures due to reuse of the tapes.

Proactive Maintenance

BizTalk solutions can be very important to an organization, and their availability is expected to be high. This is only possible if the system administration focuses on preventing disruptions and problems. As we have seen, this is very different from being ready to solve problems.

The chance that a component in your server will fail increases with the age of the component. Replacing components in business-critical servers, such as the ones that make up your BizTalk infrastructure, after a fixed period makes good sense. For example, you should replace hard disks after two years. This does not mean that you should throw them away! They can still be very useful in less critical systems, or you can sell them to a refurbisher. Alternatively, you can use heuristic management tools to monitor the server components and warn you of forthcoming failures.

Another sensible task is to take a server offline once every year, open it up, and clean the inside. Dust and lint can clog the ventilation and fans, and can cause static discharges that can destroy the CPU, memory, or the entire motherboard.

Proactive maintenance is also about keeping things structured and organized; for example, being able to find your way around documentation, logbooks, and computer rooms. Computer rooms can sometimes give the impression that a bomb went off inside, with cable bundles that look more like spaghetti on a plate, seemingly starting somewhere and going nowhere. Organized and labeled cables are a good protection from the wrong cable being detached.

Network Protection

The BizTalk infrastructure can be extensive if you tie it to the Internet, integrate it with Microsoft Commerce Server or another Microsoft .Net Server product, and link it to your back office where your ERP system is residing. Data is floating all over the place, and by default available for everybody's eyes. Network sniffers are available in abundance, so you should take care that valuable data is kept hidden for prying eyes.

The best, if not only, way to do this is by using data encryption and secured communication. Within the Windows 2000 environment, you can use Secured Socket Layer (SSL) or Internet Protocol Security (IPSec).

NOTE

Although SSL 3.0 is still widely used, it has been succeeded by Transport Layer Security (TLS), which is described in RFC-2246 (www.ietf.org/rfc/rfc2246.txt) and is supported by Windows 2000. Windows 2000 also comes with Service Pack 2 standard with 128-bit encryption. To check what the encryption level of your system is, point your Web browser to www.fortify.net/sslcheck.html.

You will use SSL to go between the IIS Server and the clients that want to contact the Web Server and it should be enforced for every user that wants to access the IIS Server, not only the ones that access the IIS Server from outside your network.

For most SSL applications, it is used to protect the client, not the server. From your standpoint, you also want conformation that the client is trustworthy, so the client, actually the user, needs a certificate too. Remember that the IIS Server forces the negotiation of a secured channel, but the client decides what type of encryption is going to be used.

You can select the security protocols in the Web browser (Figure 8.4). Go to **Tools | Internet Options | Advanced**, and scroll down to the security section.

Figure 8.4 Selecting the Security Protocols in Internet Explorer 5.5

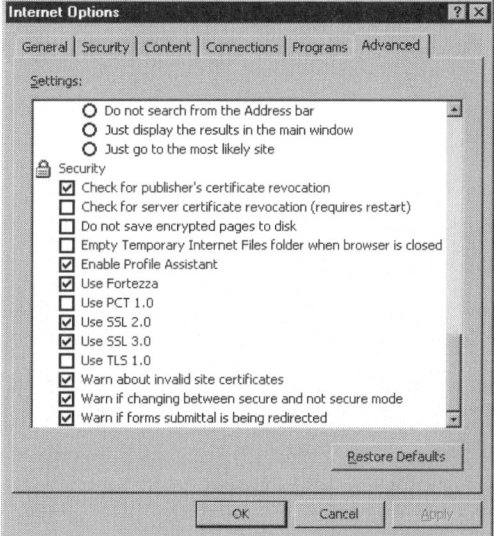

> ## Configuring & Implementing...
>
> ### Security Protocols on IIS Servers
>
> A connection between a client and a Web server only goes into Secure HTTP (HTTPS), if the server demands it. Then, a negotiation follows in establishing which security protocol to use. From the point of view of the IIS server, you might want to enforce strong security and not use PCT 1.0 and SSL 2.0. However, as you can see in Figure 8.4, the default way is the client "choosing" the protocol, and the server accepting any secure protocol. You can change that by disabling these protocols on the

Continued

server, so IIS is unable to use them. In case the client and server cannot agree on a common secure protocol, the server will deny access. As noted earlier, direct editing in the Registry is not recommended; however, in this situation, we are left with no other choice.

To disable one or more of the security protocols, you need to do the following:

1. Run **regedt32.exe**, through **Start | Run**. Do not use **regedit.exe**, since you are not able to set the correct values.

2. After the Registry Editor has started, open the following Registry folder: HKEY_Local_Machine\System\CurrentControlSet\Control\SecurityProviders\SCHANNEL\Protocols You will see five folders:
   - Multi-Protocol Unified Hello
   - PCT 1.0
   - SSL 2.0
   - SSL 3.0
   - TLS 1.0

3. Let's suppose you want to disable the PCT 1.0 protocol, so open the **PCT 1.0\Server folder**.

4. Now you need to add the binary value **00 00 00 00**. You do this by **Edit | Add Value...** For the **Value Name**, enter **Enable**, and for the **Data Type**, choose **REG_BINARY**, and then press **OK**.

5. Now the Binary Editor opens. Enter the value **00000000**, and press **OK**.

6. Do the same for all the server-side protocols you want to disable.

7. When you are finished, you need to restart the server to activate the changes.

NOTE

Remember to document these changes, since Registry modifications are not traceable.

It is clearly not advisable to let the client decide what the level of security is. However, the HTTP-based security only covers the communication between the IIS server and the clients, but not between the servers in your BizTalk infrastructure.

This is where the use of IPSec comes in, an open standard described in RFC-2401 (www.ietf.org/rfc/rfc2401.txt). IPSec comes in two flavors: Authentication Header (AH; RFC-2402) and Encapsulating Security Payload (ESP; RFC-2406). The difference is clearly stated in the RFC-2401:

- The IP Authentication Header (AH) provides connectionless integrity, data origin authentication, and an optional anti-replay service.

- The Encapsulating Security Payload (ESP) protocol may provide confidentiality (encryption), and limited traffic flow confidentiality. It also may provide connectionless integrity, data origin authentication, and an anti-replay service. (One or the other set of these security services must be applied whenever ESP is invoked.)

- Both AH and ESP are vehicles for access control, based on the distribution of cryptographic keys and the management of traffic flows relative to these security protocols.

NOTE

Within Windows 2000, AH is hyped as medium security, and ESP as high.

Setting up an IPSec connection starts a negotiation regarding the authentication methods and encryption algorithm, as described in the IKE/Oakley standard (RFCs 2409 and 2412). Before activating IPSec on your Windows 2000 Server network interface (as described in the next section), you should consider the following issues:

- Depending on the amount of communication over the network, which can be substantial for a distributed BizTalk environment, the bandwidth utilization can jump as much as 10 percent. Make sure there is enough bandwidth available before making all IP communication secure.

- Depending on the amount of network communication a server has, encryption/decryption algorithms can increase a CPU's load by around 15 percent. If the server is not equipped with sufficient CPU power, it will slow the server.

- The more secure the encryption standard is, the more CPU power it takes. As you will understand, there is a significant difference between using DES or its more secure "brother," Triple DES (3DES). Make your choice depending on the risks you run that your encryption keys are subject to *crypto-analysts* (that is the nice word for crypto-criminals).

- If you really want to go for the strongest possible encryption, it would be a smart decision to use hardware-embedded encryption and not the software version (such as that which is activated in Windows 2000). By equipping your servers with NICs that have embedded 3DES/DES encryption, encryption will be done at wire speed, and will not claim any server CPU and memory resources. To get an idea of what is available, visit the Red Creek Communications site (www.redcreek.com).

IPSec Policies

You activate IPSec in Windows 2000 through IPSec policies. You are able to make your own policies, suiting your particular needs. Here we will only look at the predefined ones:

- **Client (Respond Only)** Mostly used on Windows 2000 Professional clients that will only activate IPSec if requested by a server.

- **Server (Request Security)** Used on the server if it is not necessary to use IPSec. The server will request the client to use IPSec. If the client denies, then insecure IP is used.

- **Secure Server (Require Security)** A connection is only established if the client has at least a "Respond Only" IPSec policy activated. If the client is not able to set up an IPSec connection, the server will refuse the connection.

There are a number of ways to set up and manage IPSec policies for users, computers, and servers. The best way is to centralize the management of IPSec policies using the MMC with the IP Security Policies snap-in. You will do this on the local or domain level (Figure 8.5). Assuming you have an Active Directory domain in place, doing it on domain level makes the policies available for all computers (and users) in the domain. You can assign the policies from within every group policy. It is beyond the scope of this chapter to explain the way group policies contribute to the security of your domain. However, keep the following points in mind:

- A group policy defines settings for computers and users.

- Every time a computer boots Windows and contacts the domain controller, the settings are transferred to the computer.

- Every time users log on to Windows, the settings are downloaded from the domain controller.

- Group policies can be defined on different levels within the domain and are applied in the order of: local, site, domain, and organizational units.

- By default, group policy settings are inherited from earlier applied group policies, and can subsequently be overwritten by the group policies that are applied later.

- IPSec policies need to be explicitly assigned to users or computers from within a group policy.

Figure 8.5 Using the Microsoft Management Console IP Security Policies Snap-In

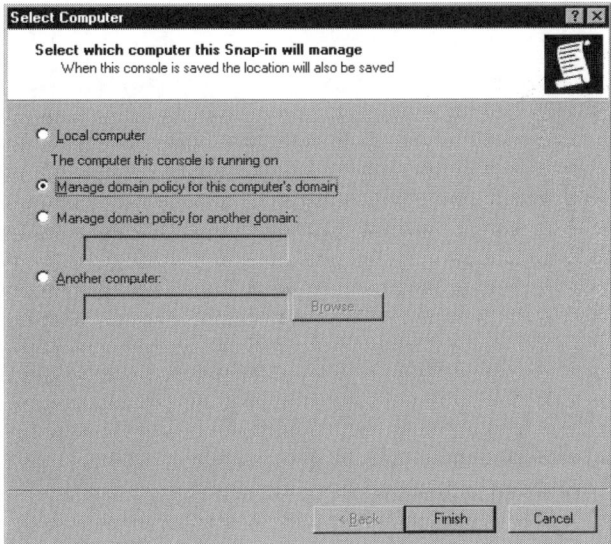

WARNING

Do not change the IPSec policies from within a group policy! Since IPSec policies are global to the domain, these changes will take affect throughout the domain. In case you need a slightly different IPSec policy, create a new one, and assign it to the group policy.

For Windows 2000 servers that are not part of a domain, you can also set an IPSec policy directly on an interface. To do so:

1. Select **My Network Places** on the desktop, and open the **Properties** window.

2. Select the **Local Network Connection** that represents the proper NIC, and open the **Properties** window.

3. Open the **Properties** dialog of **Internet Protocol (TCP/IP)** and press **Advanced...**.

4. Selective the **Options** tab, and now you are able the set the IP Security Properties.

To give you more understanding about how to activate IPSec between your servers in the BizTalk environment, we are going to look at a quick exercise. Your BizTalk environment is comprised of three servers: BizTalk-1, Tracking-1, and Database-1. They are all part of the same domain and need the same IP Security characteristics. For the sake of the exercise, let us assume all three servers reside in the same subnet and have direct communication with each other. Group the three servers in the default site and create an IPSec policy for the three servers.

To activate the IP Security policy in the group policy of the site:

1. Open the **Microsoft Management Console** and be sure that at least the following snap-ins are added to the list: Active Directory Sites and Services, and IP Security Policies on Active Directory.

2. Open **Active Directory Sites and Services**, and open the **Sites** folder. You will at least see one site in the list that is created as a default site in the domain.

3. Open this **Sites** folder, and then open the **Servers** folder. The domain controller is already in there. Now add the other three servers by right-clicking the **Servers** folder, and selecting **New | Server**.

4. Now, click on **IP Security Policies on Active Directory**. The right part of the dialog shows the available IPSec policies (Figure 8.5).

5. Right-click the **IP Security Policies on Active Directory**, and select **All Tasks | Create IP Security Policy**. This will start the **IP Security Policy Wizard**.

6. The first step in the wizard is giving the policy a name and description. In the example, the name "IPSec BizTalk" is used.

7. Next, you are asked if the policy should **Activate the default response rule**. Keep it checked. It will work as a safety net; in case other rules in the policy do not apply, the server will at least positively respond to a request using IPSec.

8. After clicking **Next**, you must decide what authentication is used by the default response rule. You are presented with three options:

   ■ **Windows 2000 default (Kerberos V5 protocol)** This option only works if both client and server are members of a trusted domain. The Kerberos server needs to validate the authenticity of the client, and server for that matter. The use of Kerberos might be regarded as the most solid solution with a Windows 2000 environment. Remember, not every environment supports Kerberos V5. (More information on Kerberos V5 can be found in RFC 1510. Since the first release of Windows 2000, there is discussion regarding if Microsoft made some modifications to their Kerberos implementation that are not described in any RFC.)

   ■ **Use a certificate from this certificate authority (CA)** This option should be used if Kerberos is not available as an authentication method. After selecting this option, you can browse through your shared key store on the server. If this is not available, you can select a predefined certificate, which is less secure.

   ■ **Use the string to protect the key exchange (preshared key)** It is advised not to use this method since is far from secure. Both parties wanting to set up an IPSec connection must enter the exact same preshared key. Additionally, this key is stored in readable— hence, nonencrypted—format.

9. Since all the servers are in the same domain, select **Windows 2000 default**.

10. After clicking **Next**, you can finish the wizard. If you want to make changes to the policy properties, keep **Edit Properties** checked. Then, click **Finish**.

11. Now you enter the IPSec Properties dialog (Figure 8.6), with two tab pages: Rules and General. In the IP Security Rules list you see one rule, the one you created with the wizard.

Figure 8.6 Use the Properties Page to Maintain the IP Security Policy

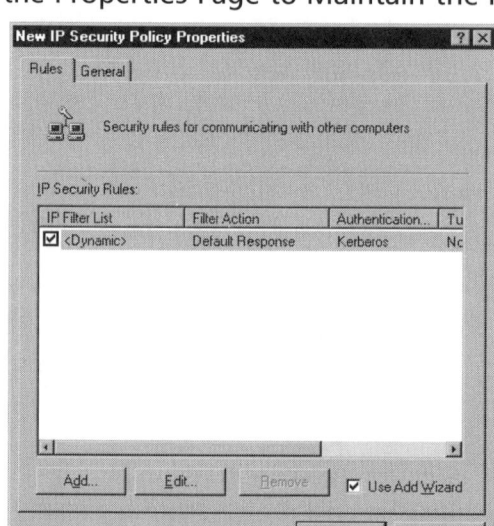

12. You see in the bottom-right corner the option **Use Add Wizard**. If you uncheck this and subsequently click **Add...**, you have to manually configure a new rule. Keeping it checked will activate the Security Rule Wizard. Without the wizard, you can configure rules in more detail, but you must have a more in-depth knowledge of how rules work.

13. To see what is behind the rule in the list, select the **rule line** and press **Edit...**. You will see the Edit Rule Properties dialog with three tab pages. The Security Methods tab is shown in Figure 8.7. As mentioned earlier during the initial phase of setting up an IPSec connection, there is a negotiation. When this rule executes, the Security Method preference order gives the sequence in which the security settings are negotiated; in our case, by the BizTalk Servers.

Figure 8.7 Editing a Rule of an IP Security Policy

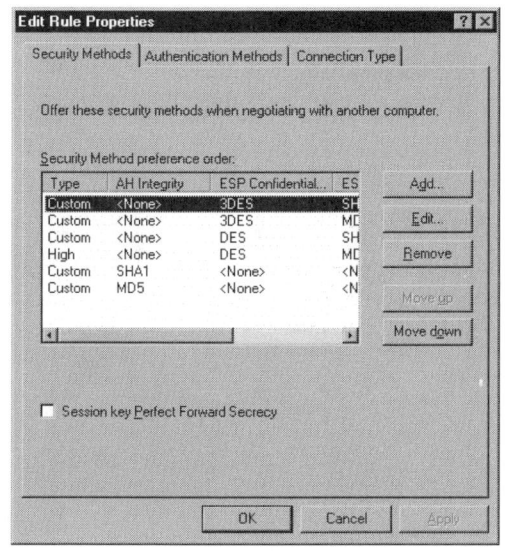

14. Now, select the first line in the **Security Method** list, press **Edit...**, and you will get into the **Modify Security Method** tab. Since Custom (for expert users) is selected, you will now press **Settings...**.

15. The **Session Key Settings** box in the dialog (Figure 8.8) allows you to **Generate a new key every** so many kilobytes or seconds. You can check the **seconds** option and leave the value at 3600. This means that every hour, the servers involved in this IPSec connection will exchange new session keys. By doing this, you make it more difficult for crypto-analysts to break your key. Figure 8.8 shows that the Security Method is set to ESP and it makes use of key hashing algorithm SHA1 and the encryption algorithm 3DES. By using these, you have enabled the most secure communication available within Windows 2000.

16. Press **OK** to leave this option, and close the **IPSec Properties** window.

17. Go back to the **Site object** where earlier you added the servers. Right-click the **site** and select **Properties**. You enter the **Properties** dialog and then select the **Group Policy** tab. A list of group policies is shown. In our case, this will likely be empty, so you have the choice of the available buttons:

- **New** With this button, you create a new group policy.

■ **Add** With this button, you can select a group policy that is already in use with the Active Directory tree.

Figure 8.8 Modifying the Session Key Settings

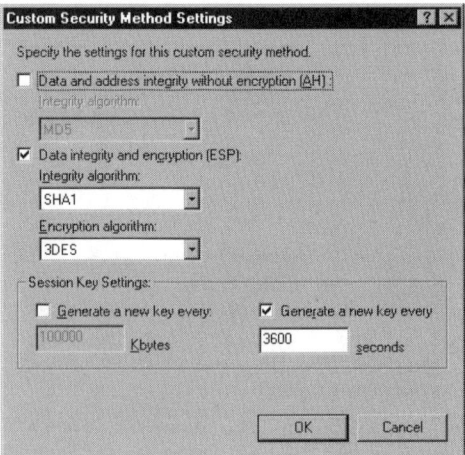

18. Select **New**, give the policy the name **BizTalk Group Policy**, and press **Enter**. Next, press **Edit** and a Group Policy dialog will open. It shows two configuration trees: Computer and User. You will use Computer.

19. Within the **Computer Configuration**, open **Windows Settings | Security Settings**. Then, select **IP Security Policies on Active Directory**. You see in the right pane of the window all the available IP security policies, including the "IPSec BizTalk" you just created. In this part, the column "Policy Assigned" will probable all state "No."

20. To activate your IPSec BizTalk policy, right-click this **policy** and select **Assign**. The **No** will turn into **Yes**. Close the window.

21. The next time the servers synchronize their settings, which you can enforce by rebooting the server right away, this security policy is activated.

We will get back to security in the section *Certificates and CryptoAPI*. In case you want to learn more about the use of Active Directory, you can read Syngress Publishing's *Active Directory for Windows 2000 Server* (ISBN 1-928994-60-1).

Equipment Access

Computer rooms should always be locked. Even so, too many people have access to these rooms. The best example is the computer room that is invaded by the cleaning person with a heavy-duty vacuum, plugging into a power outlet in the computer room and maneuvering dangerously around computers and over and under cables. In addition, external parties are sometimes given access on good faith and without supervision. The chance that someone makes a mistake or accidentally unplugs a cable increases with the number of people who can access the computer room. Here are some pointers to limit the risk of accidents:

- Limit the number of persons who have a key to the computer room(s); this must obviously be based on their job or role in the organization.

- Persons who have no key should be instructed what they can and cannot do in the computer room. External parties can only access the computer room under supervision.

- All equipment must be placed in racks that have doors that can be locked. All cabling and patch panels should also be placed in lockable racks.

- Prevent the availability of freely accessible power outlets.

- Prevent the presence of fuse boxes in the computer room.

Equipment in the offices is always accessible. This means that you must pay attention that unauthorized personnel do not have access to these computers or can gain access to them. This means:

- Put a lock on the computer cases, to block direct access to the system's innards.

- Preferably, disable diskette drives, CD-ROMs, and/or DVD-players.

- In case you allow these types of devices, disable the possibility of booting from them.

- Put passwords on the CMOS utilities, although there are utilities that can extract the password from the CMOS.

Once users are logged in, you should also build in some access limitations:

- No local installation of software.

- Administrators and developers accounts are only allowed to log on from specific computers. Since these users have extensive rights on the server, minimize the chances of inappropriate use.

Of course, these are not really security measures directly related to designing and deploying a BizTalk solution. However, the BizTalk solution might become a mission-critical application. If this happens, then every measure, even the obvious, must be considered to minimize the risk of disruption. Sadly enough, the obvious is easily forgotten when everyone focuses on the threats that splash the headlines of the news.

Securing XLANG Schedules

Up to this point, most of the discussion has been about securing the infrastructures and servers. Therefore, it is time to take a closer look at how the specific BizTalk server parts can be made more secure. Moreover, the XLANG schedule is a good starting point. There are a number of security issues involved:

- Development and deployment process
- Version control and release engineering
- File protection

Running an XLANG schedule in production involves a number of stages: development, testing, acceptance, and production (also referred to as *deployment*). In a well-designed development process, every stage has its own environment, without ties to each other. This means that files have to be transported from one environment to the other. You want to be sure that what is running in production is the same as was developed. The biggest challenge in protecting your XLANG schedules during all these phases is that the schedules are plain-text files. Additionally, you also are dealing with COM+ components that are developed and called from one or more XLANG schedules and COM+ components calling XLANG schedules. The best approach to transferring your BizTalk solution between phases is to let it be controlled by a release engineer, who should take care of version control, packaging the components and schedules into, for example, a .CAB file, and signing this .CAB file with a certificate. In this way, the chances of tampering with the files will be significantly reduced. More on packaging can be found in the sidebar *Bringing the BizTalk Application to Production*. In short, the development and deployment process should work as follows:

1. The development teams hand over the schedules, components, and database scripts to the release engineer.

2. The release engineer checks the versions of the different parts, installs them on the test environment, and rebuilds databases as needed. A test plan, preferably an extensive regression test plan, is executed where the working of the BizTalk application is tested.

3. If all problems and errors are resolved during the test phase, the release engineer packages the application, including an installation script, and signs the total package. Now he or she can hand it over to the acceptance testing team. Again, this will lead to some modifications and bug fixing.

4. The communication between the acceptance testing team and the development team(s) is conducted by the release engineer. It is his or her role to make sure that the right fixes are released.

5. If the acceptance team finally gives permission to proceed, then the release engineer finalizes the version, repackages and signs it, and hands it over to production.

6. The release engineer is, of course, also responsible for all the correct documentation that has to be shipped with the application.

Now let's focus on securing the development environment. Developers are granted far more access rights than end users are. In fact, most of the time they have administrator rights. This is not a problem, as long as the systems are properly secured.

NTFS

It is important that all servers make use of the security features of the Windows 2000 File System, still called NTFS. NTFS can help you in two ways to secure your XLANG schedules and COM+ components:

- Access rights
- Encrypting file system

Setting the correct access rights is important for the BizTalk application to work properly. In that regard, it is sensible to keep the access rights in all environments, including the development, limited to the level you will use in the production environment. You need at least a basic understanding of how access rights are granted within NTFS. For the sake of the discussion, let us assume that the format of a Windows 2000 Server file system is NTFS, by default. Experience shows that a fair amount of runtime problems during production are due to the lack of attention during development and testing. You are not only confronted with access rights of the users of your BizTalk application, but also with the role identities that are given to COM+ components and the fact that Windows 2000 users are bound to these roles. This is discussed later in the section *Component Level Security*. Remember that the BizTalk XLANG schedule engine is itself a COM+ application.

NOTE

As you work with the Active Directory, you will notice that you can set access rights within the Active Directory tree. While they look similar to the access rights you can set on files and folders, they are not! The access rights in the Active Directory are access rights to objects in the Active Directory tree, while the access rights you set on files and folders are file-system related.

The access rights in Windows 2000, also called *permissions*, extend over the ones introduced in Windows NT. These extended rights can be accessed by clicking **Advanced...** on the **Security** tab in the file/folder **Properties** sheet (Figure 8.9). The Security tab shows in the upper list box the users and/or groups that have access to the file/folder, and in the lower list box the permissions. Each permission has an **Allow** and **Deny** check box, identifying the setting of this specific permission. In case the check box is grayed out, this is inherited from a higher level. You will be able to overrule it, but cannot change these inherited permissions at this level, only at the level the access right is set. Of course, you need sufficient rights to make these changes. The modifications propagate to lower levels as the inherited permissions. Suppose you have a folder that has an inherited permission that is allowed and you check **Deny** for this permission. You will see that the Allow setting remains unchanged. However, since the Deny has been set, the Allow will be disregarded, because any Deny setting takes precedence over the Allow.

You should take notice of the option **Allow inheritable permissions from parent to propagate to this object**. By default, this option is checked. By deselecting this option, you break the inheritance chain and start a new one. Windows 2000 will warn you of this (Figure 8.10) and forces you to make a choice:

- **Copy** Creates the new chain using the same permissions as the ones that were inherited.

- **Remove** Removes all existing permissions and start with a clean sheet.

Figure 8.9 The Folder Properties Sheet

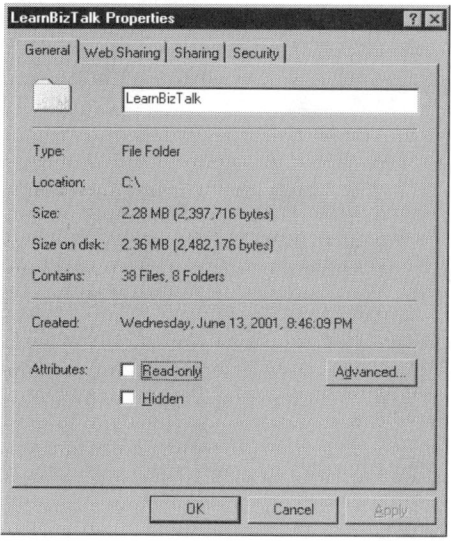

Figure 8.10 Making a Choice When an Inheritance Chain of Permissions Is Broken

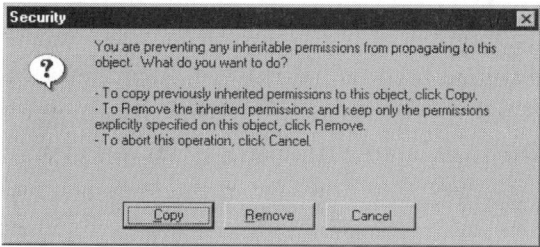

Be aware of the group "Everyone"; with default installations of Windows 2000, this group can pop up in different places having inherited rights. If you have given specific groups access rights to a file or folder, you should remove the Everyone group.

Now, press **Advanced** on the **Security** tab, and the Access Control Settings dialog (Figure 8.11) appears. The **Access Control Settings** dialog (Figure 8.11) has two additional tab pages: Auditing and Owner. The Auditing tab gives you the ability to activate auditing at selected permissions for selected users. Be prudent when using this file system auditing; since audit rules are also inherited, this can put a significant strain on the storage performance.

Figure 8.11 The Access Control Settings Window

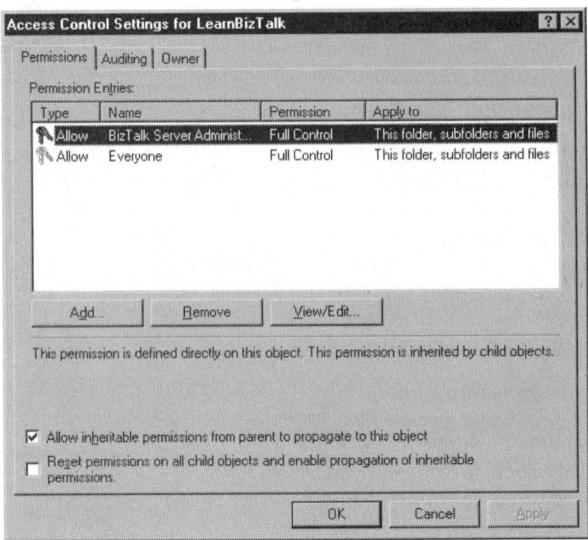

You will also see that the two lists in the previous window (Figure 8.9) are transformed into one list with Allow and Deny rules. In fact, in deciding which access rights a user has, the list is read from top to bottom. If a rule applies, the search is stopped. Here it becomes clearer that the Deny rule takes precedence over the Allow rule, and newly created rules overrule inherited ones. Below the first set of buttons, it is stated that a "permission is or is not inherited." Inherited rights cannot be removed, but you can break the inheritance chain by clearing the check box **Allow inheritable permissions from parent to propagate to this object**. This is the same option as you saw in the previous screen. The second option enables you to continue the inheritance chain on a lower level, ignoring the access rights modifications you made on the current level. If you play a bit with this option on a temporary folder tree, you will see that the inherited permissions on the child folders will be the same as those on the parent level. You should recognize instantly the numerous possibilities this brings in setting access rights. However, this can also introduce "access leaks" if you make regular use of breaking inheritance chains. The **Access Control Settings** dialog is the best way to get a detailed look in the access rights inheritance on a folder or a sub tree. Moreover, if you look at a rule in more detail, by clicking **View/Edit...**, you will see the exact permissions (the extended attributes) a user or group is given or denied (Figure 8.12).

Figure 8.12 The Folder Permission Entry Window

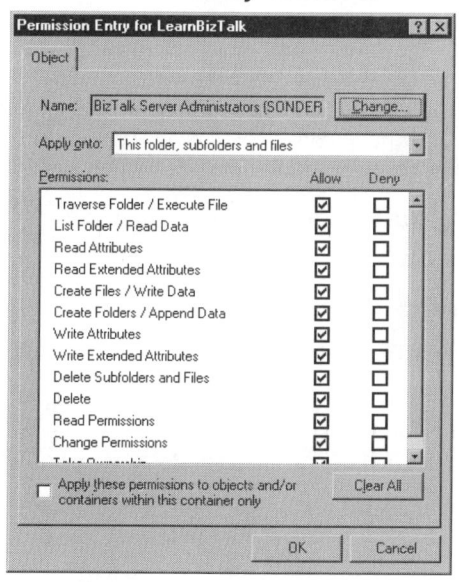

A final remark on access rights: Since Windows 95, you can use "Folder Sharing" as a means of a distributed file system. This is still possible within Windows 2000; however, use it sparsely, and do not set access rights! If you create a Share, go to the **Permissions** sheet and remove all checks on **Allow** and **Deny**. After having done this for all Names in the list, this list will be empty and the check boxes grayed out. The effect is that Sharing does not define access rights, and the permissions set within the Security tab are used. Even if you share a directory, the access control is done in one place.

A second security mechanism that comes with Windows 2000 NTFS is Encrypting File System (EFS). In the section *Certificates and CryptoAPI* you will find more information on the security infrastructure concepts, so for now, let us focus on the benefits. By encrypting files, folders, or subfolders, you prevent others from accessing the readable version of the file. Just having access to a file is not enough to obtain the readable version of the file. Only users who have access to the *certificate* that is used during encryption can decrypt the file and use it. Users who try to access the file but are not in the possession of the certificate will receive a message telling them that Windows was not able to open the file. Ones the encryption option has been set on a folder, every file that is created or placed in that folder is automatically encrypted, without the user needing to perform additional actions—it all takes place within the Windows kernel every time the file is accessed. EFS will only work if there exists at least one *recovery agent* with a *recovery certificate*; otherwise, encryption cannot be activated. This is a safeguard for situations where a certificate used to encrypt files becomes corrupted.

To activate EFS for part of your file system:

1. Go into the **Windows Explorer** and select the folder from which you want encryption to take place.

2. Right-click the **folder** and select **Properties**. This opens the **Properties** dialog.

3. On the **General** tab, press **Advanced…**, which opens the **Advanced Attributes** dialog (Figure 8.13).

Figure 8.13 The Advanced Attributes Window

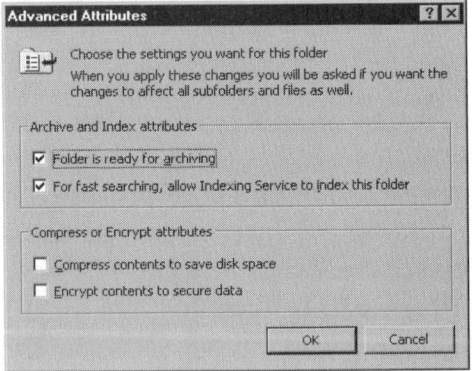

4. Select the check box **Encrypt contents to secure data**, and press **OK**.

5. In the **Properties** dialog, click **Apply**.

6. You will be asked if the encrypt attribute is for **This folder only**, or for **This folder, subfolders, and files**. Choose the appropriate one, press **OK**, and you are done. Now you can close the **Properties** window.

WARNING

If you encrypt a file, the unencrypted data will still reside on the disk in free data blocks. Up until the point these data blocks are reused for other files, someone who has the tools to scan the disk for these data blocks can gain access to the content of the file.

Microsoft has been aware of this serious security vulnerability and has finally (June 2001) released a version of the encryption program (cipher.exe) that zeroes the data blocks of the unencrypted version. Replace the current version with this one if you are planning to use EFS for any purpose. You can find more information on this revised tool and download at:

www.microsoft.com/technet/itsolutions/security/tools/cipher.asp

www.microsoft.com/technet/itsolutions/security/tools/cipherfaq.asp

Remember that access rights (permissions) and encryption are not related. A user with Delete access to an encrypted file can still remove it even if he or she is unable to read the contents.

If you are running Windows Cluster Service, the encryption functionality is automatically disabled. The reason for this is that the encryption functionality is coupled to the local system and the storage in a cluster is not related to one specific system.

The question now is, how can you use these NTFS functionalities to get better security for your BizTalk environment? By now, you might be aware that XLANG schedules are very vulnerable. Special care is needed to keep them away from prying eyes. Are you wondering how you can ensure that the compiled XLANG schedule cannot be modified without notice? Or the XLANG schedule drawings for that matter? EFS is a great way to obscure the XLANG schedule contents for anyone who is not allowed to modify it. Unfortunately, this means that everyone besides the user who encrypted the files is unable to read the files. For a development team, this means that they cannot use their colleagues' drawings. In the production environment, this means that you are not able to give every COM+ application its own service account (see the following section, *Role Definitions*). Unfortunately, file encryption currently has no working option in environments in which more than one user must be able to access a file. Let us stick to access rights and identify the steps you need to take to enhance security:

1. List all the separate working environments. Identify the root folders of these environments. In case a root is a subfolder in another environment, consider moving it to a higher level. For example, if you install BizTalk Server on a single server, the Tracking directory is installed by default as a subfolder of the BizTalk Server 2000 environment. Since you can decide the location of the Tracking "subsystem" during installation, be sure to substitute the default value with a more appropriate path. Moreover, avoid placing system and application files in the same subfolder structure.

The same goes for separating program and data files. In general, the environments you can identify are:

- The BizTalk Server 2000 parts (e.g., runtime and tracking) on every server

- The SQL Server 2000 installation on the different servers

- The Visio 2000 SR1 installation on the development server(s)

- The development, release, and production environment of your BizTalk application, including databases, on the different servers

2. For each environment, list the users who need access to these environments.

3. Group the users based on their roles. You might even consider making different developer groups; for example, for component developers and XLANG schedule designers. This helps to limit the number of users who have modification rights to the XLANG schedule drawings.

4. Determine the minimal access rights these groups need. Always identify these access rights from the root of an environment. Prevent adding or removing rights at a lower level in the environment. Never give user's Administrator rights or Full Control to BizTalk-related folders, since this will make it more difficult to keep control over the permissions being handed out.

5. At the root level of every environment, break the inheritance chain of access rights. This gives you total control of the proper access rights for the different user groups. By doing so, you prevent other users getting access to the BizTalk folders simply because an administrator gave them certain permissions at a higher level.

6. Enable auditing on the different environments. In case of development environments, you want to know at least who can delete or modify files or folders. In production environments, you want to know who makes any changes to the environment. Keep in mind that extensive auditing can slow the system, but instead of turning off auditing, it is better to beef up the server.

7. Do not make use of shares on BizTalk Server folders, especially in the production environment. If you want to use shares in the development environment, which can have its benefits, make sure no one uses the share to refer to files. If you do so, XLANG schedules and components

will not run in the production environment if the shares are nonexistent or if the path to the file is different.

8. In case you decide to make use of shares for BizTalk folders, remove all the permissions that are set with the share, so they cannot overwrite the access rights you set on the folders.

9. Component developers will only have to make use of the compiled XLANG schedules, so be sure that the compiled versions of the XLANG schedules are placed in a separate folder at a higher level. Now you will only have to give the component developers read access to this folder and not have to enter the Schedule development folders.

Role Definitions

When discussing access rights (permissions) on folders and files, you automatically talk about users and groups. When you put BizTalk Server 2000 in place and create the different environments, you want to ensure that only the people who need access to these folders get the appropriate permissions. As we discussed earlier, you have to give employees access based on the roles they play. You must refrain from giving separate users permissions on folders, since this makes maintaining the security on access rights difficult over time. However, there is an exception, which we will discuss later. Instead, link roles to groups and when a person has a different role, his or her user account will be placed in a different group. Keep the numbers of groups as small as possible. Before creating user groups for your BizTalk applications, it makes sense to discuss this with the BizTalk application designers. As discussed in the section *Component-Level Security*, access control to components is linked to business roles. By lining up the user groups on the Windows 2000 server with the roles that are defined by the components, you can make security—hence, access control—transparent.

Let's look at the User Groups that are created when you install BizTalk Server. Two groups are created with only the user who performed the installation as a member:

- **BizTalk Server Administrators** Users who belong to this group have full control of the BizTalk Server installation. To enforce this, add this group to the root folder of the BizTalk Server installation on all the servers that make up the full configuration, and give it "Full Control."

- **BizTalk Server Report Users** Members of this group are allowed to access BizTalk Tracking. In case you have BizTalk Tracking installed on a separate server, this group only needs to appear on that server. This group has to have read-only access to the Tracking folder.

Understand that these two groups do not represent all the roles you have to consider. Additional groups include:

- **BizTalk Server Component Developers** Contains all the users who are part of the team that is developing COM+ components for a BizTalk application.

- **BizTalk Server Schedule Developers** Contains all the users who are part of the development team responsible for the XLANG schedules.

- **BizTalk Server Service Accounts** This group is special, since it holds all user account that are used to start a COM+ application that is part of a BizTalk application. As discussed in more detail in the section *Component Level Security*, create a separate service account for every COM+ application. This enables you to control the context in which the COM+ application executes for every application. Additionally, it helps you to audit the operating of the application in more detail.

- **BizTalk Server Database Administrators** Since BizTalk Server uses a number of databases for different purposes, you might want to give certain users who are designated administrators for the BizTalk databases the necessary permissions to work with these databases. Remember that the databases can be running on servers other than where the other parts of your BizTalk Server application are running.

- **BizTalk Server Operators** This group can be used for the users who are responsible for the day-to-day operations of the BizTalk applications. They can make do with a subset of the permissions that the BizTalk Server Administrators have.

- **BizTalk Application Users** This group can be used in case certain components use context delegation (see the section *Component Level Security*). In that case, the user, kicking off the component, needs to have access rights to the files and folders the component needs to execute. As we will see, context delegation is a very powerful way of transferring the user context, and therefore must be handled with care.

You might even want to use different groups, based on your specific environment, but try to limit the number of groups. As mentioned earlier, you do want to give users direct permissions to specific folders when using service accounts. Again, it makes a lot of sense to create a service account for every COM+ application, automatically implying that this user has to have permission to access the folder (and subfolders) holding the application components. You could do this through the BizTalk Service Accounts group. However, that would give all the other service accounts—hence, COM+ applications—access to each other's folders; security wise, not a sound decision. Therefore, this is the only situation in which you should set permissions at the user level. You might wonder about the purpose of this group. First, the group members share the same role, owner of a running COM+ application; more specifically, a part of a BizTalk Server application. Second, they also need to access other parts of the BizTalk infrastructure, such as the BizTalk Server folder and libraries. Setting these access rights at group level simplifies managing these permissions.

Component-Level Security

We will now look at how we can apply security at the component level, and how you can link this with the security at the Windows 2000 Server level. Keep in mind that the extent and complexity of the security within Windows 2000 goes way beyond what we can discuss in this chapter. However, since COM+ is at the heart of BizTalk Server, it is important to understand the working of COM+ security and the way it ties in with the rest of the security. After installing BizTalk Server, there are four COM+ applications that we will be dealing with (Figure 8.14):

- BizTalk Server Interchange Application
- BizTalk Server Internal Utilities
- XLANG Scheduler
- XLANG Scheduler Persistence Helper

The XLANG Scheduler COM+ application is the default XLANG schedule engine that comes with BizTalk Server 2000. However, you can build your own scheduler engines, using the default as an example. When writing your own XLANG scheduler, or any other COM+ application for that matter, there are two types of security involved: programmatic and declarative. In the former, security is part of the component's code, and in the latter, security is controlled from outside the component using the administration tool Component Services

(Figure 8.14). In this section, we will only discuss the declarative security. Remember, programmatic security is as much part of the COM+ Security Model as declarative security is. In fact, the programmatic security extends the declarative security right into the component.

Figure 8.14 The MMC with Component Services Showing the Installed COM+ Applications

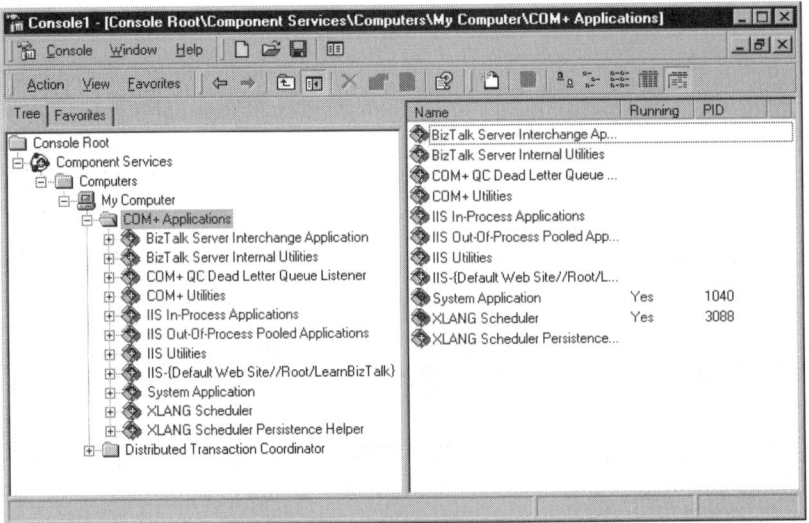

From the declarative perspective, you can control the following security aspects:

- **Access** Determines which users can access the component, interfaces, or even methods within a COM+ application. Access is controlled through roles.

- **Activation** Determines which users are allowed to start—the term *launch* is generally used—a COM+ application.

- **Authentication** Determines to what extent the COM+ application should check the authenticity of users who activate a component or the data a component receives.

- **Identity** Determines under whose security context a component is activated. Identity is comprised of two parts: the *user account* used to start the COM+ application, and the *impersonation* level that determines to what extent a component can take over the identity (through the client's credentials) of the caller of the component. Impersonation can transcend the context of a server, and even the domain the server is in, in the case the component is running on a different server. In that case, context delegation can be used where the client's security credentials are transferred to the other server. This only works if Kerberos V5 is operational.

■ **Reference Tracking** Determines if additional security checks have to be executed to prevent components from being released prematurely.

If you install a BizTalk COM+ application and do not configure the security at the COM+ application level, the machine-wide security settings are used.

Machine-Wide Security Settings for COM+

To access the machine-wide security settings for COM+ applications:

1. Open the **Microsoft Management Console** (MMC), adding the **Component Services** snap-in.

2. Expand **Component Services**.

3. Expand **Computers**.

4. Right-click on **My Computer** (or any other computer for which you want to change the settings), and select **Properties**.

5. The **My Computer Properties** dialog will appear (Figure 8.15) with the General tab showing.

Figure 8.15 The Default Properties Tab in the My Computer Properties Window

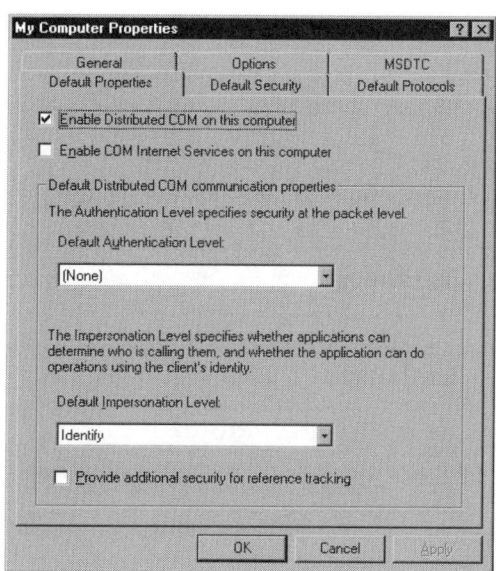

6. Select the **Default Properties** tab.

7. The tab starts with two check box options, of which the **Enable Distributed COM on this computer** drives the rest of the options on this page. Distributed COM (DCOM) is the protocol used between components running on different computers. By default, this option is selected. The second check box relates to IIS using COM.

8. Select the first check box, since this is the only place where you can enable DCOM.

9. In the frame below, you can select the default DCOM communication properties Authentication and Impersonation. If the server on which your BizTalk application is running is not used for other purposes, it is best to select the authentication and impersonation level most appropriate for the server. Select **Packet Privacy** as the default authentication level. See Table 8.1 for an explanation of the other authentication levels. Packet privacy is the highest authentication level, and can be overruled by setting a different level on a COM+ application (see the section *COM+ Application Security Settings*). The reason for this is that in case you forget to set the authentication level at the COM+ application, the application is protected from rogue data that is submitted to a component.

10. Select **Anonymous** for the impersonation level—although this seems illogical, it is not. Anonymous means that the credentials of a user are not checked when a component is called, and that a component cannot use the identity of the caller and cannot call a component on a different server. See Table 8.2 for the explanation of the other impersonation levels.

11. The last option is the check box **Provide additional security for reference tracking**. As explained earlier, this option prevents components from being released too early. Do not use this option for the BizTalk server, since it does not bring added security to your BizTalk application.

Table 8.1 Authentication Levels

Authentication Level	Explanation
None	No authentication takes place.
Connect	Client authentication takes place only when a connect takes place.

Continued

Table 8.1 Continued

Authentication Level	Explanation
Call	Client authentication takes place at every call to a component.
Packet	Client authentication takes place at every call to a component, and a check on the data completeness is performed.
Packet Integrity	Client authentication takes place at every call to a component, and a check on the data integrity (to see whether the data changed during transmission) is performed. A digital signature is sent with the data using a certificate.
Packet Privacy	Client authentication takes place at every call to a component, the data is encrypted, and a check on the data integrity (to see whether the data changed during transmission) is performed. A digital signature is sent with the data using a certificate.

Table 8.2 Impersonation Levels

Impersonation Level	Explanation
Anonymous	No identification of the client takes place, nor does the client hand over any credentials to the component. A component can never assume the identity of the client when calling another component. This is mandatory when a component on another computer is called.
Identity	The client's identity is established by the called component, and it can use this identity to perform access control checks(see the section *Access Control Lists*). Note: If a COM+ application component calls a component in another COM+ application, the calling component is the client.
Impersonate	The client's identity is established by the called component, and it can use this identity to access resources available to the client on the same server as the called component is running on.

Continued

Table 8.2 Continued

Impersonation Level	Explanation
Delegate	The client's identity is established by the called component, and it can use the full identity to access resources available to the client on the same server on which the called component is running. Additionally, the called component can use this identity to pass to another component running on any other computer.

After setting the **Default Properties**, you can set the default security properties (Figure 8.16). To do so:

1. Select the **Default Security** tab. You will see two frames: Default Access Permissions and Default Launch Permissions. Both have an Edit Default… button.

2. Press **Edit Default…** in the **Default Access Permissions** frame. A dialog called Registry Value Permissions is shown, indicating that the default access permissions values are saved in the Registry. By default, the list box will be empty. By pressing **Add**, you can add users and groups to the list, and select the type of access. The values are AllowDefaultAccessPermission or DenyDefaultAccessPermission.

3. For now, leave the list empty, and press **Cancel**. This means that the COM+ application needs to explicitly define the user's access by using roles (discussed in the section, *COM+ Application Security Settings*).

4. Press **Edit Default…** in the Default Launch Permissions frame. Again, a Registry Value Permissions dialog appears. You will probably see a number of entries in the list with the value AllowDefaultLaunchPermission. Among these are the groups INTERACTIVE and SYSTEM. By default, a COM+ application will have one of these two groups as the user who is allowed to launch the application. If you are sure that none of your COM+ applications that run on the server where BizTalk Server is installed need to have interaction with the desktop, it is a good idea to set INTERACTIVE to **DenyDefaultLaunchPermission**. Otherwise, leave it as is, and press **Cancel**.

Figure 8.16 The Default Security Tab in the My Computer Properties Window

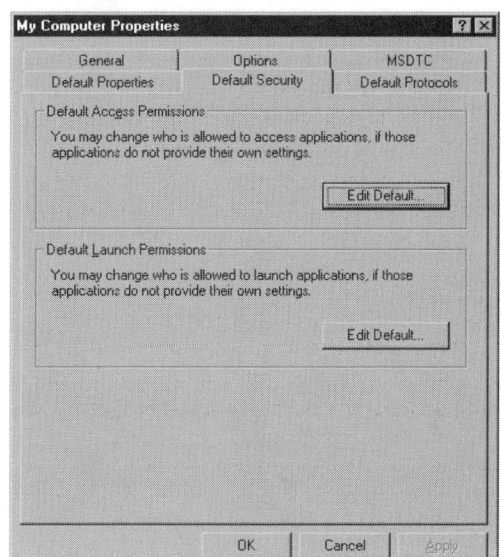

You should also check the **Default Protocols** tab that lists the protocols that can be used in DCOM. It should only list **Connection-oriented TCP/IP**. Since we chose IP Security, using any other protocol will result in unsecured communication. Enforcing TCP/IP as the one and only protocol for DCOM will prevent this. Also, make sure that on the **MSDTC** tab, the **Client Network Protocol Configuration** is set to **TCP/IP**.

COM+ Application Security Settings

Setting the security machine-wide is a safety net in case you forget certain security settings on individual COM+ applications. However, this is certainly not the optimal security setting, and you should take care that the security settings for each COM+ application within your BizTalk application are set with care. In this section, the COM+ application XLANG Scheduler is used to show the different security options. Figure 8.17 shows the partially expanded structure of the XLANG Scheduler application.

Figure 8.17 Expanded XLANG Scheduler Application in MMC

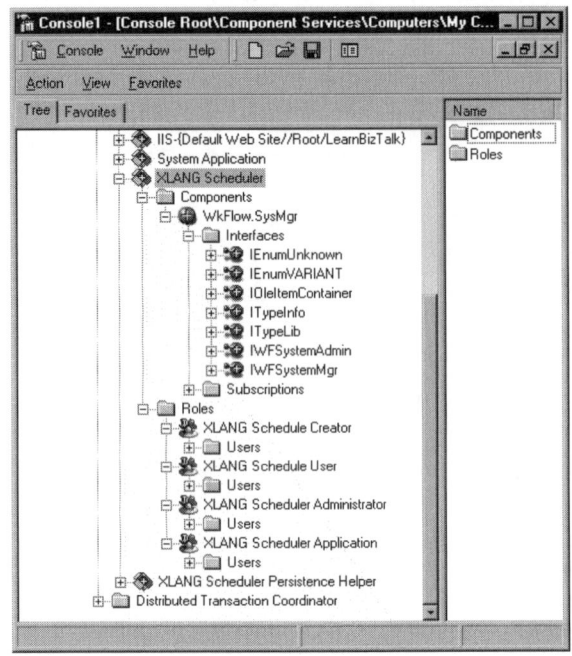

Let's see what these settings are and how you can set them:

1. Open the **Microsoft Management Console** (MMC) and add the **Component Services** snap-in.

2. Expand **Component Services | Computers | My Computer | COM+ Applications**.

3. Expand **XLANG Scheduler**. At this point, you see under the XLANG Scheduler two folders: **Components** and **Roles**. Before determining what security settings are available within these two folders, we must first look into the security properties of the XLANG Scheduler application.

4. Right-click the **XLANG Scheduler** application, and select **Properties**. The **XLANG Scheduler Properties** dialog appears. As you will notice by clicking the tabs, you cannot change any settings. These are locked to prevent them from being changed accidentally, which might result in the breaking down of running XLANG Scheduler components. Another thing to notice is the last tab, **XLANG**. This is no coincidence! If you create a new COM+ application; you will see that the same XLANG tab will appear in the Properties window. It is there to enable another

COM+ application to host XLANG schedule instances, by making an ODBC connection to an Orchestration Persistence database. You will find more information on this in the section *Database Security*. Now, before you can make changes to the Properties settings, you need to "unlock" the settings.

5. Select the **Advanced** tab, uncheck **Disable Changes** in the Permission frame, and click **OK**.

6. A warning dialog appears. You can answer by pressing **OK**, and the **Properties** dialog will close.

7. Reopen the **XLANG Scheduler Properties** dialog. You will see that all properties can now be changed.

8. Select the **Security** tab (Figure 8.18). The Security tab is comprised of three parts: Authorization, Security level, and Authentication/Impersonation.

Figure 8.18 The Security Tab in the XLANG Scheduler Properties Window

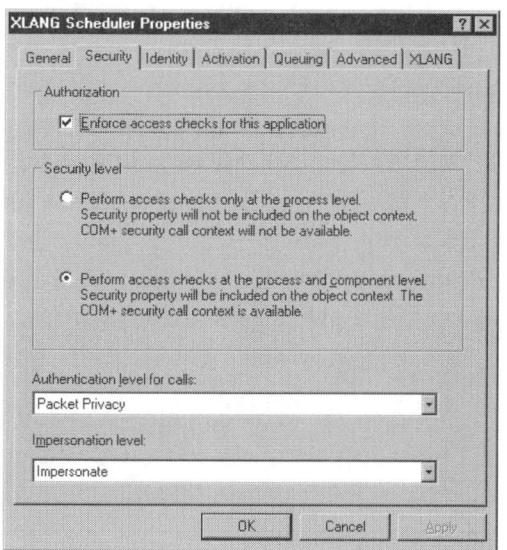

For authorization, you can check the option **Enforce access checks for this application**. By doing so, you ensure that the client's identity is checked during access and launching of the application. If no specific user is specified at the COM+ application level, the access list you defined at the **My Computer**

level is used. By default, you should check this option for all COM+ applications in BizTalk Server.

Security-level settings will only be used if you have the Authorization option checked, and are used for incoming calls. There are two possible settings:

- **Perform access checks only at process level.** This means that only calls coming from another COM+ application are subject to access checks. Calls within a COM+ application are regarded as safe. The security context will not be part of the context in which the component is running. Therefore, if the caller is allowed to access the COM+ application, access is granted without any further checks.

- **Perform access checks at the process and component level.** This means that calls within a COM+ application are checked. In this case, the security context of the caller will be part of the component context. Select this option for the BizTalk Server COM+ applications.

Authentication and impersonation levels only have leverage for outgoing calls. Refer back to Table 8.1 for authentication-level values and Table 8.2 for impersonation-level values. Select **Packet Integrity** for the authentication level. Since you will use IPSec for communication between servers, encryption of the packet is not necessary. However, this assumes that the server is safe enough that data in calls within the server do not need to be encrypted. Select **Impersonate** for Impersonation level. Only use **Delegate** in an environment in which closely linked BizTalk COM+ applications run on different servers.

The **Identity** tab enables you to select the account that launches the COM+ application, and in which context the application will run. Here is where the Service Account comes into play. In the **Account** frame, you can select:

- **Interactive user** The user who launches the COM+ application is used for the context in which the application will run. If the user logs out, the COM+ application is automatically shut down. When you select this option, the user list of the Default Launch Permissions is used.

- **This user** An existing user account on the server or within the Active Directory can be selected. You should always create this option, so the COM+ application can run even when no user is logged on. In our case, you should select the service account you created for the XLANG Scheduler. Remember to make the following changes to the account (see the section *Server Configurations* for more information):

- Enable **Act** as part of the operating system
- Disable **Deny logon** as a service
- Disable **Shutdown the system**
- Enable **User cannot change password**
- Enable **Account never expires**

Select **This user**, since this is our desired option, and then check that it is working correctly. If you enter the incorrect password, the COM+ application will not start.

The Activation tab enables you to determine "where" your BizTalk COM+ application is started. Always select **Server application**, whereby the COM+ application is run as a separate process on the server, using the context of the service account to run. This option ensures that the COM+ application cannot be torn down by any code execution in the same process the COM+ application is running in, and vice versa. Additionally, if a rogue user seizes control of the application, access to the system is limited to the service account.

Context Delegation

Context delegation is a form of impersonation first introduced in Windows 2000. It is a very powerful way to run a component in its own COM+ application process, by using the caller's identity. As discussed earlier, it makes use of Kerberos V5 (see the section *Certificates and CryptoAPI*) to get a positive ID on the client. We discussed previously how you can set context delegation by making use of the Component Services. However, this is only the declarative security, and context delegation only works if you insert context delegation programmatically into the component. You will find it worth the effort, since it adds additional security to your system, and increases the protection of your business processes. When you enforce context delegation, you always know who is initially making a call—hence, starting a business process—all along the chain of calls, even if you built a distributed BizTalk application. However, from the client's point of view, context delegation is also dangerous, since handing over your identity to a rogue component can do that person, your business, and your system a great deal of harm. You must meet the following conditions to be able to use context delegation:

- All servers, and workstations for that matter, making up your BizTalk application must be running a version of Windows 2000 and must be part of a Windows 2000 domain.

- Kerberos V5 must be running within the Windows 2000 domain.

- If the BizTalk application runs over more Windows 2000 domains, the Kerberos instantiations need to have trusted relationships.

- The client (the initial component making the call) must have its impersonation level for outgoing calls set to Delegate. You can do this using Component Services, as described earlier.

- The client account (the service account of the calling component, or the interactive user making the initial call) cannot be marked for "Account is sensitive and cannot be delegated" in the Active Directory.

- The server account (which is the service account of the component being called) must be marked for "Trusted for Delegation." This is needed to limit the risk that the component being called is untrustworthy.

Designing & Planning…

Every COM+ Application Should Have Its Own Identity

When building a BizTalk application, you will probably model it around one or more business processes. It is important to contain a complete business process in one XLANG schedule, and contain the schedule in one COM+ application. By doing so, you can limit the amount of information that needs to be exchanged between COM+ applications. In addition, limit the number of exposed interfaces to as few as possible, and put as many methods in one exposed interface as you can. Remember that the exchange of data and the exposed interface are the most vulnerable parts of your COM+ application.

This is why it is important that you run every COM+ application under its own service account, hence its own identity, and limit its access to the system. If a COM+ application is compromised, or becomes unstable, the damage can be contained and is more easily traced. Additionally, by enforcing Context Delegation you harden both the COM+ application and the business process.

Roles

Another way to protect the components being called by unauthorized users is to add roles to a COM+ application. This will only work if you determine in what capacity, or role, users are allowed to make use of a COM+ application. It is a perfect way to add business security to your COM+ application. For example, within a bank, a teller is allowed only to perform transfer transactions up to $5,000, and teller supervisors can have a transaction limit of $15,000. By adding roles to the transaction component, you can check if a user, based on his or her function, stays within his or her transfer limits.

First, let's look at how the declarative part of roles is implemented by the XLANG Scheduler:

1. Go to the **Component Services**.

2. Expand **Roles** under **XLANG Scheduler**.

3. You see four roles: XLANG Schedule Creator, XLANG Schedule User, XLANG Scheduler Administrator, and XLANG Scheduler Application.

4. Expand the four roles.

5. Expand **Users** under each role.

Three of the roles have Everyone as an assigned group (Figure 8.19). Since this is not much security, change this as soon as possible. Therefore, you need to know what these roles stand for:

- **XLANG Schedule Creator** is able to run an XLANG schedule instance. If the caller's identity—hence, user account—is not assigned to this role, it is not allowed to start a schedule; instead, an error is displayed. This unauthorized attempt will also show up in the event log.

- **XLANG Schedule User** is able to make calls to a running XLANG schedule instance; for example, to retrieve status information. Again, if the user is not assigned to the role, and he or she makes an unauthorized call, an error message is displayed and an event log entry is made.

- **XLANG Scheduler Administrator** is able to monitor and influence the running of the XLANG Scheduler engines and the active instances.

- **XLANG Scheduler Application** is the role that reflects the identity of the scheduler and is therefore the role the service account is playing.

Figure 8.19 Listing the Users Assigned to the XLANG Scheduler Roles

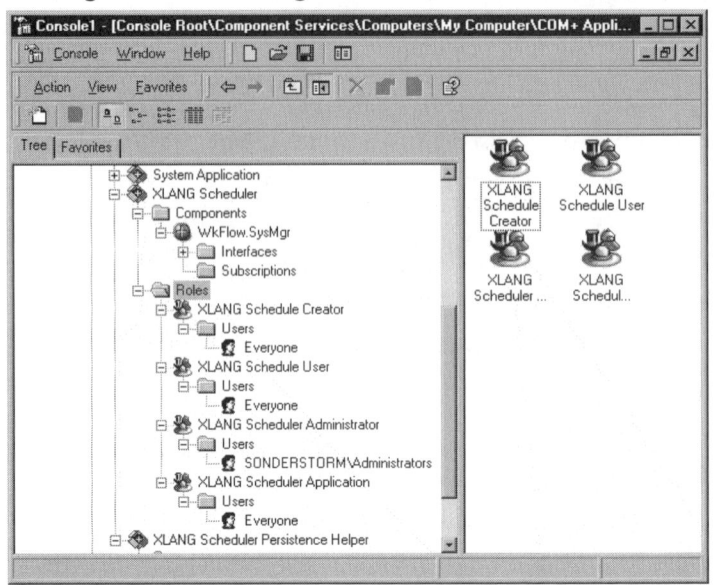

Roles can be assigned to different levels within the COM+ application:

- The component
- An interface within a component
- A method within an interface

A lower level automatically inherits the role setting from a higher level, and you always should assign roles at the highest possible level. Again, this is something you already defined in the design phase of your BizTalk application, so at this stage, you only assign users in the operational environment to the roles defined within the different COM+ applications.

First, substitute the **Everyone** in the roles to the appropriate user/group accounts. For example, you need to link the service account for the XLANG Scheduler application to the role XLANG Scheduler application. Follow these steps:

1. Select the **Users** folder of the **XLANG Scheduler Application** role.
2. Right-click the folder, and select **New | User**.
3. The **Select Users and Groups** dialog appears, and you can select the service account for **XLANG Scheduler**.

4. Press **Add**, followed by **OK**. The dialog closes and the user is added to the Users folder. Now you need to delete **Everyone**.

5. Select the object **Everyone**.

6. Right-click it, and select **Delete**.

7. A dialog appears asking you to confirm. Press **Yes**, and you are done.

Let's see how a role can be added to the WkFlow.SysMgr component, to show the ease with which you can apply roles:

1. Expand the **Components** folder.

2. Right-click **WkFlow.SysMgr**, and select **Properties**.

3. Select the **Security** tab (Figure 8.20).

Figure 8.20 The Security Tab in the WkFlow.SysMgr Properties Window

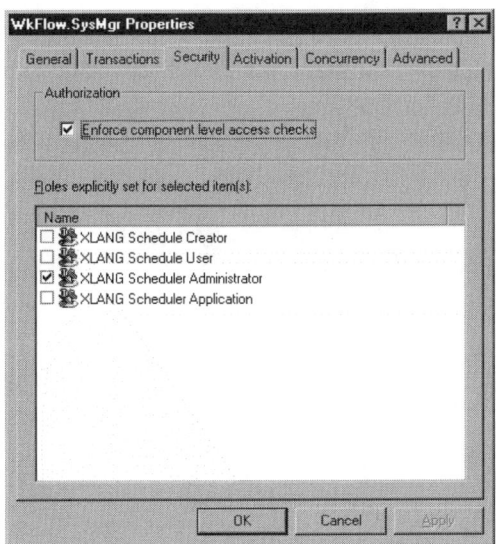

The option **Enforce component level access checks** is checked. If this option is grayed out, you did not select the option **Perform access checks at the process and component level** on the **Security** tab of the COM+ application **Properties** window. Although this option was set at application level, you can still deactivate it for individual components.

Below the Authorization option is the list of roles defined for the XLANG Scheduler application, and only **XLANG Scheduler Administrator** is checked. You could deselect this role and/or select one or more of the other roles. In case the authorization option is grayed out, you will not be able to change the role setting. Now, let us assume you want to set the XLANG Schedule Creator role for the Startup method of the IWFSystemAdmin interface.

1. Expand the **WkFlow.sysMgr** component.
2. Expand the **Interfaces** folder.
3. Expand the **IWFSystemAdmin** interface.
4. Expand the **Methods** folder.
5. Right-click the **StartUp** method, and select **Properties**.
6. Select the **Security** tab.

You see two role lists (Figure 8.21). The upper list shows the inherited roles; in our case, this only contains XLANG Schedule Administrator. The lower list shows all available roles.

1. Select the check box **XLANG Schedule Creator**.
2. Press **OK**, and you have activated this role explicitly for this method.

Figure 8.21 The Roles Assigned to the IWFSystemAdmin.StartUp Method

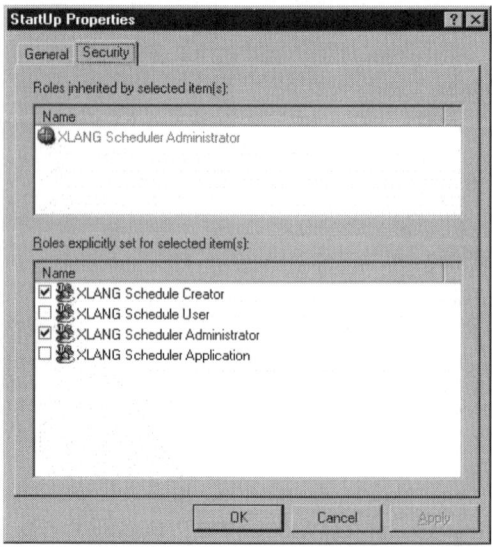

To be sure these modifications are picked up right away, restart the XLANG Scheduler COM+ application.

It is just as easy to add new roles to a COM+ application as it was to add roles to a component or method:

1. Select the **Roles** folder under the **XLANG Scheduler** application.

2. Right-click it, and select **New | Role**.

3. Enter a name for the role, and press **OK**.

4. A dialog appears with the statement: "The XLANG Scheduler application was created by XLANG Scheduler Setup. Are you certain that the changes you are about to make are supported by XLANG Scheduler Setup?"

5. Click **Yes**.

After making all the necessary changes to the XLANG Scheduler application, be sure to "lock" the properties of this COM+ application by selecting the check box **Disable Changes** in the **Advanced** tab in the **XLANG Scheduler Properties** window.

Database Security

BizTalk Server 2000 relies heavily on Microsoft SQL Server; when one of the BizTalk Server default databases falters, your entire BizTalk Server application will come to a screeching halt. Although the databases might only seem useful to the different BizTalk services, they are accessible to any SQL Server user. If this is the first time you need to set security for SQL Server, or work with SQL Server 2000 altogether, then you should read the book *Designing SQL Server 2000 Databases for .NET Enterprise Servers* (ISBN 1-928994-19-9) from Syngress Publishing. Database Security can roughly be divided into two parts: *database access* and *data loss prevention*.

Database Access

As discussed in Chapter 2, "Planning an Installation of BizTalk 2000," BizTalk Server makes use of SQL Server authentication, not Windows 2000 authentication. When you install SQL Server and BizTalk server by default, the Message Managing database, Tracking database, and Shared Queue database will use the database administrator account "sa." Since this account has full control over the SQL Server and all databases running under it, it is, for security reasons, not the proper thing to do.

Database Logins

Instead of using the "sa" database login, create a SQL user with administrator rights for every database, and limit the access of this user to one of the databases. You do this by:

1. Creating SQL server users.

2. Limiting database access.

3. Replacing the "sa" user within BizTalk Server.

Before you begin, you need to shut down BizTalk Server to prevent the interchange services being locked out, then perform the following steps:

1. Open the **SQL Server Enterprise Manager** (**Start | Programs | SQL Server 2000 | Enterprise Manager**).

2. Expand the **Microsoft SQL Servers | SQL Server Group | SQL Server | Security** folder.

3. Select **Logins**.

4. Right-click **Logins**, and select **New Login…** The **SQL Server Login Properties** dialog opens.

5. Enter a **name**; for example, for the Message Managing database, use "sa_InterchangeBTM" (Figure 8.22).

Figure 8.22 Creating a New Login Using the SQL Server Login Properties Window

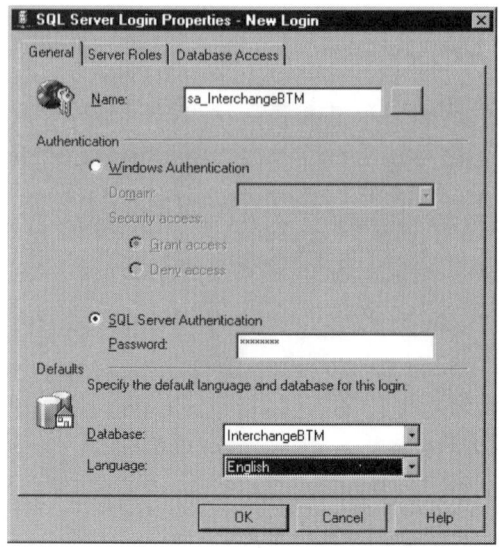

6. Under **Authentication**, select **SQL Server Authentication** and enter a **Password**.

7. Under **Defaults**, select the appropriate **database** for the user; for this example, choose **InterchangeBTM** and **English** for the **Language**.

8. Select **Server Roles** tab, and be sure that all the **Server Role** entries are unchecked.

9. Select the **Database Access** tab.

10. Place a check in the **Permit** box at the appropriate database; in our example, Interchange BTM. The login will appear in the **User** field.

11. In the **Permit in database Role** list, check **db_owner**.

12. Press **OK**. A dialog asks you to confirm the password. If it is correct, the user is created.

13. Repeat step 4 through 12 for the other two users: sa_Interchange_DTA and sa_Interchange_SQ.

NOTE

Every COM+ application that can run XLANG schedule instances, such as the default XLANG Scheduler, also has a database associated with it. This Orchestration Persistence database is linked using a data source name (DSN). Database authentication should be done through Windows 2000 authentication, not SQL Server authentication. One reason for this is that Windows authentication is regarded as more secure. Going through Windows will also allow you to use Delegate for impersonation levels, since Kerberos v5 has to be used.

As you can see in Figure 8.22, when you choose Windows Authentication, you are able to explicitly grant or deny a user or group access to the database.

Next, you need to administer these SQL Server users for BizTalk Server:

1. Open the **BizTalk Server Administration** tool (**Start | Programs | BizTalk Server 2000 | BizTalk Server Administration**).

2. Select **Microsoft BizTalk Server 2000**, right-click it, and select **Properties**.

3. Change **User name** to **sa_InterchangeBTM**, and the **Password** to whatever you choose when creating the user.

4. Click **OK**.

5. Expand **Microsoft BizTalk Server 2000**.

6. Select **BizTalk Server Group**, right-click it, and select **Properties**.

7. Click the **Connection** tab.

8. Change the **User name** and **Password** for the Tracking database and Shared Queue database.

9. Press **OK** and restart BizTalk Server.

Database Roles

As we discussed in the section "Component Level Security", you are able to define roles within the database and give them permission to access database objects. However, roles have only meaning if you link roles to database users, which is a subset of the logins. Since the users who make use of the COM+ applications are the same as those accessing the database, it would be a good decision to add all BizTalk server-related users to the database logins list. Of course, you should use the role-based groups you created in the Active Directory and not the individual users. The best way to explain how this works is to add a new role. For this example, you will also use the InterchangeBTM database.

1. Open the **SQL Server Enterprise Manager**.

2. Expand until you see the objects under the **InterchangeBTM database (Microsoft SQL Servers | SQL server Group | SQL Server | Databases | InterchangeBTM)**.

3. Select **Roles**, right-click it, and select **New Database Role...**.

4. The **Database Role Properties** dialog appears (Figure 8.23).

5. Fill in the appropriate **Name**; For our example, use **XLANGScheduleCreator**.

6. Now, choose the **Standard role** database role type. You will only use **Application role** if all access to the database is handled by the same application; hence, the application makes a one-time connect, and all access flows through this connection. The application has a sort of broker role.

Figure 8.23 Creating a New Role for the InterchangeBTM Database

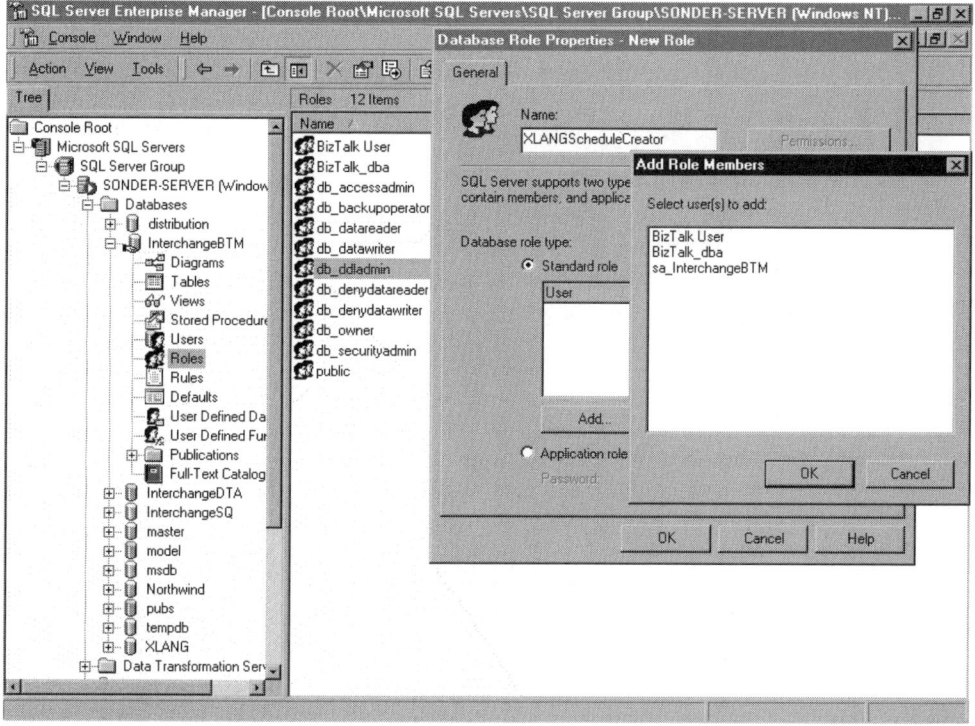

7. Click **Add...**, and the **Add Role Members** dialog appears. This list box shows all users of the InterchangeBTM database *and* all user-defined roles for the InterchangeBTM database. In Figure 8.23, you see also BizTalk User in the list. This role was created prior to the creation of the XLANGScheduleCreator role, and it does appear in the list of roles left of the Database Role Properties window. You are able to nest roles, which is not something that you should be use, since the inheritance of rights can give unwanted results!

8. For the sake of this example, add only **sa_InterchangeBTM** to the list.

When you set out to secure your BizTalk application, you will first add users to the list, before creating roles. However, you can always add new users to the role.

NOTE

Once you create a database login, you can no longer change the authentication method. The only thing to do is: create a new login, add this login to the appropriate database users lists, link it to the appropriate roles list, and delete the old login.

Once you create a database role, you can no longer change the database role type. Therefore, create a new role, add the appropriate permissions to the role, link the appropriate database users to the role, and delete the old role.

This is a very intensive operation and prone to errors, so review your database access structure before implementing it.

Database Object Access

By using database roles and linking database users to them, you have control over who can and cannot access the database. After getting access to the database, users can access all data stored there: the records (rows) stored in the tables, stored procedures, views, and so on. You might feel the need to prevent specific users from altering certain tables, executing certain stored procedures, or even certain table columns from being shown. All these items, called database objects, can be protected from users. The best way to do this is through roles.

There are two ways to set these access rights. Both work because they provide a different view on the permissions that are stored in one place in the database, a system table. The first view is taking the role as a starting point. In this case, you are shown all available database objects with the corresponding permissions. Depending on the number of objects that are defined in the database, this list can be quite overwhelming. To get a better understanding of what you are presented with, you can open the permission list of the BizTalk_dba role in the InterchangeBTM database:

1. Open **SQL Server Enterprise Manager**.
2. Expand until all databases are shown.
3. Expand **InterchangeBTM**.
4. Create a **New Database Role** called **BizTalk_dba**, and make **sa_InterchangeBTM** a member of this role.

5. Reopen **BizTalk_dba** by right-clicking it and selecting **Properties**.

6. The **Database Role Properties** dialog appears. Press **Permissions...**.

7. The current **Database Role Properties** dialog will now appear with a **Permissions** tab (Figure 8.24).

Figure 8.24 Setting Object Permissions in the Database Role Properties Window

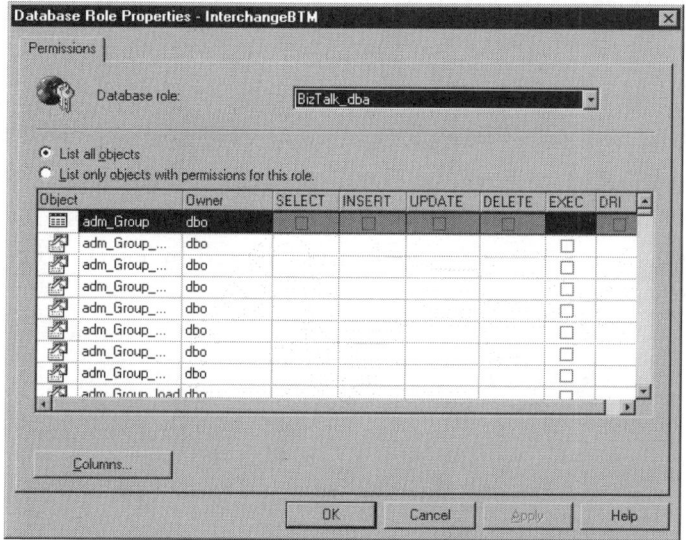

8. Notice that even you "'asked" for the permissions of BizTalk_dba, you are able to select any role available within the current database.

9. Below the Database role is a list selection. The option **List all objects** is the default, since at this point selecting **List only objects with permissions for this role** will give you an empty list.

10. The Object list is sorted alphabetically, and the Object column shows an icon indicating the type of object and its name. The next column shows the owner of the object.

11. The last six columns represent the possible permissions, with the valid permissions showing a check box in the cell. The meanings of the permissions are SQL-statement related. Let's look at them:

- **SELECT** is the role allowed to perform a SELECT-FROM-WHERE SQL statement on the table; hence, allowed to read records (rows) from the table.

- **INSERT** is the role allowed to perform an INSERT-INTO-WITH SQL statement on the table; hence, allowed to add records to the table.

- **UPDATE** is the role allowed to perform an UPDATE-SET SQL statement on the table; hence, allowed to modify records in the table.

- **DELETE** is the role allowed to perform a DELETE-FROM-WHERE SQL statement on the table; hence, allowed to remove records from the table.

- **EXEC** is the role allowed to perform an EXECUTE statement on the stored procedure; hence, allowed to run the stored procedure.

- **DRI** is the role allowed to execute Declarative Referential Integrity constraints on the table. DRI constraints enable you to ensure consistency between tables, effectuated by equal columns with the same values.

  For example, you have two tables, "Vendor" and "Products." Each Vendor record is identified with a Vendor_Id. Every record in the Products table is identified by a Product_Id and a Vendor_Id showing who is selling this product. Every Vendor_Id used in the Products table must correspond with one and only one Vendor_Id in the Vendors table. This is called *referential integrity*. A DRI constraint can be that before a DELETE on a vendor record is effectuated, it is first checked if there are still product records with this Vendor_Id. If so, the Vendor record cannot be deleted.

The ability to clamp down the access to the database is very powerful, but by its extensiveness also very prone to errors, resulting in runtime errors due to a shortage of permissions. Nevertheless, an additional level of permissions gives you even more possibilities. At the bottom of the **Permissions** tab of the **Database Role Properties** windows is a **Columns...** button. This button becomes active if the object you select is a table. Do the following:

1. Select an object that is a database table; for example, the first object **adm_Group**.

2. Press **Columns...**, and a **Column Permissions** dialog appears (Figure 8.25).

3. The dialog shows the role name (although it is called User name) and object name. Below it is the option to limit the listed columns.

Figure 8.25 Setting Permissions in the Column Permission Window

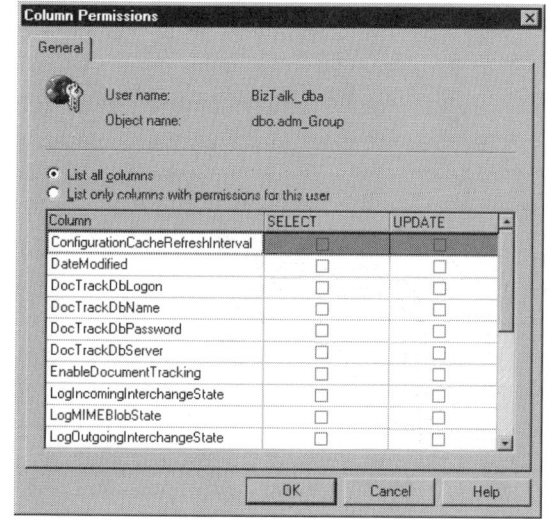

4. The list box lists all fields (columns) in the table. In each column, you can choose to allow or deny the following options:

- **SELECT**, meaning this column can or cannot be used in a SELECT-FROM-WHERE statement. If you deny SELECT access, the column will not show in a selection.

- **UPDATE**, meaning the value of this column can or cannot be changed in an UPDATE-SET statement. If you deny UPDATE access, the column value will not be changed, even if the UPDATE tries to do so.

The second way to set permissions is through the view of the object. This shows the object and all roles associated to the database, and from here you can set the same permissions. Let's see how this works:

1. Open **SQL Server Enterprise Manager**.

2. Expand until all databases are shown.

3. Expand **InterchangeBTM**.

4. Select **Tables**.

5. Select a table in the right-hand list box; for this example, select **adm_Group**.

6. Right-click it, select **Properties**, and the **Table Properties** dialog appears (Figure 8.26).

Figure 8.26 The Table Properties Window

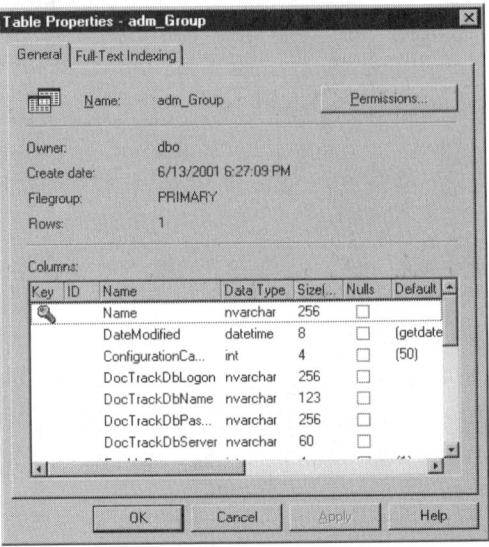

7. Press **Permissions…**, and the **Object Properties** dialog appears (Figure 8.27).

Figure 8.27 Setting Permissions in the Object Properties Window

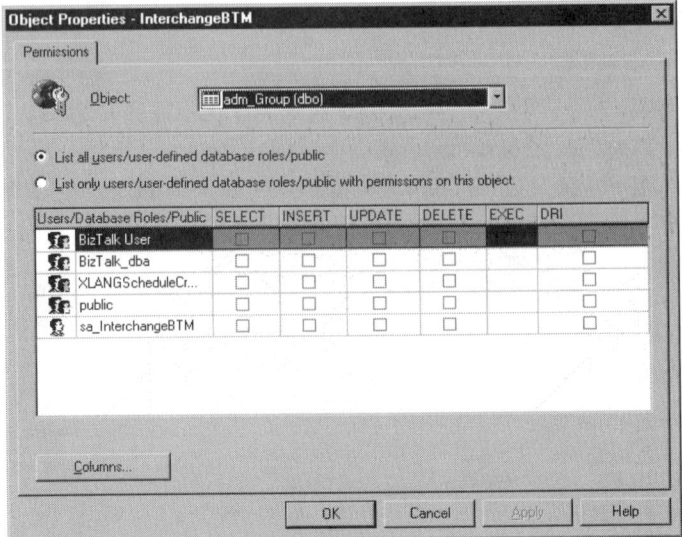

8. As you will notice, you are able to select every database object associated with the InterchangeBTM database.

9. The list box shows the Users/Database Roles/Public. The icon in front of each line indicates a role or a user.

10. Now, select the role **BizTalk_dba**, and then press **Columns....** The **Column Permissions** dialog as seen in the first view will appear (refer again to Figure 8.26).

Data Loss Prevention

Users having access to classified information is bad, but not being able to restore the database to its state just before it was corrupted or disrupted is even worse. Let's take the following example: A firmware bug incapacitates your RAID array on your database server, and you are not able to salvage the BizTalk Interchange databases that are stored on these disks. In addition, even you make a full database backup each night of every database, that backup is already 20 hours old. Conclusion: Regular periodical backups will not prevent loss of data if something goes wrong.

You need to extend your backup strategy to achieve a full recovery. You can also take another approach: keep a copy of each database online on another server, so in case things go wrong, you can easily switch databases. First, let us look at how to make your backup strategy less vulnerable.

Backup/Recovery

Setting up a recovery strategy is not something you do late on a Friday night. As the BizTalk Security Policy discussed in the beginning of the chapter, your recovery strategy is an elaborate plan on its own. If you want to know more on that subject and how SQL Server 2000 can assist you in achieving a nearly fail-safe recovery strategy see Chapter 7, "SQL Server Backup and Recovery" in *Designing SQL Server 2000 Databases for .NET Enterprise Servers*.

A good backup strategy that enables you to minimize data loss includes:

- Make a daily full backup to tape during the night.

- Every six hours, make an incremental backup to disk. Take notice of the fact that you can make backups while the database stays online.

- Every 15, 30, or 60 minutes, make a backup of the transaction log to disk, depending on the amount of transactions that take place on the database.

NOTE

While backing up your BizTalk databases, you should also back up the master and msdb databases. These contain valuable operational and historical information regarding all databases that run under the same SQL server. It will save you a great deal of time if you do not have to rebuild these databases.

If a disk pack now ceases to exist, do not panic. Check to see if the SQL server is still running, using the Enterprise Manager. If so, you can still back up the open transaction log, which saves all finished transaction since the last backup of the transaction log. The only transactions you lose are the ones that were not committed when the failure took place.

The backups you make to disk should be done to the storage of another server. What is the point in making a backup if you put it on the same disk on which your database is residing? If the disk fails, your backup files will disappear with it. Restoring the database is a reverse process:

1. Restore the full backup.

2. Restore all the incremental backups since the last full backup.

3. Replay all the transaction logs since the last incremental backup.

WARNING

In the installation documentation of BizTalk Server 2000, Microsoft advises you to enable automatic truncation of the transaction logs to improve performance. They are right about the performance issue, only they forget to tell you that you might also be throwing away your last resort in restoring a database to its last correct state, without significant loss of data. Therefore, unless you are absolutely sure that you know what you are doing, *never* turn on automatic truncation of the transaction logs in a production environment. Beefing up your server to overcome the slight loss of performance is better insurance.

Online Database Copy

There are different ways you can create an exact online copy of you BizTalk databases. The most well-known is *replication*, in which somewhere on your network runs another SQL server that has subscribed to the part of the database, or the whole one, you make available for publication.

1. Create a publication for the entire database. Be sure you make it transactional, so it stays synchronized with the source.

2. Create a Pull subscription on the other SQL server.

3. Make at least one backup a day, since bad news never comes alone.

While using replication as a means to ensure that you have an actual copy of the BizTalk databases, it is not its intended purpose. Replication, using the Publish-Subscribe method, is use to distribute data among multiple independent applications. Once the subscriber gets the data from a publication, it is no longer under the control of the publisher. Another application of replication is to have multiple places in your network, especially if data has to travel over slow links, from where the content of the database can be inquired, thereby overcoming the slow communication.

Replication does require additional processing power—in the worse case, more than double—so it can cause significant problems when the load on the SQL server is high. You need a thorough understanding of the how replication works, and the different types of replication infrastructures that are possible. In addition, understand how the primary database is used in terms of load. It is highly recommended that you execute some performance tests on the replication infrastructure to determine how replication behaves under high loads. For more information on replication, read Chapter 12 of *Designing SQL Server 2000 Databases for .NET Enterprise Servers*.

Another way to create online copies is with *Log shipping*. As the name implies, the transaction logs of a BizTalk database are shipped to another server that runs SQL Server. That server has a copy of the BizTalk database running, and every time it receives a transaction log, it replays it on the database, thereby synchronizing the copy with the original database. The copying of the transaction log can be done every time you back up the transaction log. Again, do not truncate the transaction logs.

Certificates and the CryptoAPI

We've already mentioned certificates and CryptoAPI, also shortened to CAPI. Now, it is time to take a closer look at both and see what they mean for a BizTalk application. Certificates are used to *authenticate* a user and/or the data he or she is sending, the *encoding* of data ensuring its originality and proof of not being tampered with, and encryption of data sent by a user, preventing others from reading the original data. You have probably seen the use of certificates in applications such as Outlook and Internet Explorer; however, the Encrypting File System (EFS) and IPSec are using certificates to encrypt files on disk. The applications all need to have access to the certificates that are reside in certificate stores that are system or user related. In fact, when configuring messaging ports and/or channels, using the BizTalk Messaging Manager, you can select certificates for subsequent inbound and outbound messaging. When you built a XLANG schedule engine or another COM+ application and need to securely exchange messages, make use of CryptoAPI to access a Certificate store, and use the certificates for authentication, encoding, and/or encryption purposes.

This chapter will not go into detail on how public-key encryption works. However, you can find more information on this subject in the Syngress book *Configuring Windows 2000 Server*, or go to www.microsoft.com/windows2000/technologies/security.

Certificates Services

If you want to make use of a certificate, you need to obtain one from a trusted organization. This trusted organization, called a certificate authority (CA), ensures you that the certificate is genuine and authenticates the user named in the certificate. The most used Certificate Standard is X.509, which includes:

- The version of the certificate (for example, version 1)
- The hash algorithm used for the certificate signature (e.g., SHA1, MD5)
- The serial number uniquely identifying this certificate
- The CA that issued the certificate
- The name of the certificate owner
- The public key of the owner and the algorithm (e.g., RSA 2048 bits)
- The CA's signature (thumbprint) and the algorithm used (e.g., SHA1)
- The period (from.. to..) during which the certificate is valid

When considering CAs, we usually think of companies such as like VeriSign; however, for your BizTalk environment, you can be your own CA. Let's see what steps you need to take to realize this:

1. Log on with administrator rights on the **primary domain controller (PDC)** on the **BizTalk domain**.

2. **Start | Settings | Add/Remove Programs | Add/Remove Windows Components**.

3. Check the **Certificates Services** option, and click **Next**.

4. Note the warning message (Figure 8.28). By installing Certificate Services on the PDC, it is not likely that you will run into these kinds of problems, since you will not make changes to the PDC's name or remove the server from the domain. Remember that both the CA and all certificates issued by the CA become invalid.

Figure 8.28 Warning Message When Installing Certificate Services

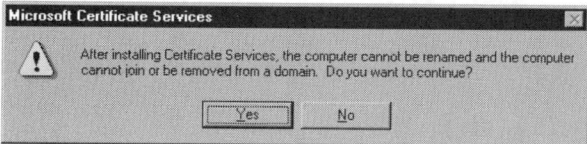

5. Since this will be the first CA in the domain, you have to make it your Enterprise root CA (Figure 8.29). Unless you are experienced with the cryptographic implementation of Windows 2000, leave the **Advanced Options** box unchecked.

Figure 8.29 Choose the Type of CA that Needs to Be Set Up

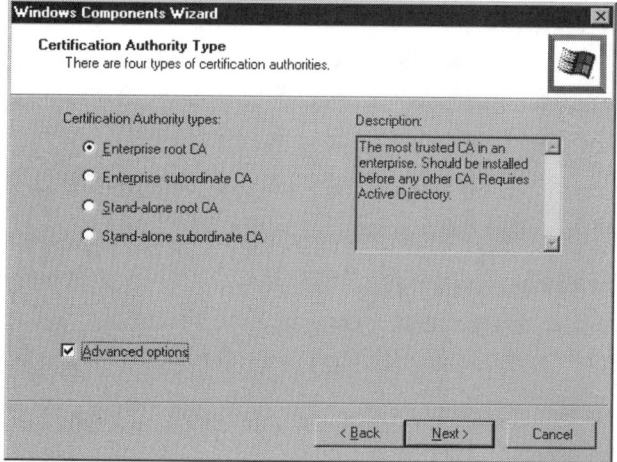

6. Follow the rest of the steps and supply the necessary information, using the defaults where available.

7. Check if the service **Certificate Services** is running by opening the Microsoft Management Console and adding the following Snap-ins:

   - **Services** for the local computer.

   - **Certificate Authority** for the local computer.

   - **Certificates** for the computer account on the local computer.

8. Open **Services**, and check if **Certificate Services** is in the list and is running.

9. Now, open **Certification Authority (Local)**. You will see an icon with the name you gave your CA. The icon should have a white circle with a green check mark, indicating that it is active.

10. Open the **CA** and you will see five folders (Figure 8.30).

    - **Revoked Certificates** Contains the certificates the CA administrator has declared invalid. In case a user or application checks the validity of such a certificate, it will be informed that it is revoked. There can be different reasons to revoke certificates, such as an employee leaving your company, or certificates that are "lost." This information will also be communicated with subordinate CAs within the domain.

    - **Issued Certificates** Contains all certificates issued by the CA. Although it may be empty at first, it will quickly populate, since functionalities in need of a certificate, such as IPSec or EFS, will automatically enroll for a certificate and be issued one. You can check this by going to an unimportant directory and encrypting it. If you now refresh the Issued Certificates folder, you will notice that a certificate has been issued.

    - **Pending Requests** Contains the requests for a certificate that needs to be issued; for example, enrollment requests sent to the CA while the Certificate Services is down.

    - **Failed Requests** Contains all the requests that could not be fulfilled; for example, technical problems or because the CA was unable to get a positive ID on the user.

    - **Policy Settings** Contains all the types of certificates the CA can issue.

Figure 8.30 The Certificate Authority Snap-In to Manage the CA

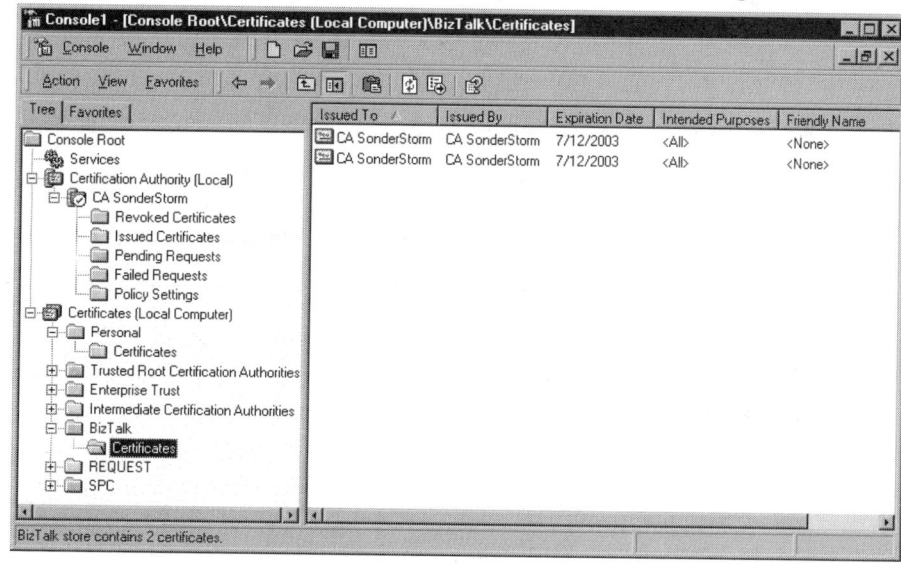

Before leaving the CA to do its work, you need to set an option that enables you to monitor and manage user certificates from within the Active Directory:

1. Select your **CA**, right-click it, and select **Properties**.

2. Select the **Exit Module** tab, and press **Configure…**.

3. The **Properties** dialog appears with a Certificate Publication tab (Figure 8.31). This tab has two options; the **Allow certificates to be published to the file system** will be checked by default. You can leave it that way.

4. By also checking the box **Allow certificates to be published in the Active Directory**, you will see that the next time you go into the AD to manage objects, the Properties window will have a **Published Certificates** tab (Figure 8.32).

Your own CA is up and running, so we can go back to BizTalk Server. You will have noticed that when configuring Messaging Ports, Channels and Envelopes, using the BizTalk Messaging Manager that you can select Certificates for inbound and outbound data, protecting the messages you send and ensuring that received messages are genuine.

Figure 8.31 The Properties Window of the CA Exit Module

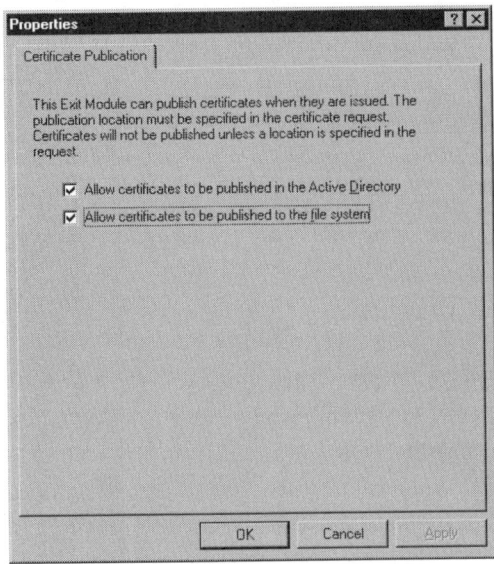

Figure 8.32 Managing the User's Published Certificates from within the Active Directory

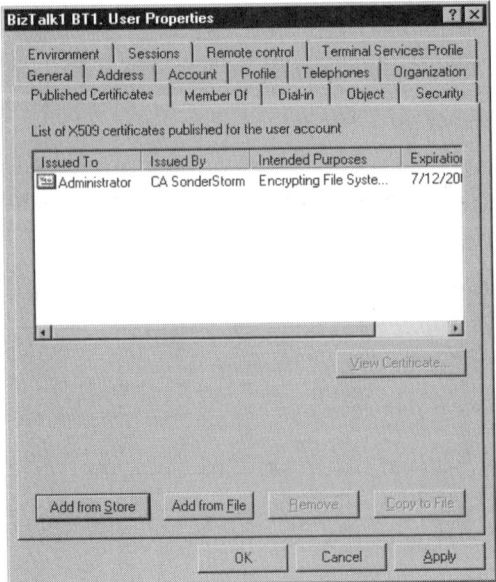

Working with Trading Partners

The definition of *trading partner* in the BizTalk Server glossary reads, "An external organization with which your home organization exchanges electronic data. The messaging ports, distribution lists, channels, and XLANG schedules that you create govern the exchange of documents among trading partners." A big part of that governing is ensuring that the messages/documents you receive from your trading partners are really coming from them, have not been tampered with, and preferably have been encrypted to keep the contents from unauthorized users. If you use SSL (for Secure HTTP data exchange) or IPSec, the data will be protected from network eavesdropping, but once it arrives on the server, it becomes readable again. The use of certificates enables you to achieve the level of security you need.

It is important to know where BizTalk Server looks for certificates. The certificates it uses to authenticate its own messages are stored in the Personal Certificate store on the local computer, the server running the BizTalk Server service. The certificates of the trading partners are kept in the BizTalk Store on the local computer. You can manage these using the Certificates (Local Computer) snap-in (Figure 8.30).

To populate the 'Personal Store' with certificates (remember that "personal" means "this computer"), you can request a new certificate or import a certificate from a file. In case you import a certificate, it also needs to include the private key, or else you are not able to use it to sign and encrypt outgoing messages/documents or secure communications.

Without going into too much detail of the use of certificates, it is important to know that they, in most cases, make use of *public key* technology. This means that you have two asymmetric keys, a public one and a private one. Simply put, the private key that is well protected by Windows is used to decrypt your messages that you receive. The public key, which is wrapped in the certificate and can be available to everyone, is used to encrypt messages that are meant for you.

To populate the BizTalk store, you need the public key—hence, the certificate, of your trading partners—and they need your public key. Before you can develop any COM+ application in which you actively work with certificates (see the section *CryptoAPI*), you must be in the possession of these public keys. You need to ask your trading partners to supply you with the certificate they are going to use in the BizTalk document exchange. In case you have a limited number of known trading partners, for supply-chain or e-procurement, and you hold a central position in these relationships, you could consider becoming the

CA for your BizTalk application. Your trading partners can enroll for a certificate, using your CA, by using the Certificate Enroll Web site application that comes with the Certificate Services (called certsrv). The advantage is that since you trust your own CA, you can trust all certificates that are issued by this CA, giving you better control over the certificates used. If you do not want to be bothered with setting up and maintaining your own CA, you should define the certificates that you accept for using with your BizTalk application:

- Which CAs do you accept?
- Which hash algorithms do you allow/support?
- What key lengths do you allow/support?
- What public-key encryption algorithms do you allow/support?

Let's clarify the enrollment, export, and import of certificates using the following example. Assume you decide to have your own CA for the BizTalk application, and you will only accept certificates issued by your BizTalk CA. You will also define certificates in your channel definitions. Perform the following steps:

1. Trading partner requests a certificate from the BizTalk CA.
2. After having received the certificate, the trading partner needs to export it to the BizTalk application.
3. The certificate has to be imported into the BizTalk store.
4. A local certificate and the imported certificate have to be selected for a channel.

The trading partner will use the Certificate Services Web site to request a certificate. To be able to access the CA, he needs a username and password within the domain. This is only a viable solution if you know your trading partners, and they are limited. However, the benefit is better control of the used certificates; hence, security. Every trading partner has to perform the following steps to obtain a certificate:

1. Open the browser and point to the **Certificates Services Web site**, by default called **certsrv**. After authentication, you enter the Web site (Figure 8.33).
2. Select the option **Request a certificate**, already selected by default.
3. Press **Next** to move to the next page, requesting for the appropriate type.

Figure 8.33 Requesting a Certificate Using the Certificate Services
Web Site

4. Select **Advanced Request**, and press **Next**. You need to select this type
   to make the key exportable, as you will see later.

5. On the **Advanced Certificate Requests**, select the option **Submit a
   certificate request to this CA using a form**, and press **Next**.

6. You are now on the second page of the Advanced Certificate Request
   (Figure 8.34) and should make the following selections:

   - For **Certificate Template**, use **User**.

   - For **CSP**, use **Microsoft Strong Cryptographic Provider**,
     although the default also works.

   - For **Key size**, use **1024**; a larger key size takes more processing power
     without providing additional security for your BizTalk application.

   - Select **Create new key set**.

   - Check the box **Enable strong private key protection**.

   - Check the box **Mark keys as exportable**. This is the main reason
     to go for the Advanced Request, or else you will not be able to

export your private key, which you will need for the application that will exchange messages/documents with your BizTalk application.

■ Check the box **Export keys to file**, and fill in a **filename**; for example, **BizTalk_Exchange**.

Figure 8.34 The Advanced Certificate Request Page on the Certificate Services Web Site

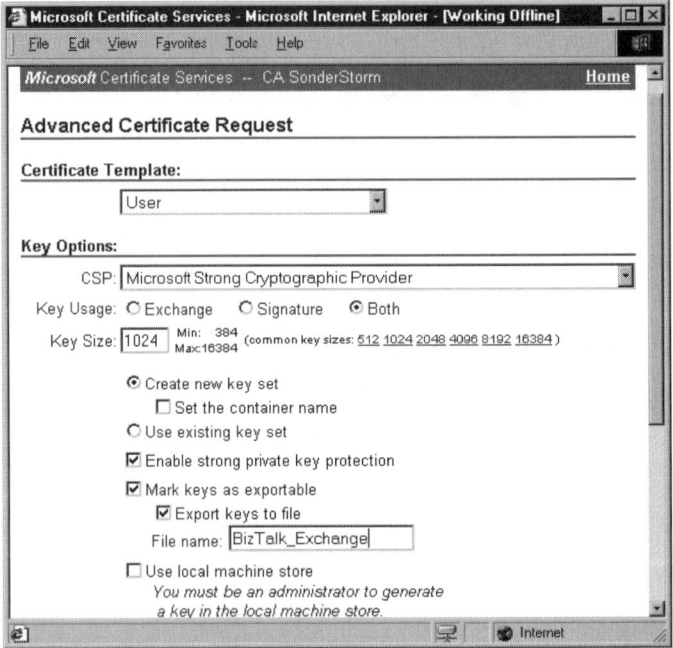

7. Press **Submit**.

8. A dialog will appear that prompts you for a password to protect the key file. Enter the password twice, and press **OK**.

9. You are now on the **Certificate Issued** page, and you can select the type of encoding. For this purpose, both will do, so keep the default.

10. Click the link **Download CA certificate**, and the Windows dialog for File download appears. Save the disk to file.

11. Close the browser.

At this point, the trading partner has a file containing the certificate, including the private key. This file can be installed on the server in the appropriate store, by double-clicking this file, pressing **Install Certificate...**, and launching the **Certificate Import Wizard**. After completing the Import Wizard, the trading partner can export the certificate by going to the **Details** tab and pressing **Copy to File…**. This will start the **Certificate Export Wizard**. The Certificate file can be send to you.

Since the trading partner needs also a certificate from you, follow the same steps and install the certificate in the **Personal store** of the local computer, being the server that runs BizTalk Server. You can request a certificate directly from the MMC with the **Certificates – Current User** snap-in. Go to the **Personal store**, right-click it, and select **All Tasks | Request New Certificate…**. You can set the same options as with the CA Web site. After the certificate is created, it automatically installs in your Personal store. You can move it to the **Certificates (Local Computer) Personal** store by cutting and pasting the certificate.

After receiving the certificate from your trading partner, you need to install it in the BizTalk store of the local computer. Do this from the MMC with the **Certificates (Local Computer)** snap-in:

1. Expand **Certificates** (local Computer).

2. Select **BizTalk** folder.

3. Right-click this folder, and select **All Tasks | Import…**. The **Certificate Import Wizard** starts.

4. Click **Next**.

5. Browse for the **Certificate file**, and select it, and click **Next**.

6. The dialog asking for the Certificate store will select the option **Place all certificates in the following store**, with BizTalk selected as the store.

7. Click **Next**, followed by **Finish**, and the certificate is installed.

In this example, we decided that an inbound document on a channel will be both encrypted and signed. Therefore, you need to select one of your own local system certificates for decrypting an inbound document on a channel, and a trading partner's certificate to validate the signing of the message (Figure 8.35).

Since you expect the inbound document to be signed by the trading partner, you must also sign your outbound documents. This certificate also needs to be picked from the Personal Certificates (My Store) of the local computer. You can do this on the Outbound Document page of the Channel Properties window.

Figure 8.35 Selecting the Inbound Document Certificates on the Channel Properties Window

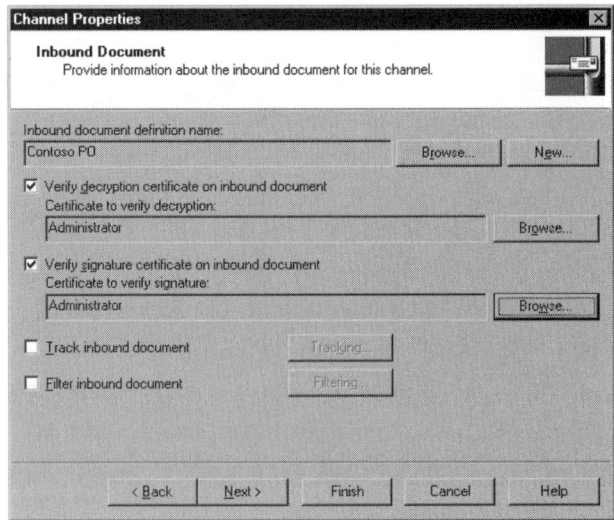

It is crucial that you select the proper certificates! The certificate that you select for decrypting purposes *must* be the same as the one you exported to the trading partner that will send your documents over that channel. The certificate to verify the signature of the document *must* be the certificate that the trading partner exported to you and will use for signing.

To make this last part more clear, let's list the steps you need to take:

1. Open **Start | Programs | BizTalk Server 2000 | BizTalk Messaging Manager**.

2. Select **Channels** under **Search for other items**.

3. Click **Search Now**.

4. Select the appropriate channel from the list in the right pane.

5. Right-click it, and select **Edit**.

6. Click **Next** twice. This brings you to the **Channel Properties** page named **Inbound Document**.

7. Check the box **Verify decryption certificate on inbound document**, click **Browse...**, and select the certificate that you selected for

this function. Note that the dialog **Select a Certificate to Verify Decryption** explicitly states that it looks in the store "My Store"; hence, Personal Folder.

8. Check the box **Verify signature certificate on inbound document**, click **Browse…**, and select the certificate that you selected for this function. Note that the dialog **Select a Certificate to Verify Decryption** explicitly states that it looks in the BizTalk store.

9. Click **Next**, which brings you to the **Channel Properties** page named **Outbound Document**.

10. Check the box **Sign outbound document**, click **Browse…**, and select the certificate that you selected for the option **Verify decryption certificate on inbound document** on the **Inbound Document** page.

11. Click **Finish**.

When selecting certificates for the channels, it is advised to create a new certificate for every channel. This allows you to revoke a certificate if a channel becomes obsolete or a trading partner no longer makes use of the BizTalk application. In this way, you always keep control over the way the certificate is used.

WARNING

To avoid a great deal of certificate maintenance, use the same certificate as the one you use for decrypting inbound messages. In this case, you have only one certificate that you have to send a trading partner, and you only need one certificate from your trading partner. This way, you keep the setup symmetrical.

This concludes the discussion of certificates from the declarative point of view. Now, it is time to look at certificates and the way you can use them from a programmatic point of view.

CryptoAPI

Cryptographic API was available in earlier Windows versions; however, the solution is now more comprehensive and ties in better with the authentication security. CryptoAPI makes the use of cryptography within applications easier, more transparent, and portable. All the C-API calls remain the same, even if you change the cryptographic service provider (CSP); however, parameter values might change. If you take a closer look at how the CryptoAPI architecture is set up (Figure 8.36), you can identify five functionality groups:

- **Base cryptographic functions** Used to connect to a CSP, creating a security context that gives you access to private keys, generation of keys, and exchanging keys. The Base functions are as close as you can get to a CSP. When creating a context, you can select the CSP you want to use, but the access to the CSP remains out of sight and within the Windows kernel. This is done to give maximum protection to the public keys. The Base cryptographic functions can be subdivided in functions for:

  - **Service provider** (Table 8.3)

  - **Data encryption and decryption** (Table 8.4)

  - **Key generation and key exchange** (Table 8.5)

  - **Hash and signature** (Table 8.6)

  - **CryptEncodeObject/CryptDecodeObject** These generalized functions do the encoding/encryption and decoding/decryption of the object referred to.

- **Certificate store functions** Enable you to manage certificates available in Certificates stores.

- **Certificate verification functions** Take care of the encryption and decryption of the data, based on the security context. In addition, the hash functions are part of this function group. All these functions start with "Crypt."

- **Simplified message functions** Used to encrypt/decrypt messages, sign messages, verify certificates. These message functions are composed using multiple low-level message functions and base cryptographic functions (Table 8.7).

- **Low-level message functions** Used by simplified message functions, and can be used to obtain more control over the message functions, although it takes more programming effort.

For information on the other CryptoAPI groups, visit the Microsoft Platform SDK site (msdn.microsoft.com/library/default.asp; **Security | Security (General) | SDK Documentation | Cryptography | CryptoAPI**).

Figure 8.36 An Overview of the CryptoAPI Architecture

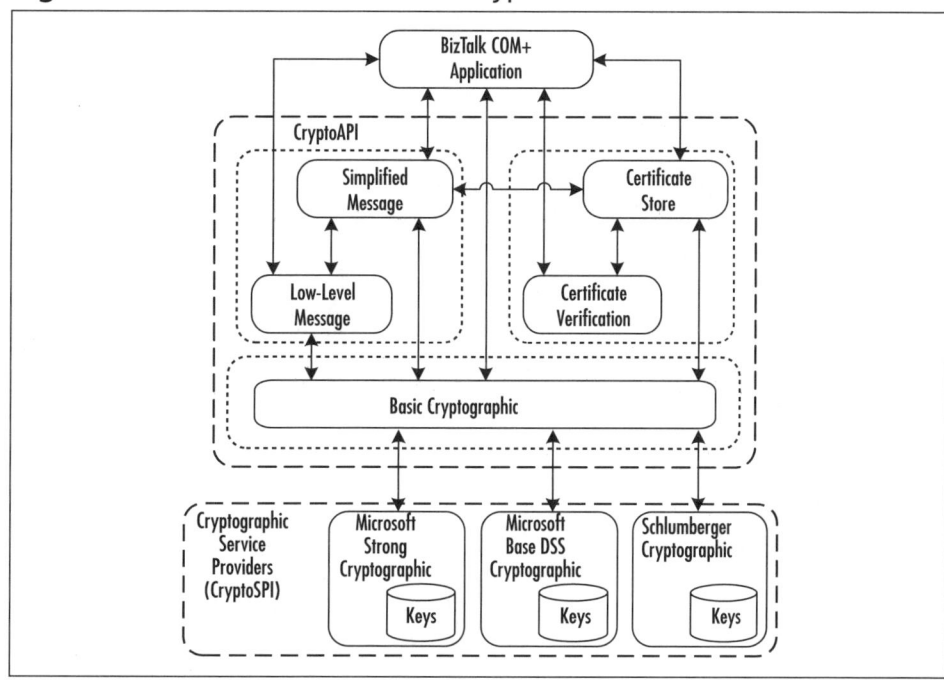

Table 8.3 Base Cryptographic Functions—Service Provider

Function	Explanation
CryptAcquireContext	Opens a security context for a specific key container, related to the appropriate CSP. Only after this functions returns a handle to this context, the CSP handle, the application is able to use the private keys.
CryptContextAddRef	Use this call if more functions make use of the same CSP handle, to prevent the context from being released while there are still functions using it.
CryptEnumProviders	Retrieves the next available CSP on the system. If you want to use the best possible CSP, you first have to find out which are available.
CryptEnumProviderTypes	Retrieves the next available CSP type on the system. Instead of going through all available CSPs and finding out what type they

Continued

Table 8.3 Continued

Function	Explanation
	are, you can first check out the type, and based on that, find an appropriate CSP.
CryptGetDefaultProvider	Retrieves the default CSP for a specific CSP type.
CryptGetProvParam	Retrieves the attributes of a specified CSP.
CryptInstallDefaultContext	Sets the context acquired by CryptAcquireContext as the default security context within a multithread process.
CryptReleaseContext	Is called by a function to end its use of the security context. If more functions reference this context, it will only be fully released if the reference count equals 0.
CryptSetProvider	Sets the default CSP for a specific CSP type. This value is the default for the user; for example, a service account of a BizTalk COM+ application that sets this value. Therefore, every time this user makes a call to CryptAcquireContext and refers to the default CSP for a specific CSP type, this provider is used.
CryptSetProvParam	Sets a specific CSP parameter (attribute) in the current security context, referenced to by the CSP handle.
CryptUninstallDefaultContext	Clears the CSP handle, set by CryptInstallDefaultContext, as the default that can be used by other threads in a process. However, if there are still threads using this context, the call will be deferred until all threads release their reference to this CSP handle.

Table 8.4 Base Cryptographic Functions—Data Encryption and Decryption

Function	Explanation
CryptDecrypt	Takes a specified block of encrypted data and decrypts it using the indicated key, being a session key or a private key.

Continued

Table 8.4 Continued

Function	Explanation
CryptEncrypt	Takes a specified block of plaintext data and encrypts it using the specified key, being a session key or a public key.
CryptProtectData	Takes a specified plaintext Binary Large Object (BLOB)—for example, an image—and encrypts it using the public data encryption key of the user calling this function.
CryptUnprotectData	Takes a specified encrypted BLOB and decrypts it using the private data encryption key of the user. If the user is different or the private key does not correspond with the public key, decryption will fail.

Table 8.5 Base Cryptographic Functions—Key Generation and Key Exchange

Function	Explanation
CryptAcquireCertificatePrivateKey	Opens a security context—hence, acquires a CSP handle—for the private key corresponding to the available certificate.
CryptDeriveKey	Generates a session key, mostly used to encrypt data, based on a hashed passphrase. As the name suggests, session keys are generated for one-time use. This function returns a hash handle.
CryptDestroyKey	Releases the hash handle and makes the session key inaccessible.
CryptDuplicateKey	Creates an identical key, as the one supplied to this function.
CryptExportKey	Makes a key available for export to a known recipient. To safely get a key from protected memory to unprotected memory, the key is encrypted generally using the public key of the recipient. The result of this function is a key BLOB that holds the exportable key.
CryptGenKey	Generates a random key, being a session key or an asymmetric key pair. This function returns a Key handle.

Continued

Table 8.5 Continued

Function	Explanation
CryptGenRandom	Generates a block of cryptographically random data, with a specified length.
CryptGetKeyParam	Retrieves the value of a specific parameter from a key referenced by the Key handle.
CryptGetUserKey	Gets a Key handle from a security context—hence, CSP handle—on one of the two default key pairs a user has: one for key exchange and one for signature purposes.
CryptImportKey	Imports a key from a key BLOB into the key database of a specified CSP. Since this is the reverse process of CryptExportKey, the key used in the import must be related to the key used to create the key BLOB.
CryptSetKeyParam	Sets the value of a specific parameter from a key referenced by the Key handle.

Table 8.6 Base Cryptographic Functions—Hash and Signature

Function	Explanation
CryptCreateHash	Returns a handle to a hash object, effectively creating an empty hash object. This object is related to the existing security context; hence, CSP handle.
CryptDestroyHash	Releases the hash handle, making the hash object no longer usable.
CryptDuplicateHash	Creates an identical copy of a hash object, as the one supplied to this function.
CryptGetHashParam	Retrieves the value of a specific parameter from a hash object, referenced by the hash handle.
CryptHashData	Takes a block of data, applies a hash algorithm on this data, and moves the hashed data into the specified hash object. The type of hash algorithm used is based on the parameters of the hash object. In case the data block is larger than can be handled by the hash function, it is possible to perform this function a number of times, using the same hash object. The already calculated hash will automatically become

Continued

Table 8.6 Continued

Function	Explanation
	part of the data that is supplied to subsequent calls to CryptHashData.
CryptHashSessionKey	Takes a session key, applies a hash algorithm on this data, and moves the hashed data into the specified hash object. The type of hash algorithm used is based on the parameters of the hash object. In case multiple keys need to be hashed, it is possible to perform this function a number of times using the same hash object. Here also, the already available hash value is added to the subsequent keys before performing the hash.
CryptSetHashParam	Sets the value of a specific parameter from a hash object referenced by the hash handle.
CryptSignHash	Signs the specified hash object, using the private key of the user's key exchange or signature key-pairs.
CryptVerifySignature	Verifies the signature of a hash object, referenced by the hash handle. It uses the public key of the sender to do the verification.

Table 8.7 Simplified Message Functions

Function	Explanation
CryptDecodeMessage	Decodes, decrypts, and verifies a cryptographic message.
CryptDecryptAndVerifyMessageSignature	Decrypts the specified message, and verifies the signature of the message signer.
CryptDecryptMessage	Decodes and decrypts the specified message.
CryptEncryptMessage	Encrypts and encodes the specified message for the recipient(s) of this message. Remember that for each recipient, the message has to be encrypted using the public key, available in the certificate.
CryptGetMessageCertificates	Gets a handle to a Certificate store that contains the certificates and

Continued

Table 8.7 Continued

Function	Explanation
	certificate revocation lists that are contained in the specified message BLOB.
CryptGetMessageSignerCount	Determines the number of "users" who signed a specified message.
CryptHashMessage	Returns a hash of a specified message.
CryptSignAndEncryptMessage	Creates a hash of the specified message, subsequently signs this hash, encrypts the content for every recipient, hashes this content and the signed hash, and then encodes both the encrypted content and the signed hash.
CryptSignMessage	Creates a hash of the specified message, subsequently signs the hash, and then encodes both the original message and the signed hash.
CryptVerifyDetachedMessageHash	Verifies a message containing a detached hash. A detached hash is a hash that is not accompanied by the original message. This decreases the amount of data that has to be sent; however, it only works if the recipient can access a copy of the original in another way.
CryptVerifyDetachedMessageSignature	Verifies a signed message containing one or more detached signatures. A detached signature is a signature that is not accompanied with the original message that is signed. This only works if the recipient has access to a copy of the message that has been signed.
CryptVerifyMessageHash	Verifies the hash of a specified hashed message.
CryptVerifyMessageSignature	Verifies the signature of a specified signed message.

As the preceding tables show, the CryptoAPI is quite extensive, since the functions in the tables only account for about half of the functions available. Before you decide to use CryptoAPI in your BizTalk application, take the time to understand the CryptoAPI, and the way secure processes, such as exchanging keys, work. CryptoAPI does help you with getting access to keys and encryption/hash algorithms. However, it does not help you to get secure processes realized. If you are still interested in using CryptoAPI, the following example will give you a better understanding of the use of CryptoAPI functions and how they fit into a process. This example is about exchanging a session key, and lists the process of acquiring a key and sending it to the known recipient.

Let's take the following situation: You are writing a COM+ application that needs to set up a secure communication with another application. It has been decided to use HMAC-MD5; therefore, you need to exchange a session key that can be used as shared key in the HMAC algorithm. The example will create a session key and send it to the other party: The program has to perform the following steps:

1. Open a Context using **CryptAcquireContext**; this will result in a CSP handle.

2. Generate a random exportable session key (type CRYPT_EXPORTABLE) using **CryptGenKey**; the CSP handle is used as input and delivers a handle to the key (key handle).

3. To export the session key, you have to encrypt it first before you can bring it from the protected environment to the application (unprotected) memory in a BLOB. This means that you have to access the public key for key exchange of the other party using **CertOpenStore** or **CertOpenSystemStore**.

4. Look up the AT_KEYEXCHANGE certificate of the other party using **CertFindCertificateInStore**.

5. Now you can extract the session key from the protected memory using **CryptExportKey**, telling it to create as SIMPLEBLOB, meaning export a session key. You will call **CryptExportKey** twice: the first time to determine the size of the BLOB and allocate the memory to store the BLOB in; and then again with a reference to the memory where CryptExportKey stores the encrypted session key.

6. Before sending it, you have to ensure yourself that nobody will be able to change it without being noticed. Therefore, you need to sign the key

BLOB you send to the other party. Call **CryptGetUserKey** to retrieve your AT_SIGNATURE key. You will use the private key of the pair to generate the hash.

7. First, call **CryptCreateHash** to create a hash object that is used to store the hash in.

8. Next, call **CryptHashSessionKey** to create the hash.

9. Then call **CryptSignHash** to leave your signature on the hash.

10. Now you can send the data, but before ending the program, you need to destroy the hash, using **CryptDestroyHash**; close the Certificate store, using **CertCloseStore**; and release the context you created in the first step, using **CryptReleaseContext**.

NOTE

In the listings of CryptoAPI functions, references to hashing are made without any further explanation. Although this is not necessary to understanding the general working of CryptoAPI, it might enhance it. Hashing is a method to derive a fixed-length string, often referred to as *Message Digest* or *Message Fingerprint*, from a variable-length data block (message). These type of hashing algorithms are referred to as *one-way hash*, meaning that the chance that you can derive the original message from just the Message Digest is nearly nonexistent. Another feature of the hashing algorithm used is that if you change 1 bit of the original message, the hash value differs. This means that by sending the Message Digest with the message, the recipient can check if the message has been changed. Of course, the digest has to be encrypted to prevent it from being replaced by attackers who want to alter the message.

Within Windows 2000, there are by default the following hashing algorithms available:

- **MD4 (Message Digest 4)** Described in RFC 1186, makes three passes over the message, resulting in a 128-bit digest. However, it was discovered that the algorithm has a weakness, making it vulnerable for attacks. Therefore, it should be considered insecure, and should not be used. MD4, a 32-bit hashing algorithm, was preceded by MD2, an 8-bit hashing algorithm.
- **MD5 (Message Digest 5)** Described in RFC 1321 is a strengthened version of MD4 and makes four passes, also resulting in a 128-bit digest. During the computation of the digest, it uses 64 32-bit constants.

- **SHA-1 (Secure Hash Algorithm 1)** Described in FIPS PUB 180-1 as an algorithm developed by the National Institute of Standards and Technology (NIST; www.nist.gov). This algorithm delivers a 160-bit digest and is regarded saver as MD5, while both algorithms look very alike, the SHA-1 algorithm is slower compared to MD5. During the computation of the digest, it uses 79 32-bit constants.

These algorithms come with an extension called *Hash Message Authentication Codes* (HMAC), described in RFC 2104. It incorporates a session key, which is shared between the sender and recipient, in the hashing process. Since only both parties involved possess the shared key, it is practically impossible for an attacker to break the hash. Additionally, with the use of the shared session key, the parties involved sign the data they send. Not only takes does the hash ensures that data cannot be changed without noticing, but it also enforces *nonrepudiation*, since only the parties who know the session can create the hash, and therefore any message must originate from one of these parties. HMAC-MD5 is described in RFC 2085.

Transport-Level Encoding

To let your BizTalk application exchange messages with other applications, they need to encode this data in such a way that information can be decoded without loss of information. This section discusses the widely used encode/decode standard *Multipurpose Internet Mail Extension* (MIME). It was developed to enable mail programs to add other types of data to an e-mail. Before MIME–aware mail programs became available, you could only send plain text with binary attachments. MIME has become an established standard and is described in detail in RFCs 1341, 1521, 1522, 2045, 2046, 2047, 2048, and 2049.

BizTalk Server 2000 relies on MIME encoding when sending messages to trading partners through the Simple Mail Transmission Protocol (SMTP). In case you use COM+ applications, or scripts such as VBScript, to construct these MIME messages, you need to understand what makes up the MIME format, and how to write programs that create them. Let's first look at the MIME anatomy. It is straightforward, starting with a header, followed by a body that consists of one or more body parts. The latter is called a "multipart" body. Every body part can be a "multipart" body. The following example uses indentation to show the use of multipart bodies.

```
 1  MIME-Version: 3.0
 2  Content-Type: multipart/mixed; boundary=
    "----=_NextPart_000_0000_01F2E43B.61E63AB0"
 3  Content-Class: urn:content-classes:message
 4    This is a multi-part message in MIME format.
 5  ------=_NextPart_000_0000_01F2E43B.61E63AB0
 6  Content-Type: multipart/alternative;
    boundary="---=_NextPart_001_0001_01F2E43B.61E63AB0"
 7    ------=_NextPart_001_0001_01F2E43B.61E63AB0
 8  Content-Type: text/plain; charset="iso-8859-1"
 9  Content-Transfer-Encoding: 7bit
            See if you can APPROVE this Request.
10    ------=_NextPart_001_0001_01F2E43B.61E63AB0
11  Content-Type: text/html; charset="iso-8859-1"
      Content-Transfer-Encoding: 7bit
            <html><p>See if you can <b>APPROVE</b> this
                Request. <br>
12    ------=_NextPart_001_0001_01F2E43B.61E63AB0-
13  ------=_NextPart_000_0000_01F2E43B.61E63AB0
14  Content-Type: text/xml; name="/xml/ReqToApprove.xml"
15  Content-Transfer-Encoding: quoted-printable
16  Content-Disposition: attachment; filename="/xml/ReqToApprove.xml"
          <NorthwindReq>=0D=0A
              <Header reqNumber="BL0211"
                  reqStatus="New" dateCreated="2000-10-24"
                  timeCreated="16:29:00" />=0D=0A
          <Shipping name="Jeffrey MacGuiness"
                      addr1="1 Berkeley Street" addr2="Suite 101"
                      city="Boston" state="MA" zip="02116" country="USA"
                      phone="(617) 266-0123" />=0D=0A
              <Items count="1" totalPrice="2385.00">
                  <Item partNo="TFT17HQ"
                  description="17-inch TFT monitor max.
                      res. 1600x1200"
```

```
                   qty="3" unitPrice="795.00" />=0D=0A

               </Items>=0D=0A

           </NorthwindReq>=0D=0A
```

17 ------=_NextPart_000_0000_01F2E43B.61E63AB0—

18 Content-Type:image/gif

19 Content-Transfer-Encoding: base64

```
           AAAFFDDlhGAGgAPEAAP/////ZRaCgoAAAACH+PUNvcHlyaWdoddCAoQykgMTk5
           NSBJRVRGLiBVbmF1dGhvcml6ZWQgZHVwbGljYXRpb24gcHJvaGliaXRlZC4A
           HgY43dfgh467DghmER7i45/rh4retyrty3578hkErFDGhe3456retysdgdhw4
           RGHr456fghsrtthESTqw342yl890879567ngfdvgbsdfEFGSDFtgawqw4e445
```

20 ------=_NextPart_000_0000_01F2E43B.61E63AB0—

Now, let's address every numbered line of the above message to explain the content of this example:

1. Every MIME-encoded file starts with the MIME-Version.

2. States what the body is going to look like; in this case, "multipart/mixed." This means that the body contains more than one body part named "multipart". Additionally, the body parts are independent and must be kept in the order as they are listed ("mixed"). This is the default multipart construction. "Boundary" gives the strings that separate the body parts, except for the first one that indicates the start of the first part.

3. "Content-Class" defines the content type of the file, and what properties are valid for this MIME-encoded content. In this case, it is the content class for a message. "urn" stands for "uniform resource name."

4. This text is contained in every MIME-encoded message. In case you use a mail viewer that is not able to decode MIME, it will break off the message as soon as it encounters "nonprintable" data. If this is the case, the recipient sees at least this text, letting him or her know why the full message is not shown.

5. This is the first time the boundary value is encountered; meaning, "here starts the MIME encoded content."

6. Since we know that the file contains more than one body part, it has to define what type the first body part is. In this case, it is also a "multipart" body part, except this time it is "alternative." "Alternative" means that the body parts are alternatives of each other, listed in increasing format

complexity. The mail viewer can decide if it will display all alternatives, or just display the most complex format it understands. In this example, we have a plaintext format (line 8) and an HTML format (line 11). Since this is a nested multipart body part, a new boundary value is defined.

7. This is the first time the second boundary value is shown, indicating the start of the first nested body part.

8. This defines the content type of the first nested body part ("text/plain") and the character set used.

9. This defines the type of encoding that is used for the text. In this case, it is "7bit", meaning that every character in this text is represented by a 7-bit code.

10. This signals the end of the first nested body part.

11. The content type of the second nested body part is HTML.

12. This signals the end of the second nested body part.

13. This signals the end of the first body part, that started at line 6.

14. This defines the content type of the second body part as being an XML, and gives the original name of the file.

15. The data encoding for transferring the data is "quoted-printable," enabling 8-bit characters to be sent using their readable hexadecimal value. For example "=0D=0A" stands for "new line."

16. The disposition field tags the way the content needs to be displayed; in this case, as an attachment with the name "ReqToApprove.xml." This content will not be shown in the message, but must be separately opened, as is the case with mail attachments.

17. This signals the end of the second body part.

18. This defines the content of the third body part as a GIF image.

19. "Base64" is used to encode messages by converting every 24 bits in four characters, where each 6 bits of the 24 bits is used as the index of a Base64 character map.

20. This signals the end of the third body part.

You can write code in your BizTalk application that creates MIME encoded message. By using the Collaboration Data Objects (CDO) for Windows 2000, you can easily accomplish this. The following Visual Basic code can be used to create the example message we just explained. The program can be written differently, but it shows the best way in which CDO helps you to quickly construct MIME-encoded messages.

```
'Reference to Microsoft ActiveX Data Objects 2.5 Library
' Reference to Microsoft CDO for Windows 2000 Library
Dim iMessage As CDO.Message
Dim iBodyPart1 as CDO.BodyPart
Dim Stream1  As ADODB.Stream
Dim Flds1  as ADODB.Fields


Sub InsertBodyPart (pBodyPart as CDO.IBodyPart
                    sContentType as String
                    sEncoding as String
                    sDisposition as String
                    sText as String
                  bFileName as Boolean)
    Dim iBp      As CDO.IBodyPart
    Dim Fields1  As ADODB.Fields
    Dim sCmpound As String

    Set iBp = pBodyPart.AddBodyPart
    Set Fields1 = iBp.Fields
    Fields1("urn:schemas:mailheader:content-type") = sContentType

    If sEncoding <> "" then
        Fields1("urn:schemas:mailheader:content-transfer-encoding") = _
            sEncoding
    End if
    If sDisposition <> ""  then
        SCompound = sDisposition
        If sDisposition = "attachment" and sFileName <> " "  then
            SCompound = sCompound + "filename=""" + sfileName + """"
            Fields1("urn:schemas:mailheader:content-disposition") = _
                sCompound
```

```
        End If
        Fields1.Update


    If sText <> "" then
        Set Stream1 = iBp.GetDecodedContentStream
        If bFilename then
            Stream1.LoadFromFile sText
        Else
            Stream1.WriteText sText
        End if
        Stream1.Flush
    End if
End sub


' Create the message
Set iMessage = CreatObject("CDO.Message")


' add the level 1 bodypart Multipart/Alternative
' set point to level 1 body part so you can create level 2 body parts
iBodyPart = iMessage.BodyPart
iBodyPart1 = 1BodyPart.AddBodyPart


' Add the level 2 body part text/plain
InsertBodyPart iBodyPart1.BodyPart, _
                "text/plain; charset=""iso-8859-1""", _
                "7bit", _
                "", _
                "See if you can APPROVE this Request. ", _
                false
' Add the level 2 body part text/html
InsertBodyPart iBodyPart1.BodyPart, _
                "text/plain; charset=""iso-8859-1""", _
                "7bit", _
                "", _
                "<html><p>See if you can <b>APPROVE</b> this Request. _
```

```
                <br>", _
                false
' set the Multipart/Alternative value,
' since by default this is set to multipart/mixed
Set Flds1 = iBodyPart1.Fields
Flds1("urn:schemas:mailheader:content-type") = "multipart/alternative"
Flds1.Update
' Add the level 1 body part text/xml attachment
InsertBodyPart iBodyPart, _
                "text/xml", _
                "quoted-printable", _
                "attachment", _
                "/xml/ReqToApprove.xml" _
                true
' Add the level 1 body part image/gif
InsertBodyPart iBodyPart, _
                "text/xml", _
                "base64", _
                "", _
                "/images/biztalk.gif", _
                true
' Now set the Message object's Content-Type header
' to multipart/mixed, even if that is the default value
Set Flds1 = iBodyPart1.Fields
Flds1("urn:schemas:mailheader:content-type") = "multipart/mixed"
Flds1.Update
```

Kerberos

Kerberos is a subject in itself; we will discuss it here in brief. Kerberos was introduced first in Windows 2000 and permits COM+ applications to delegate its security context—hence, credentials—to another server. Kerberos V5 is described in RFCs 1510 and 1964 (respectively, www.ietf.org/rfc/rfc1510.txt and www.ietf.org/rfc/rfc1510.txt) and can do more than just delegate credentials. In fact, it is a powerful yet simple distributed security mechanism that takes care of user authentication, transcending single domains and even extending authentication beyond the realm of Windows 2000. Kerberos was originally developed by the Massachusetts Institute for Technology in a UNIX environment, but based on RFC 1510 implemented in Windows 2000 as a Security Service Provider (SSP), accessible through the Security Service Provider Interface (SSPI). Other authentication mechanism as NTLM and SSL are also implemented as a SSP, accessible through the SSPI. On a conceptual level, you can compare SSP with CSP and SSPI with CryptoAPI, although SSPs make use of CryptoAPI.

Central in the Kerberos architecture is the Kerberos Key Distribution Center (KDC) that runs on every Windows 2000 domain controller, directly integrating with the Active Directory and authentication information. Kerberos V5 is enabled on every domain controller by default. The operation of Kerberos authentication works in the following way:

1. As you successfully log on to the domain, assuming Kerberos V5 is not disabled, this authentication is relayed to the KDC.

2. The KDC will issue a Ticket-Granting Ticket (TGT). The TGT allows you to apply for Service Tickets (STs) in case you want to set up a session with another server, interactively or through an application. The TGT holds information that identifies the user, including a session key that the users must use in further communication with the KDC. To secure the ticket data information, part of it is encrypted by the KDC's provide key, ensuring that this information is only accessible to the KDC. Another part of the information is encrypted with the session key, and the session key is encrypted with the hash of the user's password.

3. Once you posses the TGT, you can request STs. You need to do this every time you want to access a service. In fact, you will request a ticket to work on your local computer. Suppose the BizTalk application want to access a service on the database server. It will send a request to the KDC, with the TGT as prove of identity. To ensure that the TGT is not hijacked, the request also contains a timestamped authenticator of the user, encrypted with the session key. As you will see later, the timestamps are important within Kerberos.

4. If the KDC successfully identifies you, it will send you an ST. The ST holds information that tells the service you wants to talk to, "I have positively verified the identity of the user that presents you this ticket." The KDC does this by encrypting this authenticator with a key only known by the KDC and the specified service. This encrypted part also contains

a new session key that you and the service can use to securely exchange data. Therefore, the ST also puts this session key in the ticket encrypted with the session key that you and the KDC share.

5. The first time you address the service, you will present the ST. The service decrypts the authenticator, which you send along with the ST, to access information about you and the session key you both will share for this session. Since the service is able to decrypt the information, this proofs to the service that the information in the ST originates from the KDC. Again, the ST also holds timestamps. If the service authenticates you and checks if you are authorized to use this service, communication between you and the service will commence.

6. Suppose you have used the service and ended the session. The next time you request the service, you need an ST. However, if the ST you previously received from the KDC for this Service is still valid—the timestamp is still within the defined lifetime—you can reuse this ticket. To ensure that this ticket is still available, Kerberos has a local cache that holds all the tickets granted to you and still valid.

7. This is just half of the authentication problem! You have authenticated yourself to the service, but what tells you that the service you are talking to is not a malicious impersonation of that service? Kerberos allows mutual authentication. To achieve this, the service will send you a message that holds the timestamp you put into the authenticator when you send the ST to the service. This timestamp is encrypted with the session key you share. After decrypting this message, if the timestamp is the same one you put in your message, you know it is the true service. This simple counter-authentication is based on the trust you put in the KDC. If you do not trust the KDC, this security mechanism collapses like a house of cards! So, how do you know the service is the service just based on the timestamp?

8. Since you were able to decrypt the timestamp using the session key you share with the service, means that the service has access to the session key.

9. The service can only access the session key if it is able to extract it from the ST you sent it. The KDC encrypted this part of the ST using the session key it shares with that service.

10. This implies that the service must have access to that shared key.

11. The service can only have access to this shared key if it has authenticated itself to the KDC.

12. Since you trust the KDC and the KDC trusts the Service, you are inclined to trust the Service too!

This description only accounts for the Kerberos authentication operation if you and the service are using the same domain controller, and, therefore, KDC. If you want to use a service in another domain, you have to go by the "path of trust" that exists between KDCs. Remember that the distributed security of Kerberos only works if there is a mutual trust between KDCs. For the sake of the explanation, suppose all KDCs involved have trust relationships. Another important thing to understand is that Kerberos uses the Domain Name System (DNS), meaning that there is one KDC per DNS domain. The KDC finds its neighboring KDCs by traversing the path of DNS domains. Again, let us assume that all separate DNS domains have a KDC. To be able to communicate with a service on another domain, you need to get a ticket from the KDC that authenticated that service, but is unaware of your identity. For you to be able to get that ticket, you have to prove that you are who you are; hence, have a TGT for that "foreign" KDC. Therefore, you have to walk the path of trust:

1. You request your KDC to give you a ticket to the Ticket-Granting Service of a neighboring KDC that lies in the path to your destination service. Since these KDCs trust each other, they are allowed to issue TGTs for one another.

2. After you received this TGT, and this KDC is not the KDC that knows the service you want to use, you request a TGT for the next KDC in the path. You repeat this until you reach the KDC of the domain where the service is located, also meaning that this KDC has authenticated the service.

3. Having reached the last KDC, you can request a ticket for that Service and from then on it will work the same as if you were using a Service on a server that is in the same domain you are. Even while you are in another domain, your computer will directly communicate with the Service without the interference of any KDC, since the ticket is fully certified now.

This method seems a bit overburdened, but holds a number of advantages:

- It is a very scalable way of extending the distributed security, since KDCs only have to trust the KDCs in neighboring domains, and thereby indirectly be trusted by all other KDCs.

- The path of trust can traverse domains with different operating systems, without requiring that the method of authentication be changed.

- All tickets are cached, so if you need another service in another domain, you might already possess the TGT for that KDC.

- As long as the tickets you have are valid, you do not need to go to the domain controller to re-authenticate yourself.

- You are only involved with one KDC at a time.

- You can use delegation of identity/credentials, enabling services to act on your behalf.

Delegation works as follows:

1. Suppose you already have established a session with a service (S1), but this service needs to access another service (S2) on your behalf to fulfill your service request. Therefore, S1 needs to impersonate you.

2. S1 can impersonate you if you allow it to assume your identity; thus, you have to delegate your identity to S1. This only works if you respond to the request of S1 by sending your TGT and the session key you share with the KDC to S1. Of course, this session key is encrypted with the session key you share with S1.

3. S1 will contact the KDC, using your TGT and session key, to request a Service Ticket for S2.

4. From this point, it works like the communication between any client and KDC.

This delegation works only if the user is allowed to delegate its identity. This is done on the **Account** tab in the **User Properties** dialog (Figure 8.37). To do this, perform the following steps:

1. Open **MMC** with the snap-in **Active Directory Users and Computers**.

2. Expand **Active Directory Users and Computers**, and expand the appropriate domain.

3. Select the **Users** folder; the users and groups will be listed in the right pane.

4. Select the appropriate user, right-click it, and select **Properties**.

5. The **User Properties dialog** appears (Figure 8.37).

Figure 8.37 Setting Delegation Trust in the Account Tab of the Users Properties Window

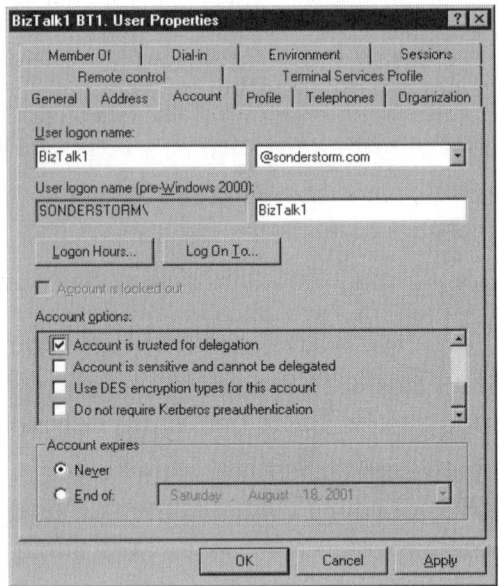

6. Select the **Account** tab.

7. Under **Account options**, scroll to the end of the list; four options are visible:

   ■ **Account is trusted for delegation** You have to check this option to let the user use delegation. You might consider this for the service accounts of BizTalk's COM+ applications that have "delegate" set as the impersonation level. This is only valid if the next option is not checked. This option is also used to give the user the ability to delegate administration tasks on a domain's subtree to another user/group.

   ■ **Account is sensitive and cannot be delegated** Prevents this account from being used for delegation.

   ■ **Use DES encryption types for this account** Activates the use of DES as a method of encryption. By default, Windows 200 uses

RSA encryption. If you are communicating with other devices or domains that only support DES encryption—for example, a KDC on a UNIX host—you should check this option.

- **Don't require Kerberos preauthentication** Used to make Windows 2000 Kerberos V5 compatible with other Kerberos implementations that do not use the preauthentication, before handing out TGTs. By default, preauthentication takes place at the time you log on to a domain controller. In an all-Windows 2000 environment, this option does not need to be set.

As you might expect, Kerberos communication can be encrypted using the session key you share with the KDC. Applications, like the logon application or your BizTalk COM+ application, using Kerberos V5 can activate encryption through the Security Service Provider Interface (SSPI). Another Kerberos feature is *data integrity*, which prevents anyone from tampering with the content of the communication. This is done by calculating a checksum over the complete packet and encrypting it with the session key you and the KDC share. If you receive a packet from the KDC, you recalculate the checksum, and if it is equal to the checksum sent with the packet, you are sure the content has not been changed.

The last subject on Windows 2000 Kerberos V5 we will discuss here is timestamps and ticket lifetimes. Every Kerberos ticket that is exchanged holds a timestamp in an encrypted form. This enables Kerberos to control the validity of tickets over time. First, you do not want a user to be granted access to a service for as long as the user exists in the domain. Second, you want to be able to prevent misuse of tickets by attackers using replay attacks. Third, delegation of identity must be restricted by time. Ticket timestamps can be serialized in time, creating validity checks on time, since an ST cannot be issued previously to a TGT. Therefore, after a user is reissued a (new) TGT, all previously issued STs become automatically invalid.

Within Windows 2000, you can set these ticket lifetimes. These Kerberos lifetime settings are set in the **Default Domain Policy** under **Computer Configuration | Windows Settings | Security Settings | Account Policies | Kerberos Policy** (Figure 8.38). In subsequent group policies, the Kerberos settings can be changed (Figure 8.39) In this case, the values in the group policies take precedence over the settings in the default domain policy. If the computer you are using runs Windows 2000 Professional, you can also set the Kerberos settings. However, from the moment you log on to a domain controller, the settings in the default domain policy overrule the local computer settings.

Figure 8.38 Kerberos Policy Settings in the Default Domain Policy

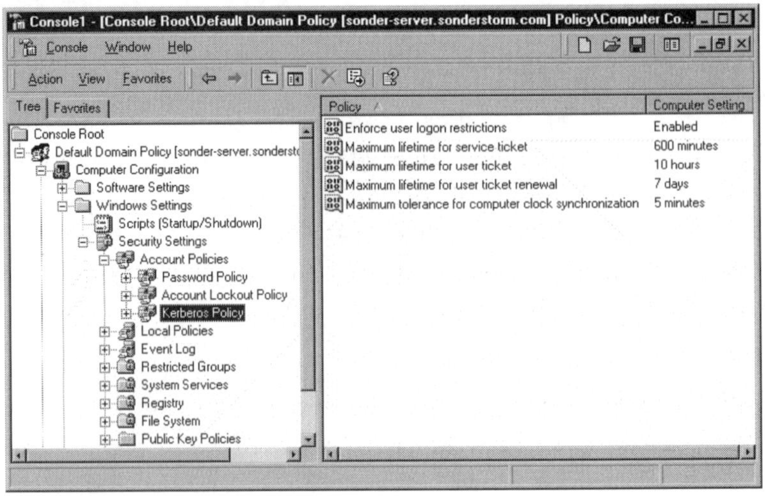

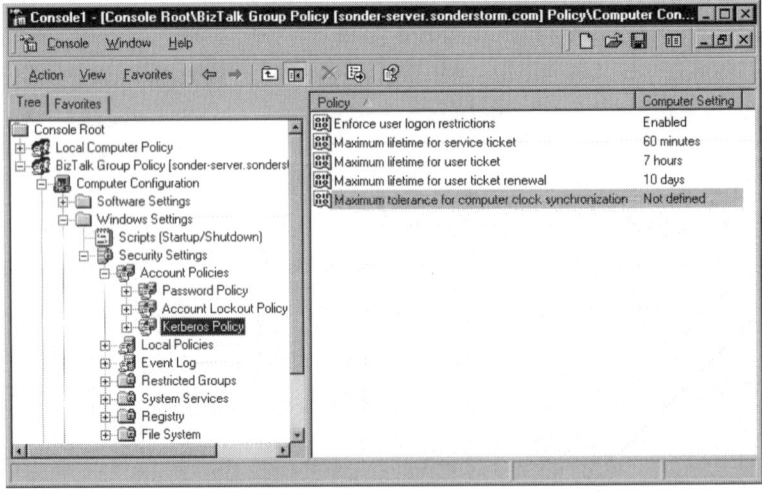

Figure 8.39 Kerberos Policy Settings in the BizTalk Group Policy

The settings have the following meanings:

- **Enforce user logon restrictions** If this option is enabled, the KDC checks the active directory on the user rights on the system the requested service is running. An ST is issued only if the user has the right to *log on locally* on that computer and is allowed to *access this computer from the network.*

- **Maximum lifetime for a service ticket** Sets the maximum lifetime (in minutes) an ST remains valid after being issued. The minimum time is 10 minutes, and no longer than the lifetime for a User Ticket, the name Microsoft uses for TGT. The default value in the default domain policy is 600 minutes.

- **Maximum lifetime for user ticket** Sets the maximum lifetime (in hours) of a TGT. This is at least one hour, but must be at least equal to the maximum ST lifetime. If the lifetime of a TGT expires, a new TGT has to be requested, unless this is within the TGT renewal time. In that case, the TGT can be renewed. The default value in the default domain policy is 10 hours.

- **Maximum lifetime for user ticket renewal** Determines during which period (in days) a user can renew its TGT. This is determined from the time the initial TGT was issued. After this period, you need to request a new TGT, and therefore need to preauthenticate yourself. The default value in the default domain policy is seven days.

- **Maximum tolerance for computer clock synchronization** Sets the amount of time (in minutes) the clock of the client and the KDC server can be out of sync. If the clocks run within the difference set by this parameter, ticket timestamps are considered authentic. Alternatively, if the ticket timestamp lies between the clock time and the clock time plus the value of this parameter, the ticket is valid. The default value in the default domain policy is five minutes.

Summary

When you install business-critical applications, such as a BizTalk Server 2000 application, security becomes a high-priority issue, not only because BizTalk can link multiple business processes and applications of your company, but can have one or more links to trading partners in a supply-chain or e-procurement relationship. If you also use BizTalk Server for business-to-consumer relationships, you should definitely take care to protect your BizTalk Server environment. Since security is only as strong as the weakest link, you need a roadmap that guides you through the implementation of security measures. This is your company's security policy, written from a business point of view, to minimize the number of disruptions. In general, a security policy goes beyond the use of a single application, but a BizTalk Server application is a good reason to build one.

The first tier of security measures holds the physical considerations of the BizTalk Server environment, ranging from the use of firewalls and proxies, to keeping your environment running even if part of it fails, to keeping your servers under lock and key. The physical security measures are fairly easy to implement; however, the challenge is to maintain them and keep the security at the same level. One of the issues that should be viewed in line of the physical considerations is the securing of the XLANG schedules, since they form the engine of your BizTalk application. Additionally, you have the XLANG schedule drawings that are made and maintained in the development stage, and the compiled XLANG schedules that are needed to run in the test and production environments. Keeping the XLANG schedules coordinated and protected from uncontrolled changes is very important, even though the compile schedules are in XML format.

The next level involves securing applications at a system level. The first one is the security of the COM+ applications that form the program base of the BizTalk Server, especially the XLANG schedule engines. COM+ applications have various ways to tune the security and protect themselves from ill-fated use. Especially the possibility to limit the access of COM+ component has to the Windows 2000 environment access prevents the component from running havoc on your server. Assigning Windows 2000 users to the roles that you define at the component level does this. As important as it is to protect the components in the runtime environment, it is equally important to protect the data that drives your BizTalk application. Since the XLANG schedule engines handle a continuous and persistent flow of data, this data is stored in different databases. It is necessary to protect the data in the databases from being accessed by unauthorized users; therefore, the access control of the components needs to be extended to the SQL Server databases. In fact, the same role-based access control model of the components can be implemented at the database level, where you can control the access not only in tables, but also in fields. Of course, it is important to safeguard SQL Server databases from data loss by having an up-to-date copy of the databases at hand.

The last level of security concerns the security providers implemented in Windows 2000, and the way they assist you in creating a secure environment. The use of certificates is central to this, enabling users and applications to communicate in a safe way. Windows 2000 even lets you be your own certificate authority (CA) issuing certificates to your users and trading partners. Note that certificates are pivotal to the security of many applications, like Encryption File System (EFS), IP Security (IPSec), and Kerberos V5. The latter is used to enable COM+ components to allow the delegation of user credentials/identity. Windows 2000 comes with a CryptoAPI that enables you to have the applications you develop use certificates and cryptographic algorithms for encryption and hashing of data. Additionally you can use the Security Service Provider Interface (SSPI) to let your applications directly access the SSPs, such as Kerberos V5.

Solutions Fast Track

Defining Your Security Policy

- ☑ The most important role of a security policy is to raise security awareness within your organization.

- ☑ Implementing risk analysis and risk management enables you to control the security measures to take directly related to your business goals.

- ☑ Defining and implementing security audits is a way to keep your operational security measures on their defined levels.

- ☑ Defining and implementing a contingency plan enables your company to act quickly when things go wrong.

- ☑ The most underestimated part of the security policy is a test plan that guides you through how changes should be tested before being taken into production, thereby preventing unexpected disruptions.

- ☑ Each employee performs at least one role in your organization, and each role has to have access to certain applications and data. By defining these roles and access levels and mapping them in user groups limits the employees from accessing data they are not authorized to see.

☑ Develop a policy on how you should deal with security patches and security packs that come available from time to time.

Physical Security Considerations

☑ The use of routers, firewalls, and proxies can enhance the security within your BizTalk infrastructure, if placed in the proper places and configured in a thorough and rigid way.

☑ The server configurations that should be used for an BizTalk infrastructure is determined by a number of factors. First, what type of hardware components you are going to use. Second, to which extent does a server need to have fail-over capabilities at hardware and/or software level. Third, how is it accomplished that the Windows 2000 platform will adequately installed, configured and tuned to support its tasks.

☑ To prevent people from eavesdropping on the communication between servers, you need to put network protection in place, which primarily means encrypting the communication with encryption protocols, such SSL and IPSec, that also take care of authentication of the parties involved.

☑ The most obvious, but many times forgotten, aspect of physical security is equipment access, not only of servers and the computer room, but also the systems in the workspaces. People have a tendency to bolt the doors, but leave the windows open.

Securing XLANG Schedules

☑ Securing XLANG schedules, drawings, and compiled schedules is about strict version control, and you can use release engineering to accomplish this.

☑ The best way to physically protect your XLANG schedules is by strictly controlling the access, making full use of the access rights that the Windows 2000 file system (NTFS) incorporates.

☑ The Windows 2000 functionality of Encryption File System (EFS) is a perfect way to keep the content away from prying eyes. Unfortunately, EFS is not a feasible solution in a BizTalk development and production environment that needs to share XLANG schedules among users and XLANG schedule engines, since only the user that encrypts a file or folder can decrypt it.

☑ Use different BizTalk user groups to distinguish the different roles within the BizTalk Server environment. These groups can later be mapped easily based on the role definitions for the BizTalk COM+ applications.

Component–Level Security

☑ You can secure access to COM+ components using roles and mapping them to users in the Windows 2000 domain.

☑ By setting authentication levels and impersonation levels per COM+ application, you can control the security environment in which the COM+ components run.

☑ Security settings should be done at the COM+ application level; however, by setting COM+ security at machine level you create a safety net in case you fail to set certain settings at the application level.

☑ Create a separate service account for every COM+ application to control the access the application has to the server, and be able to audit their behavior in detail.

☑ The security settings of the BizTalk Server COM+ application after installation are minimal.

Database Security

☑ The Message Managing database, Tracking database, and Shared Queue database all use SQL Server authentication. Only the XLANG Scheduler persistent database uses Windows authentication.

☑ By default, BizTalk server uses the SQL Server system administrator account ("sa") to log in to the database, giving the COM+ applications that use these database unlimited access. By creating a separate SQL Server user account for each of these databases as the owner of the database, a more restricted access is achieved.

☑ By creating database roles, which are in line with the roles you defined in the BizTalk COM+ applications, you can restrict access to database objects such as tables, views, or stored procedures, or even table columns (fields) in a database. Database users are members of one or more roles, giving them limited access to the database.

☑ Different strategies enable you to prevent, or at least minimize, the loss of data in case of a database failure. This can be achieved by a well-designed backup/recovery strategy, or by creating and enabling database replication, through a Publish/Subscribe configuration.

☑ Windows 2000 Kerberos V5 is a distributed security protocol that has its own way of delivering authentication, data integrity, and data privacy without using certificates. The CryptoAPI is used in generating session keys and encrypting data. The Kerberos Key Distribution Center runs on every domain controller and gives out tickets that enable users to access services on services, even if these services run in other domains or on different operating systems.

Certificates and the CryptoAPI

☑ Windows 2000 Certificate Services allows you to become your own certificate authority (CA) for your domain, or BizTalk environment. Certificates issued to users can be managed from within the Active Directory.

☑ Certificates are used in every authentication and encryption method within Windows 2000. Within BizTalk Server 2000, you can set certificates on inbound and outbound documents on BizTalk channels.

☑ Certificate Services come with a Web site from which your trading partners can request a certificate, in case you decide to control the certificates that are used in the BizTalk Server environment.

☑ CryptoAPI is the powerful interface that enables your BizTalk application to make use of the certificate service providers (CSPs) that are available on the Windows 2000 server.

☑ A secure exchange of compound messages between a BizTalk server and a trading partner can be achieved by encoding them in MIME format and sending them by Secure MIME (S/MIME).

Frequently Asked Questions

The following Frequently Asked Questions, answered by the authors of this book, are designed to both measure your understanding of the concepts presented in this chapter and to assist you with real-life implementation of these concepts. To have your questions about this chapter answered by the author, browse to **www.syngress.com/solutions** and click on the **"Ask the Author"** form.

Q: Why do I need a security policy when I want to implement BizTalk Server 2000?

A: You do not need a security policy to implement BizTalk Server; in all cases, it will work just fine. The issue is that BizTalk Server is used to take over business processes, tie different information bases together, have direct links to trading partners, and even drive your e-commerce Web site. If that is the case, you have an application that is critical to your company. Your company should feel inclined to secure business-critical applications such as BizTalk Server. Implementing and maintaining adequate security touches not only the BizTalk Server infrastructure, but also every part of your organization. A well-defined security scheme only works if all the parts come together, thus requiring a security policy. This security policy is your roadmap when implementing, and, even more crucial, maintaining the established security. Another important property of a security policy is that it should be designed with the business goals in mind, since you are actually securing your business from being disrupted. Eventually, you have to put technical measures in place, but only if they are viable to the company's needs. Security is all about risk management, risks that can hurt the company. To know which technical security measures you need to take for your BizTalk Server environment that make sense to the company, you need a security policy.

Q: Isn't it enough to install a firewall to protect hackers from accessing my BizTalk Server environment?

A: Many small organizations have to scramble to protect themselves from threats that come from the outside world; in other words, the Internet. The installation of a firewall is indeed an important step to take, but you must be sure that it is correctly configured, or else it gives the company a wrongful feeling of security. Most external attacks are annoying, but they are well-documented and, in many cases, predictable. Having a firewall in combination with an intrusion detection application allows you to intercept most attacks. However, fencing off your BizTalk environment from the outside world just solves one part of the problem. What about internal attacks? These distinguish themselves from the outside attacks in a major way, since the attackers have access to the BizTalk environment and their attacks are unpredictable.

In general, inside attacks go unnoticed for a longer period of time, thereby increasing the damage. Therefore, you need to increase security awareness within your organization, and take adequate technical measures. To simplify security, since it is already difficult enough, you should not make an explicit difference between internal users and external users. Implement different security levels/tiers that apply to every user, known or unknown, who wants to access the BizTalk environment. Do not implement a firewall as the one and only means of security. Think about creating a demilitarized zone (DMZ), using a proxy to break up a single session into different independent (sub)sessions. Only permit authenticated users, and eventually distribute certificates through your own certificate authority.

Q: How can I control all the security measures you describe without losing track?

A: This is a genuine problem! Not only do you have to take security measures in different areas, but also in most organizations, more than one engineer/administrator is involved. Unfortunately, there is no quick solution for this situation; however, I can give you some guidelines that can ease the situation. First, many IT departments are organized around the work method of solving problems. This reactive way of operating makes it even harder to control security. An IT department can make a leap forward to restructure itself by becoming an organization that prevents problems from occurring. This proactive way of operating is more organized, and uses the knowledge and skills of engineers/administrators much better. Here are the guidelines to help you keep track of security measures:

- Document security measures in a structured way, and make sure that all involved in keeping the security measures "alive" understand the information. This will be the heart and starting point of your security.

- Every change you need to make regarding security should be drafted in a one-page memo. Give this to your colleagues to review; you might have overlooked something!

- Draft a protocol that describes the way the change should be installed, tested, and uninstalled. Again, let you colleagues review it. It is important that all engineers/administrators are critical in a constructive way; this leverages the overall quality of your work and the IT facilities.

- Perform an actual test of the protocol to determine if it is working according to your expectations.

- Apply the change in an environment that resembles your BizTalk production environment.

- Perform a regression test of this environment.

- Never make these kinds of changes and tests on your own; involve at least one colleague.

- If the test is completed with the desired result, it can be deployed at a suitable time.

- After deploying, update the documentation to reflect the changes made.

I have a pretty good idea of what your response will be: "Not realistic!!" If this is indeed your response, then your organization works in a reactive way, since one of the symptoms of a reactive IT department is that nobody has time to document, review each other's work, and apply changes. Everybody is genuinely scrambling to solve problems, problems that might have been prevented if there was more time to discuss longer-term solutions amongst engineers/administrators and have documentation that gives a better understanding of the environment. Remember that a BizTalk application can turn into a business-critical application, and a 24x7 application. This reduces the time to apply fixes significantly.

Chapter 9

Performance and Monitoring

Solutions in this chapter:

- Planning for High Availability

- Configuring BizTalk Server Groups

- Monitoring Performance with the System Monitor

- Integrating with Application Center 2000

- Web-Based Enterprise Management

☑ Summary

☑ Solutions Fast Track

☑ Frequently Asked Questions

Introduction

Building a manageable business-to-business (B2B) or enterprise application integration (EAI) solution with BizTalk is important but incomplete without an ongoing plan to monitor and optimize any bottlenecks that may occur. In this chapter, we cover how to monitor a BizTalk solution and how to provide a reliable, flexible, and scalable BizTalk implementation. We also address the ongoing tasks of maintainability and monitoring.

Planning for High Availability

When you made the decision to place BizTalk Server 2000 into your infrastructure, you may have made a great choice in a product, but what happens when that product becomes "critical?" What if it is deemed "mission critical" where an absence would cause your company to lose money?

This is when you start to plan for the redundancy High Availability (HA) of services and make them safe from mission-crippling events that can and eventually will occur by duplicating them. When you are implementing HA, you become proactive in either avoiding these events (for example, a system crash) from occurring, or easing the pain and damage of these events when they do occur. HA through the use of either clustering or load balancing can provide such relief. Let's look at the fundamentals of why you would design and deploy an HA implementation of Microsoft BizTalk Server using the cluster service component of Microsoft Windows 2000 Advanced Server.

Clustering

Now that we know why we need to have an HA solution, we need to understand the basics of clustering. Clustering is what is used to create such HA solutions. In simple terms, clustering is the grouping of machines (also called nodes) together. Of course, a cluster is a "grouping," but the reason for this is for redundancy in case of catastrophic system failures. You at least need two or more nodes to create a cluster. Both nodes exist together, but in many cases, only one is doing work while the other node sits idle. One server is responding to all the client requests and then it has a hard disk problem. The server goes down and you as the administrator are paged to come fix it. The clients never knew what hit them because the server that was previously idle began working the instant the first server crashed. Although at first this sounds simplistic, upon further research it becomes more complex. When you get into the details of passive/passive states and active/passive states, a node can either just site there and help out with the load, or it can sit and wait for the other node to cease working, at which point it will take over. Although this is not a book about clustering, it is important to know how it works in general; if you are going to set up a cluster, you will need to do further investigation. This section will explain to you how to design your BizTalk implementation in a HA solution.

Clustering Services and Return on Investment

The Microsoft Clustering Service will allow for at least a minimum of two machines to be clustered together. Windows 2000 Advanced Server and DataCenter Server include this component. Clustering uses the WLBS, or Windows Load Balancing Service, found with Advanced Server and later. Your decision to design the use of the cluster service depends on two things:

- The amount of tolerable business or company downtime
- The budget available for the hardware and software that will be needed to create such redundancy

It is important to realize that if you want optimal performance and reliability, you need to pay for it. The Return on Investment (ROI) if you cannot afford any downtime is well worth the initial cost simply because you save the money when the systems do fail. This is also very important if you're a business that claims a Five Nines (99.999%) uptime policy as part of a service level agreement, or SLA. To set up a typical cluster with Windows 2000, you would want at least two servers and, as shown in Figure 9.1, a virtual IP address and physical MAC address that both servers share. This way, failover from one node to the other is transparent to the clients using the server's services. Again, this is not a book on clustering; we're just giving you the basics to help you understand how to design for the deployment of a highly available BizTalk Server 2000 solution.

Load Balancing

So now that you have a fundamental knowledge of clustering, what about network load balancing? *Load balancing* is a term coined for the use of dividing the services that a server must provide among multiple peers or nodes in a group. This way, if you wanted to host a Web site—or in this case, multiple BizTalk Servers—the servers can work together to provide better service to you by sharing the load. Load balancing uses an algorithm to dynamically send client requests to each member in the load balanced group so that no one node becomes overwhelmed with requests. You might want to install Application Center 2000 (covered later in this chapter) and its Health Monitor to monitor the performance of such load-balancing events. Again, BizTalk might need to be load balanced to respond and reply to many document exchanges. Figure 9.2 shows a typical design to allow for load-balancing servers for client access.

Figure 9.1 Clustered Nodes Set for Failover with a Virtual IP and MAC Address

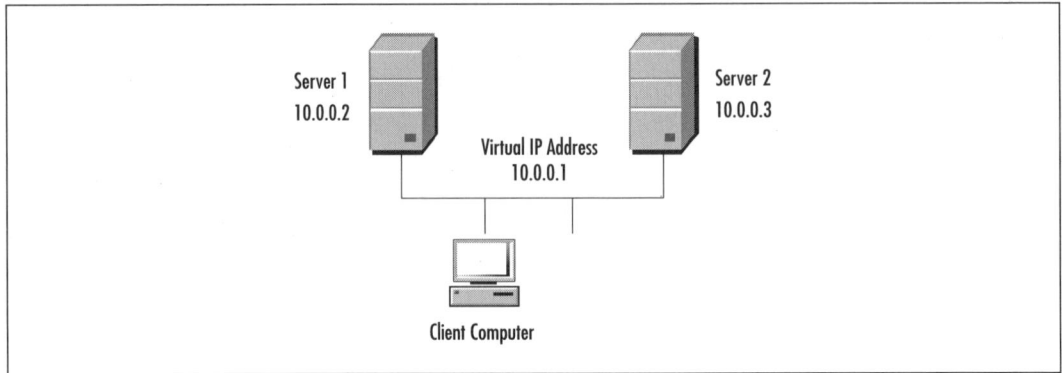

Figure 9.2 Nodes Set for Load Balancing and Sharing the Requested Load

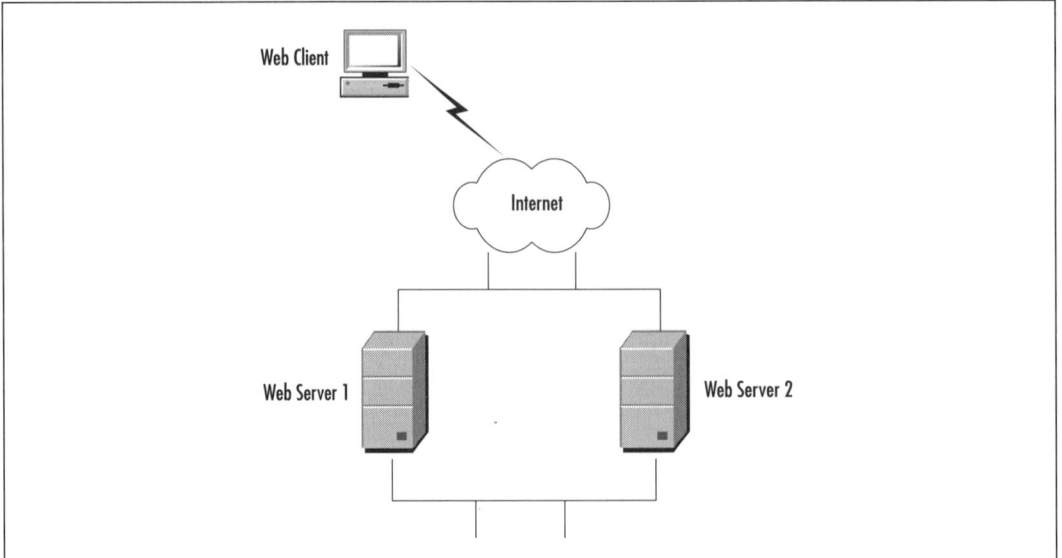

BizTalk Load Balancing and Clustering

So, how do clustering, load balancing, and HA work with BizTalk? With BizTalk, you might be surprised to know that this product accommodates these features very well. BizTalk can be configured to allow all the servers within a group to access one BizTalk Server database server over the network.. If a BizTalk server fails, then another can be accessed with a connection to the same database. What if the database server then crashes? The simple answer is to design redundancy into that area as well with a second cluster. Again, the cost continues to climb but so does the reassurance in your equipment and services being available. Figure 9.3 shows a simple design of load balancing BizTalk with a clustered database solution. This will certainly influence the infrastructure design toward top performance and HA.

Figure 9.3 Load Balancing BizTalk and Sharing a Common Database

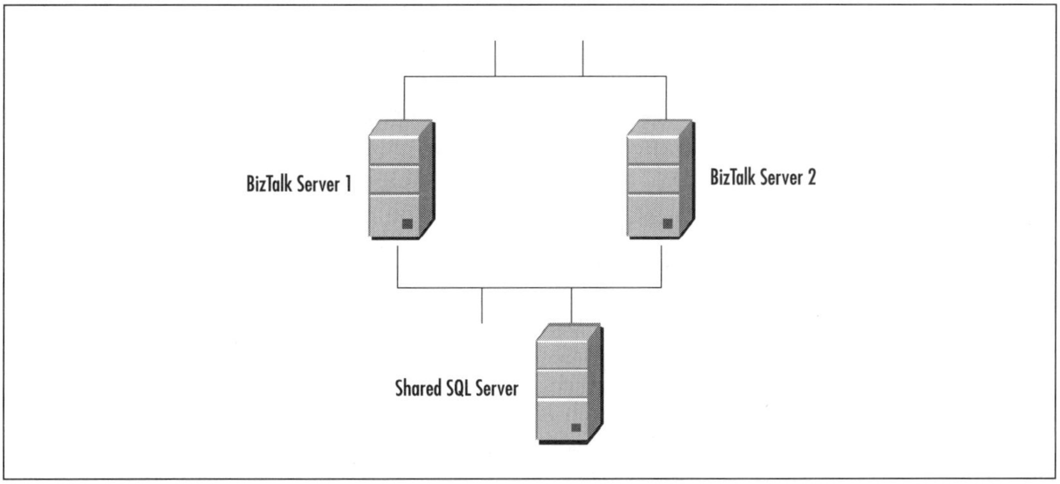

Failover Clustering with BizTalk Server

The primary purpose of failover clustering is to guarantee uptime for a server that is used to persist data on its disk subsystem. To completely protect BizTalk Server against hardware failures, failover clustering should be implemented in the areas listed in Table 9.1.

Table 9.1 Areas to Implement Failover Clustered Solutions

Message queues	Message queues should be looked at with a critical eye due to the importance of queuing. BizTalk receives or sends its critical data using Microsoft's Message Queuing (MSMQ). Queues are used where high throughput and reads and writes are very important, if not critical. MSMQ can be clustered and should be worked into your clustered BizTalk design.
SQL Server databases	We learned in previous chapters and doing installs of BizTalk that BizTalk Server needs four databases to function properly: Message Management, Shared Queue, Tracking, and Orchestration. You would of course want to cluster the database on which these essential databases reside.
File shares	BizTalk will store, send, and receive text files as part of the processing service of BizTalk. If these files are not available, BizTalk Server cannot process this data. A file share can optimize the ability to perform after a failure and keep the server running. It is most important to protect against this by clustering the files by clustering a share.
The WebDAV repository	Document specification, which we learned about in earlier chapters, is critical to BizTalk production work. If the WebDAV repository is either unavailable or damaged, how can business continue? Set failover-based clustering to make sure you have a redundant repository. The WebDAV (Web Distributed Authoring and Versioning) repository for BizTalk Server must have a reliable storage clustering in case of failure.

NOTE

If you do not intend to use either flat files or Message Queuing queues, then it is unnecessary to cluster these resources.

Scale BizTalk Up and Out

You might hear that you can optimize BizTalk performance by scaling it. What exactly is scaling, and should you choose to scale out or up? Scaling *out* is adding more servers to the equation so that you can expand out. You can also scale *up*, which means using more powerful hardware such as CPUs and memory to increase performance.

Optimizing Service with BizTalk Server Groups

BizTalk Server Groups are key to optimization within BizTalk Server Administration. You need to create these groups to add to the performance optimization of your systems. If you create a group, the actual server group is centrally managed (optimized to one administrator's management), configured, and monitored, which is also good because monitoring allows you to see problems as they occur. The Event Viewer is also snapped right into the BizTalk Administration console as shown in Figure 9.4.

Figure 9.4 BizTalk System Administration Console and Event Viewer Monitoring

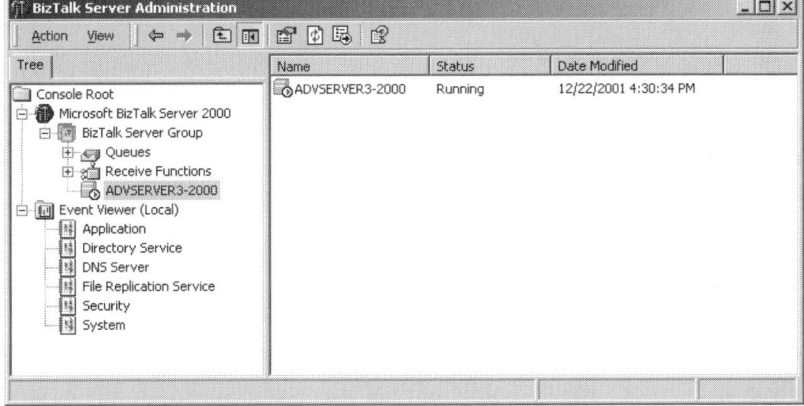

Servers in a BizTalk Server Group have approximately four things in common:

- **Shared queue database** Persists all documents until they are successfully processed.

- **Tracking database** Used to log document and interchange activity and to run reports.

- **Receive functions** Used to set the receive functions.
- **All other components** Components that the server requires when processing documents and interchanges.

A centralized BizTalk Messaging Management database will allow the management of multiple servers so that they share the same configuration information. To configure, you simply need to specify the same BizTalk Messaging Management database for each server installation so that you can remotely administer each server and group from the administration console as shown in Figure 9.5. In addition, if you are setting up multiple server groups for scalability and improved performance, use only one central BizTalk Messaging Management database. You need to do this because if you don't, these servers won't share the same BizTalk Messaging Management configuration.

Figure 9.5 BizTalk Server Groups in the Administration Console

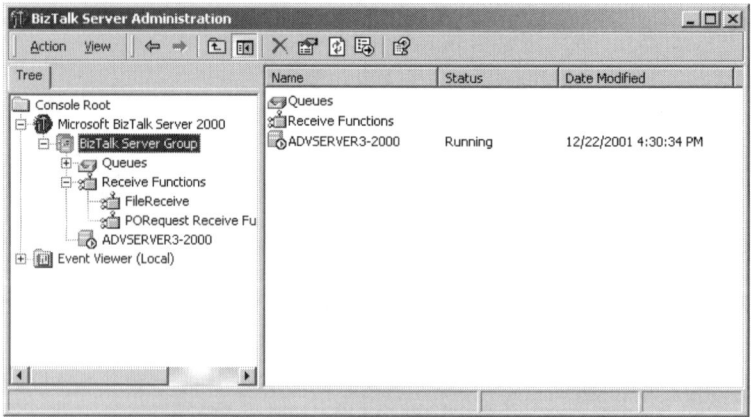

NOTE

Each installation of BizTalk Server 2000 must have at least one server group.

Adding a Server Group

In this section, we look at how to add, remove, and configure a Server group in BizTalk Server 2000.

1. Open the **BizTalk Server Administration console** by going to **Start | Programs | BizTalk Server**, and open the **MMC**.

2. Once the console is open, highlight (by clicking on it) the **Microsoft BizTalk Server 2000** icon in the left-hand pane of the MMC.

3. On the **Action** menu in the console's toolbar, point to **New**, and select **Group**.

4. The New Group dialog box appears as shown in Figure 9.6.

Figure 9.6 New Group Dialog Box

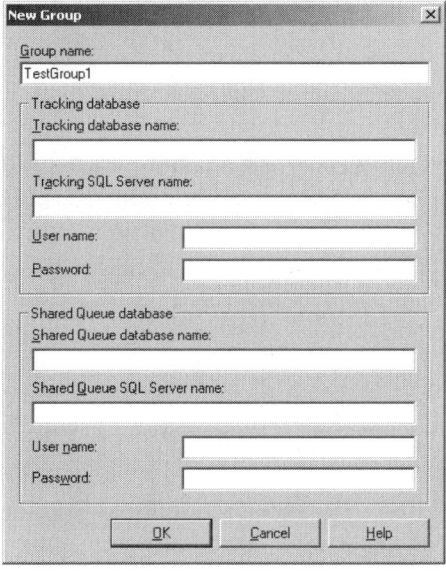

5. Type the name of the new server group in the Group name.

6. Next, apply the name of the Tracking database for the server group. Put this in the Tracking database name space.

NOTE

If you change information in the Tracking database or Shared Queue database areas, you must complete the following steps:

1. Stop all servers in the Microsoft BizTalk Server 2000 node.
2. Shut down the BizTalk Server Interchange Application.
3. Restart all servers in the Microsoft BizTalk Server 2000 node.

---

7. Type the name of the server on which a Tracking database for the server group is located in the **Tracking SQL Server** name box.

8. In the **User name** and **Password** boxes, type the Microsoft SQL Server logon username and password that are used to connect to the server where the Tracking database is stored.

9. Also note that **User name** is a required field and must be completed.

10. **Password** is in fact an optional field; in other words, a password is not required to connect to the server, although this is not a great idea.

11. Click **OK** to finish adding and configuring the group.

NOTE

You should remain security conscience and know that this along with many SQL Server passwords of the same nature can leave you with many holes in your security infrastructure. Be aware that they exist and how to protect them. Assign a password if needed.

Make sure that if you change any values in the Tracking database area, you must remember to update the connection string in the Connection.vb file with the new Tracking database information. The Connection.vb script can be found in the **\Program Files\Microsoft BizTalk Server\BizTalk Tracking\ VBScripts** folder on your BizTalk Server.

Developing & Deploying...

Connection Strings

The connection string in the Connection.vb file is:
```
Const g_ConnectionString = "Provider=SQLOLEDB.1;Persist
Security Info=False;User ID=dta_ui_login;Password=;Initial
Catalog=<databasename>;Data Source=<servername>;Connect
Timeout=15"
```

Server Group Status States

With BizTalk Server Groups, you will have visible "status" states in the Administration console. BizTalk Server Administration will show the server groups and if a group can connect to the Tracking and Shared Queue databases. Clicking the Microsoft BizTalk Server 2000 icon at the top of the console will show you the group state under the status bar in the details pane as shown in Figure 9.7. This Status seen here is "Connected."

Figure 9.7 Viewing the BizTalk Group State in the Administration Console

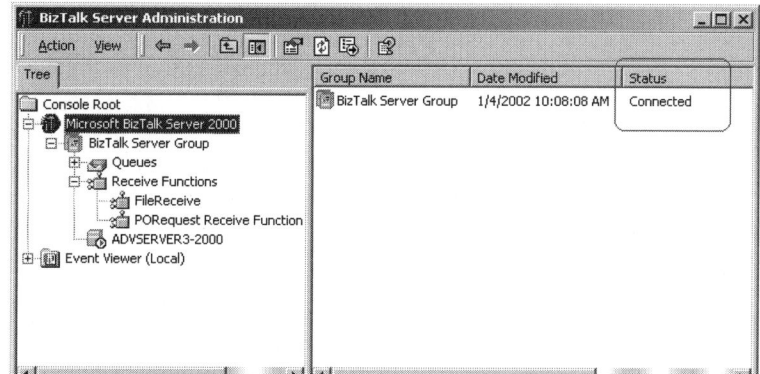

The group states are as follows:

- **Connected** specifies that the group is connected to the Tracking and Shared Queue databases.

- **Tracking connection failed** specifies that the group is not connected to the Tracking database.

- **Shared Queue connection failed** specifies that the group is not connected to the Shared Queue database.

- **Tracking and Shared Queue connections failed** specifies that the group is not connected to the Tracking and Shared Queue databases.

Planning and Watching Performance

You need to thoroughly understand the results of planned performance, because without a solid plan, your performance will be affected. They technically go hand in hand and need to be addressed together. Most technicians who do not plan suffer with a poorly performing design. A good understanding of where the most likely bottlenecks could occur (e.g., I/O, CPU utilization, redundant paths, and other redundancy and scalability constraints) will alter your entire architecture and will aid you in designing what you need to succeed. Part two of this equation is to monitor your design and make sure it is functioning properly.

NOTE

For a detailed list for planning your cluster requirements, refer to Microsoft Windows 2000 Server Deployment Planning Guide on TECHNET.

Hardware Design Considerations

When looking at a cluster design, you need to consider hardware and cost. You might need to implement a RAID solution for total redundancy, and improve performance of disk reads and writes with striping. It is wise to implement either a RAID 5 (striping with parity) or a RAID 10 (both striping and mirroring) as shown in Figure 9.8, and use a dedicated external storage system for the clustered nodes to share.

Figure 9.8 Common RAID 5 Configuration with an External Storage Device

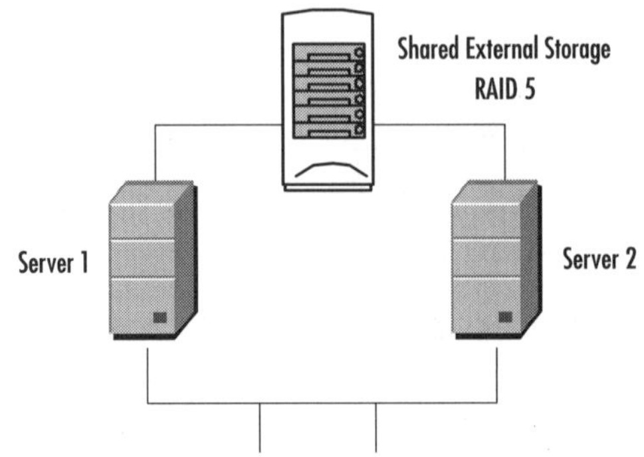

More expensive solutions such as storage area networks (SANs) offer a much more flexible approach involving fiber channel switching. SANs can also improve

speed and performance by having high-speed fiber channel connections between the server nodes and the external devices.

To increase efficiency, you might also want to implement a three-disk array so that when performance is crucial, you can add an additional cluster group so that SQL Server and the BizTalk Orchestration systems can run on the other cluster node.

NOTE

You might want to consider implementing your SQL servers and databases on the external storage systems to increase speed, performance, and efficiency.

Optimizing BizTalk Server Group Properties

In the BizTalk Server Administration MMC you can specify more properties in the BizTalk Server Group. These properties include setting better refresh intervals and disabling unneeded or unwanted services. Let's look at these in detail. These little tweaks can really help you increase BizTalk services and performance.

Messaging Management object cache refresh interval (seconds) Here is where you can set the interval to a maximum of 300 seconds. BizTalk Server 2000 caches configurations such as channels and messaging ports and envelopes in server memory so that it does not have to make a call to the database each time it is requested. With this tweak, you can increase performance because if you find that these objects are not changed regularly, you can set the value to 300. This will reduce the number of read/writes to the database. This change will take effect as soon as you apply it within the refresh interval.

Disable document tracking The Tracking tab as shown in Figure 9.9 can be used to enable or disable document tracking. To do so, go to the **BizTalk Administration** console and highlight the BizTalk Server Group you want to modify. Go to the **Action** menu and select Properties. Select the **Tracking** tab.

If you are positive that tracking is not in use, feel free to disable this field, which will then minimize the number of read/writes to the database for a single transaction. As with the other tweaks also mentioned, most tweaks come to read/write performance settings, which can and will slow performance. If you do have this enabled, then BizTalk Server will connect to the database and begin to log data. *Do not* disable this field unless tracking is not needed. Actually, it is *highly recommended* that document tracking stay on and enabled. You might want to use this service, and it is not going to account for much optimization if you have the right hardware installed on your systems. This is, of course ,only a recommendation.

Figure 9.9 Document Tracking Tab

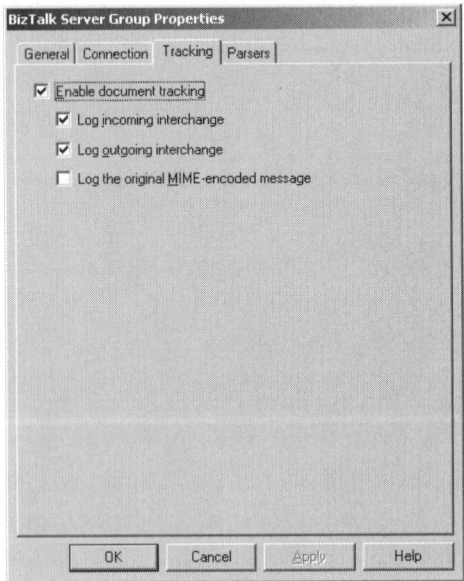

NOTE

The performance of BizTalk Server will be affected if the size limit for tracking interchanges is exceeded.

Monitoring Performance with the System Monitor

To successfully optimize performance, you have to scale the BizTalk server and databases. How do you go about making that decision if you do not know whether you should scale up or out? With System Monitor (a tool integrated in Windows 2000 Server), you can easily map out problems, monitor them, set base-lines, and make accurate decisions about the current performance both for common use and under heavy stress. To do this correctly you need to set up a monitoring plan—it is important to know both what you are looking for and for how long, and when you want to view the result of the monitored events. You can use the Performance console by going to **Start | Programs | Administrative Tools | Performance**. You can now see that the System Monitor lies within the Performance MMC. The System Monitor is shown in Figure 9.10.

Figure 9.10 Monitoring Performance with the System Monitor in Windows 2000

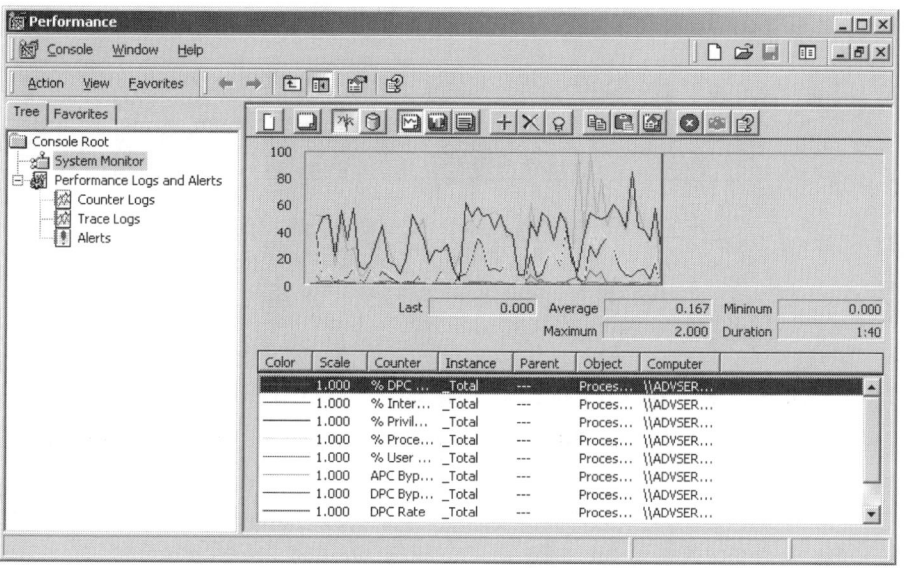

To correctly monitor the performance on any service or item within the base server operating system of Windows 2000 or in the .NET platform Server service of BizTalk 2000, you must set counters to monitor such events such as CPU usage and performance or disk I/O.

Configuring Counters

In order to monitor system performance, you need to configure counters. To configure Performance counters, open the **Performance** console and add what you want to monitor. To open the Performance console and access the System Monitor, go to **Start | Programs | Administrative Tools | Performance**. Selecting the Performance menu option will open the Performance MMC where you will see the System Monitor and the Performance Logs and Alerts tool as shown in Figure 9.10.

To configure a counter, simply click on an icon and add what counters you need. It's that simple, and more importantly, it is critical to the performance and optimization of your systems. Many times you want to make changes to a system, such as add RAM or a more powerful CPU, because you "think" that is the bottleneck on the system. Well what if it was the network interface card (NIC)? With the System Monitor, you can monitor performance and optimize what you need to and not upgrade components on a whim.

To add a BizTalk-related counter, follow these steps:

1. Go back to the open Performance console as shown in Figure 9.10. On the top toolbar (Figure 9.11) is a "plus sign."

Figure 9.11 System Monitor Toolbar

2. Add a counter.

3. When you click **ADD**, you will be presented with the Add Counters dialog box as shown in Figure 9.12.

Figure 9.12 System Monitor Add Counters Dialog Box

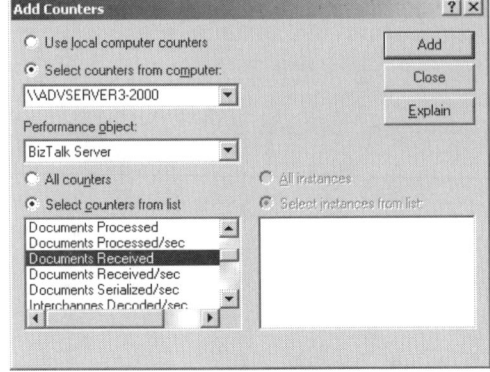

4. To remove the counters, simply click on the **X** right next to the plus sign. This removes whatever counter you have highlighted at the bottom of the System Monitor.

Once the Add Counters dialog box is open, you will want to look at the options within. First, there is an option to select a Performance object. This is important because this is where you are going to find your BizTalk Server option. Once you select BizTalk Server, you will see the available counters that are specific to BizTalk.

Other counters to monitor are actually server related, but make sure that they are also monitored for reasons that should be self-explanatory. The system, memory, and physical disk parameters should also be monitored closely for lack of performance needed to run your BizTalk Server implementation.

Recommendations for Increasing Your System's Performance

In this section, we provide general recommendations for optimizing system settings and include topics for optimizing BizTalk Server 2000 settings to increase performance. This is important when you need to get all you can out of a system, and what better way to see what it can do than with monitoring tools and optimization designs? To optimize Windows 2000 settings you can make the common changes and setting enhancements such as not running unnecessary services or protocols. One out of five servers running probably has unneeded services running on it In our experience, we have found many unneeded services and protocols running that when removed or disabled, increased performance noticeably. Make sure that these are definitely not being used before removing and disabling them.

Another option for major optimization is to not have the "mainframe" mentality (place everything on one box) while setting up a design. Allow separate servers to do separate functions. Make your BizTalk servers only for BizTalk, and place the databases on a separate SQL server. Again, this is just a design and performance optimization; if you needed to, you could place them all on the same server. Many techniques used to optimize Windows 2000 can also be used to optimize BizTalk Server.

Developing & Deploying...

Binding Order

You might want to check your binding orders if running multiple protocols. Try to make TCP/IP (or the protocols most used) the first protocol to be looked at first when bound to the NIC cards by placing it at the top of the binding order in you network and dial-up connections settings. This can be found in the **Advanced** menu under **Advanced Settings**....

If you want to monitor and then optimize performance, you might want to look at transport between your services. This is important because you might have a bottleneck on the network and think it is a server-related issue (or vice versa). You should incorporate high-speed, reliable and redundant connections between BizTalk services such as the BizTalk Orchestration Services and BizTalk Messaging Services, especially if you have a separate database server (or servers). We recommend that you go as fast as possible, but for design purposes, we would not suggest anything under 100MB switched between services for LAN. In addition, make sure you not only monitor wide area connections such as Frame Relay and the Internet, but also work with your Telco or ISP to see what your level of service is. There's nothing like going from 100MB switched to a 16K CIR-based Frame Relay circuit. Make sure you are actively involved by monitoring the network yourself, or have someone help you if that is not what you are trained to do.

NOTE

For more information about optimizing Microsoft Windows 2000 settings, see Best Practices in the Windows 2000 Help system.

For clustered services, of course, you should use multiple NICs and run at 100MB switched with separate VLANs (one for the management or heartbeat network and one for client access).

This will make for an increase in performance and for better throughput and less traffic on the LAN.

> **NOTE**
>
> Make sure you optimize the LAN and WAN connections. If you don't know much about networking, it is we highly recommend that you work with a network engineer (if you are not one) or your Telco. A slow connection will make any fully loaded server go nowhere.

Integrating with Application Center 2000

To round off the performance and optimization plan or design you should consider Application Center 2000, which is Microsoft's .NET-based HA solution for the .NET enterprise server platform. With Application Center 2000, you have the power of deployment and management with a tool that provides high availability for Web applications—and the entire service is installed and built on the Microsoft Windows 2000 operating system.

To get the HA that you want with the monitoring tools incorporated, you will need to invest in Application Center 2000, which makes managing groups of servers as simple as managing a single computer. You manage the Cluster Controller and push application updates to it, which in turn updates the other nodes in its grouping. Application Center 2000 will streamline your application deployment because you can deploy applications to entire groups of servers from one staging server.

HA comes from the fact that load balancing (discussed at the beginning of the chapter) is implemented through Application Center 2000. You can implement load balancing with Windows 2000 Advanced Server and later, but you can install Application Center 2000 on Windows 2000 Server and later and "manage" them together as a grouping. You can also load balance COM+ components with component load balancing (CLB).

You can also easily scale servers with Application Center 2000 because you can add nodes to the group without affecting the rest of the nodes. It equates to 99.999% uptime, and the more you add (if needed), the better your performance.

Finally, Application Center 2000 provides tools that monitor the cluster and its servers. One of these tools, which is covered in the next paragraph, is the Health Monitor. Full integration with Application Center 2000 and BizTalk Server 2000 is "hinted" to be in the Redmond pipe for BizTalk Server 2002.

Health Monitor

Microsoft Application Center 2000 includes a tool called Health Monitor. Health Monitor supercedes the functionality of the Windows 2000 Event Log and system monitor tools and allows administrators to set up monitors as shown in Figure 9.13.

Figure 9.13 Application Center 2000's Health Monitor

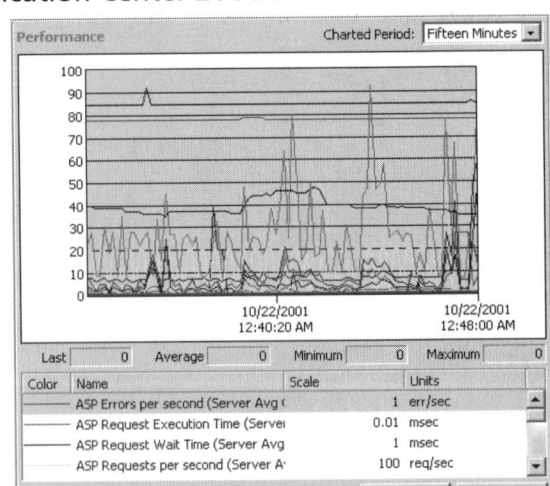

These monitors include checking TCP/IP, performance monitor counter thresholds, Event Log errors, and Windows Management Instrumentation (WMI) events. Conditions can be configured for these monitors so that when certain criteria are met—for example, when a threshold of 90 percent on a CPU is met or exceeded—an action occurs such as a taking a server offline or sending an e-mail message to an administrator. These tools can be used to proactively monitor and maintain the performance of BizTalk Server 2000.

Understanding WMI in BizTalk Server

WMI is a tool integrated into Windows 2000 (it can also be added to NT and 98) that allows for Web-based management of services. For example, you can build an ASP page and use WMI to use a Web page to manage the BizTalk Messaging Service remotely. BizTalk Server also uses WMI to access services such as the SQL Server database.

When you use BizTalk Server Administration to change group, server, queue, and database management settings, the new values are stored in the BizTalk Messaging Management database through the BizTalk Server WMI provider. One thing you should know is that the WMI provider uses a Microsoft SQL Server database to store administrative objects. The WMI provider acts as an intermediary between WMI and BizTalk Administration objects.

The WMI provider will gather information from a managed object to make it available to manage applications through the WMI API. The BizTalk schema can use the managed object format (MOF) and put information in a **.mof** file so you can submit it to the MOF compiler, which is the **Mofcomp.exe**.

You can find MOF code examples in the **InterchangeProvSchema.mof** file, which can be found in the **\Program Files\Microsoft BizTalk Server\Setup** folder. This file as well as the **SrvEvents.mof** will contain the BizTalk Server namespace and the provider, provider registration, and schema class definitions. The contents of the **SrvEvents.mof** file is shown here:

```
// The namespace is shared with InterchangeProv.mof


//********************************************************
//***  Creates namespace for MicrosoftBizTalkServer schema ***
//***    under the Root namespace.
//********************************************************
#pragma namespace ("\\\\.\\Root")


instance of __Namespace
{
    Name = "MicrosoftBizTalkServer";
};


//********************************************************
```

```
//***  Changes focus to new namespace
//**********************************************************
#pragma namespace ("\\\\.\\Root\\MicrosoftBizTalkServer")

class DocSuspendedEvent : __ExtrinsicEvent
{
    string stringSuspendedGuid;
};

instance of Win32PseudoProvider as $P1
{
    Name = "BizTalkServerEventProv";
};

instance of __EventProviderRegistration
{
    Provider = $P1;
    EventQueryList = {"select * from DocSuspendedEvent"};
};
```

Summary

This chapter discussed the fundamental knowledge you will need to either monitor or optimize the performance of BizTalk Server 2000. We touched on the high availability (HA) of critical services to give you a solid understanding of what it is you might need to implement to keep your systems running in time of crisis. This, of course, depends on budget and what amount of downtime is acceptable. Clustering and load balancing can help achieve this high availability, as well as segmenting services such as putting databases on separated clustered servers. We also delved into the topics of configuring BizTalk Server groups, which were used to centrally manage multiple resources. Making performance gains by using the right amount of bandwidth on LAN and WAN links and making sure you do not have significant bottlenecks in those areas were also discussed to help in optimizing services. We looked at specific system tweaks in order to get the last little drops of performance out of your BizTalk Server system. Performance optimization was monitored through the Performance console's System Monitor, and we set up counters to review and monitor specific system resources. We also looked at configuring BizTalk-specific counters. Finally, we covered the fundamentals of Application Center 2000 and Web-based management with WMI.

Solutions Fast Track

Planning for High Availability

- ☑ High availability (HA) is the assurance that your systems will be "available" when there is demand, and when disaster strikes, those same systems are up and running.

- ☑ Clustering is the use of two or more machines (or nodes) and setting them up in a group where one can failover on the other in the case of a system crash. There are two types of clustering setups: the first is Active/Active, where both nodes are active and handle requests, and when one node fails, the other takes over at half the normal response. The second is Active/Passive, where one node lies dormant awaiting the other to fail. They use a common virtual IP address to achieve transparent failover for a client.

☑ Load balancing is the use of two or more nodes to distribute client requests load among the nodes in the group.

Configuring BizTalk Server Groups

☑ BizTalk Server groups are configured in the BizTalk Server Administration console.

☑ BizTalk Server groups are used to "centrally manage" resources, making administration that much easier.

☑ BizTalk Status states are Connected, Tracking connection failed, Shared Queue connection failed, and Tracking and Shared Queue connections failed.

Using the System Monitor

☑ The System Monitor is located within the Performance console and is used to monitor the performance of a running system.

☑ The System Monitor monitors specific items based on configurable counters that you can add to the monitor to include, and are not limited to CPU, memory, and I/O usage.

☑ There are many BizTalk-specific System Monitor counters to monitor documents and BizTalk services.

Integrating with Application Center 2000

☑ Application Center 2000 is Microsoft's HA-based platform to help you scale services and applications on your network.

☑ Application Center 2000 includes a tool called the Health Monitor, which can aid in centralizing the management of resources.

Web-Based Enterprise Management

☑ Windows Management Instrumentation, or WMI, is a tool integrated into Windows 2000 (it can also be added to NT and 98) that allows for Web-based management of services.

☑ BizTalk uses WMI directly in some of its services to transparently access and use database functions.

Frequently Asked Questions

The following Frequently Asked Questions, answered by the authors of this book, are designed to both measure your understanding of the concepts presented in this chapter and to assist you with real-life implementation of these concepts. To have your questions about this chapter answered by the author, browse to **www.syngress.com/solutions** and click on the **"Ask the Author"** form.

Q: I attempted to delete a BizTalk server from the BizTalk Server Group in the BizTalk Server Administration Microsoft Management Console (MMC) snap-in and received the following error message: "The server cannot be deleted because of a failure returned from the BizTalk Server WMI provider: The "MACHINENAME" server cannot be deleted because it is the processing server for at least one receive function." What is the problem, and what can I do to fix it?

A: BizTalk Server requires that each receive function is assigned to a processing server. If you need to delete a BizTalk server from the BizTalk Server Group, you must either delete the receive function or functions that are assigned to that BizTalk server, or reassign the receive function to another BizTalk server in the same BizTalk Server Group.

Q: When running BizTalk Server 2000 in a normal production environment during month-end processing when our system is under very heavy stress loads, many issues arise with server performance, among other things. It seems like the entire server is slowing. What could be the problem?

A: When BizTalk Server is under stress, you might encounter problems with server performance, event sequence, and user event marshalling. You might also receive Access Violations. To resolve this problem, obtain the latest service pack (2) for Windows 2000. For additional information, see article Q290619 in the Microsoft Knowledge Base.

Q: I need to make sure that the databases I created for my BizTalk servers to access are safe from failure. We already had a hard disk failure on one of our servers, which corrupted the database, and we were down for a while fixing it. What could I have done to prevent this from happening so I can prevent it from happening again?

A: You will need to take the databases that BizTalk uses and move them to another machine so that you can isolate the databases on a clustered set of SQL servers. This way, if you have a server crash, the databases are always protected.

Q: I want to optimize my BizTalk server because it just seems to crawl at times. I am not quite sure why, and I am not sure where to even begin looking. What would I do to start trying to find my problem?

A: To optimize your machine, you will need to first determine "where" and "what" the problem is. It might be network related, it might be hardware related, it might have nothing at all to do with BizTalk, or it could be BizTalk Server's doing. You need to open the Performance monitor and start monitoring your system with counters and alerts to obtain a baseline of normal use, and then see what is not working well. It might just need a memory upgrade—either way, this monitor will help you.

Q: I can't get the BizTalk Server Group to connect . What can I check or view to make sure it is a BizTalk-related problem and not something else?

A: Take a look at the BizTalk Server Group State. Make sure that it is in the "Connected" state; if it is not, you might have failure in that area. You can find the BizTalk Server Group state by clicking on the BizTalk Server Group found in the BizTalk Server Administration console.

Q: I would like to remotely manage my BizTalk Server via the Web. I would like to at least monitor the services from my desktop via a Web page, and I am not quite sure what to do to configure it.

A: You can configure the WMI piece of BizTalk to write an ASP page that allows you to remotely access BizTalk Server to check to see if its services are running, or to stop and start them if needed.

Chapter 10

Troubleshooting

Solutions in this chapter:

- **Process Profiling**
- **Troubleshooting Means Service Packs**
- **Troubleshooting Permissions**
- **Locating the Errors**
- **Troubleshooting Message Queuing**
- **Interchange Size Limits**
- **Refreshing the Elements**
- **Managing Receive Functions**
- **Debugging XLANG**
- **Working with WebDAV**
- **Miscellaneous Issues**
- ☑ **Summary**
- ☑ **Solutions Fast Track**
- ☑ **Frequently Asked Questions**

Introduction

With any new product to market, there are always hidden features waiting to cause you trouble. Unfortunately, this usually happens right before a demonstration or the night before a system goes live. Without quality assurance, things would be exponentially worse, but nothing or no one is perfect. The key to maintaining a successful implementation is your prowess at troubleshooting problems and taking the appropriate actions to accommodate these anomalies. By structuring these updates into timed releases, with the ability to provide hot fixes if necessary, a client or trade partner can plan to keep systems up for maximum availability.

BizTalk 2000 has already logged some items into Microsoft's online knowledge base, and appears to have some features working just a little under par. The release of BizTalk Server 2000 Service Pack 1, as with all service packs, is acknowledgment that this software is a work in progress. This chapter is based on personal experiences and hours of scouring online knowledge bases and newsgroups to bring together, at this time, a complete listing of major problems. We will also provide some interesting information on configuration settings that might assist you in your design and implementation of BizTalk 2000.

This section is designed to help the BizTalk developer address and avoid problems that arise during development. It cannot be a complete list of all troubles, of course, but is instead a discussion of some of the most common or most critical situations that you as a developer are likely to encounter. Ideally, the information provided here will help you troubleshoot your application before spending hours in the help files, the knowledge bases, and the newsgroups.

Process Profiling

BizTalk Server 2000 solutions are distributed applications. As with all distributed applications, you as the developer need to look at the individual components of the application, as well as the big picture—the components all working together. Let's first discuss the elements that comprise a BizTalk solution, and then briefly review ways to analyze the process as a whole.

Interchanges as Objects

To start troubleshooting the BizTalk application, it might be best to get in the right frame of mind. Let's first look at a basic unit of BizTalk work, the *interchange*. A single interchange could comprise a Receive function with a preprocessor, a channel, and a messaging port to an AIC. In this interchange, you have the opportunity to introduce your own code, probably in the form of a COM object, at:

- The Receive function's preprocessor
- The channel's map
- The messaging port's AIC

As far as BizTalk is concerned, however, that is all for one interchange. Fortunately, it is very easy, almost natural, to completely view this interchange without any regard to the rest of the world. Analogous to the COM concept, this interchange has a finite number of "interfaces," namely the inbound document definition and the outbound document definition. As long as the schema of these document definitions is honored, other processes can view the interchange as a closed system. We can essentially treat it as its own component.

Given that, we then address it in the same way that we analyzed our components of distributed applications in the past. We can test it thoroughly in isolation before testing it within the complete application.

Let's consider an extremely simple sample BizTalk application, where Company A needs to send data to Company B1 and Company B2. Company B2 needs a different format than B1 needs. A's data is gathered from its database using a custom COM and converted to an XML document. (This document is defined with a BizTalk specification.) The document is then passed through a BizTalk Orchestration (XLANG) schedule, where it sends the document to one channel for Company B1 and to a different channel for Company B2. Each channel converts the document and posts the data to each company's receiving ASP URL, using its messaging port's HTTP transport.

Because the data component knows that its output must be an XML document conforming to the BizTalk specification defined, it can be designed, tested, and refined without ever talking to BizTalk. Likewise, the channel and messaging port can take any XML document conforming to the specification and perform the conversion. For early development, the channel can simply pick up dummy files via a Receive function and dump them out via the messaging port's file transport service. This affords us a convenient opportunity for testing as well. Your tester (of course, this is not you) can generate numerous files, good and bad, and then can simply be dumped in a Receive folder at any volume desired. This gives us the ability to run all the testing, performance monitoring, and so forth in relative isolation. Since your two final destinations have BizTalk specifications designed for them and they are represented by document definitions in the messaging port, you know that the end results match the "interface" of whatever will be receiving the documents at company B1 and B2, respectively. It is not until you are completely satisfied with the interchange internally that you need to introduce the HTTP transport.

Viewing the Complete System

The Performance Monitor, discussed in Chapter 9, exposes several counters for the BizTalk Server and can be the best tool for monitoring speed of interchanges, and so forth. However, it might not tell you what you would like to know about how the various components of your interchange are interacting.

Once you have put it together to complete the interchange, you might wish to introduce a higher-level analysis tool such as Visual Studio Analyzer (VSA). Visual Studio Analyzer is available in the Enterprise version of Visual Studio 6.0. Those who plan to use VSA for BizTalk analysis should be aware of a COM+ issue that can arise in cases where an installation of Visual Studio is present before upgrading from NT 4.0 to Windows 2000. Further details can be found in Microsoft KnowledgeBase article Q257378 INFO: Visual Studio Analyzer Does Not Collect MTS Events.

One of VSA's strengths is the ability to watch the interaction of various COMs within the context of the complete process. By selecting the right events to watch, you can see potential memory leaks, faults, bottlenecks, and the like. This can expose problems that are introduced by bringing the components together to perform the work in the interchange.

A word of caution: As you might know from experience, VSA introduces a lot of activity, and can sometimes overwhelm the system you are testing. You need to be selective as to what events you are watching. When discussing BizTalk interchanges, maps can introduce a special concern. During one interchange, you will likely watch the preprocessor and the AIC without much trouble. However, suppose you needed to reference a very small COM in the custom script of a functoid in your map. That functoid is connected to at least one record, and if your document contains 4000 instances of that record, your little COM will be created and destroyed 4000 times. That can be much more activity than you were seeking.

VSA does require you to write custom code to instrument your component to capture custom events. If you can justify it, you might want to look into more traditional profiling tools that can automatically instrument your code.

This discussion has been interchange centric. Often, however, one interchange represents a small piece of your BizTalk solution. When that is the case, BizTalk

Orchestration is often used as the "glue." The XLANG schedule, a COM+ entity in itself, gives the user the opportunity to introduce even more custom components into a solution. Obviously, they should be tested independently as well, but as the solution becomes more complex, the more a tool such as VSA can be valuable. XLANG also introduces some new behaviors, like long-running transactions, which tools such as VSA and the Performance Monitor don't exploit as well. Fortunately, Microsoft has given us XLANG Monitor to fill the voids when analyzing XLANG schedules.

Using XLANG Monitor

While other tools for analyzing distributed applications have existed for some time, Microsoft has provided us a new troubleshooting tool with BizTalk Server 2000 known as the XLANG Monitor. XLANG Monitor gives us the ability to manage our XLANG schedule instances and capture XLANG events.

XLANG Monitor "installs" itself during a standard BizTalk Server 2000 installation, but does not appear on any menu or icon, so it can be easily overlooked. It is merely copied to a location on your disk. In a default installation, it appears as \Program Files\Microsoft BizTalk Server\SDK\XLANG Tools\XLANGMon.exe. As file locations go, it has been seemingly given the rank of a sample file or small utility, but XLANG Monitor can be a very useful and powerful tool, so much so that you will probably want to consider adding a shortcut to it in your BizTalk menu.

XLANG Monitor specifically addresses XLANG schedules. When you start to use XLANG schedules, it does not take long to start asking yourself questions such as, "Is my schedule running?" "What happened?" "It seems to be running … how can I stop it?" All of these questions, and many more, can be answered by using the XLANG Monitor, so let's look into using it.

Start XLANG Monitor by simply double-clicking the XLANGMon.exe file. When you start XLANG Monitor, the first screen displays a tree, with the name of the machine as top element, followed by any COM+ application hosting XLANG schedules (Figure 10.1). By default, XLANG schedule instances are hosted in the COM+ application XLANG Scheduler. However, as you know from earlier material, any custom COM+ application can be configured to host XLANG schedules. Appropriately, XLANG Monitor can display information on schedules that are being hosted in any COM+ application, XLANG Scheduler or otherwise. Under each COM+ application are two folders, Running and Completed. These two folders represent the two basic states of XLANG schedule instances. Within these two categories of state are five more detailed statuses, listed in Table 10.1.

Figure 10.1 Displaying Schedule Statuses in the Main Screen of XLANG Monitor

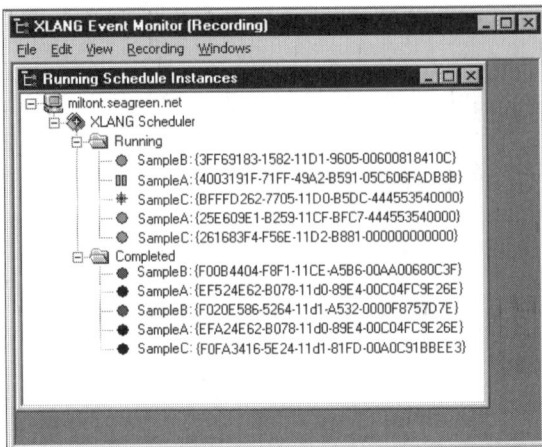

Table 10.1 Defining Schedule Status Displayed in XLANG Monitor

Icon	State
Green dot	Running XLANG schedule
Blue lines	A suspended/paused schedule
Blue snowflake	A dehydrated schedule
Red dot	Complete schedule—with errors
Black dot	Complete schedule—successful

When an instance of an XLANG schedule is in one of the states listed in Table 10.1, they will appear in the appropriate folder. Each instance will be represented by the icon in the table, the name of the schedule (".skx" file), and a GUID. If you recall from earlier material, each instance of each schedule adopts a GUID to enable individual identification. Here you see it displayed.

XLANG Monitor also gives you the ability to *manipulate* schedule instances. You can start, suspend, or terminate from this screen. You can start an application in one of two ways:

- Highlight the **COM+ application** that will host the schedule, select **Instance**, then **Run** from the menu, and type in the full name to the skx file.

- From the **Windows Explorer window**, drag the .skx file of choice and drop it on the **COM+ application** that will host it.

Following either method, a new instance of the schedule will appear under the Running folder. Each will have a green dot signifying that it is running. To suspend a schedule instance, highlight the **running schedule**, and then from the menu select **Instance** and then **Suspend**.

Since we are talking about XLANG schedules, which tout their ability to dehydrate, it should be clarified that a schedule suspended in this interface is *not* the same as dehydrated. The only way to resume a suspended schedule is through this interface. If you were looking to rehydrate a schedule, this is not the application for that. Instead, that functionality exists on the XLANG tab of the COM+ application that is hosting the schedule. This can be accessed through the Component Manager (Figure 10.2). To terminate a running or suspended schedule, highlight the **schedule** and from the menu select **Instance** and then **Terminate**.

Figure 10.2 Rehydrating an XLANG Schedule

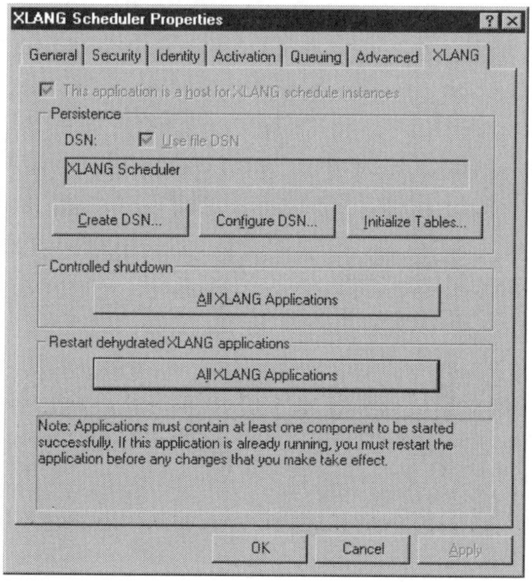

In addition to providing XLANG instance monitoring and control, XLANG Monitor displays events of XLANG schedules. To view the events available, double-click the **schedule** of interest. The Event window will open, showing two panes. The upper pane is a simple list of all events subscribed to. By selecting any one of these events, details for that event will show in the bottom pane.

NOTE

During your early development time, don't be surprised if you open this application and find *many* green dotted GUIDs in your Running folder, indicating many instances of a running schedule. It is very common to get schedules initiated and then "hang." At this point, be thankful we have this tool, because of the ease with which you can terminate the rogue schedules.

If your list of events is confusingly long, you will likely want to limit the list. This functionality is available in the Event Filter window. Access this window by selecting **View** and then **Events Filter** from the menu.

This new window shows a tree of many events. Figure 10.3 shows only the ScheduleState and Errors nodes expanded; there are many more under each heading. This window gives you the ability to limit the list of events that will be reported to you in the Event Viewer. It should be noted that this is just a viewing filter. Behind the scenes, the XLANG Monitor is still subscribed to all events. Table 10.2 is a simple list of the XLANG events from which you can choose.

Figure 10.3 Selecting XLANG Events to View in XLANG Monitor

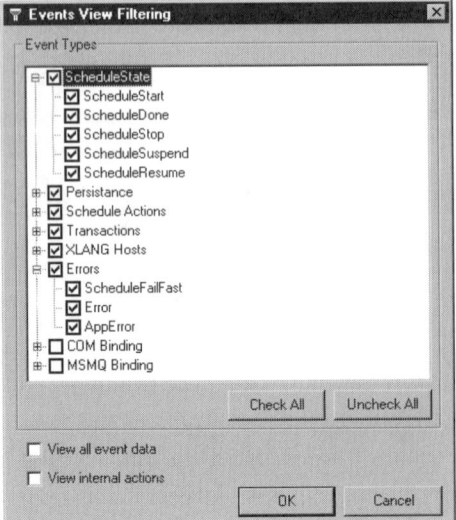

Table 10.2 XLANG Events Exposed by XLANG Monitor

ScheduleState	Schedule Actions	Transactions	COM Binding
ScheduleStart	SourceEnter	TransactionBegin	ProxyEnter
ScheduleDone	SourceLeave	TransactionEnd	ProxyLeave
ScheduleStop	SinkEnter	ContextEnter	ComSinkCall
ScheduleSuspend	SinkLeave	ContextLeave	ComSinkReturn
ScheduleResume	PartitionEnter	ContextAbort	ComSourceCall
	PartitionLeave	ContextCompensate	ComSourceReturn
Persistence	ConnectEnter		
SchedulePersist	ConnectLeave	**XLANG Hosts**	**MSMQ Binding**
Dehydrated	CallEnter	Shutdown	MSMQDeliver
Rehydrated	CallLeave	Startup	MSMQReceive
	ReturnEnter		
	ReturnLeave	**Errors**	
	TaskEnter	ScheduleFailFast	
	TaskLeave	Error	
	SwitchEnter	AppError	
	SwitchLeave		
	CaseExecute		

Since BizTalk is an enterprise application, common sense and good design will tell you that one XLANG host on one machine is not sufficient to tell the story of a complex BizTalk solution. XLANG Monitor considers this as well by giving you the ability to add machines to your sources of events. On the **Recording menu**, click **Stop Recording**. This is assuming you were in Recording mode (as denoted in the title bar of Figure 10.1). Now, on the **Recording menu**, click **Event Sources**. The Select Event Sources dialog opens, shown in Figure 10.4.

This dialog gives you the ability to add more computers and add more COM+ XLANG hosts within each computer. (It's a good policy to click **Refresh** first when entering this window, and when adding or removing computers.) Once the list is built, you can easily choose what you will be viewing at any given time.

XLANG Monitor will likely be promoted to a more formal application in future releases. It is an invaluable tool when XLANG schedules fall within our troubleshooting path.

This might be a good place to remind the reader that prior to BizTalk Server 2000 SP1 and Windows 2000 SP2, the XLANG Monitor could display some interesting behavior. Many experienced *no* running instances showing in the window when at least one was definitely running, or showing *no* event information until a second instance was started. Regardless of the error, these two service packs went a long way in making XLANG Monitor a stable and valuable tool, and you the developer would be wise to make sure they are installed on your BizTalk machines.

Figure 10.4 Selecting the XLANG Event Sources in XLANG Monitor

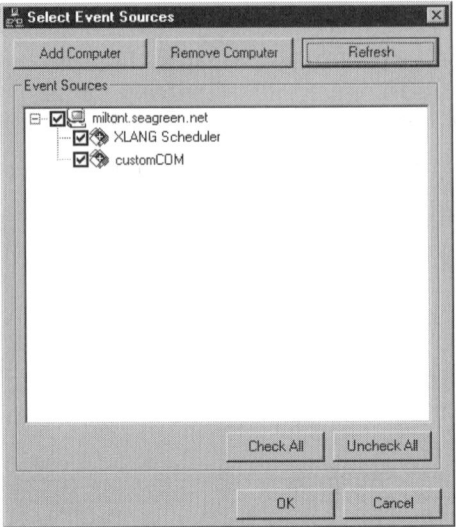

Troubleshooting Means Service Packs

Before going too far down the road of troubleshooting, it is best that we pack the right gear. In the case of BizTalk Server 2000, that gear would include BizTalk Server 2000 Service Pack 1, and Windows 2000 Service Pack 2. While it is comforting to know that you are not the only one suffering from a particular problem, there are few things more frustrating than trying to solve the unsolvable. Following is a brief discussion on both service packs.

BizTalk SP1

At the time of this writing, Microsoft had just released BizTalk Server 2000 Service Pack 1 (BTS SP1). You can get complete information about this service pack at the Microsoft site at http://support.microsoft.com/support/kb/articles/Q299/6/64.ASP. The following is a partial list of some of the items addressed in the service pack that users are most likely to encounter. While this is not meant to be a complete list, it might benefit you to quickly scan these items to more easily determine if you should have hope that SP1 will cure your problems:

- WebDAV Does Not Work After You Install Office XP

- BizTalk Editor and Mapper Do Not Start and Fail to Load Schema Files After MSXML 4.0 Beta Is Installed

- BizTalk Service Fails If Microsoft Distributed Transaction Coordinator Fails

- BizTalk Server Never Purges Persistence Database

- BizTalk Server Does Not Purge or Archive Tracking Database

- Failed Documents Are Sent to the Suspended Queue Instead of the Retry Queue

- Documents in the Suspended Queue May Fail to Resubmit

- Documents Processed by BizTalk Server Are Stuck in the Work Items Queue

- XLANG Errors Occur When You Run BizTalk Server Under a High Load Condition

- XLANG Monitor Sample Does Not Record Events Until You Start a Second Instance

WARNING

All BizTalk Servers in a group must be running the same version of BizTalk. Therefore, you must apply the service pack to all the servers before bringing them back into the group.

Windows 2000 SP2

BizTalk Server 2000 is a heavy user of COM+, and during its early stages, a few bugs came up that were purely COM+ related. Hotfixes addressed these up to the point when they were consolidated into the current Windows 2000 Service Pack 2. Both products have been well received, with negligible negative feedback on the newsgroups and so forth, so we recommend that you install both on your system, regardless of any trouble you might have.

Troubleshooting Permissions

Does this scenario sound familiar? You have been working on your development machine with great success for some time now, and you are ready to move your BizTalk configuration over to a server. You install BizTalk Server 2000 on the server, migrate all of your configuration elements, and run your process to see that it works on the server. However, later when you try to run the process remotely, or on a schedule, nothing happens. Moreover, there is no information in the Event Viewer.

The problem is very simple in concept, and the solution will come as no surprise, but it continues to be an extremely common issue: BizTalk does not have permission to execute.

You might recall that during installation, there were some prompts for user accounts for which you might have accepted the default of Local System Account or Interactive User. Well, remember, you are on a server now, and it is time to enter some actual accounts that will do the job. Following is a brief compilation of the places you need to go to adjust the identity or logon information to allow BizTalk to operate in a remote setup.

In **Computer Management | Services and Applications | Services:**

- BizTalk Messaging Service
- XLANG Schedule Restart Service

In **Component Services | COM+ Applications**:

- XLANG Scheduler

For the two services, it is easy to scan the Log On As column of the details section in the MMC window. If it shows LocalSystem for these two services, you will need to change them. Figure 10.5 shows the Log On tab of the Service Properties dialog.

For the COM+ components, just open the **Properties dialog** of the listed components and select the **Identity tab**. Keep in mind that you will need to uncheck **Disable changes** in the **Permissions** section of the **Advanced tab**, make the identity change, and then re-check **Disable Changes**.

Three other default COM+ applications are added by BizTalk that require identity information, but it should not be necessary to change them from the default. Depending on your situation, however, you might wish to change them. These applications are:

- BizTalk Server Interchange Application
- BizTalk Server Internal Utilities
- XLANG Scheduler Persistence Helper

Figure 10.5 The Log On Tab in BizTalk Messaging Service

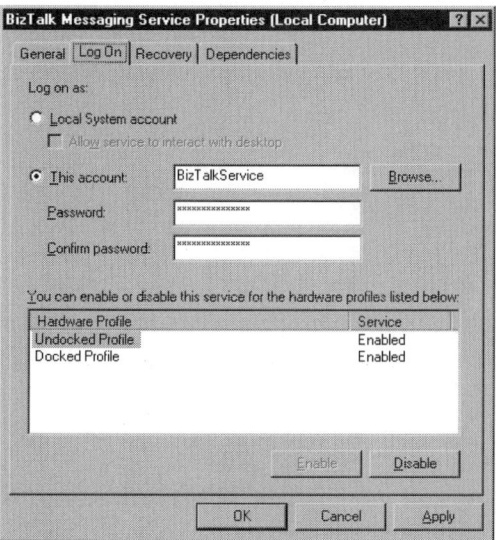

NOTE

Make sure that the service account(s) you create for operating BizTalk does not have expiring passwords. You can be completely diligent in giving all the components proper identity, log on, and then have the password expire and bring the entire thing to a halt. If the password expires on your BizTalk service account, BizTalk will simply not start. This can be the most difficult problem because unless you have configured some error reporting outside of the BizTalk application, you will not be notified that your process is simply not initiating. In cases of XLANG or custom COM components, the applications will likewise not start, but you might have some clues in the event log because your BizTalk process had at least begun.

As discussed previously, BizTalk is integrated with SQL Server, and so it follows that if SQL Server is not running, BizTalk will fail. Therefore, you should ensure that the following SQL services have proper identity information as well:

- MSSQLServer
- SQLServerAgent

In addition, in your efforts to get your identities correct, don't forget your custom COM+ components. You will undoubtedly design and use a few, and like the BizTalk COM+ components, they require the proper identity to execute.

If it does not otherwise violate your security policies, it is wise to explicitly, not via other groups, add any account that will execute or administer BizTalk configurations to the BizTalk Administrators User Group. Even just viewing your channels, ports, and so forth in the BizTalk Server Administration MMC requires the user to be a member, and since it is likely that sometime down the road you or another will log on to the server with the service accounts you use for executing BizTalk, it would help to be prepared. For more detailed information on changing identity and account information, see Chapter 8.

Locating the Errors

Now that we have discussed situations in which BizTalk doesn't even start, let's move our attention to when BizTalk starts generating some errors. The first order of business is to locate those errors; for this, you will primarily visit two locations:

- Event Viewer
- Suspended Queue

You can find both in the BizTalk Server Administration MMC. The default BizTalk installation displays an Application log view in the Event Viewer where the significant BizTalk errors will be logged (Figure 10.6).

Almost every error that takes place in BizTalk will be reported to the Event Viewer, so this is the first place you want to look, and often will be the last. Errors regarding document validation, failing COM objects, missing queues, and almost everything else will appear here. The following is a sample message for a document validation error.

```
Description:
An error occurred in BizTalk Server.
```

```
Details:

------------------------------

The XML document has failed validation for the following reason:
Element content is invalid according to the DTD/Schema.
Expecting: LineItem.


The following channel configuration setting is not valid: "Channel
    to convert Inbound to Outbound"


The server could not finish processing the document.


Suspended Queue ID: "{FEB7E4B9-A8D1-4823-9333-7C4E6C4AC5F4}"
```

Figure 10.6 Finding Errors in the Suspended Queue and Event Viewer

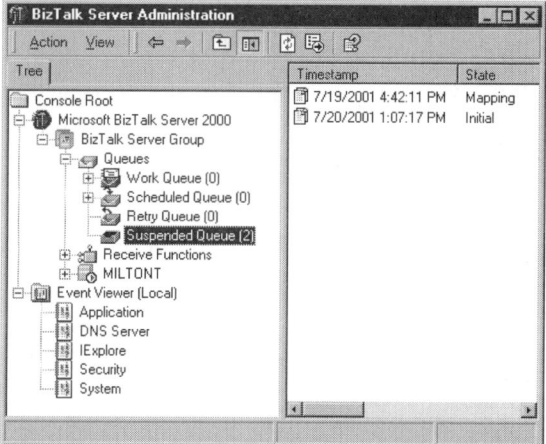

Let's review this sample error message. Under "Details:" the first paragraph contains the detailed description of the error. The second paragraph is the configuration object in which the failure took place; in this case, a channel. The third item is further status, and the fourth is the GUID of the interchange document that now rests in the Suspended Queue.

This takes us to the second step in our error search, viewing the Suspended Queue. The Suspended Queue is the final resting place for interchanges that could not complete successfully. Knowing that, it will not come as surprise that it can become fairly populated during development time. Within the details section of the MMC, several columns can be helpful as a summary of what failed and where in the process. When you are looking to correlate a particular document with a particular error found in the event log (which is usually the case), go to the last column, Interchange ID, and look for the GUID that was referenced in the event log error.

For each entry in the Suspended Queue, two actions will help you along your way. With one of the items selected in the queue, either select **Actions** from the menu or right-click on the item. The menu that appears has two key items at the top, View Document and View Error Description. The latter, View Error Description, is unfortunately often populated with messages such as:

```
"Validation of this document against its specification failed.
See the event log for more information."
```

There is certainly nothing wrong with that statement, but it doesn't really add anything to what you obtained from the error log. The first action, "View Document," will display the XML document as it was when the process failed. This can be very helpful when experiencing errors with document validation and mapping. In our previous example, the document failed validation because it was expecting a certain element, but in a large document, that can leave a lot of room for investigation. A nice trick is to copy this document out to a file, and then use BizTalk Editor to "Validate Instance…". BizTalk Editor will then tell you exactly where in the document, line number and position, the problem lies. For more information on this process, see the sidebar, *Getting Ready for a Channel*.

NOTE

Messaging ports contain primary and backup transports. Many applications absolutely require the use of a backup transport to maintain a mission-critical flow, but for those applications where it is not relevant, consider using the backup transport as a form of debugging. If, for instance, you need to know when a primary transport is not available, you can simply send the data along the backup transport, such as an e-mail to you. That way, without writing any code per se, you have an automatic method of alerting you that the primary transport failed.

Designing & Planning…

Getting Ready for a Channel: Getting Your Spec and Map Correct Before Entering an Interchange

Converting from one XML document to another is one of the key services BizTalk Server 2000 provides, so as a BizTalk developer you can expect to do this often. As you know, the conversion takes place using a map, which takes place within a channel. However, before we create a channel or send in a document and hope that it processes successfully, there are several things we can do to increase our likelihood of success.

First, make sure you have valid inbound and outbound documents. Without ever leaving the BizTalk Editor, you can verify that your schema is valid, assuming you have a sample data file with which to work. BizTalk Editor offers "Validate Instance" as a tool, and if you can't get your schema to validate your sample data file, there is little point in moving on. In outbound schema cases, you should create a sample file with another tool, especially with flat files, since BizTalk Editor cannot create a flat file instance as it can an XML instance. Your outbound schema must be able to validate the flat file you created; otherwise, there is no chance it will be able to create a good one through an envelope.

With two good specifications, we can focus on the map. When you think you have a good map, test…test…test. The Mapper gives you the ability to plug in values for each field and watch the results. Testing will test the functoids as well. This can be especially valuable when using custom script functoids.

A behavior that can surprise the developer is that the output from a Mapper testing is still not 100-percent compatible with the outbound document specification. The output is *not* validated against the specification. One easy way to work around this is to copy the contents of the Output tab window (it's a browser, so right-click in the **Output tab window**, select **View Source**, and then **Save**) to a file, and then use BizTalk Editor to validate this XML instance. This can expose certain issues, such as missing required attributes or the wrong number of elements, that would show up later in the Event Viewer as a document validation error when you tried to run the conversion through a channel.

By observing some of these guidelines, you can greatly reduce the occurrence of errors in your channel, a significant source of overall errors in the BizTalk process.

Troubleshooting Message Queuing

BizTalk Server 2000 can use message queuing heavily. It's a key element in what gives it its flexibility and scalability. Therefore, it is important to ensure that message queuing is configured properly. The following are a few items that are worth discussing.

Installation Issues

First, you would not be alone if you installed BizTalk Server 2000 and forgot to install message queuing. It is a separate Windows component and it is up to you to get it on your machine. When attempting to use BizTalk services that use message queuing, you might receive errors that are not necessarily clear as to this being the source of the error.

Properties

If you are planning to use message queuing, you should consider creating transactional message queues. Creating private queues is quick and easy, and despite Transactional being the only option in the dialog, it can be easy to disregard. Figure 10.7 shows the very lean dialog where you have the opportunity to check **Transactional**.

Figure 10.7 Messaging Queue Creation Dialog

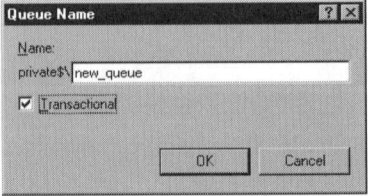

When message queues are used as transactional, they guarantee that all messages sent within the transaction, if they can be delivered, will arrive exactly once, and in the order in which they were sent. If one of the operations fails, the transaction is aborted and changes are rolled back to the state when the transaction was invoked. Therefore, for data reliability, you would choose to use transactional queues.

Similarly, if you plan to implement a message queue in an Orchestration transaction, the queue will need to be transactional. When using transaction shapes in orchestration, their transactional properties are dependent on the components implemented. If you have designed a transaction in Orchestration, and a port within that transaction implements a *non*transactional message queue, you in fact do *not* have a transaction. The queue (as well as the other implemented components) must be transactional for the XLANG schedule to implement transactions.

So, why would you *not* choose transactional message queues? One reason could be that transactional message queues must be local queues on the BizTalk Server. If your application requires the use of remote queues, transactional will not be an option. Another reason could be that transactional message queues require more resources, so if performance were a driving factor, you would need to consider nontransactional message queues.

Naming

Message queues can be used in Receive functions, messaging ports, and XLANG schedules. Unfortunately, referring to a queue uses slightly different syntax depending from where it is referenced, and this can lead to some frustrating moments. Table 10.3 is a quick review of the ways to reference the queue shown in Figure 10.7.

Table 10.3 Referring to Queues

Referring from...	Prompt	Syntax
Receive function	Polling location:	DIRECT=OS:.\private$\new_queue
Messaging port	Primary transport address:	DIRECT=OS:.\private$\new_queue
XLANG schedule	Enter the queue name:	.\private$\new_queue

Interchange Size Limits

If your process is working, but behaving very slowly, you might be flirting with some of the size limits within BizTalk. Details on the size limits are available within the BizTalk documentation, so this section will just be a consolidation to serve as quick reference.

BizTalk Messaging can support an interchange of up to 20MB. This means that any interchange exceeding this size will cause severe performance issues. However, as you approach 20MB, you will certainly begin to see the effects. If your process can live without it, disable document tracking in the BizTalk Server

Group Properties. If you need it, consider scaling down to the minimum tracking needed. Flat files can lead to some questions regarding size. The size limits stated are all in terms of XML documents. Remember that before BizTalk can flex its processing muscle on the document, it must first convert it to XML. Therefore, after adding all the necessary tags and so forth, the equivalent file can be larger.

NOTE

When reviewing the size of flat files, consider a 3-to-1 ratio as a fair approximation. In other words, a 1MB flat file could turn into approximately a 3MB XML file.

Messaging queues, however, have a limit of only 4MB (2MB if you are using Unicode), so be cautious. If you foresee large documents, you might need to avoid using queues in your configuration objects.

In cases where you do need to use BizTalk Orchestration with file sizes greater than 4MB/2MB, you need to get the message into Orchestration while bypassing the use of the message queues. One way to do this is to take advantage of the noninstantiated COM component at one of your ports.

Let's discuss this approach in terms of a simple example. First, create a simple component with a method SubmitDoc. The code would look like this:

```
Sub SubmitDoc(xmlstring)

End sub
```

The method contains one parameter and no code. Into the parameter *xmlstring* will be passed the complete XML of the XML document/message. Then, in Orchestration, create a new schedule (LargeDoc.skx) and implement a port (FirstPort) with this component using "No instantiation." Figure 10.8 shows the dialog where you select this option for COM objects in BizTalk Orchestration. Connect the first action of the schedule to the SubmitDoc method of this port. The schedule is instantiated by using the following pseudocode:

```
ScheduleURL="schedule://ThisServer/LargeDoc.skx/FirstPort"

Set Schedule = GetObject(ScheduleURL)

Schedule.SubmitDoc(strxml)
```

Figure 10.8 Binding a Component with No Instantiation

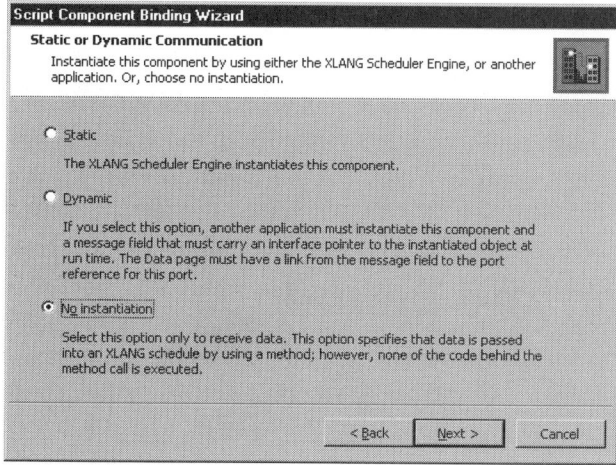

In this case, `strxml` is the large XML document you want to submit. The rest of the orchestration will now have access to the XML passed in through the method's parameter (Figure 10.9).

Figure 10.9 Submitting a Large Document through XLANG

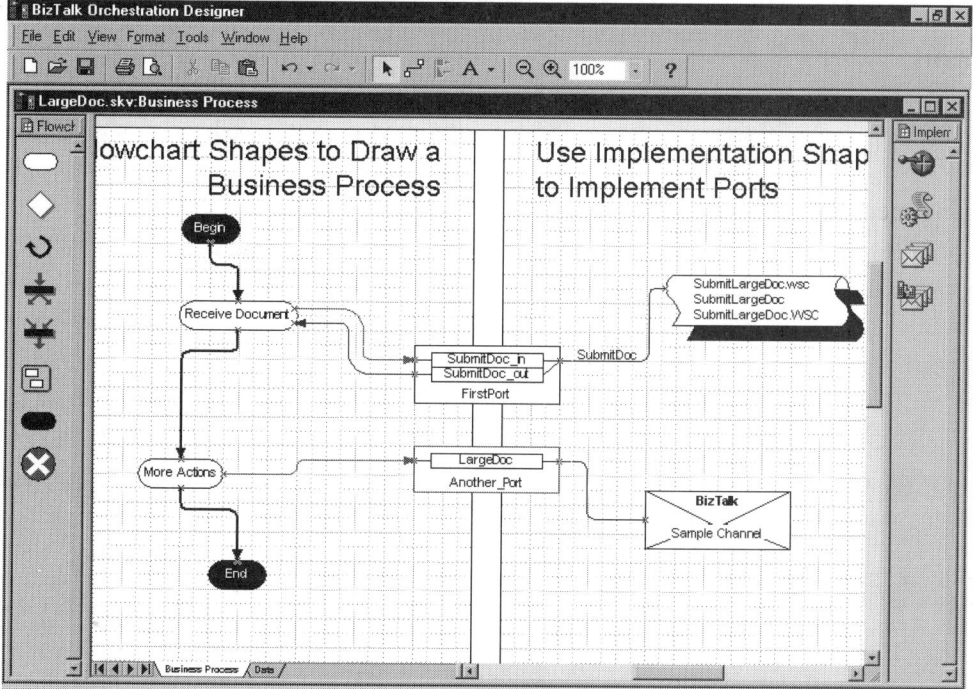

Now, you might be asking yourself, "But I am not using the message queuing implementation shape in my schedule, so why am I limited?" Remember that message queuing is how BizTalk Messaging and BizTalk Orchestration communicate with one another. Thus, when you activate an XLANG schedule by a messaging port, and you have the BizTalk Messaging implementation used in your schedule, you are using message queuing behind the scenes. Therefore, even though you have not expressly called for message queuing, you are using it, and are correspondingly bound to the 4MB/2MB limitation.

Refreshing the Elements

BizTalk Server 2000 has a few features that we might affectionately call "disconnects." Let's not call them problems because they can have good justification, but that doesn't change the fact that they can really frustrate the developer. Let's consider an exemplary BizTalk interchange case of receiving a flat file and mapping it to a new XML file. For this interchange, you will require:

- A file Receive function (let's have it refer to a channel in this example)
- An envelope to parse the flat file
- A specification for the incoming document
- A specification for the outbound document
- A map to do the conversion.
- A channel referring to an inbound document definition, an outbound document definition, and the map
- A messaging port referred to by the channel

Let's say everything is working, and now you need to make a change to one field in the inbound spec, and one change in the outbound spec. These changes will also affect a change in the map. Let's first make the change in the inbound spec. You do this in BizTalk Editor and save the file using **File...Save**. Now, in BizTalk Editor, you make the change in the outbound spec and save the file. Next, you open the map. The map that depends on these specs does not reflect the changes you made because you must reload the specifications. After reloading both specifications, you make the map change, and save the map. You then try to run the process and nothing changes. Why?

First, the Receive function references an envelope. The envelope depends on the inbound specification, but envelopes can only reference specifications kept in

WebDAV. Therefore, for the envelope to be current, your spec in WebDAV must be current. In the channel, the map can only reference maps kept in the WebDAV as well. Therefore, the map, too, must be saved to the WebDAV. In addition, within the channel, the inbound and outbound specs refer to document definitions, which in turn only refer to specs in the WebDAV. In case that wasn't enough updating, when you make a change to a map, the Channel dialog needs to be explicitly opened and resaved to update the map that is actually cached for use.

Confusing? Let's summarize. When you make a change to BizTalk specifications or maps, you should:

- Save all changes to WebDAV.

- Open and save any document definitions dependent on the changed specs.

- Reload specifications into dependent maps.

- Open and save any channels dependent on changed maps.

Make no mistake, this does require a lot of clicking, but your diligence will provide smoother modification processes.

Managing Receive Functions

So, you have been a good developer and made sure that all of your specs and maps are validated and tested, yet every time you drop a document into a folder for a Receive function, you get a validation error. Even worse, you only get a validation error occasionally. Assuming the error message you get resembles that shown earlier in the section, *Locating the Errors*, pay special attention to the line that reads:

```
The following channel configuration setting is not valid:
"Channel to convert Inbound to Outbound"
```

Is that really the channel you are testing? No? If the wrong channel is getting the message, don't be surprised if that is telling you that the wrong Receive function is picking up the message. Remember, a Receive function polls for a particular type of file in a particular location, so there are two ways in which Receive functions can overlap. Multiple Receive functions might look in the same folder for different file types. This can be a perfectly good design—consolidating all incoming messages in one place. Multiple Receive functions can also poll for the same file type in different locations. Perhaps all PO★.xml files for Company A are sent to FolderA, and all PO★.xml files for Company B are sent to FolderB. This is also a perfectly viable solution to perhaps the two different POs needing to be processed differently. The trouble occurs when multiple Receive functions are polling for the same type of file *and* in the same location.

During development time, it is easy create many different Receive functions for many different purposes, and along the way, inadvertently create this problem. Unless you disable the Receive function, each will try to pick up the file type it is looking for, and as a result, send a perfectly good message to a perfectly wrong channel, and the first sign of trouble is a document validation problem. To make matters worse, you will not know which of the competing Receive functions will pick up the file first at any given time.

NOTE

Two practices will help avoid competing Receive functions. First, take the time to create a unique folder for each file Receive function, and a unique message queue for messaging Receive functions that you create during development. Give them meaningful names, so they provide more clues as to their purpose. Second, disable Receive functions that you are not currently using. These two strategies should help keep Receive functions out of your debugging path.

Up to this point, we have discussed Receive functions that refer to channels, but the same problem can arise when using self-routing documents that depend on organizations and document specifications. Obviously, any set of data that is designed to determine a processing route is subject to duplication, which leads to competing Receive functions. Let's clarify, however, that this is a completely separate topic from duplicating Receive functions across multiple servers to improve performance. Receive functions in that case are meant to grab the *same* messages and send them to the *same destination*.

Remember also that Receive functions are always listening, and as soon as they "hear" the type of document they are looking for, they will pick it up. So, what happens if you are sending an asynchronous DOM message to a message queue, or building an XML file by incrementally writing text to the file? The message or file could qualify for the Receive function *before* it is complete, and thus, the Receive function grabs what it can. The result is a document validation error, of course, and this type of error could send you down a completely inappropriate troubleshooting path. To prevent this problem, write your DOM messages to a queue with Async=False, and don't "build" files where they are to be received. Build them elsewhere, and copy the complete file over to the Receive Function folder.

Now, what if you can't get any Receive function to pick up a file. Go back to BTS Administration and check that the Receive function you had in mind is, in fact, enabled. BizTalk Receive functions have a fairly rare quality in that if they encounter a problem, such as a file location not existing, they will disable themselves, but they will not re-enable themselves. This is very practical when you think about, but since you might not necessarily notice when it disables, you might not think to check on it. If the Receive function continues to disable itself when you re-enable it, it is merely telling you that you have not found the problem parameter yet.

Debugging XLANG

An XLANG Orchestration schedule, in itself, does not provide methods of debugging. You can have many actions, messages, and implementations without being able to pause the schedule to look at the value of the variable. Perhaps this will be offered in future versions, but for now, you *can* go a long way with the tools you have in debugging a schedule. The answer here lies in COM implementation.

Make yourself a simple "debugging" component (I like to use the Windows Script component for the simple ones because it takes minimum work on my part), with at least one method whose sole purpose is to display a message box. Add as many actions with references to this COM as you deem necessary, and on the data page, simply point the particular pieces of data that you want displayed to the method. In Figure 10.10, the component BTSUtility.wsc is added in the flow only for debugging purposes. It has only the one method MessageBox. However, always use good judgement when using message boxes and working with servers that can operate unattended.

NOTE

When using a debugging component, consider using the Constants fields in the data page to store text such as the schedule name. When a value is displayed or logged, it is far more comforting to be reminded what XLANG schedule you have instantiated, and by using the constants, you only need to type it once per schedule (Figure 10.11).

Figure 10.10 BizTalk Orchestration Business Process Diagram

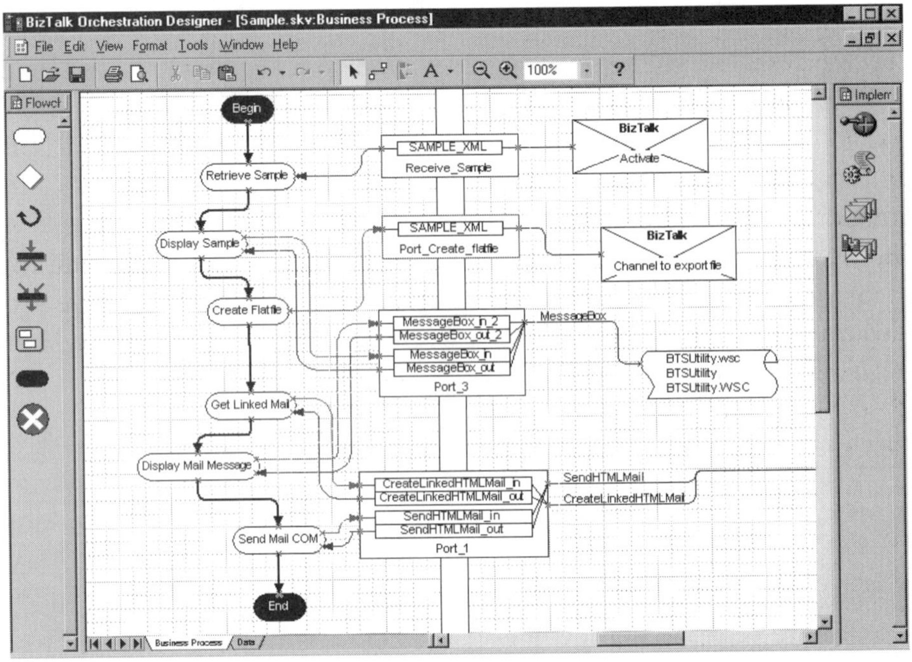

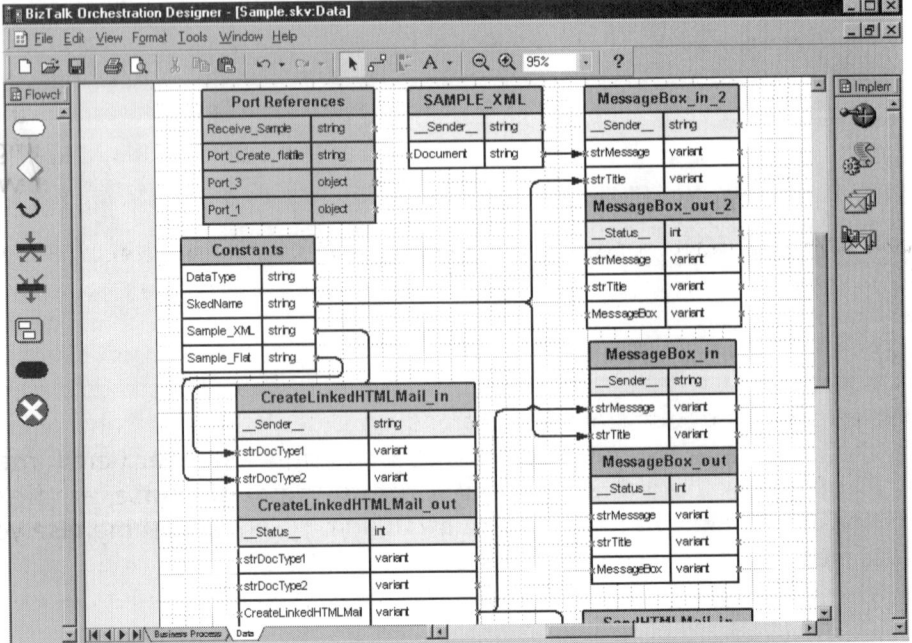

Figure 10.11 Using Constants Fields to Aid XLANG Debugging

Taking this concept a step further, consider adding a method to your COM that logs values and messages rather than displays them. You could keep them in an XML file, an SQL database, or just e-mail them. Regardless of your preferred approach, this would be a single COM that you could reuse for every schedule you design. Ultimately, when the bugs are worked out, you simply remove them from your schedule and recompile. It's worth the programming time to build one of these handy components.

Now, when your trouble lies within a complex (or otherwise) COM object, it is likely that it is written in a language such as Visual Basic. That being the case, don't forget about your language's debugging environment. As you have probably done in so many other solutions in the past, go ahead and open the code for your COM, put some breakpoints in there, and then run it. When the COM is fired from the XLANG, it will instantiate your COM and halt execution at your breakpoints, allowing you to watch the values.

Debugging...

Self-Serving XLANG: Using Orchestration to Handle Errors

As BizTalk developers—well, actually, as developers period—we spend our time designing solutions for various departments while enjoying working with the new tools. There is no reason that we shouldn't use this tool for ourselves as well. What we are discussing here is error handling.

As we know, the better we design our error handling, the faster we can solve our problems. Sometimes, in the very distributed applications we design, good error handling can be a challenge in itself. So, why don't we take advantage of this slick new tool, BizTalk Orchestration, and put it to work for us.

In a BizTalk solution, you have a number of COM components: pre-processors, AICs, and the components connected in the XLANG, all waiting to break and tell us something.

Consider the following scenario: Let's design a standard error message and make it a BizTalk schema. In this schema, of course, are fields for the COM name, the application it is serving, and everything else you need. Let's make all components in this solution (or any others if you wish) send their conformant XML error messages to a single queue. A

Continued

> BizTalk Receive function retrieves these error messages and activates a central XLANG schedule. In this schedule are branches based on the COM name, the application name, or whatever is important to you. Then, each branch can call a BizTalk channel/port combination to, at the least, e-mail to a distribution list. If you can foresee corrective action for certain errors, you can call the components that will perform these actions from this schedule as well.
>
> This approach gives us the loosely coupled nature of using message queues and the workflow design tool of BizTalk Orchestration. There is no reason that only the users should benefit from these new tools.

Working with WebDAV

Let's begin this section with one of the most popular error messages in the BizTalk community, the warning shown in Figure 10.12. While this warning happens to reference localhost, anyone who has fought this error knows that under the right (or perhaps more properly, wrong) conditions, it doesn't matter what server name is used. You also know from either working with BizTalk or reading this book that if you can't get into WebDAV, you will not be building a BizTalk solution.

Figure 10.12 Confronting a Very Common WebDAV Error

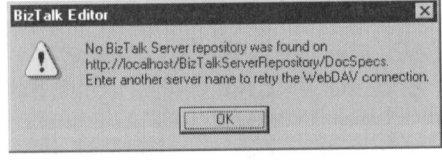

Some of the following information is readily available in the BizTalk documentation, and some is the result of experience. It should also be noted that many of the problems with WebDAV have been addressed in the BizTalk Server 2000 Service Pack 1, and feedback seems to be positive as to its efficacy. Nevertheless, because of the frequency and importance of this issue, a brief review is included here. Note that issues existing before SP1 *should* no longer be necessary:

- Do not install OfficeXP or SharePoint on the same machine as WebDAV.

- Un-register and re-register MSDAIPP.dll and MSDAURL.dll (typically found in C:\Program Files\Common Files\System\Ole DB\).

- Get the latest version of the MapEdit.OCX file from Microsoft, replace the old file with this new file, and register the OCX.

- Issues that still apply after SP1: (The following should default correctly during installation, but they should be checked during trouble.)

    - Give the BizTalk repository virtual directory (usually BizTalkServerRepository) read, write, and directory browsing permission.

    - Disable FrontPage Server extensions.

    - Disable IIS authoring. (MS support also suggests that it be turned off *before* installation of BizTalk.)

    - Ensure that World Wide Publishing is running.

Miscellaneous Issues

There is no limit to the trouble that we as developers will encounter with any product. However, over time, certain issues will arise more often than others. In addition to the most common challenges presented earlier, the following are brief discussions on issues that still appear frequently enough as to deserve mention.

XLANG Message Type

It is more than clear that in the BizTalk realm, document validation is critical. Therefore, proper reference to the proper document definition or schema would follow as obvious. While using BizTalk Messaging, it is very simple to refer to a document definition where prompted because we click a button, and are shown a list from which we can select one. However, in the BizTalk Orchestration world, we need to be a little more careful. In BizTalk Orchestration, when working with the XML Communication Wizard, you have to enter the proper message type to use, and it does not offer a list. This is not stressed in the Microsoft documentation and the samples provided. Figure 10.13 shows the dialog where you enter the information. The name you enter should match the root node in the XML document, which should match the name of the message in the message queue, shown in Figure 10.14. It is very easy to enter an arbitrary name, and when you do this, XLANG now looks for a document that contains a root node matching the arbitrary name. Since you are not sending an arbitrary message, the XLANG schedule doesn't see a conforming message and thus does nothing, but stay active.

There will be no error messages, because nothing is "wrong." You will eventually open XLANG Monitor and terminate it. Save yourself the steps and enter that Message Type appropriately.

Figure 10.13 Using Proper Message Type in BizTalk Orchestration

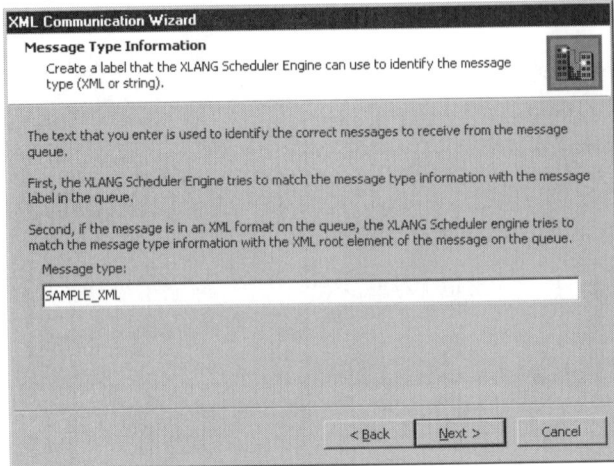

Figure 10.14 Using Proper Message Label in Queue

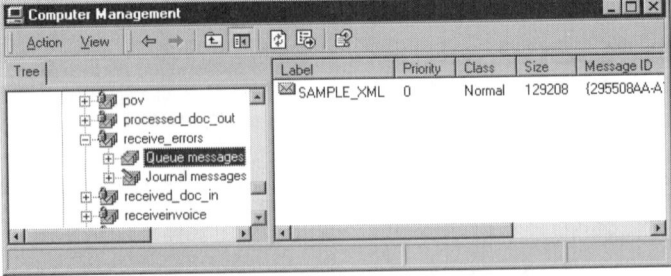

Distributed Transaction Coordinator

Distributed Transaction Coordinator (DTC) is required for BizTalk. Since it is a separate service that can be shut down for any number of reasons outside of BizTalk, make sure that it is running. Typically, this problem will produce references in the event log to "MSDTC Client," so you will have clues. Nevertheless, we mention it here because in a typical server environment, someone outside of the BizTalk team might have had some "influence" on DTC without your knowledge.

As suggested in the Microsoft documentation, many BizTalk configurations will be comprised of BizTalk Server installed on one machine, and the SQL Server database installed on another. In this scenario, MS Distributed Transaction Coordinator (MS DTC) must be running on the SQL server. If it is discontinued, BizTalk will fail, with errors such as "Can't access InterchangeSQ."

Slowing Interchanges

If you are experiencing a high demand on resources and performance is suffering, take notice of how you are instantiating the interchange. Instantiating the interchange as a COM object from code can be part of your problem. The BizTalk documentation states: "Using Receive functions provides better performance than using the Submit method to call the Interchange object because the Receive functions run within BizTalk Services and can cache the internal state of objects. Whereas, the Submit method runs out-of-process and has to rebuild its internal state for each call." This is discussed in more detail in the section, *Optimizing BizTalk Messaging Services* of the BizTalk documentation.

Document Tracking Database

Perhaps when trying to use the document tracking interface, you receive errors regarding Office Web Components. While these are installed automatically with BizTalk, frequent uninstalling and installing of some other Microsoft products can unregister the components that BizTalk needs. These are:

`Msowc.dll`

`Msowcf.dll`

Simply reregister these files when you encounter these errors. Another note on the document tracking. The document tracking database can become very large, even with minimal tracking enabled. BizTalk SP1 includes stored procedures that allow selective purging of this database. Take advantage of these to keep your tracking database within a reasonable size. As is always the case, an overly large database will result in slower performance.

Enveloping Flat Files

If you are using flat files, at some point you will probably forget to use an envelope. Whether this is on the inbound side, as in the Receive function, or outbound, in the message port, an envelope is required to convert XML to text, and vice versa. Missing envelopes on the inbound side will typically result in document validation errors, and the outbound side will typically give you a successful XML output rather than a text file output.

E-Mail Server

Don't forget to identify an SMTP host. It is easy to forget, and until you are ready to try e-mailing a message, you might never think about it.

Antivirus Software

While the reported errors are varied, running anti-virus software can lead to problems. Be sure to try the BizTalk process with these software disabled to see if indeed that is the source of your trouble.

Summary

BizTalk Server 2000 is a powerful new product poised to solve many enterprise needs. It has a solid COM+ foundation and exploits the benefits of distributed applications. Even the new elements it offers, such as the interchange, are fairly modular. Developing a solid BizTalk solution requires the same diligence in pursuing performance and faults as any distributed application. The same tools, such as the Performance Monitor and Visual Studio Analyzer, will work well with BizTalk. In addition to the existing tools, BizTalk provides us with XLANG Monitor, a new tool to manage the events of the BizTalk Orchestration objects.

With all new software comes all new places to stumble and fall. When it comes to BizTalk, we do ourselves the greatest favor by upgrading our machines to BizTalk Server 2000 Service Pack 1 and Windows 2000 Service Pack 2. We have seen that you must be diligent in assigning the proper identities to the various BizTalk and SQL services so that BizTalk Server can operate smoothly in a server environment.

When a BizTalk interchange does suffer an error, the first place we must go is the Event Viewer. Here we will get the most detailed information available, followed by the Suspended Queue, which makes the document available in the its last state before the error. Size limits on interchanges can affect both success and performance. BizTalk Messaging supports 20MB documents, whereas Message Queuing only supports 4MB documents. BizTalk Messaging has a few surprises to keep us vigilant. Document definitions and channels do not automatically use the last version of their specifications, so you must manually "refresh" each one when you are making changes. During development and testing, you might build up a collection of Receive functions that eventually might have the same targets, thus competing with one another.

BizTalk Orchestration and XLANG Scheduler provide us with a nice development environment, but not much of an inherit testing environment. However, with intelligent use of our own COMs placed in the schedules, we can watch and extract almost any information we need as the schedule executes. Combine that with the XLANG Monitor, and we miss "setting breakpoints" a little less often.

A basic unit of work in BizTalk is an interchange to convert one document type to another. This depends on specifications and maps, all which can be thoroughly debugged using BizTalk Editor and BizTalk Mapper, *before* introducing them into a channel/port combination.

Finally, there is no way any book can cover the knowledge available from all the developers already working with the product. Unlike some more popular or generic topics, newsgroups on BizTalk are not yet so crowded as to be tedious, but are popular enough to attract knowledgeable and helpful people. Table 10.4 addresses some of the more common problems and their solutions.

Table 10.4 Troubleshooting Quick Reference

Type of Problem	Reason	Remedy
Document validation error	Changes to schema have not been updated through document definitions.	Manually open and save every document definition that should reflect the changes to the schema.
Wrong channel receiving message	Probably indicates wrong Receive function picking up the file. Rare: Message received before complete.	Disable competing Receive functions. Don't build a file in the Receive folder or send an asynchronous message to a queue.
Mapping is not accepting changes	Dependent channel needs to be explicitly refreshed.	Open channel and click Finish to manually refresh.
Nothing is happening	One or all of the BizTalk services and COM applications do not have permission to execute in noninteractive mode.	Check all BizTalk and XLANG services and components to ensure they are using a service account with permissions.
Interchange too large	XML message has exceeded BizTalk 20MB limit, or message queue 4MB limit. Flat file is small enough, but the equivalent XML grows to exceed the limit.	Break up files into smaller files. The can often require the use of custom COM components. If restricted by queues, remove them from the solution.
WebDAV not accessible	Many possibilities. Very common and documented.	Install BizTalk SP1 and review documentation.
Process is increasingly slower	Memory leak.	Decompose solution into smaller components, and test and monitor.

Continued

Table 10.4 Continued

Type of Problem	Reason	Remedy
XLANG schedule is running, but it won't take the message	The message is not labeled or referenced correctly.	"Message Type" in BTO and message label in queue should both use the root node of the message as a value.
XLANG Monitor doesn't show any schedules at all	A confirmed bug.	Install Windows 2000 SP2.

Solutions Fast Track

Process Profiling

- ☑ Treat the interchange as its own distributed application to decompose and find performance problems.

- ☑ Use a profiling tool such as Visual Studio Analyzer to track the interactions among the many COMs that will be introduced in a BizTalk solution.

- ☑ Use XLANG Monitor to get detailed information on XLANG schedule state and events.

Troubleshooting Means Service Packs

- ☑ Installing BizTalk Server 2000 Service Pack 1 might solve many of your problems.

- ☑ All BizTalk servers in a group must be working with the same version. Therefore, upgrade them all at the same time.

- ☑ Installing Windows 2000 Service Pack 2 might also serve to take care of many of the more common problems you will encounter.

Troubleshooting Permissions

- ☑ Create a service account with the necessary permissions to execute all of the BizTalk services.

☑ In a server environment, ensure that BizTalk Messaging Service, the XLANG Schedule Restart Service, and the XLANG Scheduler COM+ application are configured to use a service account.

☑ Ensure that the SQL Server services MSSQLServer and SQLServerAgent are configured to use a service account.

Locating the Errors

☑ The primary location for errors is the Event Viewer. In a default installation, the Application log will display the BizTalk and XLANG error messages.

☑ The second important location is the Suspended Queue. The error message might not add anything to the Event Viewer information, but it will contain a copy of the interchange document before it failed.

☑ For document validation errors, you can copy the document in the suspended queue to a file, and validate it using BizTalk Editor to get a specific location in the file where the validation fails.

Troubleshooting Message Queuing

☑ Ensure that Message Queuing is installed; it is separate from BizTalk.

☑ When creating message queues, ensure that they are transactional.

☑ When referring to queues, keep in mind that different configuration objects use different syntax. "DIRECT=OS:" might need to prefix the private queue ".\private$\new_queue".

Interchange Size Limits

☑ BizTalk Messaging supports interchanges of up to 20MB. Performance will slow significantly around that limit.

☑ Messaging Queues support messages of only up to 4MB (2MB Unicode).

☑ Flat files will be converted internally to XML, resulting in an increase in size; roughly, a 3 to 1 growth.

☑ If you need to use XLANG with >4MB interchanges, you will need to implement via COM. BizTalk activation requires message queues behind the scenes.

Refreshing the Elements

☑ When changing document specifications, always save to WebDAV.

☑ Open and save any document definitions based on the changed specifications.

☑ Reload specifications into dependent maps.

☑ Open and save any channels dependent on changed maps.

Managing Receive Functions

☑ Beware of competing Receive functions.

☑ Try to use unique locations and unique document types for each Receive function.

☑ Receive functions can disable themselves. If the Receive function finds a problem, it will disable itself until you re-enable it.

Debugging XLANG

☑ Report errors, variable values, and so forth in XLANG schedules by implementing custom COMs.

☑ Make the COMs simple and generic to easily use in all schedules.

☑ Use the Constants fields of the XLANG schedule to report static items such as the schedule filename or application name.

Working with WebDAV

☑ Ensure that BTS SP 1 is installed.

☑ Ensure the BizTalk repository virtual directory has read, write, and directory browsing permission.

☑ Disable FrontPage extensions.

☑ Disable IIS authoring.

☑ Ensure that World Wide Publishing is running.

Miscellaneous Issues

☑ The Message Type in the XLANG schedule must be the same name as the root node of the document and label used in the message queue.

☑ Distributed Transaction Coordinator must be running.

☑ Using Receive functions is more optimized than calling the Submit method on the COM object.

☑ When using flat files, you always need an envelope.

☑ Remember to enter an SMTP host for your BizTalk Server Group when implementing SMTP transports.

☑ Beware of using antivirus software on a BizTalk Server.

Frequently Asked Questions

The following Frequently Asked Questions, answered by the authors of this book, are designed to both measure your understanding of the concepts presented in this chapter and to assist you with real-life implementation of these concepts. To have your questions about this chapter answered by the author, browse to **www.syngress.com/solutions** and click on the **"Ask the Author"** form.

Q: I receive a validation error when I submit a document, but the document is large. How can I find out where the error is?

A: Copy the document from the View Document window from the Suspended Queue, save it to a file, and then use BizTalk Editor to validate the instance. It will give line and position numbers.

Q: I migrated my BizTalk solution from my development box to the server. However, when I schedule it to run, nothing happens. I don't see any errors.

A: You must make sure that the various BizTalk services and applications have sufficient permission to execute when there is no interactive user.

Q: I make a change to my map, but the changes don't seem to take effect in the outbound document. I've tested the map and it works fine. What's wrong?

A: You must go through the formality of opening the channel that uses the map, and re-save it. This will bring the new map into use.

Q: How do I find out if my XLANG schedule ever started or ever stopped.

A: Use the XLANG Monitor.

Q: I can't access my WebDAV. What do I do?

A: First, install BizTalk SP1. Then, check the documentation for the more specific elements of the fix.

Index

U

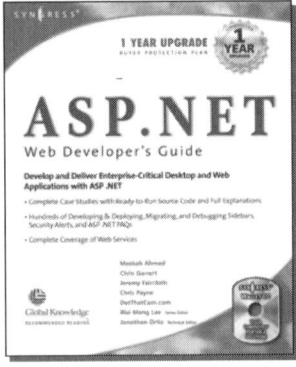
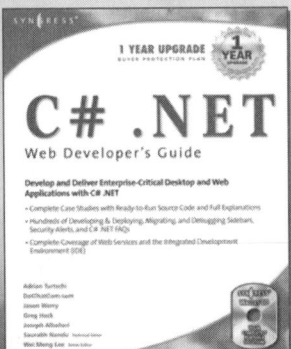